Allow L

CW00537917

Ulf Poschardt was born in 1967. He lives and works in Munich as Editor-in-Chief of Süddeutsche Zeitung Magazin, the supplement of Germany's leading daily. DJ CULTURE became a major success when first published in Germany.

'A fascinating masterpiece: the art of mixing sounds from two turntables transformed into 400 pages'
Neue Zürcher Zeitung, Zurich

'A substantial contribution to the writing of pop history'
Profil, Vienna

DJ-CULTURE

ULF POSCHARDT

TRANSLATED BY SHAUN WHITESIDE

QUARTET BOOKS

First published in Great Britain by Quartet Books Limited in 1998
A member of the Namara Group
27 Goodge Street
London W1P 2LD

Originally published in Germany in 1995 under the same title

Typography and design by John Warwicker, Tomato

A catalogue record for this book is available from the British Library

ISBN 0 7043 8098 6

Phototypeset by FSH, London
Printed and bound in Great Britain by C.P.D. (Wales) Ltd, Ebbw Vale

In memory of Olaf Dante Marx (1957–1993)

For my parents
For Moritz, Oschi and Susanne

CONTENTS

1. FOREWORD, INTRODUCTION, PREHISTORY

FOREWORD   15

INTRODUCTION   19

The bias thing   19

The underground thing   21
The technology thing   30
The writing thing   32
The history thing   35

DJ CULTURE – THE PREHISTORY   40

The radio pioneers – the first DJs   40
The first star DJ   45
Play my music, man!   48
The hit parade – the birth of top 40 radio   49
Top 40 radio   52
Alan Freed – the inventor of rock'n'roll   57
The DJ and corruption: payola   63
'Pop is here to stay' – DJs in the pop industry   66
Mucho Maas – the DJ in Thomas Pynchon   68
The victory of pop culture   72
Murray the K – 'the king of the jockeys' (Cohn)   74

78   Going underground – the sound of a youth rebellion
83   Dissidence and integration – the black DJ
95   DJs – the development in Europe

2. THE HISTORY

A. DISCO

101

101 Disco – the beginnings
103 The twist
107 Francis Grosso – the first DJ author
112 Disco – a gay thing
116 The roots of disco music
119 Disco fever – incubation period
122 The remix and the eternal return of the same
126 Saturday Night Fever – Nik Cohn and the Faces and a
      number of attempts to discover the hipster on the
      dancefloor
129 The hipster in changing times
135 Welcome to the disco – Studio 54 and the rest
140 *Saturday Night Fever* – the film
142 *Young Soul Rebels* – another Saturday Night Fever
144 Don't believe the hype – DJs, clubs and the record
      industry
145 Back in the underground
147 Disco – the end, not an end

B. HIP-HOP

148

148 Word up
150 Roots of rap
155 Roots of rap – roots of reggae: the Jamaican sound
      system
159 The first rap DJs
160 Kool DJ Herc and the breaks
167 Grandmaster Flash: mix, scratch and beatbox
175 Afrika Bambaataa and the Zulu Nation
181 The man from Harlem – DJ Hollywood
182 Words to the beat: the beginning of rap
186 Word up – what can language do for the DJ?
192 The road to success
197 Hip-hop turns into pop (I): the black will to power

Hip-hop becomes pop (II): the white accomplices 203
Always curious: Blondie commits Rapture 204
All art history: Malcolm McLaren – a white intellectual 205
    discovers hip-hop
Wild Style: hip-hop in/as film 213
Always new: hip-hop innovations 215

DIGRESSION: WELCOME TO THE TECHNODOME 219

Aura or record box 219
Beatbox, drum machine, drum computer 222
The first German B-Boys: Kraftwerk 224
The digital record box 228
Don't sweat the technics – a record-player writes 234
    musical history
The mixing desk 237

C. HOUSE 239

Disco goes back underground 239
Hi-NRG 240
The birth of house in Chicago 242
The home of house music 247
The idea of salvation and release in house music 254
The family tree 257
Harmony or rhythm? Harmony and rhythm! 258

D. DANCEFLOOR PLANET 1987–1995 261

The journey from pop to M/A/R/R/S 261
After old school – the new hip-hop 268
'Beat Dis' and friends 272
Sampling in the age of its absolute usability 275
England – the start of the European dancefloor scene 284
Acid house 285
Summer of love 287
Rave 289
Rare grooves, acid jazz, modern soul 292
Strictly turntablized: from Soul II Soul and Massive 293
    Attack to Tricky and Mo'Wax
Dancefloor style 302
Rainald Goetz – literature under the DJ's desk 305
Techno – the new heavy 313
Techno – the family tree 316
Belgium – the leap from industrial to EBM and techno 319

322 England – subsonic basses and a wunderkind
326 Germany – Westbam and the rest
328 Love Parade

3. ATTEMPT AT A THEORY

335 Brief remark on the pop researcher as parasite
336 The big ideas
337 History and progress
340 Cultural progress as political progress?
347 Nonetheless: the project of progress
347 Technical progress
370 Aesthetic progress
373 The death of the author/artist
384 Self-referentiality – the goal of Modernism, quite natural for the DJ
388 Complexity of the system and production
391 Avant-garde goes pop
393 High Modernism – not postmodernism
398 Progress for mankind: life in the subculture
406 New dawn

BONUS TRACK ('97 MOODY DUB)

410 Reawakening
416 I rock the party that rocks the body
428 Homework
434 The new normality

441 Bibliography
455 Magazine articles
461 Index
473 Acknowledgements

»REALITY USED TO BE A FRIEND OF MINE« PM DAWN

1

DJCULTURE FOREWORD INTRODUCTION PREHISTORY

FOREWORD

In July 1877 Thomas Alva Edison yelled his first 'Hello' into the mouthpiece of the telephone, and had the sound recorded by a phonograph machine. This was the beginning of the history of the recording of sounds and noises, and also of the history of the gramophone – the instrument with which the DJ would bring about a revolution in pop music. In 1887 the stanniol-coated cylinder on Edison's phonograph was replaced by the wax-covered zinc plate invented by Emil Berliner. Shortly before the turn of the century, Deutsche Grammophon Gesellschaft produced the first gramophone records. In 1906, in Brant Rock, Massachusetts, electrical engineer Reginald A. Fessenden played a record of Handel's *Largo* in the first ever radio broadcast, becoming the ancestor of all DJs in the process.

In the late 60s the DJ first saw the (murky) light of day both as an artist and as a 'music-musician' in the New York clubs. Disco, hip-hop and house turned the DJ into a composer.

The transition of the DJ from someone who played records into a musician forms the core of this book. Like artists in the Middle Ages, DJs were at first defined as craftsmen. The DJ as star and author has only existed for a short time. But the future of pop music lies in DJ culture[1] as Neil Tennant of the Pet Shop Boys is quite sure: 'In the long run two record-players and a mixing desk are more exciting than five guitar strings.'[2] The DJ questions the traditional concept of the artist,

1. The title is a reference to the song 'DjCulture' which the Pet Shop Boys recorded in 1991, and which threw up the idea and the first definition of this book. With this song, which entered the charts, the term became widely accepted.

2. USLAR, Moritz von: 'Wir haben prima Laune. Aber wir sind nicht geisteskrank.' In: SZ-MAGAZIN, 21 January 1994, p. 22.

Pet Shop Boys: DjCulture (1991)

blows it apart and re-establishes it in overhauled form. The DJ is by definition eclectic and a 'music-musician'. Just as the film-maker Jean-Luc Godard describes himself as an organizer of pictures and sounds,[3] the DJ appears on the music scene to interrogate and partially destroy the archaic notion of art that has managed to survive into the aesthetics of the late 20th century. The artist as the creator of his work, as an autonomous genius, came into being in the Renaissance, and has repeatedly had his status confirmed by the idealist aesthetic: as an *alter deus* and a superman.[4] Only the avant-gardes of the 20th century shook this idea to its foundations. Duchamp, Picabia, Warhol and others scorned the idea of the artist as genius, and were still unable to avoid merely modernizing the concept of the artist as author. The DJ occupies exactly the same ambivalent place between the destruction and preservation of the idea of the artist. He radically unmasks his material: his record box is the starting-point of all his production. He organizes material that has already been created and builds artworks into a new whole. He is a second-level artist.

For a long time the artist was either an expressionistic, autistic figure, producing art out of himself, almost as a 'neurotically' compulsive act, or a conscious creator who saw himself as working in the tradition of art history as a whole This type 'transcended' previous production in the Hegelian sense: which is to say that he negated, preserved and elevated it at the same time.[5] Now the DJ transcends music produced previously in the materialist sense: he collects and archives it as raw material for his own work. In so doing he enters directly into a relationship with music history, and is thus able to tinker with it. He can bring together sounds, beats and melodies from various songs, by various composers, even from different eras, juxtaposing or combining them. Old music is put in new contexts; the contexts are transposed. Old pieces of music (both whole songs and elements of songs) are endlessly reinvented. Musical history seems to lose its linearity: the potentially boundless access to old material makes everything run towards the present, the moment of synthesis.

The method used by DJs is not so much rational as

3. That's why my name isn't in the titles. I didn't make the film. I'm its conscious organizer.' GODARD, Jean-Luc: quoted in: Nouvelle Vague – Presseheft, p. 16.

4. Cf. WOLFF, Janet: The Social Production of Art, p. 26ff.

5. Cf. HEGEL, G.W.F.: Phenomenology of Spirit, p. 124.

geared towards abandoning oneself entirely in music, as the well-known song title suggests: 'Lost in Music!' There is no DJ poetics expressed in abstract concepts or theoretical reflections on the DJ's own work. He tends rather to see himself as a craftsman and a music-lover. A lot of interviews and statements given by DJs make it plain that they are both able and willing to get by without concepts. They have devoted themselves entirely to music and consider it a complete waste of time to draw up a theory for their own activities. And any kind of reflexive process can weaken their immediate passion for music. 'It all comes from here!' declares star DJ David Morales in an interview, putting his hand on his heart.[6] Most DJs don't feel the slightest need for intellectual mediation. Anyone who wants to understand them has to go to the club. The truth about DJs has to be experienced by watching them at work and dancing to their music. This text can speak of facts, actions and ideas – in the club, such words are mute and impotent.

The philosopher of science Michel Serres assumes that the human or social sciences are only familiar with 'police methods'. This, he argues, is the true danger for those who deploy them: they run the risk of acting as the method or theory dictates.[7] 'We must see discourse as a violence that we do to things,' warns Foucault, 'and at the same time a practice that we impose upon them.'[8] 'The world is not an accomplice of our knowledge,' he writes, there is no pre-discursive providence 'which disposes the world towards us'[9] – particularly when we are dealing with such a non-verbal piece of the world as DJ culture. A few exceptions aside, the DJ has remained untouched by academic study and any kind of scientific inquiry will demand that we 'surrender to the life of the object'.[10]

DJs tend towards laconic autism. This makes them pliant objects for any theorist and academic who approaches them. He can pull his conceptual blanket over their heads and press them into the structure of his theory without having to take any counter-reactions into account. In this case police methods are dealing with a submissive victim. But the victim is more and/or

6 . Cf. PHILLIPS, Dom: The World's Biggest Remixer, in: MIXMAG 7/1993, p. 46.

7 . Cf. SERRES, Michel: L'Hermaphrodite, p. 61.

8 . FOUCAULT, Michel: L'Ordre du Discours, p. 55.

9 . Ibid.

10 . HEGEL, G.W.F.: Phenomenology of Spirit, p. 32.

T-shirt with Keith Haring motif

11. Cf. GODFREY, John: Nightclubbing, in: Godfrey (Ed.): a decade of i-Deas, p. 163.

12. GEORGE, Nelson: Hip-Hop's Founding Fathers Speak the Truth, in: THE SOURCE 11/1993, p. 50.

less immune to the attacks of the researcher; DJs generally don't much care what is written, thought and said about them. They are one of the producers of a new age who place no value on the theoretical superstructure of their work, and so are friendly and open to the parasite. Not because they hold him in high esteem, but because he means absolutely nothing to them.

It is by no means enough simply to place the DJ within an aesthetic context. The history of technology and media locate the DJ as an aesthetic phenomenon, the history of pop and the subculture positions the DJ musically and socially. The more or less agitated history of the past twenty years has placed him not just at the top of the cultural avant-garde, but also at the centre of modern life-practice. In 1990 one of the most important magazines of club culture during that period, *i-D* magazine, declared clubs, fashion and music to be the triumvirate of the past decade, bound so close together that one was not imaginable without the other. As the engine of this triumvirate, the DJ span, scratched and mixed himself into the forefront of a youth culture that was richer and more diverse[11] than that of any other decade.

Only in this context of hip fashion, cool clubs and the all-important beats and grooves do we ever hear the less-than-workmanlike utterances of DJs. Within this context some DJs break their self-inflicted vow of silence to impose a kind of intellectual order on their little world. This also provides certain points of contact for the academic working on a history and aesthetics of DJ culture. One of the innovators of hip-hop, DJ Grandmaster Flash, stresses that only those actively involved in a scene can tell its story. 'Either you can hear his-story, or history, and the only way you gonna hear the real historical views on it is by the people who were actually there – who actually took it from nothing and built into whatever it became to be.'[12]

INTRODUCTION

THE BIAS THING

This work is biased. A historiography of the DJ is, like any historiography, also an act of selection and evaluation. Every form and phenomenon of the DJ is interesting, but the most fascinating and important are the figures of revolt, resistance and rebellion who have turned from respectable record-spinners into complex structured artists. The history of the DJ is not least the history of the exceptional DJs, who had a vision of a new kind of music they wanted to play and a new way of playing it. Who turned their faces from the mainstream and conformity and became heroes of the great, universal pop revolt which, from the very start, turned this music into something rebellious and exciting.

The DJ has become a cult figure, celebrated by writers from Thomas Pynchon and Tom Wolfe to music historians like Arnold Shaw and Nelson George. The DJ is more than someone who spins records, he is one of the new 'culture makers' (Wolfe).

Science has to strive for objectivity and neutrality. How can the academic approach a cult figure without depriving him of his aura? How can the academic take on the spirit of a cult figure without distorting it by the use of false concepts? In 1887 Nietzsche wrote that science 'is a hiding place for every kind of discontent, disbelief, gnawing worm, *despectio sui*, bad conscience,'[13] and informed by the discontent prompted by a lack of ideals and the lack of great love. The topic of the DJ cannot bear this 'dissatisfaction', disbelief and above all this lack of love'.

'Do not define it,'[14] warns Michel Serres, calling science to order by appealing to its heart. For Serres, one of the most cheerful of contemporary thinkers, the fruitfulness of a work emerges from the positive, with no empire, no rulers, no contradiction. The creator within the thinker is challenged: 'Onwards, onwards, take the proffered hand, go on and confidence will come... If you want to write, drop criticism. Leave theory, method, all the intellectual and emotional famines...'[15]

These epistemological challenges are particularly important for a theorist acting on 'opposing' fields: who both knows about the DJ as a scientist and has at the same time played records for years as a house DJ, and still feels committed to the dancefloor underground. This text tries to do justice to both sides. Any academic work has its individual epistemological problems, and must leave both the topic and its description alive. This book on DJs strives to circumvent rigid categorizations and restrictive conceptual arrangements, to avoid 'the pedantry that turns its back on the object'[16] which is there to be described and explained.

The book is written with passion, as befits the underground DJ. Fortunately the author has good reasons to concentrate his expositions upon the underground – because it is this that has propelled the development of the mainstream. Like the avant-gardes in classical Modernism, the rebels have altered and shaped the face of both high and popular culture. Particularly in popular culture, a rebellious, often aggressive practice has been constitutive since the very first.

13. NIETZSCHE, Friedrich: On the Genealogy of Morals, p. 147.

14. SERRES, Michel: L'Hermaphrodite, p. 83.

15. Ibid.

16. SERRES, Michel: Esthétiques sur Carpaccio, p. 114.

THE UNDERGROUND THING

'The ideas of the ruling class are in every epoch the ruling ideas: i.e. the class which is the ruling *material* force of society is at the same time its ruling *intellectual* force,'[17] Marx and Engels write in 1845–6 in *The German Ideology*. 'The Class which has the means of material production at its disposal, consequently also controls the means of mental production, so that the ideas of those who lack the means of mental production are on the whole subject to it. The ruling ideas are nothing more than the ideal expression of the dominant material relations, the dominant material relations grasped as ideas; hence of the relations which make the one class the ruling one, therefore, the ideas of its dominance.'[18]

Marx and Engels waste barely a word on cultural dissidence. They merely observe that the existence of revolutionary ideas in a particular age 'presupposes the existence of a revolutionary class'.[19] This was written in an age of civil war, of revolutions and of class struggle. Pop culture begins in the 1950s, when the western, civilised world began to enjoy a state of peace and prosperity. And from the very start this pop culture was at once the product of the ruling ideology and the expression of absolute rebellion. The roots of the first pop music, rock'n'roll, lay in the rhythm'n'blues, jazz and gospel of the oppressed blacks, and in the 'schmaltzy songs of the whites'.[20]

Pop culture was always a youth affair, and its primary goal – as a biologically determined avant-garde – was symbolic patricide, the rejection of the old and the battle for the new and the independent. Young people rebelled until they had won and themselves became the establishment. According to Greil Marcus, pop knocked holes in traditional cultural assumptions. The dominant assumptions about how the world works were called into question – peaking in punk as pop that had an effect on everything: 'the milieu where, commuting to work, doing one's job in the home or the factory or the office or the mall, going to the movies, buying groceries, buying records, watching television, making love, having conversations, not having

17. MARX, Karl/ ENGELS, Friedrich: The German Ideology, p. 22.

18. Ibid.

19. Ibid. p. 23.

20. COHN, Nik: AwopBopaLooBopALopBamBoom, p. 10.

conversations, or making lists of what to do next, people actually lived.'[21] Unbearable life was made bearable.

Pop rebellion didn't seem motivated by political considerations, but by a longing for more freedom and self-determination; a longing, then, that had hitherto helped to constitute every bourgeois democracy. In the 50s no one was interested in the idea that this yearning might contain genuinely political interests – what mattered was private life, the personal existence. In the early 1960s young people's aggressions were slowly building up against the restrictions and repressions of a society in need of reform, and at the end of the 60s they finally exploded. The 'children of Marx and Coca-Cola' (Godard) now no longer tried only to change their own little world, but the rest of the world at the same time. As a dream of free love, equality, liberty and fraternity with a hint of socialism, the pop rebellion was to end in a real revolution. But the project failed politically; socially, it made the battered western nations fit for the new age. Everything became supposedly more liberal, generous, tolerant. The values of the post-war age were overhauled, and the establishment was given a modern lick of paint.

The political utopias were finally exhausted, and there was a widespread lack of direction. Were the 70s the end of pop culture? No, because the future of pop was beginning in dark little gay clubs in New York. Disco was born, and with it a new strategy of resistance. A minority (gay and/or black) tried, on a separatist basis, to construct a new world of its own in murky garages, neon-lit clubs and bars, without having to react directly to the 'real', hostile (outside) world. While the discourse of the 60s was based around a loud and dramatic 'no', disco culture put its money on a loud and euphoric 'yes'. Contradiction and critique only entered the field indirectly, involuntarily. The disco underground was underground because it clearly separated itself off from the rest of the world, and because it was borne by people whom the rest of the world discriminated against, and whose passions were suppressed.

As in rock'n'roll, soul and funk, the music became a free space outside society – with one difference, that the rebellious character that had been to the fore

21. MARCUS, Greil: Lipstick Traces, p. 3.

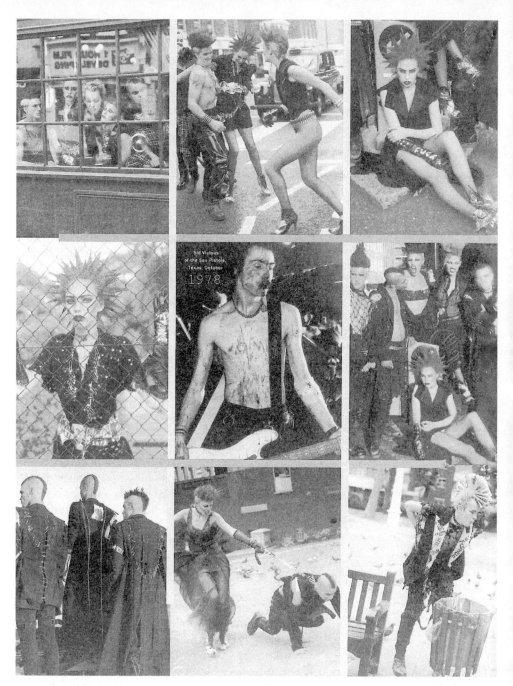

Picture of Sid Vicious in the middle of a fashion spread in Interview 10/1993

disappeared in disco culture. It was all about looking good, cool dancing and having fun. Disco culture didn't adopt an offensive position towards the rest of the world, but ignored it and tried to construct a new world of its own. A fundamental posture that was to shape all subsequent dancefloor subcultures.

Just as disco was experiencing its commercial high point in 1977, the punk revolution was raging in London. Their music, their style and their appearance made the punks warriors of a nihilistic guerrilla army that the rest of the world wanted not to ignore but to destroy and then forget.

For Greil Marcus, who, in *Lipstick Traces*, puts punk in a line with the most important cultural avant-gardes of the 20th century, punk changed the world. The 'no' of the punks was so loud and irreconcilable that it had to change the lives of those who really adhered to it, something Greil Marcus experienced in person. After the Sex Pistols' final concert on 14 January 1978 in San Francisco his life was changed. Everything could start over once again. He was 32 years old. Nine years of work on *Lipstick Traces* followed.

The desire to change the world began with the demand to live not as an object but as a subject of history – to live as if something actually depended on one's actions – and that demand opens onto a free street. Damning God and the state, work and leisure, home and family, sex and play, the audience and itself, the music briefly made it possible to experience all those things as if they were not natural facts but ideological constructs: things that had been made and therefore could be altered, or done away with altogether. It became possible to see those things as bad jokes, and for the music to come forth as a better joke. The music came forth as a no that became a yes, then a no again, then a yes: nothing is true except our conviction that the world we are asked to accept is false. If nothing was true, everything was possible.[22]

This attitude that Marcus attributes to punk can, with a few shifts, be transferred to disco culture. While the punks demonstrated their concerns aggressively, the makers and disciples of disco ignored God, state, work,

22 . Ibid. p. 5f.

home and family. They made themselves subjects of history, creating a space in which they could be happy, defining themselves in an unalienated way. Disco already had the 'no' behind it, and was able to start straight off with a 'yes'. Nonetheless, punk became an important starting-point for subsequent (youth) subcultures, particularly for the (European) dancefloor scene.

Punk had ended the world, 'or anyway their own'.[23] And after this ending there was plenty of space to create new things. After the symbolic destruction, the symbolic reorientation began. The shocks of punk extended into art, literature, film and the graphic arts. Young and not-so-young people everywhere began to pursue their own ideas of beauty, art and design. It was the beginning of a phase that lasted until the late 80s.

British academic Simon Frith, writing about punk, asked whether, to make revolutionary music, musical traditions and language had to be revolutionary, and whether the avant-garde was the only radical art form. Frith says yes to both. 'The avant-garde is by definition the art form that closes itself off to the cultural usability of the capitalist system.'[24] Frith wrote this in 1978, and only a year later punk outfits were the latest fashion at the most expensive hairdressers and boutiques. The punk wave lapped in even the most remote provincial department stores, distorted to the point of unrecognizability and perverted to the point of mere form. Radical resistance to all the rules of the establishment was richly absorbed by that same establishment. The German Princess Gloria of Thurn and Taxis turned up at a show-business party with a wildly back-combed punk hairdo. The power of resistance and the violence of anger (as intended by punk) were transformed into positive energies that could be tapped by the system: like creativity, originality and cheekiness (the desirable counterpoint to rebellion). The ambivalence of punk between absolute rebellion and cynical nihilism was deliberate – Malcolm McLaren, punk's Svengali, described the whole thing as 'The Great Rock'n'Roll Swindle'. As in the revolts of '68, by the end of punk the old society had been given a modern lick of paint, promising more tolerance and an altered (more libertarian) value

23. Ibid. p. 17.

24. FRITH, Simon: Zur Ideologie des Punk, in: GÜLDEN, Jörg/ HUMANN, Klaus (Ed.): Rock Session 2, p. 31.

25. According to the subtitle of the *i-D* logo.

26. GODFREY, John (Ed.): op. cit., p. 9.

27. WELSCH, Wolfgang: Zwei Wege der Ästhetisierung, in: HUBER, Jörg (Ed.): Wahrnehmung von Gegenwart, p. 55.

system, but without changing its fundamentally restrictive underlying characteristics. Everything stayed as it was, but it looked nicer now and seemed to promise more fun. After the glorious liberation, this experience of rapid appropriation and complete sell-out informed the subcultures that followed on from punk. What was needed was a new strategy of resistance, and what came was the impressive semiotic war of the 80s. One of the most important magazines to emerge from this revolt was the British *i-D*, which was founded in September 1980, and which since then has been reporting on 'i-Deas, Fashion, Clubs, Music, People'[25], with crazy layouts, eccentric pictures and passion-driven articles. In 1990 the makers of *i-D* assembled an encyclopaedia of the 80s and took stock:

The 80s was the decade when everybody dealt in ideas. From the pages of magazines, the catwalks, art galleries, music to nightclubs, the energy that punk unleashed at the end of the 70s became the rationale of a decade. Broken glass stuck on canvas became art, records were made in bedrooms, magazines bred like rabbits, anything and everything became fashion... Ideas were reworked with such speed that nothing ever stood still, and the information technology that evolved made sure that everybody knew what was happening then, even if it couldn't predict what was going to happen next. Popular culture became a game in which anybody could join in, and everybody broke the rules.[26]

In the creative zones of capitalist society, resistance to norms became the norm. The new freedom, paired with the affluence-related boom of aesthetics, created an inflation of cultural innovations. Everything seemed to be getting bright, beautiful, postmodern. The masses, the affluent 'two thirds'[27] of society, started to take an interest in the finer things of life. Refinement, elegance, exoticism, even glamour lost their strictly elitist aftertaste.

Against the background of these developments, which culminated particularly in the second half of the 80s, pop culture had to come up with new strategies. After punk and its melancholy aftermath in new wave, it was the pop of '82 that was to provide new directions. The

German pop journalist, thinker and prophet Diedrich Diederichsen thought the 'project of putting a new kind of pop music on its feet through the historicization and relativization of all the elements of music'[28] a successful one: 'No one believed in natural expression any longer. All the elements were referential, referring to the history of pop culture, nothing was innocent, everything was exaggeratedly deliberate, intellectual, camp and yet beautiful and charming... The Roxy Music project of a pop music that was no longer yelled but, like the system of language, organized from significant musical and non-musical signs, had come into its own.'[29]

Pop music was now – in a classically postmodern way – doubly coded. For many people it was simply pop, for the rest it was a complicated play of signs: with references, allusions and considerations that turned pop into a critical theory of pop. Bands like ABC, Spandau Ballet and Heaven 17 produced pop in the knowledge of pop's function within a capitalist society, and the dangers to which it can give rise. A new, left-wing pop audience grew up, one which no longer enjoyed pop with innocent euphoria, but with thoughtful euphoria, and which would 'vouch for the values of word, history, politics and beauty'.[30] From this audience emerged the new, left-wing pop criticism based around the German magazines *Sounds* and *Spex*, and the literature of Lottmann, Diederichsen, Glaser and Goetz.

The pop of '82 didn't last long, but its consequences did. From now on mainstream pop was measured against its media realism, the precision with which the conditions of the production process and its connections in the music, in styling, in interviews, videos and concerts were inscribed within the product itself. Madonna became the prime example of this. On the one hand she was the perfect embodiment of the 'whore' of the system, not only being taken up by it but also exploiting it; on the other hand, though, Madonna never lost contact with the dancefloor underground. The strict separation between her personality and her pop image (which could change by the hour) turned her into the figurehead of the new critical pop intellectuals. Bands like New Order and the Pet Shop Boys worked

28. DIEDERICHSEN, Diedrich: Sexbeat, p. 41.

29. Ibid.

30. Ibid. p. 42.

in a similar way; the latter were, tellingly, founded by a pop writer. Pop's emergence into consciousness is comparable to the development in the cinema of the 50s, when young film journalists came together in Paris and passed through theory and writing and love of film to cinematic practice. The nouvelle vague, with their thoughtful 'film-films', took cinema's innocence from it and at the same time rescued it from barrenness and stultification.

The pop intellectuals, whether working as journalists or as musicians, used the field of pop music, relatively untouched by critical and reflective approaches, and beneath the cloak of affirmation they began a refined campaign of double coding within the entertainment industry. Diederichsen describes the 'rejection of the always dialogical structure of critique or protest in favour of fake affirmation or affirmation'[31] as one of the central artistic practices that can be seen as subversive. Clever, doubly-coded pop is not concerned with integrating itself critically into the opinion-forming processes of the bourgeois public, but simulates an apparently boundless agreement with the exercise of power; 'for it is more grounds for delight that the shit should stay identical with itself... than if, through dialogue with oppositional forces, it wins the chance to present itself as pro-reform'.[32] Instead, energies are fed directly into the underground. Madonna keeps her contact with the blacks and the gay Latinos and gives them lucrative commissions, the Pet Shop Boys financed the work of the HIV–positive film-maker Derek Jarman, whose career had been damaged by Clause 28, until his death in 1994.[33]

A very different strategy was pursued by the independent bands, which, fully in the spirit of punk, avoided the large record companies and their processes of marketing and production. The indie bands presented the consumer with a broad spectrum from experimental electronic music, industrial and conceptual sounds via punk rock, metal and EBM (electric body music) to guitar pop and eccentric mainstream. Through the breadth and quality of what was on offer, the indie labels quickly established true competition with the majors. When distribution problems were solved in the mid-80s, indie bands

31. DIEDERICHSEN, Diedrich: Subversion – Kalte Strategie und heisse Differenz, in: Freiheit macht arm, p. 35.

32. Ibid. p. 38.

33. In 1988 the British Conservative government led by Margaret Thatcher banned all forms of homosexual propaganda on the cultural level. During the period of AIDS hysteria, Clause 28 led to the defamation and suppression of gay films, writing and art.

Madonna: film still from In Bed with Madonna (1991)

invaded the upper reaches of the charts. Unknown groups that had grown up with indie labels stayed loyal to them even once they had become successful, and thus gave them greater financial play. But successful indie bands kept being bought off with money from the major labels, and – once the initial euphoria had faded – the indie scene started to dry up.

The late 80s brought user-friendly and cheap production technologies like synthesizers and samplers. These, together with the development of dancefloor music, helped to revivify the idea of the independents. Labels like Rhythm King, Big Life, Gee Street, Chicago Trax, Strictly Rhythm and Warriors Dance turned good profits with their hip-hop and house productions. Many dance acts work on two levels, releasing their more difficult projects on small labels, while the productions with a chance of being a hit are brought out on major labels. Directly or indirectly, the profit returns to the subculture. By the early 90s the dancefloor underground had become the biggest and most profitable area of the independent scene. The spectrum of music extends now from acid jazz via the countless variations of hip-hop to all kinds of house music. The meaning of underground within the dancefloor movement varies enormously: in hip-hop the tradition of black soul and funk rebellion is linked up with all possible political and metaphysical ideologies. The black house scene saw itself in the tradition of disco culture and insisted on rigid separatism. The white house scene, from acid to techno, combined the impetus of punk with the affirmative attitude of disco and pop. The acid jazz movement, on the other hand, saw itself as the avant-garde of good taste, and thus primarily as a lifestyle guerrilla force. What all these movements have in common is the fact that they began to change the face of music in the mid-80s, and that they now form the most innovative, exciting and progressive areas of pop culture. One of the most important motors within all these subcultures was and remains the DJ. This book will show how great the influence of the DJ on the development of music has been – and it hopes to prove that the DJ must remain connected to the underground.

THE TECHNOLOGY THING

'Media determine our situation, which (despite or because of this) deserves description.'[34] With these words Friedrich Kittler began the introduction to his *Grammophon Film Typewriter* in 1985. In his research he describes how new technologies have changed perception, particularly literary perception. In addition, Kittler set out to discover how many new methods of perception and production of the artistic avant-garde have profited from earlier technical inventions. Many of the 'revolutionary creations' of the avant-garde were relativized with regard to the history of technology, because the new methods of making art – as writer–philosopher Klaus Theweleit has observed – 'were originally invented by engineers'.[35] New working methods in artistic production were thus 'more or less a copy of new technologies'.[36] It might be said that without earlier technical invention 'the human brain could not think certain thoughts, or make certain perceptions'.[37]

The dominance of technology, which Heidegger considered 'the supreme menace',[38] is particularly apparent at the turn of the century, when many inventions were first made or widely accessible for the first time, making a certain impression on practising artists. Kittler writes: 'In the early days of technological media, their horror was so overwhelming that literature recorded it with greater precision than in the apparent media pluralism of today... What made its way into the pages of startled authors between 1880 and 1920, on the subject of gramophone, film and typewriter, the first technical media, therefore provides a spectral image of our own times, conceived as the future.'[39]

Kittler tells of the dissolution of man, a 'recent invention', 'erased, like a face drawn in sand at the edge of the sea',[40] and making way for the 'rule of the *Gestell*', or 'frame'[41] (as Heidegger metaphysically referred to the whole of modern technology). For Kittler, man can be made through the new technologies. 'His being makes the transition to machinery. Machines take over functions of the central nervous system, and no longer only, like all previous machines, the

34. KITTLER, Friedrich A.: Grammophon Film Typewriter, p. 3.

35. THEWELEIT, Klaus: Buch der Könige, p. 371.

36. Ibid.

37. Ibid. p. 371f.

38. HEIDEGGER, Martin: Die Technik und die Kehre, p. 26.

39. KITTLER, Friedrich A.: Grammophon..., p. 4.

40. FOUCAULT, Michel: The Order of Things, p. 387.

41. HEIDEGGER, Martin, op. cit., p. 28.

musculature. And only thus... comes about the clean separation of matter and information, of the real and the symbolic.'[42] Kraftwerk, the German sound engineers whose music is the predecessor of all DJ music, tried to experience this transition to machinery from the early 70s onwards. In an interview Ralf Hütter admits that Kraftwerk's musicians have a very friendly relationship towards their machines. 'If you treat them well, they work, and they treat us well. It's a real collaboration: we play our music machines, and sometimes they play us... I ride a racing bike as well, and that's the same – sometimes "it" does the riding. We've composed a lot of pieces like that: we didn't actually make the music ourselves, it happened by itself.'[43] Authorship moves towards the digital circuits of the music machine, and at the same time it moves away from the brains of the artists. But Kraftwerk think it fatal to divide man and machines, nature and technology in that way. The only possibility for survival is 'to achieve a positive relationship towards the world. And technology isn't anything strange, it's part of our world. There's a destructive force in that strange way of thinking in terms of division – exploit something here, throw away something there. It can only stop when a unified thought process takes place.'[44] Kraftwerk want to contribute to the thought and construction of this courageous sense of technology.

At the end of the classical subject as constructed in the 18th century there is a breakdown 'into physiology and information technology'.[45] Kittler historically reconstructs the hardware of consciousness from typewriters, calculators, record-players and cameras. Hardware today is completely digitally equipped: 'All streams of data flow into the N states of Turing's Universal Machine, numbers and figures are (in defiance of romanticism) keys of all creatures.'[46] This book about DJs might also prove the extent to which the world of the symbolic has become the world of machines. Since its beginnings, the DJ aesthetic has been closely connected with the development of technology. Into the 70s, DJs just played records using two record-players and a small mixing desk. With disco, hip-hop and their mixing, scratching and cutting

42. KITTLER, Friedrich A.: Grammophon..., p. 29.

43. Anon.: Wir sind die Roboter, in: SZ-MAGAZIN, 31 October 1991, p. 40.

44. Ibid.

45. KITTLER, Friedrich A.: Grammophon..., p. 29.

46. Ibid. p. 33.

techniques, came the crucial breakthrough to an artistic use of turntables and records. With the introduction of sampling, the scratching of the DJs became a process that could be achieved at the press of a button. The digital storage of sounds together with compositional software granted the DJ inexpensive access to the world of the music producers. Given the contemporary rate of technical development, it is hard to predict how DJs will produce music in five to ten years, and which new machines they will use at their club appearances. The fate of pop music lies in the hands of both the engineer and the artist.

THE WRITING THING

Anyone who writes usually sits alone at his computer. His only companions are the books and magazines piled up on his desk. The writer communicates with other writers about their texts, and thus begins to become less lonely. He recognizes his own thoughts or is stimulated to think. The old idea that everything has to come out of oneself seems pathetically far away in 1995. Anyone who writes needs the rest of the world, or else their text remains impoverished and autistic. The DJ is similarly alone when he sits at home by his turntables spending the days with his records. But more than the writer by his text, the DJ is freed from loneliness by the music. Music is more of a beloved than a text can ever be, because music speaks directly to the heart. Music is the medium of absolute immediacy, while text, mediated through words and symbols, is oriented towards the intelligence. The DJ produces songs from loneliness, the writer texts, the thinker thoughts and theories. Maybe all artistic products are at the same time the conquest of loneliness, finding in isolation the strength to escape one's own isolation and into the world.
Creation is always drawn on thousands of causes and sources of power. This book about DJs will attempt to take its euphoric method of production, full of love and enthusiasm, and introduce it into its own work on the text. The first and most fundamental form of deejaying

is the mixing of two records to effect the creation of a third thing. Writers can mix existing texts, and thinkers can fuse existing thoughts and theories. This will happen to a very great degree in this work, because any thinker or writer whose work can be used or tapped into for this project is welcomed with open arms. DJs practise a mix until it sounds good, until the idea they have put into it becomes audible. This is exactly what happens in this text: everyone from Adorno to Tate gets a hearing, and they're all interlinked and mixed together, fragmented and mingled to the point of unintelligibility, generating a new intelligibility. Each of the decks is autonomous; on one there might be Beethoven's 'Eroica', on the other a wild-pitch remix by DJ Pierre. There are no discernible rules to this, apart from the one which says that something new must arise out of the synthesis, and that at the end of the synthesis the two mixed productions are no longer alien to one another. Thus Adorno and Greg Tate must fertilize one another by communicating and ceasing to be alone.

The second major art of the DJ is the remix. Growing out of the synthesis between the two decks, the remix came into being in the mid-70s, as a way of reinterpreting an existing song in a creative form of reproduction. The aim of most remixes is to ensure that the existing piece works in the context of a discotheque, and harmonizes more successfully with the other elements of the DJ mix. The remix, then, is the deliberate diversion of a piece towards a particular context, a particular purpose. The remix brings a greater or lesser amount of the old piece into a new form, and according to the remix one might speak of a new song or a carefully renovated form of the old song. Walter Benjamin or Karl Marx lend themselves to remixing as well, because a remix can not only adapt to a new context, but also make an old (and brilliant) idea contemporary. In most cases the remix is prompted by love of the original, along with the belief that this original creation can and should be reconsidered, varied and enriched. The remix seeks to give the original new life, to reinforce its influence and preserve its idea. The remix serves the original without forgetting its own interests. Even more than this: it serves the original in the knowledge that it is thus declaring and clarifying its own interests. Marx and Benjamin are remixed in devotion and love of the original. Remixes without that love and devotion are generally pale things, miserable and boring. The great thing about remixes is that you don't have to take all of the original, just the parts which you've been seduced by, parts that will work in a new context. The remixer isn't concerned with salvaging authenticity, but with creating a new authenticity.

Sampling technology became the third important element of DJ compositions. Without scratching, mixing and remixing, sampling in this form would probably never have entered musical history. Sampling makes possible the digital storage and manipulation of all kinds of sounds. From simple whirring noises to whole melodic sequences – everything can be sampled with developed technology. Sampling makes it possible to insert original sounds at any desired point. Sampling makes the original flexibly and rationally usable. Sampling makes it possible to transfer authentic sounds from the world into the emerging artistic product. And in this work a lot of sampling is done with this very view in mind. Sampling of quotations and images from books, magazines, songs and films designed to give the text colour, power and heterogeneity. The work should glitter and shine in as many colours and materials as possible. The unity of language is preserved by the context. The form of quotation, however, is different from many works, in which the uniqueness of the foreign language is swallowed and the foreign thoughts are quietly subsumed by the sampler's language. I hope that this happens only rarely in this work; the idea is for as many voices to be heard as possible. *All Samples Cleared* was the name that rapper Biz Markie gave his last LP, referring to the fact that samples must be identified as such. Similarly, in academic writing there are footnotes and bibliographies. Most of this work is historiography, and nothing is more dangerous than arguing historiography without samples, or with disguised samples. Samples give the reader and user the opportunity to put the author's observations to the test, and anyone who wants to remix the text can use the samples for his own purposes.

The DJ is very familiar with the favourite passages in

his records, if he is to insert them properly into his remixes. The same is true of the writer and thinker, who underlines his favourite passages in books, or writes down his favourite ideas on filing cards.

All these three DJ arts share the fact that they not only collapse the restrictions of their own design, they do not even permit any such restrictions to occur. The DJ is not tolerant, but utterly devoted to everything that he likes, and he throws together his own work from the totality of his personal preferences. The same should happen in writing: everything the writer likes and likes to think is mixed, remixed and sampled.

THE HISTORY THING

When this book was first thought through, the chief idea was to put together an aesthetic of the DJ phenomenon. In the course of the research and the months spent going through the material, the original idea underwent a fundamental shift. It became apparent how little had been written about the history of the DJ, and how indistinct, imprecise and even contradictory that writing was.

Historiography in pop music is the retelling of myths. The most important stopping points are the well-researched pop histories of Greil Marcus, Arnold Shaw and David Toop, and the clever pop reflections of Nik Cohn (myth-making) and Diedrich Diederichsen (myth-deconstructing). A vast number of books and magazine articles were minutely examined and collected for this history of the DJ. This thorough quotation turns the history of the DJ into a history of language/texts about the DJ, which can be seen as the documentation of the DJ phenomenon. The historiography is divided into two: the first part deals with the history of the DJ, before he became a producer and artist, and extends from 1907 to the end of the 60s. The extent to which the DJ exerted an influence on the history of music and helped to write the history of pop is demonstrated with reference to the most important DJ personalities. The second part represents the actual focus of the book, and marks the DJ's transition from record-spinner to artist, but it would be unthinkable and unimaginable without the prehistory that goes before it. Thus much of this work must remain dry historiography, even if the DJ himself has been fortunate enough to prompt euphoric language from otherwise dried-up sociologists, let alone the writers like Cohn, Wolfe and Pynchon who devoted their attention to the DJs in the 60s.

Throughout the work on this book, the enthusiasm for the crazy reinterpretations of pop intellectualism – an essential part of the work of the pop intellectual since the 70s – has abated somewhat. Many clever ideas about pop music are pleasant to read, but often they are devalued by the most breathtaking ignorance. Clever ideas are only clever when they are based on a knowledge of the subject.

Of course this work is also ideology, metaphysics and theory, but I have never forgotten that this tends to be dangerous and totalitarian.

Tricia Rose, the African-American academic who formulated a theory of rap music, encouraged me to write down the identities upon which my work (amongst others) is based. I am happy to go along with this practice, which has become usual among left-wing academics in the USA over the past few years[47]: I am a representative of the white European middle class, male, heterosexual and somehow left wing. Previously, intellectuals of that background and socialization have hardly ever thought it necessary to provide information on the subject.[48] Only the intellectual representatives of minorities have pointed out how narrow-minded this is. This definition of the author seems particularly important in a book whose focus is a historiography and theorization of minority and underground culture.

The inherent theoretical critique blows holes in the tight network of prescriptive thought, making ideology within historiography permeable, improvable and subject to criticism. Extensive quotation and the resulting heterogeneity of the text are intended to support inherent ideological critique. Despite the aforementioned techniques of writing and quotation, the intention is, of course, never to lose sight of one's own writing. The academic's ego writes the work, but the ego is no longer a problem if it is aware that it is a

47 . Tricia Rose refers to herself as 'an African-American woman of biracial parentage with second-generation immigrant parents' and as 'a pro-black, biracial, ex-working-class, New York-based feminist, left cultural critic'. (ROSE, Tricia: Black Noise, p. xiii.)

48 . One exception, for example, is Andrian Kreye, who begins his book about the escalation of racial conflicts in America with the sentence, 'I am white,' and continues: 'Before I first came to New York I never really thought about it. I lived in Germany... which was homogeneous and organized, a monoculture the like of which the world had never seen, a place of safety and affluence that was so colourless, and yet so pleasant and simple.' (KREYE, Andrian: Aufstand der Gettos, p. 11.)

product and clearly displays the conditions of its production to anyone who wishes to know of it. In pop music, this transparency of the conditions of production is taken as a trademark of the underground,[49] in academic writing it should be taken for granted after the critiques of academia, language and texts in the work of Serres, Barthes and Foucault. 'The observer makes the observed disappear by bringing along his noisemakers,'[50] writes Serres, referring to the scientist's language. Language, mixed, remixed or sampled with other things, gives the observed object the opportunity to express itself. The object is asked whether it has a language of its own, or whether it knows a language in which it recognizes itself. Once the observer is alone again, he can go on thinking undisturbed. Then the historian once more becomes the philosopher.

The idea of progress, as apparent itself in the history of art and literature as a product of the avant-garde, seems to encounter limits at many points within cultural production. Ideas are abstractions of reality, and for that reason one decides either to follow an idea or not. 'Philosophy affords the... insight that nothing is actual except the Idea,'[51] writes Hegel in the *Philosophy of Right*; and if this were a purely philosophical work devoted entirely to ideas, the DJ theorist could sink into the sphere of speculation. A historiography with a strongly philosophical bent, however, must provide an account of its ideas, particularly when it deals – in the age of postmodern historical scepticism – with such a grave and profound concept as that of progress. Historiography is, like any form of scientific knowledge, called into question by textual, linguistic and ideological criticism from Nietzsche to Foucault. The constructed nature of the idea of history and the relation between that constructedness and the interests of the dominant society have rendered historiography problematic in many different ways. That historiography – despite all ideological reservations – is important was made particularly clear by Foucault, who, as one who denounces terror in the field of knowledge, uses the history of science to identify tyranny and the discourse of power within the

49. Cf. DIEDERICHSEN, Diedrich: Vom Ende der Wahrheit, in: KONKRET 5/1990: 'Since pop music has existed, the innovative faction linked to the underground or the real world has always meaningfully deployed its means, never leaving the listener in any doubt about that and what they are using, while the regressive side always veils its means.'

50. SERRES, Michel: The Parasite, p. 236.

51. HEGEL, G.W.F.: Elements of the Philosophy of Right, p. 20.

humanities. That this historiography is itself part of a scientific project takes nothing away from its strength and significance, but makes it clear that to renounce historiography would be to abandon criticism, and would thus bring an end to the hope that there might be a counter-discourse to the discourse of power. Foucault the archaeologist, archivist and historian salvages from the torture chamber of human scientists the tools that might be used for the continued writing of a great humanitarian project.

Just as violent as Foucault's attack on the framework of the intellectual sciences was that of Deleuze and Guattari which – according to Foucault – turns both against 'the pitiful technicians of desire – psychoanalysts and semiologists of every sign and symptom – who want to force the multiplicity of desire under the yoke of the twofold law of structure and lack'.[52] But another arch-enemy of the 'Anti-Oedipus' was fascism. And not just historical fascism in Italy and Germany, 'but also the fascism within us all, in our heads and in our daily behaviour, the fascism that makes us love power, that makes us desire precisely that which rules and exploits us'.[53]

Against the background of a universal knowledge, Deleuze, Guattari, and – albeit in a more playful way – Serres actively seek out all forms of power and violence, thus becoming something like the *Amnesty International* of the academic community. But ideological criticism, as apparent only in the tradition that considers itself left wing, need not necessarily put its own project in jeopardy. The great French critics of the terrorism of knowledge have all, since the Second World War, nailed their flags to the mast of left-wing resistance, and fought on behalf of the oppressed and disenfranchised. Before any ideological criticism operating within the realm of the mind and philosophy, there must be a political attitude that places itself directly in relation to political events. Particularly at a time when nationalism, the far right and neo-Nazism are celebrating a grim renaissance in Russia, in Italy and in Germany, so the critique of power must be done in a more direct way.

52 . FOUCAULT, Michel: 'Der "Anti-Oedipus" - eine Einführung in eine neue Lebenskunst, in: BARCK, Karlheinz, et al: Aisthesis, p. 431.

53 . Ibid.

Ideological criticism need not lead to the impossibility of historiography, particularly when it concerns itself with the underground. The history of minorities must be told, to prevent its traces being erased from the history of the mainstream.

While disco and house are particularly dependent on this help, the artists of hip-hop culture have taken the telling of their history into their own hands.

54 . DONSBACH, Wolfgang/
MATHES, Rainer: Rundfunk, in:
NOELLE-NEUMANN et al (Ed.):
Fischer Lexikon Publizistik
Massenkommunikation, p. 331.

DJ CULTURE – THE PREHISTORY

THE RADIO PIONEERS – THE FIRST DJS

The history of the DJ begins with the history of the radio. In 1906, eighteen years after the discovery of electromagnetic waves by the German physicist Heinrich Hertz, and ten years after the transmission of Morse code signals on the basis of that discovery by the Italian Guglielmo Marconi, the two American engineers Reginald A. Fessenden and Lee DeForest succeeded in broadcasting uncoded sound signals. The conditions for broadcasting music, language and sounds to a number of receivers were now in place: on Christmas Eve 1906 came the 'birth of radio as a publicity medium',[54] when ships equipped with radios on the East coast of the USA were able to receive the first radio programme. From Brant Rock (near Boston) in Massachusetts Fessenden broadcast a contemplative programme consisting of readings from the Gospel of St Luke, embellished with songs and violin solos by the radio pioneer. But with his Christmas programme Fessenden also became the first DJ, when he broadcast a recording of Handel's *Largo* through the airwaves.[55] He was the first DJ because he wasn't just playing records for himself or his family, friends or acquaintances, but in a medium which, while it was still a long way from being a mass medium, was still ideally suited to reception by the public. And the playing of the record was part of a programme of entertainment and contemplation.

Before the invention of clubs and discotheques during the Second World War, DJs had their only sphere of activity in the radio. Nineteen years after its invention by Emil Berliner, the mass medium of the record had gained both a new enemy and a new propagandist. An enemy because radio was initially concentrated on live performances; a propagandist because live music was not always possible and the record had to serve as a substitute. Mass-produced media of broadcast and recording were gradually to bring the record to global domination in the world of sound.[56] The radio 'injected a full electric charge into the world of the phonograph',[57] but without the DJ that charge would have faded uselessly away. The radio, the record and the DJ entered a fruitful symbiosis. The DJ could assemble his music programme independent of big orchestras, difficult artists and human imponderables of every kind. Records didn't contradict you, they didn't demand a royalty and they played all kinds of music.

But it was to be some time before the DJs could claim their final victory in the radio stations. Not only Fessenden, but also DeForest claimed to be the first DJ. In 1907, for his first radio broadcast from a laboratory in the Parker Building in New York, he used a record of the overture to Gioacchino Rossini's opera *William Tell*. 'Of course there weren't many receivers in those days. But I was the first disc jockey.'[58] After DeForest many more radio pioneers chose to see themselves as the ancestors of all DJs.

In the period leading up to the First World War there was no shortage of hobbyists and handymen who held radio to be the medium of the future, and who wanted to be part of that future. America was full of radio enthusiasts, known familiarly as 'hams', who

55. Cf. BUSBY, Linda/ PARKER, Donald: The Art and Science of Radio, p. 6; ERB, Ernst: Radios von gestern, p. 45; PASSMAN, Arnold: The Deejays, p. 26; AITKEN, Hugh G.J.: The Continuous Wave, p. 74f, p. 469.

56. Cf. KITTLER, Friedrich A.: Grammophon..., p. 146.

57. McLUHAN, Marshall: Understanding Media, p. 272.

58. Cf. PASSMAN, Arnold, op. cit., p. 26.

59. Cf. BUSBY, Linda/ PARKER, Donald, op. cit., p. 6.

60. Cf. AITKEN, Hugh G.J., op. cit., p. 469.

61. Cf. PASSMAN, Arnold, op. cit., p. 23f.

62. Cf. BUSBY, Linda/ PARKER, Donald, op. cit., p. 10.

63. Cf. PASSMAN, Arnold, op. cit., p. 24.

transmitted on all frequencies, as yet unencumbered by legal regulations.[59] In January 1909, Charles D. 'Doc' Herold installed his own radio station in San José, after distributing crystal receivers to his neighbours and the inhabitants of the region. Herold's station played interviews, news and records. From 1909 until 1917 he regularly broadcast an entertainment programme.[60] At around the same time Thomas E. Clark from Detroit was playing records for the steamships on Lake Erie which were equipped with telephone receivers. For the first radio pioneers playing records was the only possible way of putting a programme together. The most important condition for assembling a programme, in fact, was ownership of the whole thing; most of these 'radio transmitters' were one-man enterprises. The man behind the microphone had only to reach into his record cupboard and the whole world of music was at his fingertips. One man who recognized the wealth of possibilities on offer early on was Dr Elman B. Myers, who became the first full-time DJ in the wake of all the part-time DJs. As early as 1911 he was broadcasting an eighteen-hour programme in New York City, in which he played almost nothing but records. In 1914 his wife Sybil M. True became the first woman to put together a radio programme, and the first female DJ. She bought her music in the record shop next door, chiefly to win over younger radio listeners to the new medium. She played contemporary hits, and the next day teenagers would go out and buy their favourite records.[61]

During the First World War, radio engineer Dr Frank Conrad transmitted a music programme from his garage in Pittsburgh each Wednesday and Saturday evening.[62] Conrad soon got feedback from listeners criticizing his limited selection of music and calling for more variety. Along with the praise and requests that flooded in, he also received an impression – albeit a vague one – of the needs of his listeners. His audience grew after the war, and with it grew the influence of Conrad's selection of music. The shops in the region registered an increase in demand for records played on the radio the previous evening, and on 29 September 1920 one shop provided a complete list of the pieces previously played on the radio.[63]

In the same year the owner of the small garage

broadcaster Station 8XK became the founder and first director of a commercial radio station. Conrad, who worked for the electronics company Westinghouse, developed radio transmitters and receivers. The high frequency transmitter KDKA, built on the company grounds in East Pittsburgh, soon became famous for its reports on the 1921 presidential elections between Harding and Cox. From 2 November 1920 the first licensed radio transmitter broadcast a programme which included not only music but also sport and politics.[64] In Canada, the Marconi Company's XWA station had gone into operation at the same time.

Things didn't happen so fast in Germany. From the start the development of radio was the province of the state and the military. Even in the German Empire, broadcasting technology was 'located exclusively within the sovereign realm of the state',[65] beginning with the Imperial Telegraph Law of 1892.[66] In 1914, at the beginning of the First World War, broadcasting occupied three areas: military radio broadcasting (army and marines), world radio and shipping broadcasting, a public and colonial service, and an official service. Before the First World War 5500 officers and 5800 private soldiers worked for the telegraph troops; in 1918 the information troop had grown to 4381 officers and 185,000 private soldiers.[67] These numbers testify to the extent to which the First World War was a media war. 'But exponentially growing broadcasting units also wanted to be entertained,' suggests Kittler, who describes the war in the trenches as 'sensory deprivation'.[68]

From May 1917 a radio programme was broadcast to the trenches, organized by AEG engineer and later German head of radio, Hans Bredow. Here too music on records was used, broadcast in alternation with the monotonous reading of newspaper articles. So the first German radio DJ was a member of the military, not a particularly promising start to the history of the disc jockey in Germany. When higher authorities learned of the radio experiments – as a supposed misuse of army equipment – the experiments in distraction and entertainment were rapidly suppressed. In the Weimar Republic the radio was placed in the hands of the Post

64. Cf. ERB, Ernst, loc. cit., p. 77.

65. DONSBACH, Wolfgang/ MATHES, Rainer: Rundfunk, in: NOELLE-NEUMANN, Elisabeth, loc. cit., p. 331.

66. Cf. BAUSCH, Hans (Ed.): Rundfunk in Deutschland, Vol. 1, p. 30.

67. Cf. RIEDEL, Heide: 60 Jahre Radio, p. 9.

68. Cf. KITTLER, Friedrich A.: Grammophon…, loc. cit., p. 149.

Office. Hans Bredow was the Secretary of State for Post and Communications, and responsible for the development of radio in Germany. From 1920 onwards there were regular experimental broadcasts from the main transmitter in Königs Wusterhausen, and from 29 October 1923 the 'Deutsche Stunde', a programme closely linked to the Post Office and the Foreign Office, broadcast from the Vox-Haus in Berlin. Both the technical organization and the contents of the radio station were kept under close surveillance by the state.

In the middle of the 20th century radio stations were set up in almost all European states, but America remained the country of the radio avant-garde. In the United States the number of broadcasters grew within six months from 60 (in March 1922) to 564 stations (in November). The six hundred major stations were joined by one thousand more, run by radio hams.[69]

With the emergence of large, powerful and affluent radio stations, the DJ slowly relinquished responsibility for drawing up the list of radio programmes. The broadcasters could afford big orchestras, which played live on major shows. Music played on records was only permitted in an emergency. Concerts and performances were put together on the spot for radio, but the radio DJ never quite disappeared from the stage.

In his book *The Deejays*, the first book about DJs, Arnold Passman draws attention to the constant presence of DJs on the radio. In 1926 and 1927 the number of records played on the radio grew swiftly, and when the recession set in, many of the large radio stations fell back on their cheap music supplies.[70] The consequence of this was that the record industry and station operators were constantly arguing about the payment of copyright royalties. Again and again there were prohibitions, limitations and legal procedures.[71] Muscians, as well as the record companies, felt they were being given short shrift by the playing of records. Trade unionists James Caesar Petrillo of the American Federation of Musicians described DJs as destroyers of live musicians, and became one of the most assiduous adversaries of DJs.[72] Other organized musicians argued that radio stations that played records were obliged to employ musicians in the station.

69. Cf. ERB, Ernst, op. cit., p. 77.

70. Cf. PASSMAN, Arnold, loc. cit., p. 36.

71. Cf. DeLONG, Thomas A.: The Mighty Music Box, pp. 263–267.

72. Cf. MEYER, Hazel: The Gold in Tin Pan Alley, p. 124ff.

The argument about the value of DJs in the music business continued apace. What remains inarguable is that even then the propaganda qualities of DJs were being exploited, and the first bribes paid to ensure that the DJ would actually play the records being promoted. 'Pay-to-play', or payola, became the set term for bribes paid to DJs. At the end of the 50s this custom turned into an enormous scandal in the United States (see the payola chapter, pp. 63–5). The early payola payments were a sign that DJs possessed power, influence and charisma.

The DJ was 'somebody', even though most radio stations preferred their DJs to work anonymously. The voice between the records had to lead inconspicuously from one piece of music to the next, and above all it had to incorporate all the advertisements into the broadcast. The DJ as a personality had to remain in the background where the products and the music were concerned, which didn't work, because the first radio DJs who broke out of anonymity were heaped with fan mail.

73. Cf. SHAW, Arnold: Rock'n'Roll, p. 69.

74. DeLONG, Thomas A.: op. cit., p. 272.

75. Cf. PASSMAN, Arnold, op. cit., p. 47f.; CHAPPLE, Steven/ GAROFALO, Reebee: Wem gehört die Rockmusik?, p. 68.

THE FIRST DJ STAR

The first real star among the DJs was Martin Block. In the early 30s former travelling salesman Block had jobbed on almost twenty radio stations, until he settled with the small New York radio channel WNEW in 1934. According to legend, on 2 February 1935 Block began to play records when waiting for news during the Lindbergh kidnap trial. At that time the radio station archive didn't have a single record.[73] Block had bought the first ones in the Liberty Music Shop around the corner, all of them by the band-leader and trumpeter Clyde McCoy. So Block didn't play a 'hodgepodge'[74] of records, but put on one song by McCoy after another, thus imitating the programme of a concert or a dance. Between the songs Block held a fantasy conversation with the musician, and gave the presentation a new quality: it was show, journalism and music programme at once.[75] Block was not the inventor of this type of radio show, but had copied it from a DJ named Al

Jarvis in Los Angeles. In 1932, working for the radio station KFBW in Los Angeles, Jarvis had already begun to put records on in such a way as to give the listeners the illusion of being at a concert. Al Jarvis called his show, embellished with imaginative verbal dexterity, *The World's Largest Make-Believe Ballroom*. The title mixed megalomaniac boasting with a cheeky admission of fraud, but Block was to be the first to turn the mixture into a massive success. Jarvis remained an averagely famous Californian DJ.

Block's *Make-Believe Ball* rapidly became a talking-point in New York. Block found himself a sponsor of his own, a company that produced slimming pills. His famous advertising slogan ('be fair to your husband by taking the reducing pill'), spoken in a highly seductive voice, ensured that only a day after the first broadcast six hundred orders came in to the radio station. By the end of the first week the number had risen to 3,750.[76] The sceptics in charge of WNEW, who didn't really want to have a 'disc show' in their programme, broke with their dogma of broadcasting only live music. And rightly so, because within only four months, the average audience of the *Make-Believe Ballroom* had risen to four million. Up to twelve thousand fan letters a week landed in Block's office.[77]

The music industry and the advertising agencies understood: Martin Block was 'hot, and so was his show'.[78] In the same year the popular fake dance-hall broadcast was extended to two-and-a-half hours. The record industry supplied the DJ with records, interviews and stars. Block, who was highly interested in the background of the music business, played records in his broadcasts, and in between he spoke to the musicians and producers about their work, their problems and enthusiasms.

For the first time, the idea of the disc jockey showed that it had an incredible potential.[79] The sponsors queued up to get one of the quarter-hourly slots of Block's broadcast – the advertised products sold regardless of whether they were pills, cigarettes or freezer cabinets.[80] Block wasn't just someone who played records, he was above all an advertising man. He wrote the advertising slogans for his sponsors himself, and was proud of it. His slogans for Lucky

76. PASSMAN, Arnold, op. cit., p. 48.

77. Cf. HALPER, Donna L.: Radio Music Directing, p. 28.

78. Ibid.

79. Cf. Ibid.

80. PASSMAN, Arnold, loc. cit.

Martin Block (l.) with Benny Goodman

Strike ('Lucky Strike Means Fine Tobacco') and Chesterfield cigarettes ('Always Buy Chesterfields') were milestones of media marketing. In 1938 his selling abilities became legendary, when Block managed to sell 300 freezing cabinets for a store in Newark, New Jersey, in the middle of a snow storm.

The listeners' trust in their DJ seemed limitless. The media philosopher Marshall McLuhan described one immediate aspect of radio as a 'world of unspoken communication between writer–speaker and the listener'.[81] 'A private experience', whose deep psychological sources of resonance McLuhan attested: 'The subliminal depths of radio are charged with the resonating echoes of tribal horns and antique drums. This is inherent in the very nature of this medium, with its power to turn the psyche and society into a single echo chamber.'[82] And what could be more obvious for a clever former salesman and born entertainer than to exploit the echoing character of the 'the tribal drum' (McLuhan) for advertising? Block, 'a crooning, serious on-the-air type,'[83] combined the role of the entertainer with that of the salesman, presenting his records, radio texts and advertisements in a single uninterrupted flow. The same man who had spoiled the listener with his favourite music and perhaps the occasional gag, seconds later became the man recommending a cigarette or a laxative: the same crooner's voice, the same person, the old familiarity. The DJ called himself an entertainer, who exuded a feeling of closeness and neighbourliness as if it was the most natural thing in the world.

Block's success was a perfect example of what Horkheimer and Adorno described as the merging of advertising and the culture industry. 'In both cases the insistent demand for effectiveness makes technology into psychotechnology, into a procedure for manipulating men. In both cases the standards are the striking yet familiar, the easy yet catchy, the skilful yet simple...'[84] It is possible that Adorno and Horkheimer had even heard Block, because in their essays on radio, the 'progressive latecomer of mass culture', the Chesterfield advertisement (Block's?) is identified as paradigmatic. 'Chesterfield is merely the nation's cigarette, but the radio is the voice of the nation.'[85] That

81. McLUHAN, Marshall, op. cit., p. 319.

82. Ibid.

83. CHAPPLE, Steven/ GAROFALO, Reebee, loc. cit., p. 68.

84. HORKHEIMER, Max/ ADORNO, Theodor W.: Dialectic of Enlightenment, p. 163.

85. Ibid. p. 159.

Block never saw himself as a producer of culture, and didn't see any problem in the merging of radio programme and advertising, makes him all the more valuable as an example. In obscene transparency, he embodies the merging of advertising and culture industry after the 30s.

Passman stresses that Block's success as a salesman and a DJ must be understood against the background of the recent Depression. At this time the selling of a product was taken as a 'summum bonum'.[86] Block's gallant mixture of formal ('Ladies and Gentlemen') and intimate ('For you, and you, and especially, *you!*') resulted in a trust and understanding, otherwise paid only to the President.[87] Block was so popular that he was even able to sell his broadcast to other broadcasters. This makes him the first DJ whose work, syndicated as a 'commodity', entered the world of business.[88] Block is the forerunner of all the populist DJs who were less concerned with expressing their musical taste, their hipness and their individuality than with having success with the correct mixture of music, advertising and small-talk.[89]

Block remained successful as a radio DJ for a long time. During the war he took over a number of programmes that could be heard not only in New York but in many other states besides. After the war Block was one of the top earners in the entertainment business. In 1948 he earned almost two million dollars[90] simply for the syndication of the *Make-Believe Ballroom* to thirty stations, an incredibly large amount for the times. In 1954 Block was bound to the radio broadcaster ABC by a contract worth millions of dollars,[91] but by that time his audience share was already in decline. Block's heyday had been the late 30s, the whole of the 40s and the early 50s – he was unsympathetic towards the arrival of rock'n'roll and the new DJ superstar Alan Freed, and became one of the keenest critics of the pop music that was just coming into being.[92]

PLAY MY MUSIC, MAN!

The DJ was influential – musicians were quick to

86. Cf. PASSMAN, Arnold, loc. cit., p. 65.

87. Cf. Ibid.

88. CHAPPLE, Steven/ GAROFALO, Reebee, op. cit., p. 115f.

89. Ibid. p. 65f.

90. Ibid. p. 115.

91. Ibid. p. 188f.

92. SHAW, Arnold: Dictionary of American Pop/Rock, p. 40.

recognize that as well. In 1948 the band-leader Art Mooney sent his version of the ballad 'I'm Looking Over a Four-Leaf Clover' to the leading radio DJs. One copy made its way with a personal dedication to the jazz expert and enthusiast Albert (Jazzbo) Collins in Salt Lake City. He played the cheerful and rather banal ballad in his popular, jazz-purist programme without hearing the record, because he was flattered by the artist's friendly note. The song began with a banjo solo that was torture to the ears of jazz fans. Collins listened to the end of the record, and, horrified, groaned into the microphone: 'I don't really believe this, but maybe I'm wrong. Let's listen again.'[93] The phones started ringing in the radio station, and everyone wanted to know what the music was. Collins was furious at the bad taste of his listeners and played the song all afternoon.[94] He kept giving it different names until the telephone lines jammed and the police were alerted, causing a scandal in Salt Lake City that made headlines all across America for days to come. 'Pop history was written that afternoon',[95] said Hazel Meyer in 1958 in one of the first books about 'pop' music. Art Mooney's mediocre ballad became one of the four most successful best-sellers of the year.

'I don't care what it is. I want to make hits':[96] that was how Cleveland's Bill Randle described his function as a DJ in 1949. Randle discovered Johnnie Ray and Tony Bennett. He had one of his 'earliest demonstrations of power'[97] when he played the R&B song 'Saturday Night Fish Fry' by Louis Jordan and broadcast the positive audience reaction live. He repeated the song every quarter of an hour and plugged it that way. Randle was so influential that he gave the record companies advice on distribution, and his judgement became the deciding factor for many record sellers and buyers when they were ordering records.[98]

93. Ibid. p. 72.

94. Arnold Shaw says he did it for three-and-a-half hours altogether. (Cf.: SHAW, Arnold: Rock'n'Roll, p. 70.)

95. Cf. MEYER, Hazel, loc. cit., p. 133.

96. SHAW, Arnold: Rock'n'Roll, p. 71.

97. Ibid. p. 72.

98. Cf. Ibid.

THE HIT PARADE – THE BIRTH OF TOP 40 RADIO

While Martin Block was beginning his triumph as a

99. CHAPPLE, Steven/
GAROFALO, Reebee, loc. cit., p. 46.

100. Ibid.

101. EBERLY, Philip K.: Music in
the Air, p. 130.

102. Cf. Ibid. p. 127.

103. Cf. PEATMAN, John Gray:
Radio and Popular Music, in:
LAZARSFELD, Paul F./ STANTON,
Frank N.: Radio Research 1942–1943,
p. 362f.

disc jockey, a broadcasting format was being developed which was to bolster the position of the disc jockey as a record-spinner and reduce his position as a dictator of taste: the hit parade. The idea of the hit parade has always been that of playing the most successful singles and long-playing records within a certain time, and to play the hits in reverse order to number one. Local hit parades came into fashion in 1934,[99] and in the same year the NBC Red Network in New York launched the 'Lucky Strike Hit Parade', to become the top-rating show within four months.[100] From 20 April 1935 until 24 April 1959 *Your Hit Parade*, subtitled 'America's Taste in Popular Music', was broadcast on Saturday evenings.

At the time of the great male vocalists like Frank Sinatra, Perry Como and Nat 'King' Cole, the popularity of the hit parade was at its peak. The stars needed the hit parade as a forum, and the hit parade needed the stars as their heroes and crowd pullers. The radio historian Philip K. Eberly claims that stars like Frank Sinatra would not have become what they were without the hit parade. Once America joined the war, Saturday night became 'the loneliest night of the week' for the girls whose boyfriends and husbands were in the army, and Sinatra was a real beacon.[101] Sponsored by Lucky Strike, Sinatra became the superstar of the 40s. In the early days, the hits were played by a radio orchestra with a strong brass section and solo singers, and later records of the hits were used. Top 40 radio adopted the hit parade idea as a programme ideology for the whole format of a station.

The question of how the chart was to be drawn up was vexed from the start. Sales of records and sheet music were evaluated, along with the frequency with which the songs were played on the radio. What was questionable was how the three factors were to be evaluated. In the 30s the trade magazine *Variety* often came to different conclusions in the chart placements from the Lucky Strike hit parade.[102] The sociologist John Gray Peatman, who examined the hit parade for the communications expert Paul Lazarsfeld and his studies into radio, found another two factors for chart evaluation: jukebox plays and audience requests to band-leaders.[103] Compared with the three main coefficients, however, these two factors remained a side-issue. What was important was only that no one be told of the sequence before the broadcast. When Frank Sinatra visited the White House, President Roosevelt is supposed to have asked him which song would be at the top of the charts the following Saturday.[104]

In 1940, a study by CBS showed that about forty-six million men and women listened to the hit parade on average 2.9 times a month.[105] That meant that just more than half of all adults in the United States were among the audience of the hit parade, not just the girls and boys under eighteen. The number grew continuously, according to a long-term study of the years 1939–42.[106] The music industry's ideal was to make a hit. In Lazarsfeld's radio studies in 1941, Duncan MacDougald pointed out that the lifetime of a record was reduced by radio. While a 'best-selling song' was 'alive' for eighteen months in the early 30s, by 1941 it only lasted four months.[107]

The consequence of this was that the music industry produced more music more quickly, and had to take its bearings more from popular taste if it was to achieve a calculated success. In 1941 this meant – according to MacDougald – '(1) that the melodic line be 'simple and easy to sing and play'; (2) that the lyric be 'romantic', 'original', and/or 'tell an appealing story'; and (3) that 'the melody of the chorus be thirty-two bars long'.[108] Once the song was produced, it became crucially important to place it on the radio. Programme directors, musical directors and the DJs in the radio stations were key figures in the struggle for market share. A new song could only be a hit if it had airplay. The mechanism of pop culture took that which was known and made it something familiar – into a hit that potentially everyone wanted to buy.

The song would then be hammered into the heads of the listeners, as MacDougald sadly sums up: 'The public at large – more specifically the radio audience – has been led more and more to the point of merely accepting these songs as standardized (musical) products, with less and less active resentment and critical interest... Thus it may be assumed that this controlled repetition and manipulated recommendation seem to tend to the standardization of the tastes of the

104. Cf. SHAW, Arnold, Rock'n'Roll, p. 74.

105. Quoted in: PEATMAN, John Gray, loc. cit., p. 353.

106. Ibid.

107. Cf. MacDOUGALD, Duncan Jr.: The Popular Music Industry, in: LAZARSFELD, Paul F./ STANTON, Frank N.: Radio Research 1941, p. 71.

108. Ibid. p. 81.

109. Ibid. p. 109.

110. In the foreword the editors thank Adorno: 'Special thanks is due Dr. T.W. Adorno for his advice on all the studies in this volume related to music.' (LAZARSFELD, Paul F./ STANTON, Frank N.: Radio Research 941, p. xii)

111. Cf. MacFARLAND, David T.: Up From Middle America: The Development of Top 40, in: LICHTY, Lawrence W./ TOPPING, Malachi C.: American Broadcasting, p. 399.

listener and the subsequent gradual eradication of these tastes.'[109]

Overall, the radio studies directed by Paul F. Lazarsfeld and Frank N. Stanton tend to be a critical evaluation of popular music and its media and industrial context. Their similarity to the critique of the culture industry as formulated by Adorno and Horkheimer is obvious: the critics' complaint that culture has become pure business, and a great deception of the masses, underlies, like a subtext, the studies and statements of the American sociologists.[110] From that point of view, infected by the European hubris of electronic culture, they have become strangers in their own (pop) culture, although it must be borne in mind that at that time almost all intellectuals had a detached and critical relationship with mass culture. But the far-sightedness of their prognoses is demonstrated by a new phenomenon in the organization of radio programmes: the ideological pure form of popular music, the hit parade, develops throughout the 50s into a dictatorship of the music mainstream, Top 40 radio.

TOP 40 RADIO

When television triumphed in the early 50s, the radio stations looked for new forms of programming to keep the population tuned in to the radio. In the 40s most independent radio stations had broadcast a loose mixture of music and news, generally presented by DJs.[111] Top 40 radio was something like the 'music-and-news' idea taken a stage further; it tried to adapt itself more closely to the listening habits of the masses, and make the DJs' decisions of taste irrelevant.

David T. MacFarland, who studied the origins of the Top 40 radio format, traced the success of mainstream radio back, amongst other things, to social changes after the Second World War: there was, for example, the rapid growth of the suburbs, which meant that more and more commuters were spending more and more time in the car. Time that was often spent listening to the radio, in accordance with Horkheimer and Adorno's dictum that '(a)musement under late capitalism is the prolongation of work.'[112]

More important for the success of Top 40 radio, in all likelihood, was demographic development in the USA. The average age of the population constantly declined from the end of the Second World War. Adding to this the Baby Boom, the consequence was that the youth market became increasingly attractive. Nik Cohn saw the rise of the 'youth market' as one of the most important factors behind the rise of pop: '...businessmen had never before seen teenagers as independent commercial units, as having entirely separate needs and tastes from the rest of the community. Now the possibilities hit them like a prophetic vision and they moved in fast, fawning like mad.'[113]

Top 40 radio was a product of the media and music industry, and pure fawning it was. Young people got to hear what they wanted to hear. And the music producers single-mindedly found out what they wanted to hear. The 50s were years of modest but broad affluence in the USA, and a large proportion of the growing income was spent on the products of the new media industry.[114] The music industry designed music solely for the market and hoped it would hit gold at some point. In April 1954 it happened: when an ageing country'n'western singer called Bill Haley made a record called 'Rock Around the Clock'. A year later it was a hit in the United States, then in England and finally in the rest of the world. For Nik Cohn the 15 million records sold by Haley were the birth of pop music.[115]

It is certainly no coincidence that this birth of pop music coincides with the rise of the Top 40 format. Before 1949 music policy on the radio consisted of a mishmash of hits and all kinds of other music such as classical, marching and folk music. In 1949 the KOWH transmitter in Omaha, under the directorship of Todd Storz, began to play only popular music – the music that had succeeded in terms of record sales and juke-box plays. The most successful singles were then taken on to the format of the Top 40 stations. In 1953 the first pure Top 40 shows appeared on WTIX in New Orleans and KOWH in Omaha, playing various versions of the most successful songs. Some time later, they began to seek

112. HORKHEIMER, Max/ADORNO, Theodor W.: op. cit., p. 137.

113. COHN, Nik: op. cit., p. 9.

114. Cf. MacFARLAND, David T.: The Development of the Top 40 Radio Format, p. 7.

115. Cf. COHN, Nik: op. cit., p. 10.

out the 'best' version of the hit song, and leave out the others. The next step towards the Top 40 format was the inclusion of the hits from the Top 40 even outside the 'countdown' programme. In 1956, KOWH and then the other Storz stations started up the 'true limited playlist' ,[116] making the most popular records the most heard on the radio as well. A direct proportionality between the sales figures and radio airplay became apparent.

The music that sold well in the mid-50s was all at the service of the 'rock revolution' (Shaw): the Top 40 hits of 1955 included Bill Haley's 'Rock Around the Clock', Chuck Berry's 'Maybelline' and El Dorado's 'At My Front Door'; in 1956 Elvis Presley dictated chart events with hits like 'Don't Be Cruel', 'Heartbreak Hotel', 'Hound Dog' and 'I Want You, I Need You, I Love You'. Along with him, pop rebels like Fats Domino, Gene Vincent and Carl Perkins stormed the charts.[117] Top 40 radio lived off the momentum of popular music, as did the music industry, which almost trebled its income from record sales in the five years from 1954 to 1959.[118] With a mixture of rock'n'roll, Doris Day and country sounds, the charts documented a broad social consensus in the USA. It seemed that hit songs couldn't get enough airplay. The 'totality of the culture industry' consists 'in repetition',[119] as Horkheimer and Adorno had recognized as early as 1944, and now Top 40 radio started to make this totality a reality. But radio and record company managers also lived off the fact that their entertainment industry contained within it the new pop music scene. Where Top 40 radio abolished the individual not only in the form of DJs, but also in the form of dissident artistic products, a new form of individualism was coming into being, and one that was able to formulate itself within the context of different kinds of standardization. The otherwise predominant practice of 'making the average the heroic'[120] collapses in the face of outstanding productions of pop music. But at first little of that was heard in the largely claustrophobically narrow formats of Top 40 radio.

Only a few DJs felt constrained by the restrictions of the Top 40 format. Although the position of the DJ – the only possible presenter of hit broadcasts – was more solid than ever, his influence on programming was in

116. MacFARLAND, David T.: Up From Middle America: The Development of Top 40, in: LICHTY, Lawrence..., p. 401.

117. Cf. POLLOCK, Bruce: When Rock Was Young, p. 195ff.

118. In 1954 213 million dollars was taken in record sales, while by 1959 the total was already 603 million dollars (cf. GILLETT, Charlie: The Sound of the City, p. 39).

119. HORKHEIMER, Max/ ADORNO, Theodor W.: op. cit., p. 136.

120. Ibid. p. 156.

noticeable decline. The DJs were at the mercy of the taste of the populace. The managers and owners of the radio stations became crucially important figures: they decided the direction of the station, they designed its format, and they looked for DJs to fit the format. Top 40 radio didn't want too much talk between the songs, no DJ personalities and certainly no musical didacticism à la Block or Jarvis.

No wonder that many DJs who had enjoyed great popularity in the 50s criticized the dictates of Top 40 radio. Their right to select records and design the programme was in decline. More and more stations devoted themselves to profitable populism, and the DJs' laments grew louder. On 12 March 1958 *Variety*, one of the most important entertainment papers in America, carried the headline: 'Deejay: Performer or Puppet?'[121] The article by Herm Schoenfeld painted a gloomy picture: 'The disc jockey is now in a fight for survival. Hailed as a hero in radio's surging boom in the face of television competition, the deejay now feels himself being cut down to size in the machine of "formula radio".'[122] The article followed on from a DJ convention in Kansas City, in which a record manager from Columbia confronted the DJs with the demand for their mass resignation.

In April 1958 the conflict between the DJs and the Top 40 stations intensified. KLAC in Los Angeles announced that it would, henceforward, do without live DJs, and only broadcast pre-recorded introductions. With these short, sober introductions 13 per cent more music could be played. The pages of the music magazine *Billboard* at the end of 1958 contained a discussion about whether the DJ could survive. Some of the famous DJs had thrown in their jobs, others had yielded to the dictates of the format. The DJ legends Martin Block and Bill Randle took to the barricades to prevent the DJ becoming a dying species.[123]

At a symposium in the spring of 1959 the question was asked: 'Is the personality DJ craze on the wane?' One programmer gave a clear answer:

If the personality DJ is the golden-tongued, $100,000-a-year, lethargic, loquacious, self-styled music critic, the answer is 'yes'. The modern DJ is a man who knows

121. Quoted in: MacFARLAND, David T.: The Development of the Top 40 Radio Format, p. 379.

122. Ibid.

123. 'Sparks Still Fly in Format Fracas', BILLBOARD, 15 December 1958, p. 63, quoted from: ibid, p. 382.

where he is going, what he is going to say, and – most important – knows why. He is a highly trained specialist, who, so unlike Stanislaski, demands motivation for any action. He realises that only the merest minority give a damn about his pontification on the pros and cons of every record... The job of the DJ today is to establish his personality between records. He must say what he has to say in a brief, bright, entertaining manner.[124]

124 . 'Is the Personality DJ Craze on the Wane?' SPONSOR, 18 July 1959, p. 46, quoted from: ibid. p. 383.

125 . Ibid.

In July 1959 the foundation of the National Disc Jockey Association (DJA) was held in Milwaukee. DJs and music programmers with at least two years' professional experience, along with radio managers, were permitted to take part, but not representatives of the record industry. At the same time as the foundation of the DJA, the payola scandal made the headlines. Rather than attacking the policy of the radio managers, the DJA had to defend the DJs against the accusation of corruption.

The payola scandal brought the guild of DJs severely into disrepute. The corruption deals seemed to confirm the radio owners and managers in their suspicion of DJs and their record selections, and consequently also in their trust in the Top 40 radio format. The DJ had lost a great deal of credit in the public eye. MacFarland: 'In the 1950s, disc jockeys ran the gamut from being considered among the "saviors of radio" in the early period to the "Judases of jukedom" at the end of the decade.'[125]

And so the DJA turned into a mere PR company that was supposed to overhaul the image of the DJs, tainted by the payola affair; it didn't succeed. It was individual DJs who saw their job as a vocation and who felt urged to join in with the bright new pop world, they were the ones who popularized the DJ and kept him alive as a glittering personality.

ALAN FREED –
THE INVENTOR OF ROCK'N'ROLL

Despite the imposition of a format on the radio programme, despite the payola scandal, the DJ couldn't be defeated as a profession, a myth and a youth hero. The DJs were familiar figures who were honoured despite being known only by their voices. In George Lucas's film *American Graffiti* the DJ is a substitute father, a substitute friend, a substitute therapist and a substitute matchmaker, who takes care of all the characters in the film. DJ Wolfman's programme also acts as the external frame of the melancholic film about youth, growing older and life in an American town in the early 60s.

Wolfman's music, his speeches and not least his social function as a messenger, although he is only seen once and then very briefly, make him central to the meaning of the film. Wolfman holds the characters as close together as he is able, as the herald of a working youth culture defining itself through clothes, music and cars. He provides the soundtrack to the senselessly heroic journeys through the streets of the city one Saturday evening. DJ Wolfman conveys greetings and messages, and the various young people on the streets of the city are brought together via the car radio. He's a DJ legend; no one's sure what he looks like, whether he is white or black and where he broadcasts his programme from. Wolfman Jack, born Bob Smith, plays himself in the film. He was a cult figure in America into the 1980s, but he was only an imitator of a DJ who helped to invent rock'n'roll and launched the pop revolution. A man of whom Wolfman said that he directly touched the heart of his listeners, that he prompted feelings, and that there was always something magical about him: 'He was a CRUSADER. I ain't crusading no more for rock and roll, because rock and roll IS. And it's gonna be FOREVER.'[126] The DJ who turned twelve-year-old Bob Smith into a thief of record-players and tape-recorders was Alan Freed.

The 50s were the infancy of pop music. In the 30s and

126 . JONES, Allen: Howl of the Wolfman, in: MELODY MAKER, 6 September 1975.

DJ Wolfman in American Graffiti

40s country blues had turned into rhythm and blues. R&B was the music of the blacks, as jazz and blues had been before. And it wasn't long before the whites began to come closer to this music.

Freed, born in 1921 in Johnstown, Pennsylvania, grew up in Ohio and began his radio career in 1945 with a station in Pennsylvania as a classical music DJ. After moving a few times, Freed ended up at the station WJW in Cleveland in 1951. It was there that record-shop owner and radio sponsor Leo Mintz confronted Freed with R&B. It was the time when R&B was beginning 'to filter through to white kids'[127] – the post-war generation seemed slowly to be abandoning its fundamental fear of black culture and music. The number of lovers of R&B was greater than that of jazz-lovers in the 30s. The American pop historian and philosopher Robert G. Pielke speaks of a powerful 'underground, barely discernible, halting fascination with black culture'.[128]

Freed's visit to Mintz's record shop is pop history. In 1951 Freed saw teenagers dancing to black R&B there, and he noted the enthusiasm with which they were buying the records. He was shocked: 'I heard the tenor saxophones of Red Prysock and Big Al Sears. I heard the blues-singing, piano-playing Ivory Joe Hunter. I wondered. I wondered for about a week. Then I went to the station manager and talked him into permitting me to follow my classical program with a rock'n'roll party.'[129] One of the most famous radio programmes in America was born: the *Moon Dog Show*, on which Freed played almost nothing but black R&B.

In his carefully researched biography of Freed, John A. Jackson contradicts this legend. The myth of the sound of rock'n'roll crossing racial boundaries was false, particularly as regards the beginning of Freed's activities. Both Mintz's record shop and Freed's programme 'at first attracted an audience that was nearly all Negro',[130] as Freed later admitted. The first concerts he held were also attended almost only by blacks. But the situation changed thanks to his work. The more Freed devoted himself to R&B, the more whites he was able to win over to the new music. This was clear in the concerts he organized in the Cleveland Arena, where both artists and audience often included

127. COHN, Nik: AwopBopaLooBop..., p. 7.

128. PIELKE, Robert G.: You Say You Want a Revolution, p. 25.

129. NEW MUSICAL EXPRESS, 23 September 1956, quoted from GILLETT, Charlie, loc. cit., p. 13.

130. JACKSON, John A.: Big Beat Heat, p. 34.

Alan Freed

whites as well as blacks. To avoid what Freed called 'the racist stigma of the old classification', he avoided the phrase R&B, and invented the term rock'n'roll.[131] Whether Freed actually did think up the term or whether he borrowed it from a 1947 song[132] is arguable. What is certain is that it was Alan Freed who popularized it, until Bill Haley's 'Rock-a-Beatin' Boogie' finally brought it into its own as the expression for a musical trend.

The 'all-black' audience: Moon Dog Shows with Alan Freed 1952–3

Freed became Moon Dog, a kind of 'mid-American Steppenwolf',[133] who pronounced black language in a black way and, with his rock'n'roll collection, became a prototype of the 'White Negro' – as Norman Mailer was later to call the white hipster. Freed's vocal cords had been injured during a polyp operation, and so he always sounded hoarse like a 'blues shouter,'[134] he howled along with songs and beat out the rhythm with his fist on the telephone book. There had never been anything like it on white radio: passion, charm and rebellion rolled together in one powerful package. Despite or because of this unusual mixture, Freed became famous.

His 'missionary arrogance'[135] made him popular among young people, but Freed was a thorn in the eye of his radio competition, the conservative, racist environment of the McCarthy era and the church. He converted young people to rock'n'roll and was 'intolerant'[136] of

131. COHN, Nik: AwopBopaLooBop..., p. 13.

132. KNEIF, Tibor: Rockmusik, p. 118f. In the same book Kneif indicates that Freed 'didn't invent the term "rock'n'roll", despite his own claim, but first heard it from his friend, the record dealer Leo Mintz in Cleveland' (p. 275). In his cover copy for one of his compilation LPs Freed claimed to have started using the term in 1951, and not to have invented it. Arnold Shaw explains that 'rock and roll' actually comes from blues language, and was used as a euphemism for sexual intercourse. After the Second World War the term, or just the 'rock', turned up in more and more R&B numbers, semantically referring both to sex and to dancing. (Cf. SHAW, Arnold: Rock'n'Roll, p. 116f.)

133. PASSMAN, Arnold, loc. cit., p. 177.

134. SHAW, Arnold: Rock'n'Roll, p. 117.

135. KNEIF, Tibor: Rockmusik, p. 275.

136. Ibid.

cover-versions by white interpreters, who were thought to take the black power and authenticity away from the original. Many black hits were covered for the white market, and 'castrated'[137] at the same time, as Cohn put it, because 'Right through the early fifties... white stations persisted in blocking the r&b off their airways and the biggest names were still people like Doris Day, Perry Como and Frankie Laine.'[138] Freed was one of the few who was able to break through those reactionary restrictions.

137. COHN, Nik: AwopBopaLooBop..., loc. cit., p. 7.

138. Ibid.

139. HALBSCHEFFEL, Bernward/ KNEIF, Tibor: Sachlexikon Rockmusik, p. 275.

140. PASSMAN, Arnold, loc. cit., p. 201.

141. Cf. SKLAR, Rick: Rocking America, p. 19.

Despite the beginnings of Top 40 radio and a racist media policy, Alan Freed's success continued. In 1954 the New York WINS station employed him, and Freed was able to battle on more effectively with his 'crusade'.[139] After only four months with the station, Freed was seen, in Passman's words, as 'the major factor in metropolitan radio as the r'n'b influence crossed all colour lines into the general pop market.'[140] Rick Sklar, programme director of WINS, declared Freed's record collection consisting of hundreds of 45 rpm singles, uncatalogued and piled up chaotically in an old cupboard, to be the most influential sound archive in commercial radio.[141]

Freed's working method is described as that of a

passionate Expressionist. His slight build and curly hair seemed to have an electric charge, along with his hectic movements when he rummaged around in the records and found his selection. The sole criterion of his selection was his own taste. The dramatic structure of the programme was random. 'There were no categories such as fast or slow records, no alternating of male and female singers with groups, and no pacing of the show based on song popularity.'[142] Freed's responsibility for his programme came from a passion and love for rock'n'roll, and made no compromises where the music was concerned. It was Freed's good fortune to be successful with this kind of programme: his listening figures and the multiple syndications of his programme gave him – contrary to all the trends – great freedom.

Freed also organized his parties in New York, where they enjoyed similar success to those in Cleveland. What was particularly surprising was that most of those who attended to the concerts were young black people, despite the many reservations that sections of the black community had towards someone who imitated blacks.[143] With his commitment as a concert organizer, Freed also opened up a further field of activity for DJs. 'DJs were ideally suited as concert promoters. They had unlimited access to advertising opportunities over the radio, daily contact with managers and artists, and they were in many cases themselves "celebrities".'[144] Freed was one such celebrity. In the 1956 rock'n'roll film *Rock Around the Clock*, which tells of the rise of Bill Haley, Freed played himself as the DJ who helped Haley make his breakthrough. In the same year he played a leading role in Will Brice's *Rock, Rock, Rock*. In *Don't Knock the Rock* Freed played himself once again. He also appeared as co-writer of fifteen rock'n'roll songs including Chuck Berry's 'Maybelline'. What remains questionable is whether this 'collaboration' was anything other than the advertising that he did for the records, and thus only an opportunity to pay payola – cleverly disguised as co-authorship – to Freed.[145] On the other hand it should be pointed out that Freed was a 'skilled arranger',[146] who had composed two solid-selling successes with 'Tongue-tied Blues' and 'Nadine'. Alan Freed felt 'every beat of every note of the music

142. Ibid.

143. SHAW, Arnold: Rock'n'Roll, p. 119.

144. CHAPPLE, Steven/ GAROFALO, Reebee: Rock'n'roll is Here to Pay, p. 138.

145. Cf. Ibid. p. 59.

146. SHAW, Arnold: Rock'n'Roll, p. 119.

147. PASSMAN, Arnold, loc. cit., p. 178.

148. SHAW, Arnold: Rock'n'Roll, p. 118.

149. PASSMAN, Arnold, loc. cit., p. 237. In Jackson's biography, Freed contradicts this statement, saying that he didn't want to say the police were directly responsible, but just spoke of 'they'. (Cf. JACKSON, John A., loc. cit., p. 195f.)

150. SHAW, Arnold: Rock'n'Roll, p. 122.

151. MARCUS, Greil: Mystery Train, p. 4.

that he played',[147] his fellow DJ Bill Randle put it. In other areas too Freed was considered passionate. When his wife said something he didn't like in the radio studio, he threw a full water jug at her, despite the fact that Arnold Shaw was there in the studio and Freed was on air. He was reserved in his reactions to the large record companies and supported the small independent labels (as did most coloured musicians).[148] When he appeared at a dance event in May 1958 with Jerry Lee Lewis as the headline, the police turned on the lights in the hall mid-show to keep watch on the dancing teens. As there had been riots in other cities, and protests from the Catholic Church, the police wanted to keep a close eye on the supposed rebellion. An unimaginable affront for Freed, who commented, 'Hey kids, the cops don't want you to have a good time!'[149] After the show there were disturbances in several parts of the city. Freed was arrested and charged, because in the opinion of the city authorities he had driven the teens into riot and anarchy. After his return, when the people from the station carpeted him unsympathetically, he furiously resigned and changed to their local competitor WABC. There Freed's career slowly came to an end after various payola-related accusations and trials. Freed had set new standards as a DJ. 'He brought to DJ broadcasts, a level of excitement and enthusiasm which were unknown before him, and which were a true expression of the music he represented.'[150] The DJ was – thanks to Freed's model – not just a record-spinner, entertainer, advertising expert or speed-talker, but first of all the agitator, initiator and motor behind a new musical trend and youth culture. For American pop intellectual Greil Marcus rock'n'roll should be seen 'not as youth culture, or counter-culture, but simply as American culture'.[151] In this sense Freed is certainly an American cultural monument – one of the new 'culture makers'. In 1973 the American–Canadian group The Band made an album entitled 'Moondog Matinee' – a homage to Freed and his rock'n'roll radio show, which all the band members had listened to.

In the 50s the DJ had become a central confidant for teenagers. George Lucas showed this in *American Graffiti*: the DJ is the authority who shapes and defines the sense of life with his music, talk and greetings – he provided 'tribal identity'.[152] Rock'n'roll began with a DJ, and pop music began with rock'n'roll. From the very first the DJ had taken his place within the history of pop, and its best days were yet to come.

THE DJ AND CORRUPTION: PAYOLA

Payola was the abbreviation of 'pay for play',[153] and a word invented specially for DJ bribery. Most people had never heard of it before corruption among DJs became a scandal, and it was even the subject of a Congress Committee in 1959. But corruption within the music industry was by no means a post-war invention; the two had gone hand in hand from the start, and adapted to changing media and marketing strategies. During the First World War and the 20s, it was the Vaudeville singers who were sponsored by the music industry. In return they were expected to take the latest numbers from the record companies and make them popular.[154] When radio became the medium which decided the fate of a song, band-leaders and singers were the first to be bribed. When the DJ assumed the role of the hit-maker, payola became a semi-institutional nexus between the record industry and DJs.

In the mid-50s the bribery of DJs was publicly discussed for the first time. The accumulated complaints and charges led in 1959 to the introduction of an investigative committee in the American Congress to clear up the allegations. The courts went to work. 207 people, most of them DJs, were charged with taking a total of a quarter of a million dollars in payola. Over 4,068 radio stations, each of which had an average of six DJs, this would mean that the overwhelming majority of DJs were 'clean'.[155] The two most famous DJs accused of corruption were Alan Freed and Dick Clark, whose television programme *American Bandstand* started in 1957 on ABC, and was shown on 105 stations a year later. Clark admitted his involvement in the corruption scandal, and confessed to the Committee of the House of Representatives that he had been involved in thirty-three (!) businesses within the music industry, including labels, music

152. COHN, Nik: AwopBopaLooBop..., p. 9.

153. EBERLY, Philip K., loc. cit., p. 286.

154. Cf. the excellent chapter on the early days of payola in MEYER, Hazel, loc. cit., pp. 154–185.

155. Ibid.

publishers and record pressing plants, but that he had already parted from them. Clark had done this chiefly so that he would be allowed to go on presenting the successful programme *American Bandstand*. The committee rewarded Clark's insight and regret with a clearance certificate: he was not pursued further.

156. Jo-Ann Campbell, a pop starlet and a close confidante of Freed, reports how much he suffered from these scandals: 'Everything just piled up on him and hurled him down into the ground. He literally died of a broken heart. He was quite young and he was stone broke, and that's the way he ended.' (POLLOCK, Bruce, loc. cit., p. 97f.)

157. Cf. PIELKE, Robert G., loc. cit., p. 32.

Dick Clarke and his American Bandstand

Alan Freed's case was quite different. When, on 8 February 1960, he had been examined by a sub-committee of the House of Representatives, Freed had already lost his radio and television programmes. Previously he had refused in principle to sign a declaration on oath giving the assurance that he had never received payola. Apart from this Freed did not appear before the investigative committee. When he was brought before a New York criminal court, Freed used the right of silence, and was then charged with twenty-six cases of corruption. In the trial, which took place in December 1962, he admitted guilt in two cases, and was fined four hundred dollars and given a six-month suspended sentence. In March 1964, as a consequence of the verdict of corruption, Freed was also charged with tax evasion. But no judgement was passed – Freed died, embittered, on 20 January 1965.[156] Freed had been most severely punished, a symbolic scapegoat for the community of those who had beaten a path for wild teen music into the cultural heartland of America.

With Freed, the establishment had put to death the man who had devoted himself entirely to rock'n'roll, a kind of music that had no wish to conceal its black roots and rebellious character. And this at a time when McCarthyism had created a climate of fear and intolerance with anti-Communist, nationalist and anti-Semitic persecutions that blocked any form of rejection and rebellion. Demonstrations against rock'n'roll were taking place in many American cities.[157] The scandal surrounding Jerry Lee Lewis' marriage to his 13-year-old cousin in 1958 infuriated the moral majority and racist reservations about any form of black culture were still very much part of American mainstream culture.[158] The Church saw rock'n'roll as the devil's music, and feared the moral danger to innocent young people from the relatively open sexualization of the music and the lyrics. Freed, as a rock'n'roll promoter, was for the puritan fundamentalists an agent of evil, whose punishment could only be a matter of time.

Dick Clark appeared quite the opposite, looking like a puritanical WASP antithesis to the instinctive Jewish hipster Freed. Clark backed rock'n'roll when it had already gained popularity, and even then he only played songs that were entirely harmless. The accusations that black pop historians made against Alan Freed as a traitor and destroyer of rhythm'n'blues, seem to apply more accurately to Dick Clark. Clark gave rock'n'roll a clean white image, and made no secret of his lack of enthusiasm for the new music. 'I'm an observer, and I present,'[159] Clark used to like saying,[160] thus emphasizing his detachment from pop culture. For Nik Cohn Clark was 'like an all-American choirboy': in his television show he 'preached God, America, Mother, True Love and Washing Behind Your Ears'.[161]

158. What is interesting is that the black pop historian Nelson George, in *The Death of Rhythm & Blues*, which describes the history of the watering-down and self-alienation of black music within a predominantly white music industry, sees Alan Freed as a conformist and business-minded white man. He imitated blacks, masked the black origin of rhythm'n'blues, and sold it to white teenagers as rock'n'roll: 'But as Freed knew, rock & roll wasn't a music but a marketing concept that evolved into a life-style' (GEORGE, Nelson: The Death of Rhythm&Blues, p. 67.) Similar accusations were discussed in New York's black community in 1954, but many of the young black people came to the dances that Freed organized in Manhattan. The prominent black band-leader Lucky Millinder also defended Freed: 'He has the fire and the enthusiasm of the Rev. Billy Graham, and he sure isn't going to make fun of the language of the blacks.' (SHAW, Arnold: Rock'n'Roll, p. 119.)

159. SHAW, Arnold: Ibid, p. 183.

160. In 1981, in the foreword to his history of rock'n'roll, Clark retrospectively declared himself a fighter for the rebel music: 'It became abundantly clear that rock was the music of the young and that it was looked upon by many older folks as "bad"... Obviously, a lot of people like rock and have made it an American institution. I've had my share of criticism because of my role in the development of rock and roll. I've also had my share of praise. But there's one comment of which I'm really proud: "Dick Clark was there when rock and roll needed him – he helped to keep it alive." (USLAN, Michael/ SOLOMON, Bruce: Dick Clark's The First 25 Years of Rock & Roll, p. 1.)

161. COHN, Nik: AwopBopaLooBop..., p. 50.

'POP IS HERE TO STAY' – DJS IN THE POP INDUSTRY

162. Ibid. p. 16.

163. Ibid.

164. SHAW, Arnold: Rock'n'Roll, p. 175.

165. COHN, Nik: AwopBopaLooBop..., p. 20.

166. Ibid. p. 24.

Clark's contribution to the great pop circus remains that with his television show he brought many visual aspects of the subculture to American teenagers. Thanks to *American Bandstand*, the teeny-boppers in the most remote villages of the mid-west knew what a teenager was supposed to look like, if he wanted to survive in the glamorous world of pop. The provincial teens saw the clothes, the hair, the movements of the stars, and were then able to style themselves more knowledgeably. Although the reactionary Dick Clark always laid great value on conservative new fashion (no jeans!), the influence of *American Bandstand* was enormous. The pop world – at least in America – rapidly became the national pop village.

Pop music began to draw up its own rules. Pop as 'exclusive teenage property'[162] (Cohn) spawned its own style 'in clothes, language and sex, a total independence in almost everything'.[163] From the vague rebellious gesture that rock music had previously been there emerged a new world order. In the song 'Blue Suede Shoes', Carl Perkins (and later Elvis in the more famous cover-version) explained to teenagers throughout the world what was important: clothing, style. 'You can do what you like with my house (set fire to it), with my car (steal it), my whiskey (drink it), but don't you step on my blue suede shoes.'[164]

What could the rest of the world do to his enchanting new blue suede shoes? For Cohn this is 'the first hint at an obsession with objects – motorbikes, clothes and so on – that was going to become central'.[165] Pop music defined the various fetish objects such as motorcycles, leather trousers, suede shoes and jukeboxes, and consequently, of course, the structures of meaning within youth culture.

The lyrics of early pop music were kept simple – a mixture of plain speaking and subcultural jargon. The lyrics became something like a 'secret teen code', they were 'almost a sign language, that would make rock entirely incomprehensible to adults'.[166] In his history of pop Cohn describes how he bought his first record: 'Tutti Frutti' by Little Richard. He listened to the record, and 'at one throw it taught me everything I ever need to know about pop. The message went: "Tutti frutti all rootie, tutti frutti all rootie, tutti frutti all rootie, awopbopaloobop alopbamboom!" As a summing up of what rock'n'roll was really all about, this was nothing but masterly.'[167]

Pop has its own language and poetry. Its power lies in euphoria, and in euphoria lies the power of taking pop seriously, because it is the euphoric bliss that the teenager never finds elsewhere in life, presented like that: infinitely stylized and yet so near.

The Big Bopper's real name was Jape Richardson, he was a Texan, and in 1959, at the age of 29, he suddenly became famous. In fact J.P. Richardson was a radio DJ and a programme director with KTRM, a small radio station in Beaumont, Texas. After a number of unsuccessful attempts in the music business, Richardson alias Big Bopper recorded a song on a B-side about a teenager who wants to persuade the girl he fancies to come on a date. 'Chantilly Lace' was a huge hit, and topped the charts in more than forty countries.[168] Richardson missed out on much of his fame. On 3 February 1959 he died in a plane crash along with Buddy Holly and Ritchie Valens. What he left behind was 'one of the very best'[169] singles in pop music: 'Apart from being funny and good, "Chantilly Lace" was a big step – it was the first time ever that white popular music owned up to lust...'[170]

DJs as pop stars, DJs as co-producers, DJs as song-writers – in the 50s DJs were central figures in the music business. Vivian Carter, a black woman, was at best average as a DJ, but her Vee-Jay label, which she co-founded with her husband James Bracken, was to have far-reaching consequences. Between 1954[171] and 1964,[172] the records of the Four Seasons and Gladys Knight and Pips appeared on the label. The Four Seasons were a model for the Beatles (cf. 'Paperback Writer') and the Rolling Stones (cf. 'Dandelion') because of their vocal techniques[173] – for Cohn they 'weren't only pop, but the greatest POP pop ever'.[174]

167. Ibid. p. 25.

168. Cf. GRAVES, Barry/ SCHMIDT-JOOS, Siegfried: Das neue Rocklexikon, p. 84.

169. COHN, Nik: AwopBopaLooBop..., p. 41.

170. Ibid.

171. In 'Soul', Arnold Shaw writes that Vee Jay was founded in 1954 (p. 131), while Charlie Gillett gives the date as 1953 (Cf. GILLETT, Charlie, loc. cit., p. 84.)

172. Nelson George dates the Vee-Jay bankruptcy as 1965 (Cf. GEORGE, Nelson: The Death..., p. 84.)

173. Cf. GRAVES, Barry/ SCHMIDT-JOOS, Siegfried, op. cit., p. 289.

174. COHN, Nik: AwopBopaLooBop..., p. 78.

Gladys Knight and the Pips were a family project based around the brother-and-sister team of Gladys and Merald Knight. With their vocal sound dominated by the vibrant, exciting voice of Gladys Knight, the Pips established the style for the beginnings of the soul label Motown, to which the Pips switched in 1967. The group, which had played together since 1952, when the members were children, maintained its presence in pop music until the late 80s.

Other important acts on the Vee-Jay label were the still unsuccessful Beatles, John Lee Hooker, Little Richard, Jimmy Reed and Jerry Butler. But despite a number of good-selling top ten songs, the Vee-Jay label of DJ Vivian Carter collapsed. Nelson George attributes this to the fact that Vee-Jay were not as shrewd 'at watching the bottom line as they were at spotting talent'.[175] Vee-Jay may have been 'extravagant and wasteful',[176] but nonetheless, the merits and qualities of the now-forgotten label were particularly important for the development of soul.[177] After the company's collapse, Vee-Jay left a gap not only in the record scene 'but in the history of black music',[178] a gap that would not be filled. It remains one of the best labels that have been set up by DJs.

MUCHO MAAS – THE DJ IN THOMAS PYNCHON

It was Thomas Pynchon who brought DJs into literature. In his mid-60s novel, *The Crying of Lot 49*, the protagonist Oedipa Maas is married to Mucho Maas, a DJ. Probably not Oedipa's great love, but her only choice: 'He was a disc jockey who worked further along the Peninsula and suffered regular crises of conscience about his profession. "I don't believe in any of it, Oed," he could usually get out. "I try, I truly can't," way down there, further down perhaps than she could reach, so that such things often brought her near panic.'[179]

Mucho is too sensitive for Oedipa. In his previous life he was a car salesman, with slim buttocks, clean-

175. GEORGE, Nelson: The Death..., p. 84.

176. GEORGE, Nelson: The Death..., loc. cit.

177. Cf. SHAW, Arnold: Soul, p. 131.

178. Ibid, p. 85.

179. PYNCHON, Thomas: The Crying of Lot 49, p. 7.

shaven and miserable about his job, in which he had to swindle the poorest of the poor. 'To Mucho it was horrible.'[180] He called out the used-car special offers over the loudspeakers, and a friend, who was also advertising manager with a radio station, discovered him for KCUF. Mucho left his used-car lot and became a disc jockey. He had believed in the cars, too much in the lot, 'he believed not at all in the station.'[181]

In a typical situation in a medium-sized radio station in the early 60s, two hundred top hits and the local news are the format within which the DJ has to operate. Mucho Maas as a person is dissolved in this format. The listeners are manipulated, not with violence, but lulled with pleasant music – a perfidious betrayal that torments Mucho Maas more than his swindles on the used-car lot. There it had been a matter of broken silencers, fiddled mileometers and brushed-over rust patches. Things that were visible, tangible and absolutely material. In the radio, consciousness becomes the touchstone of swindle, the format and the local news have the soft power of washing out brain-cells. 'Is it any wonder the world's gone insane, with information come to be the only real medium of exchange?'[182] asks the protagonist, Tyrone Slothrop, in Pynchon's *Gravity's Rainbow*. The future belongs to 'information machines',[183] and the first of these is a radio format that threatens to replace the DJ with a record chart. The last of them, since the 80s, have been computer programmes which synthetically assemble radio programmes according to the structure of the format and the station.[184]

Mucho tries to believe in his job.

Was it something like this he felt, looking through the soundproof glass at one of his colleagues with a headset clamped on a cueing the next record with movements stylised as the handling of chrism, censer, chalice might be for a holy man, yet really tuned in to the voice, voices, the music, its message, surrounded by it, digging it, as were all the faithful it went out to; did Mucho stand outside Studio A looking in, knowing that even if he could hear it he couldn't believe in it?[185]

180. Ibid. p. 8.

181. Ibid. p. 9.

182. PYNCHON, Thomas: Gravity's Rainbow, p. 258.

183. Ibid.

184. A development that ushered in the end of Medium Wave radio in America. In 1982, when the music broadcast format was changed to pure talk and news programmes, the DJs of New York's WABC channel declared that this was a 'consistent' step. 'For a long time now it has been hypocritical... to claim that one is still a music channel, a top 40 station, when we're just playing 18 hits and these aren't even selected by the disc jockey but by the computer.' (BORROMINI, Franco: Bye, bye, Phil!, in: FAZ, 23 March 1982.) And DJ legend Wolfman Jack said in a 1981 interview: 'They can't control my mouth, but they control the music I play. These days it's decided not by the DJ but by the music director or the programme director or the computer they keep in the office.' (DENSLOW, Robin: Here comes the Wolfman, in: THE GUARDIAN, 27 October 1981.)

185. PYNCHON, Thomas: The Crying of Lot 49, p. 15.

186. Ibid. p. 25.

187. Ibid. p. 26.

188. Ibid. p. 28.

189. PYNCHON, Thomas: Gravity's Rainbow, p. 71.

190. KITTLER, Friedrich A.: Medien und Drogen in Pynchons Zweitem Weltkrieg, in: KAMPER, Dietmar/ REIJEN, Willem van: Die unvollendete Vernunft, p. 255.

191. PYNCHON, Thomas, The Crying of Lot 49, p. 98.

For Mucho, and in Pynchon's novel, radio is a medium of betrayal and gentle agitation. The characters whistle songs, sing, listen to bands and are absorbed by the music.

Like a DJ, Pynchon mixes text and music together, the music becomes part of the novel, plays around passages of text and gives a rhythm to the body of the novel, along with the other foreign bodies like book titles, dramatic passages, articles, letters, footnotes, quotations, signs and messages on the toilet wall. But while Pynchon can depict the symbol of W.A.S.T.E. (a circular twist, a triangle and a trapezium), along with the outside texts that can be mixed into the larger text of the novel, songs cannot be depicted in the novel. Pynchon's pen is not a stylus, his references to the music are those of an arranger, composer or lyricist. What remains are the song lyrics, references to a fade-out or the underlying melody, as well as the stock phrases with which (pop) music tends to be described. There is the 'shuddering deluge of thick guitar chords',[186] the 'tireless shivaree of voices and guitars'[187] and a 'massive sax section'.[188] The music remains silent, however, language isn't its medium.

As far as the band called the Paranoids are concerned, their English accents and appearance give us an idea of what their music might be like. The needle goes down in the reader's unconscious, tapping into the memory of music, and the reader mixes in melodies and notes from his own song archive into the narrative. 'Tape my head and mike my brain, stick that needle in my vein,'[189] are the lyrics of a song in *Gravity's Rainbow*. The media have conquered the heads and bodies of their users. For Kittler, songs and records in Pynchon's novels are a 'medium of stupidity'.[190] Even more than that, they are agents of stupidity in the hands of DJs and programme-makers, who level out advertising and music in the service of capitalism.

When Mucho and Oedipa go into a pizzeria, Mucho is impressed by the music. They are exposed to a constant stream of it, 'seeping in, in its subliminal, unidentifiable way since they'd entered the place, all strings, reeds, muted brass'.[191] Mucho, as a DJ in a formatted station, an agent of Muzak, can identify the notes with obsessive precision. One of the seventeen violins is being played by a non-studio musician whose E string is a few cycles sharp. For Mucho he is a hero: 'Figure out what his ear is like, and then the musculature of his hands and arms, and eventually the entire man',[192] someone whose playing is not in the slightest synthetic, and who is thus rebelling against the signs of the times.

At the same time Pynchon was writing this, from the early to mid-60s, the American engineer Robert A. Moog was developing his first synthesizer, a generator of tones that was able to change sounds in every parameter: a rhizome of sound beyond artistic subjectivity. Mucho Maas is familiar with this future of music, when he explains to Oedipa that one can get by very well these days without living musicians. 'Put together all the right overtones at the right power levels so it'd come out like a violin.'[193] Mucho can take apart what he hears in his head and put it back together again. 'I can break down chords, and timbres, and words too into all the basic frequencies and harmonics, with all their different loudnesses, and listen to them, each pure tone, but all at once.'[194]

Mucho dreams of all the things that DJs have been able to do on their own in the studio from the 80s onwards, with their samplers, sequencers, computer programmes and synthesizers. Mucho's ideas are very far-reaching. For every tone you get an extra channel. 'And if I need more I just expand. Add on what I need. I don't know how it works, but lately I can do it with people talking too.'[195]

He establishes that advertising texts make the speakers of the texts identical to one another, just as the spectra of power are identical. 'Everybody who says the same words is the same person if the spectra are the same only they happen differently in time...'[196] If one puts together the various speech acts, you could have a choir several hundred million people strong 'saying "rich chocolatey goodness" together, and it would all be the same voice'.[197] Absolute identity – a gloomy vision of pop culture.

Characterlessness as a broadcasting format – Mucho sees himself and each of the DJs as 'a whole roomful of people'.[198] As a DJ for a station formatted for the Top 200, Mucho is a part and a representative of the taste

192. Ibid.
193. Ibid.
194. Ibid.
195. Ibid.
196. Ibid. p. 99.
197. Ibid.
198. Ibid.

of millions of people. Identity through pop also gives a sense of security. Every time he puts on the headset he understands exactly what is flowing into him: 'When those kids sing about "She loves you", yeah, well, you know, she does, she's any number of people, all over the world, back through time, different colours, sizes, ages, shapes, distances from death, but she loves. And the "you" is everybody. And herself.'[199]

Pop music means everyone and no one. Its indifference makes it a global language. In Pynchon's work there are only two possibilities open to the DJ. He oscillates between desperate attempts to take his bearings from concrete things and to believe them – failed attempts in Mucho's case – and no less desperate attempts to yield to indifference and dissipate oneself in global pop discourse. 'You're an antenna, sending your patter out across a million lives a night, and they're your lives too.'[200] At the end Mucho's dreams are different from before – pop music and LSD have made him quiescent – the torments are over.

Mucho Maas disappears from the novel, listening to a mysterious melody. The DJ calls out, 'Oh, listen,' but Oedipa Maas doesn't recognize anything. As far as she is concerned, her husband has broken down, succumbed to Muzak – a gullible foot-soldier of pop culture.

THE VICTORY OF POP CULTURE

The year 1955 marked not only the beginning of pop music, but also the beginning of pop art. Jasper Johns painted his first flags, Andy Warhol drew his brightly-coloured shoes, and Roy Lichtenstein worked on his dollar notes. An iconography of the ordinary had come into being. In Paris, Roland Barthes tried to 'reflect regularly on some myths of French daily life':[201] 'The media which prompted these reflections may well appear heterogeneous (a newspaper article, a photograph in a weekly, a film, a show, an exhibition), and their subject-matter very arbitrary: I was of course guided by my own current interests.'[202]

199. Ibid.

200. Ibid.

201. BARTHES, Roland: Mythologies, p. 11.

202. Ibid.

On 30 September 1955 Jimmy Dean died, and twenty-six days later Nicholas Ray's *Rebel Without a Cause* premiered in New York. Rock'n'roll as an attitude had finally gripped Hollywood. Elvis celebrated his 20th birthday.

In the high arts, pop culture first conquered visual art, and only much later literature. In 1962, James Rosenquist and Andy Warhol painted the lips of Marilyn Monroe, while Peter Phillips and Richard Hamilton painted her in a bikini. Coke cans, flags, cigarette packets, hearts and comics followed. In the early 60s urban pop art, which brought the glittering, never banal everyday world of affluent late capitalism into the galleries and museums, called the running. After the esoteric and existentialist discourse of Action Painting and other kinds of abstract painting, full, concrete life – from the supermarket via sex and comics to the glittering world of the media – returned to the artists' studios.

203. KITTLER, Friedrich A.,: Medien und Drogen in Pynchons Zweitem Weltkrieg, in: KAMPER, Dietmar/ REIJEN, Willem van, op. cit., p. 240.

204. WOLFE, Tom: The Kandy-Kolored Tangerine-Flake Streamline Baby, p. 15.

Literature alone had difficulty finding a 'poppy' form: it seemed speechless in the face of the avalanche of pop. The task of the poets was performed by the hack writers, whose jobs and attitudes brought them closer to everyday life. The New Journalism of Tom Wolfe, Norman Mailer and Truman Capote was a hybrid of literature and journalism. From journalism they had taken the directness of language, a certain proximity to the people and an interest in the *Zeitgeist*, from literature a certain narrative freedom and the possibility of poetry and reflection.

Tom Wolfe was a Yale graduate who started writing for the 'New York Herald Tribune' in the early 60s. Once again, literature proved to be culturally behind the times. And where Thomas Pynchon tried 'to read the signs of the times as a novel' in techno-mystical adventures,[203] Wolfe attempted to capture the new culture: 'Artists for the new age, sculptors for the new style and new money of the... Yah! Lower orders. The new sensibility – *Baby baby baby where did our love go?* – the new world, submerged so long, invisible, and now arising, slippy, shiny, electric – Super Scubaman! – out of the vinyl deeps.'[204]

For Wolfe, the DJ is one of the new culture makers. The piece 'The fifth Beatle' is an article about the New

York disc jockey Murray the K (Kaufman), the 'king of the Hysterical Disc Jockeys'.[205] Like Pynchon, Wolfe had recognized by the early 60s that the figure of the DJ was interesting from the literary point of view. But where Pynchon is more interested in theories of technology, Muzak and society, Wolfe turns his attention to the power and charm of the feeling of pop. Pynchon's DJ is a tragic figure, Wolfe's DJ a pop star.

205. Ibid. p. 41.

206. Cf. PASSMAN, Arnold, loc. cit, p. 246.

207. WOLFE, Tom: The Kandy-Kolored..., p. 43.

MURRAY THE K – 'THE KING OF THE JOCKEYS' (COHN)

In the major histories of pop music, Murray the K appears – if at all – only on the margins. While Martin Block established the DJ in America's collective consciousness, and Alan Freed gave him the role of a musical agitator and trendsetter with the fame of a star, it was Murray the K who made the image of the DJ comparable to that of the pop star.

Murray the K's real name was Murray Kaufman, and he began his show career as a child in a vaudeville theatre – an influence that was to determine his career as a DJ, just as Block's past as a salesman and Freed's past in music had influenced them. After a number of DJ posts, in 1958 Kaufman ended up in New York at Freed's station WINS. He began with a Monday evening programme, right after Freed's show. Kaufman promoted his programme on television, and people noticed him. Kaufman now gave himself a typically black abbreviated name,[206] which was to make him unique, Murray the K. Wolfe: 'It doesn't mean anything, but it signifies something, a kind of nutty hipsterism.'[207] He called his show *Murray the K and the Swinging Soiree* and started to develop a style that was very much his own. Even more than that: he developed his own language.

His programme director, Sklar, called it *Meussuray*: 'a new way for teens to doubletalk. It was simple and silly and involved adding an "eus" after the first consonant or diphthong of a word, or before the word if it began with a vowel. In a few weeks all the kids were speaking Meussuray.'[208] Murray the K grew more and more wild and hysterical, often leaving language far behind and losing himself in indefinable sounds. Sklar: 'Over the air he began doing nonsensical shouts that sounded like old Indian rain chants: "Ahbay, ahbay, ooh wah wah, ahbay, ooh wah wah, koowee summa summa." [209]

For Tom Wolfe Murray was a genius. 'He was probably the original hysterical disc jockey and in any case he was the first big hysterical disc jockey. Murray the K doesn't operate on Aristotelian logic. He operates on symbolic logic. He builds up an atmosphere of breathless jollification, comic hysteria, and turns it up to a pitch so high it can hypnotize kids and keep them frozen to WINS through the commercials and everything else.'[210]

Murray formed the soundtrack for the teens of the early 60s. Along with the other DJs he produced an 'endless burble background for teenage daydreams' (Cohn). 'It was all music, no speech and no interruptions allowed – kids didn't like talk, they flipped dials fast to another station. So the only way a deejay could survive was to develop a spiel so fast, so smooth that it became music on its own. No message, no sense to impart. It was pure noise.'[211]

In his foreword to a pop book for young people, Murray explained that DJs on radio and television had to revolutionize their presentation of music if they were to keep pace with the musical explosion. 'Today's songs reflect attitudes of children born after the close of World War II, whose psyche was fathered by the atom bomb!'[212] Murray took up this challenge. His wild stammering of syllables, fragments of words, black slang, and meaningless, rhythmical burbling was the perfect transition from one song to the next. Then there were all the sound effects stored on tape: 'freight trains, cavalry charges, the screams of men plunging down an abyss, nutty macaw laughter from the jungle, anything,'[213] which enabled Murray the K to keep the excitement of one song going into the next. And with his sound-groove he mixed the songs together, as dancefloor DJs would later do with mixing desks and record-player pitchers. This gave the DJ performance a magical draw. 'It was like electricity, it was like glass. It

208 . SKLAR, Rick, op. cit., p. 44f.

209 . Ibid. p. 45.

210 . WOLFE, Tom: The Kandy-Kolored..., p. 43.

211 . COHN, Nik: AwopBopaLooBop..., p. 85.

212 . In: PECK, Ira: The New Sound/Yes!, p. viiif.

213 . WOLFE, Tom: The Kandy-Kolored..., p. 44.

Murray 'the K' Kaufman

was just there,'[214] Nik Cohn eulogized. It was the vision of an endless artificial, beautiful, radiant world whose meaning came into being in a parallel universe to the teen reality, and radiated over to them. It was pure bliss.

For Cohn, dancing and radio were the core of American teen romanticism: 'Millions of kids up in front of their bedroom mirrors, getting hip to the Pony with the Good Guys on station WMCY... Or sipping coke through Murray the K's Monkey on 1010 WINS. That's the way the fantasy went. It was a self-contained cycle, twenty-four hours each day, DJs spieling like maniacs all across the nation and music splintering and feet shuffling, butts twitching by the megaton. It didn't ever have to end, it needed no improving. It was perfection.'[215]

Murray the K's favourite phrase was 'It's what's happening baby', which he repeated over and over again, and which became his trademark: a meaningless triple exclamation mark, a loud and dramatic yes to the Now,[216] the present.

Soon Murray the K's style was copied all over the place, and the imitators were often crazier and more exciting than the original. Murray's popularity began to decline, and the station started cutting his show: half an hour of news before him and a talk show after him. According to Cohn, 'By early 1964, he was definitely on the slide.'[217]

In the same year the Beatles came on their first tour to the USA. On 7 February there was a notable encounter between Murray the K and the four Liverpudlians on their way to conquer America. A meeting that inspired Tom Wolfe to write an article about the DJ.

Thousands of young fans and hundreds of media representatives were waiting for the Beatles to show. The press conference had been delayed, and everyone wanted an answer to himself, but it was Murray the K – dressed in a straw hat and an overcoat – who made the running. He sat at the Beatles' feet in the cramped press room and fired questions at them until they reacted with an answer. While the other media men had to make do with scraps, the New York DJ managed to get proper answers out of the Beatles. The

214. COHN, Nik: AwopBopaLooBop..., p. 86.

215. COHN, Nik: op. cit., p. 85.

216. The Now was very important for pop. Cohn: 'You were young, flash, international *Vogue* said you were. Now.' (op. cit., p. 84.)

217. Ibid. p. 86.

whole press conference turned into Murray the K's show, as he won over the Beatles with his language, his looks and his lack of respect. The other journalists 'were just some kind of a chorus'.[218] The next evening Murray went out with the Beatles, 'and from then on he was the Beatles' guide, Boswell, buffer, playmate throughout their American tour...'[219] For the league of disc jockeys, according to Wolfe, it was 'a historic scoop'[220] comparable to the Cuba crisis or Vietnam: a disc jockey had taken over the greatest pop band of all times, and he'd done it in front of thousands of cameras, microphones and note-pads. After this Murray the K had a monopoly on the Beatles. Journalists called him up if they wanted to know something about the Beatles. And the Beatles trusted the eccentric DJs so much that Murray the K was able to share a Miami hotel room with George Harrison. Wolfe: 'There and everywhere else Murray the K was making tape recordings a mile a minute. He had all the Beatles, one by one, saying anything he wanted into the tape recorder.'[221]

The consequences for the declining DJ were enormous. Cohn: 'By the end of the tour, Murray was right back on top again and stayed that way. He made one hundred and fifty thousand dollars a year. Sold Murray the K T-shirts and hosted albums of Murray the K's Golden Gassers.'[222] For Tom Wolfe he had become the 'Fifth Beatle'.[223]

His shows turned into a surreal Beatles theatre with wildly edited cut-up dialogues, which Wolfe thought had a 'wacky jumpy quality'.[224]

Murray the K: '"Hey Paul, baby, what's happening, baby?"

"I dunno, Murray, everything's happening sort-of-thing."

"Paul, somebody asked me to ask you – I mean they asked me, some of your fans, they asked me to ask you, so I'm going to go ahead and ask you, What is your favorite color?"

"Well, uh, it's kind of, you know, black.'

"Black."

"Yeah, you know, black. John is going to jump off the ladder now."

There is a round of applause.

218. WOLFE, Tom: The Kandy-Kolored..., p. 47.

219. Ibid.

220. Ibid.

221. Ibid.

222. COHN, Nik: AwopBopaLooBop..., p. 87.

223. WOLFE, Tom: The Kandy-Kolored..., p. 41.

224. Ibid. p. 48.

"They applaud," says Paul. "Sounds like a cricket match."
"You're what's happening, Paul baby."
Symbolic logic, baby! Who cares what's happening? The Beatles are there, and Murray the K is in there with them, tight.[225]

And this closeness to the Beatles helped Murray the K to get right to the top of the popularity stakes among Radio DJs. For Tom Wolfe this was reason enough to include him in the literary pantheon of pop culture. Murray the K had thus finally become a legend and one of the great DJs in the history of pop music: not so much because of his use of music as because of his ability to project himself and hold his own with the pop stars in the all-deciding battle of images.

225. Ibid.

226. MARCUS, Greil: In the Fascist Bathroom, p. 12.

227. MARCUS, Greil: Mystery Train, p. 103.

GOING UNDERGROUND – THE SOUND OF A YOUTH REBELLION

With Alan Freed and the payola scandal the golden age of rock'n'roll came to an end, in Murray the K Freed had a successor who was a star DJ, but no one who was willing to fight for the new teen soundtrack. Murray the K took care of the hits, and saw himself more as an entertainer than the herald of a new kind of music: a star DJ who used the mainstream as the background for his own self-dramatizations.

In the same year that Murray's connections with the Beatles made him immortal, the American Air Force began its bombing raids on North Vietnam. Greil Marcus characterized the 60s in America as a bleak time of 'assassination, riot, war, and the cold gloom of Richard Nixon'.[226] The passionate Marcus, who had an almost blind trust in the American dream, describes this period as a great crisis in the land of unlimited possibilities: 'Too much war and too much public crime has poisoned the country to be easily put to rest by any kind of reform or vengeance. There is simply too much to forget. Our (!) politics have robbed the good words of ethics of their meaning.'[227]

According to Marcus' thesis, American (pop) culture split into the state-supporting, conformist mainstream and a critical left-wing underground. Not forgetting the progressive music of the blacks, whose struggle for equality and civil rights was growing increasingly radical during this period (see also the chapter on black DJs, pp. 83–94), and was becoming linked to the movement against the Vietnam War. The non-mainstream was far from unified in its manifestations. Since the beginning of the 60s, particularly in New York's artists' district, Greenwich Village, there had been an active folk scene, whose 'topical songs' dealt with all areas of left–liberal politics, from the poverty of the workers to racial discrimination (Bob Dylan, Joan Baez, Phil Ochs, Pete Seeger). Then there was the West Coast acid rock (based in San Francisco) which, influenced by drugs, advocated drug consumption and sought to add a soundtrack, with psychedelic sounds and surrealist lyrics, to the expanded consciousness (Grateful Dead, The Byrds, 13th Floor Elevators). And finally there were the underground bands that came from the milieu of New York bohemia, like the Fugs and the Velvet Underground, whose guerrilla operations were rooted, aesthetically and intellectually, in the world of art and literature. The wildest of all were the proto-punk bands like the Stooges and MC5, who tried, with Nazi uniforms and self-mutilation, to pervert not only bourgeois politics but the whole dominant order of meanings and morals. There were also the many black bands and musicians who used soul, funk and classic R&B to agitate against all forms of racism and oppression.

What they all had in common was the understanding that existing society and existing politics must be changed, even perhaps revolutionized. Their political interests were as disparate (sex, revolution, drugs, racial discrimination) as their aesthetic. In *Rock Power*, a 1972 essay on pop music and the counter-culture, Helmut Salzinger declared the political value of this revolt in pop music, 'in line with the internal disparity of the movement',[228] to be vague: 'The only thing that is certain is that the predominant idea of politics here is not the daily practised, system-based idea of the western parliamentary democracies.'[229]

228. SALZINGER, Helmut: Rock Power, p. 36.

229. Ibid.

In the late 60s, young people in almost every country in the first and second worlds rebelled against the dominant order. And almost all of these revolts were concerned not only with questions of political organization, but also with questions of lifestyle, of co-existence, of ethics. These youth revolts had much more private concerns than all the revolutions of the 18th, 19th and 20th centuries. It might be suggested that the rebellion of puberty which occurs in everyone's life, and which is aimed at the rules of the parental generation was, for the first time, spread out over the whole of society and given an underlying political structure.

The personal nature of these political demands resulted from the lifestyles practice of the rebels: many of them lived in communes, enjoyed drugs and free sex and listened to pop music.

Purple Haze, an American film by David Burton Morris from 1982, is set at the end of the 60s and tells the story of Matt, a boy who loses his best friend and his bearings in life through the Vietnam War. In 1968 he is expelled from Princeton and rejected by his father. He joins the Army to be with his friend Jeff, but Jeff dies in the training camp. Matt deserts.

The very title of the film refers to the music of the time; it's the title of a piece by Jimi Hendrix. Apart from Hendrix, Matt is constantly accompanied by the songs of Cream and Steppenwolf, at parties, in the camp and with friends. And as in *American Graffiti* the DJ has an important role. Once again, it is a radio show on an FM underground station that provides the background of sound and meaning to a youth melodrama. When Matt learns that Jeff has died, he first turns to a radio DJ at their favourite station, because he wants to have a final song played as a memorial for Jeff. A request with which the DJ immediately complies.

The DJ is the closest confidant and friend, the first person to talk to and the organizer of the underground; his work brings together his disparate audience into an ideological and private unity – none of his listeners are strange to him. He sympathizes with the fate of each individual.

In the 60s the role of the DJ had clearly changed. Where, in the early 60s, in *American Graffiti*, he had been invisible as a rebel and an exciting mystery, by the end of the 60s he was in active rebellion against the establishment. He was accessible, he could be talked to – a centre of the subcultural network – not only through his programme, but directly, in his studio, where people met up to smoke dope. For pop sociologist Simon Frith the underground DJs were, more than anything else, 'real', friends, confidants and thus the exact opposite of the quick-witted insincerity and sales patter of their mainstream colleagues.[230] Where Wolfman had to hide in the American provinces, the revolutionary acid rock DJ swam in the Californian hippie scene like a fish in water.

Top 40 radio was supported by the idea of a social consensus: the charts were the collective (un)conscious of American society. With the lost of social consensus, successful mainstream radio was called into question. Almost all the mainstream stations were received on the AM waveband, and most car radios had AM frequencies. The FM stations had been ordered, by a decision of the Federal Commission for Communications (FCC), to broadcast completely different programmes from the AM stations: above all jazz, academic courses, foreign language broadcasts and classical music. This changed at the end of the 60s, thanks to a former Top 40 DJ. Tom Donahue (1925–1978) had deejayed since the late 50s, and since 1964 he had run his own record label. His first top five hit was 'C'mon and Swim' by Bobby Freeman. The song had been produced by the young black DJ Sylvester Stewart, later famous as Sly Stone.

Tom Donahue controlled the music scene in the Bay Area with his radio shows, his label and his big package shows. But the big success never came. In 1967 Donahue sold his Autumn Records to Warner Brothers and left the Top 40 business. He founded a psychedelic nightclub and took over the FM radio station KMPX. In so doing, Donahue was right within the trends of the time. Marcus: 'By early 1967 the hippie bands of the Haight had the ear of the nation, and San Francisco geared up for the crunch of the summer of love.'[231] Donahue, with his partner Larry Miller, began playing the music that didn't fit within the format of Top 40 radio. Chiefly the LP versions of songs by the bands

230. Cf. FRITH, Simon: Sound Effects, p. 122.

231. MARCUS, Greil: Mystery Train, p. 80.

who rejected the dictates of the mainstream: no singles, no chart hits and no constant repetitions. The DJs were not figures dependent on the station format, but fans of the new music. They played what they felt like, and talked the same way as all hippies during the summer of love and thereafter. As in the days of Alan Freed, the DJs once again stood for a new music and a new aesthetic without making any great compromises.

The extent to which they were a part of the new subculture was also apparent in their massive drug consumption during the radio broadcasts. As a result it wasn't only the initiated who could clearly hear the DJ drawing on a joint between his words[232] – as seen several times in the film *Purple Haze*. Then there was the 'hipspeak',[233] the jargon of the subculture that was to create an identity on the scene through a special language, and at the same time restrict or obstruct access to the subculture to the uninitiated. The 'hipspeak' of the underground DJs was not an extrovert self-projection as it had been with Murray the K, but the cultivation of group-specific verbal codes.

Along with musicians, the DJs became the biggest role models in the underground. The underground DJs didn't only play the new music, they were also the ones who drew the boundaries between the underground and the mainstream. They divided the traditional show-business artists from those of the hip and alternative underground, who represented the future. Only the Beatles, Bob Dylan, the Stones, the Byrds and the Lovin' Spoonful managed to escape these categories.[234] The DJs were thus part of the ideological command of the new rock underground, and stylistically influenced the development of the music.

Donahue's station invented underground radio[235] and at the same time a new radio format that was taken over by many mainstream stations years later: the Album Oriented Rock format, abbreviated to AOR. KMPX became the model for many small FM stations devoted to the 'offbeat'.[236] By playing local, unknown bands without record contracts, like Jefferson Airplane and the Grateful Dead, KMPX became a moving force within the acid rock movement. The frequency with which these bands appeared on the airwaves first made

232. Cf. Ibid.

233. BARNES, Ken: Top 40 Radio, in: FRITH, Simon (Ed.): Facing the Music, p. 15.

234. Cf. GILLETT, Charlie, loc. cit., p. 352.

235. Cf. SHAW, Arnold: Dictionary..., op. cit., p. 396.

236. In his 'Dictionary of American Pop/Rock', Arnold Shaw defines 'offbeat' as 'outside the normal, traditional, or expected. Weird, bizarre, grotesque.' (Ibid. p. 265.)

them regional celebrities, who were then taken under contract by the record companies and finally, within a few years, became superstars.

Despite his success, Donahue rowed with the management of KMPX and, along with his fellow dissidents, took over the FM station KSAN with the same programme as KMPX. These two stations fundamentally altered the basic construction of the whole American music industry, and many similar stations sprouted up all over America, particularly in the cities. And yet 'freeform' radio was 'more of an aesthetic revolution than a commercial one',[237] because audience numbers rarely competed with those of Top 40 radio. The FM stations simply extended the musical spectrum on the radio dial.

And a short time later the underground stations, with a few exceptions, began to abandon their 'freeform' approaches, introducing playlists and assuming an image that was attractive to advertisers. Economically this image was successful in the short term, but meant that the FM stations were soon barely distinguishable from the AM stations. In the meantime we might almost talk in terms of a re-evaluation, because the FM stations broadcast primarily the Top 40 or Top 100 hit parades, while the AM stations have radically changed, and their programmes are now closer to those of the earlier FM radio stations.[238]

237. Ibid.

238. Cf. HALBSCHEFFEL, Bernward/ KNEIF, Tibor, op. cit., p. 140.

DISSIDENCE AND INTEGRATION – THE BLACK DJ

The beginnings of pop music were black. Rhythm and blues came into being in the 40s, and was a mixture of various black musical trends: the emotional power of gospel, the drive of big band swing, the rhythm of boogie-woogie and the shuffle along with the melancholy of the blues. Because of the scarcity of black records, R&B existed almost solely as live music – played in the ghetto for the people who lived there. The new regard that the blacks enjoyed throughout society for their patriotism during the Second World

239. SHAW, Arnold: Black Popular Music in America, p. viii.

240. GEORGE, Nelson: The Death..., p. x.

241. Ibid. p. xiii.

242. Cf. NEWMAN, Mark: Entrepreneurs of Profit and Pride, pp. x–xiii.

243. Advertising is 'not only the financial basis of radio, it is also a determinant of programming.' (Ibid. p. xi.)

244. Ibid. p. xii.

War gave them a cultural and economic boost, however modest it might have been. In New York and Los Angeles a series of black labels, known as 'race' labels, came into being, which produced only black music. These records made R&B accessible to people outside the ghettos, and as in jazz it wasn't long before young whites noticed how exciting and cool black R&B was. The record shops recognized that R&B was a good deal, and finally the white DJ Alan Freed discovered his passion for R&B and turned it, as rock'n'roll, into the first real pop music.

White musicologists like Arnold Shaw think that American pop music is neither black nor white, but a successful fusion, the result of a free interaction.[239] Black pop theorist Nelson George, on the other hand, describes the history of pop as a constant exploitation and distortion of black culture. For him R&B 'died' when it left the ghetto.[240] In his book *The Death of Rhythm & Blues* he tries to draw up the history of the erosion of black culture after the Second World War, and places black radio at the centre of his studies. For him, radio embodies one of the most important elements 'in shaping black taste and opinion'.[241]

In his history of black radio, with the deliberately programmatic title *Entrepreneurs of Profit and Pride*, Mark Newman points out that radio was the only mass medium that had an established and institutionalized 'black appeal'. It thus acted as a 'provider of business and culture' within the black community.[242]

The first radio programmes to play race music in the 20s were racist in outlook, in that they served to sell typical ghetto goods to blacks. The sponsors advertised second-hand furniture, chitlings and patent medicines, and ensured themselves better profits in the ghetto from their links with black music.[243] In the 30s there were still no black stations, but more and more radio announcements were trying to achieve recognition on both sides of the racist society, between black slang and white middle class speech.

The first black stations were not founded until the 40s. The number grew from a handful of stations with black programmes before 1940 to over four hundred in 1954.[244] Black radio stations sprang up in Los Angeles, Atlanta, Louisville, Memphis, New Orleans, Miami,

Nashville and St. Louis, playing R&B, blues, gospel and jazz and supporting the rising black labels.

WDIA became the first 'all-black' radio station in Memphis in 1948. The radio revolution in Tennessee meant that for the first time south of the Mason-Dixon Line there was a black DJ who was able to publicly admit that he was black. An estimated ten per cent of the whole population of America listened to WDIA, and thus the black radio station was not only an important opportunity for the black community in Memphis and the entire mid-South to represent itself, but also a political power in the segregationist 50s. The economic success of the radio station was only exceeded by its cultural power. 'It served as a musical launch pad to blast local talent into the orbit of stardom,'[245] as Louis Cantor put it in his history of the radio station. The later superstars B.B. King and Rufus Thomas started their careers as DJs with WDIA. Artists like Johnny Ace and Roscoe Gordon recorded their first records in the WDIA studios. Carla Thomas and Isaac Hayes sang in the station choir. But pop history was also indirectly influenced: one of the most assiduous WDIA listeners, for example, was a white boy called Elvis Presley. From that point of view B.B. King was right when he called the station a 'prominent leader'[246] that brought blacks and whites closer together. But the reality was less idyllic. WDIA was more the product of a rigid segregation than of incipient integration. But the programme (and the success) of the radio station promoted the origin and growth of a positive black identity at a time when this was otherwise only possible in sport.

Black radio also saw the growth in the influence of the disc jockeys, some of whom were just as exciting as the artists they announced. Although most of the stations had white owners, it was not they but the DJs who made up the profile of the stations, and thus drew in advertisers. And whites worked alongside blacks as DJs for the R&B stations. The whites were hipsters who were keen on black music and acknowledged by blacks as 'white negroes', and discriminated against by whites. What they shared was their crazy way of presenting their shows, and their own language.

These verbal distortions, which were to become an art

245. CANTOR, Louis: Wheelin' On Beale, p. 2.

246. Ibid. p. v.

WDIA advertisement 1949

form in their own right, were among the origins of rapping. Berry Gordy, the founder of the Motown label, describes the black radio DJs as 'original rappers' at a time when rapping was still the way a man spoke when he hit on a woman:[247] a crazy mixture of scat, which introduced the voice into the music as an instrument, and adventurous jive lyrics[248] full of exaggerations and nonsense.

Lavanda Durst alias Dr Hep Cat was one of the first DJs who–according to David Toop – returned 'the live feel to recorded music':[249]

If you want to hip to the tip and bop to the top
You get some mad threads that just won't stop[250]

Tellingly, Dr Hep Cat was also a musician and a pianist, and even published a dictionary entitled *The Jive of Dr Hep Cat*.

Another DJ of this kind was Daddy-O-Daylie, who Dizzy Gillespie claimed had invented a more hip (secret) language[251] than the inventor of bebop, Gillespie himself. Daylie saw the verbal experiments, the shifts in meaning and neologisms as a part of his work in giving an appropriate presentation of contemporary black music. To win the attention of his audience he tried to give free rein to his feeling for language: 'I would always try and use the bop phrases to help sell the music, to showcase modern music – modern jargon.'[252] Black verbal art – hitherto an everyday poetry restricted to the inside of the ghetto – was also made accessible to white radio audiences, particularly to white radio DJs, who constantly tried to copy this authentic hipness.[253]

There was the adventurous story of the black DJ Dr Daddy-O (alias Vernon Winslow), who was employed by a station in New Orleans to teach a white man to speak black. Winslow wrote scripts, chose the music and even gave the white DJ his name. The show became the station's greatest success, but when Winslow dared take the microphone himself he was fired. Six months later Winslow was hired as DJ, and his programme 'created havoc in radio'.[254] Suddenly everyone wanted to have his own jive-talking DJ.

In December 1947 the black magazine *Ebony*

247. Cf. GORDY, Berry: To Be Loved, p. 134.

248. Arnold Shaw explains jive as 'black talk meaning to flatter, not with sincerity but with the purpose of gaining something. Also to doubletalk or kid.' (SHAW, Arnold: Dictionary..., p. 197.)

249. TOOP, David: Rap Attack, p. 38.

250. Quoted in: TOOP, David: Rap Attack, p. 38.

251. GILLESPIE, Dizzy/ FRASER, Al: Dizzy – To Be Or Not To Bop, p. 281. Gillespie puts this practice of hip talk into a larger context of the black sense of language: 'As black people we just naturally spoke that way. People who wished to communicate with us had to consider our manner of speech, and sometimes they adopted it. As we played with musical notes, bending them into new and different meaning that constantly changed, we played with words.' (Ibid.) See also DIEDERICHSEN, Diedrich: Freiheit macht arm, pp. 65–96, and the standard work by Henry Louis GATES Jr.: The Signifying Monkey. A Theory of African-American Literary Criticism.

252. GILLESPIE, Dizzy/ FRASER, Al, loc. cit., p. 281.

253. 'You had, back to that time, people saying, 'Daddy-O's talking hippy-dippy talk', and they were trying to come up with some negative vibes. But then when Arthur Godfrey started using it, a white radio personality, they accepted it. Arthur would use things that I would say, and after he put his stamp on it, they started saying Daddy-O was a great dude.' (Ibid.)

254. TOOP, David: Rap Attack, p. 38.

discovered that of the three thousand DJs in the USA only sixteen were black.[255] But success quickly changed this, because the black DJs guaranteed the advertisers and sponsors the ideal setting for spots and advertising slogans. There were two kinds of black radio DJs: those who 'pass(ed) for white'[256] and those whom 'any self-respecting upwardly mobile black would view as a discredit to the race'.[257] One of the latter was Al Benson, a former preacher, who twisted his words and stammered and thus tried to trample the English language with expressions like 'modren' and 'more lovelier'.[258] At the height of his career Benson had managed to get five shows and twenty hours of programming, had his own record company (Parrot Records), was a major concert-organizer and earned a great deal of money as a radio DJ.[259] Like Martin Block, Benson was a brilliant salesman who also saw his advertising work as an opportunity to spare blacks humiliation when shopping. Firms, restaurants and shops that advertised on black radio were interested in black customers, and thus had a material interest in treating those customers well. Newman, who, in his book, closely links the development of black entrepreneurship with developments in media, culture and society, sees the economic factor within deejaying work as the basis for its social function. 'If black disc jockeys could sell their sponsors' products to black consumers then they could sell race pride.'[260]

Because of his political statements and actions Benson was under constant surveillance. His dislike for the racist decrees moved him to actions that were the expression of rebellion as well as stardom. Thus, for example, he held a party with other blacks in the most elegant club in Chicago, ignoring the club's strict segregation policy. In 1950 Benson hired an aeroplane and dropped anti-racist leaflets on the city hall of Jackson, Mississippi. Like most other black DJs, Benson used his authority actively to represent the interests of the black minority. And thus the DJs became 'race heroes, not just because of their status behind the radio microphone but because of what they said and did'.[261]

By the 50s, the cultural hegemony of white culture and white language was undermined. One of the most

255. GEORGE, Nelson: The Death..., p. 41.

256. Ibid.

257. Ibid.

258. PASSMAN, Arnold, op. cit., p. 224.

259. About two million dollars between 1945 and 1965 (cf. NEWMAN, Mark, loc. cit., p. 83.)

260. Ibid. p. 141.

261. Ibid. p. 143.

successful verbal distorters and master of black 'doubletalk' was the New Yorker Douglas 'Jocko' Henderson, called 'the Ace from Space' who, in his show *1280 Rocket,* indulged in crazy verbal manipulations which, in their wildness and spontaneity, resembled the improvisations of free jazz. 'The idea happens in the mouth,'[262] declared Tristan Tzara in a Dada manifesto, and Jocko gave his mouth free rein to think. He mixed everyday and artificial language, and thus achieved unconventionally beautiful rhymes.[263] One of his phrases, 'Great gugga mugga shooga booga', even entered New York slang[264] and later turned up on a number of Jamaican Ska records.[265] One often quoted example of his rhyming art anticipates the rhythm and power of the hip-hop lyrics of the late 70s:

Be, bebop
This is your Jock
Back on the scene
With a record machine
Saying 'Hoo-popsie-doo, How do you do?'
When you up, you up.
And when you down, you down
And when you mess with Jock
You upside down.[266]

The lyrics of the DJs were highly self-referential and influenced by the use of studio technology. The attitude of constantly rethinking the relations between the creative self and the supporting technology were later taken on board by rap poets. In *Rap Attack* David Toop makes it plain that the DJs had direct influence, via numerous channels, on the development of black music. Not only via the music that they played, but also, and more importantly, about the manner of their presentation and their verbal distortions. The black R&B DJs developed new dancing styles and inspired ragga artists and the P-funker George Clinton, who, in 'Mr Wiggles', has a rapping under-water DJ called Mr Wiggle the Worm, who paraphrases quotations from Jocko Henderson.

Nelson George quotes a story by the New York DJ Gary Byrd, telling how the DJ veteran Bill Curtis promoted the Drifters song 'We Gotta Sing':

262. TZARA, Tristan: Sept Manifestes Dada, p. 71.

263. A mixture given exemplary form in the following 'poem': 'From way up here in stratosphere, we gotta holler mighty loud and clear ee-tiddy-o, and I'm back on the scene with the record machine, saying oo-pap-doo and how do you do!' (PASSMAN, Arnold, op. cit., p. 225.)

264. GEORGE, Nelson: The Death..., p. 43.

265. Cf. TOOP, David: Rap Attack, p. 39. Toop describes how great the influence of black radio DJs was on the development of Jamaican sound system music. Only when it met black radio programmes did the tradition of Jamaican toasting begin, which has continued through to today's Ragga music.

266. Ibid.

First he'd be playing the music and he'd slow everything down and start talking. And he'd tell the story about these guys who he had met sometime ago back in the days they were unknown and the guys turned out to be the Drifters and... blah, blah, blah, their new record and boom, boom, boom, first in the world to play their record. The record would come on. Well, as the record is playing, he'd be punctuating it with an "Ohh" at all the critical points where the excitement was. Then when he'd finish it, he'd go into this whole thing of "It's so bad, it's so bad. Oh, I just don't believe it." While he's saying he's rescuing the record. At the end when he's finished he says, "And then one more time." Ironically it was kind of like a forerunner of the whole idea of extending the record which occurred later, on the disco trip. He was just extending the groove. And then the phones would start lighting up and people were saying, "What is that record? Can I get it?" And the record stores would be calling because people are calling them asking, "Do they have this record that was just played on WUFO by the Drifters?"[267]

The radio DJs were central figures for the black communities. This even went so far that the Chief of Police in Atlanta asked DJ Jack Gibson to persuade people to calm down over the radio when there were disturbances in the ghetto.[268]

The confidence of the black DJs grew quickly with the success and the authority that they had achieved. And soon the first of them set about establishing themselves in the young pop business. One of the most famous of them was Riley B. King, who, as B.B. King, played 'maybe the best blues guitar in the world'.[269] Other ex-DJs who became stars were Rufus Thomas and Sly Stone.

Despite their popularity and power, black DJs were badly paid in comparison to their white colleagues. Consequently payola was a matter of life and death for black DJs. The radio stations constantly threatened to fire them, so even pathetic bribes were gladly accepted. Nelson George even goes so far as to claim that 'their rapid-fire bravado masked economic and social insecurities'.[270] Black DJs were expected to market and

267. GEORGE, Nelson: The Death..., p. 43.

268. Ibid. p. 46.

269. COHN, Nik: AwopBopaLooBop..., p. 122.

270. GEORGE, Nelson: The Death...., p. 55.

promote themselves and bring in their advertising contracts.

Payola gave R&B DJs the chance to take a share in the flourishing record business, and 'get a piece of the pie, a pie made sweet by their talents'.[271] Dave Clark, a representative of the record industry and a 'friend of the DJ' (George) argued that many DJs would not have survived without payola. Often all it took to get black DJs to promote a record was a much-needed pair of shoes.[272]

For George, the inequality of money and power was one of the causes of the collapse of black music and the death of R&B. The mid-50s saw the beginning of the rise of Alan Freed who, in George's view, used black rhythm and blues to make his career. Freed's record albums showed George 'that if anything truly defined rock'n'roll for Freed, it wasn't any particular style of music. To Freed, it purely and simply meant money.'[273] According to George the rapid decline of real rhythm and blues begins with rock'n'roll. 'White Negroism' took over the music and perverted its actual sound. 'The generational schism and teen-eye view that has always been the crux of the rock & roll ethos was mostly foreign to black consumers, young as well as old... rock'n'roll was young music; R&B managed to be young and old, filled both with references to the past and with fresh interpretations, all at the same time.'[274] And while George sees most subsequent black music (e.g. Chuck Berry) as a betrayal of the black cause, Arnold Shaw sees the same black music as a special achievement: bringing white interpretation (rock'n'roll) of a black music (R&B) back into a black context, and at the same time synthesizing it into a new music, one that was both black and white.[275]

Shaw writes his history of pop as one of integration and reconciliation between black and white,[276] while George assumes a separatist position[277] and lays great stress on the pre-eminence and creative authorship of blacks in pop music.

Soul as a mixture of R&B and gospel was at first uncompromisingly black. The first soul star was Ray Charles. 'This sound, not yet called soul, emphasized adult passion – the actions of people dealing with cars,

271. Ibid.

272. Cf. Ibid. p. 56.

273. Ibid. p. 68.

274. Ibid.

275. Cf. SHAW, Arnold: Black Popular Music in America, p. viii.

276. Here is the core of Shaw's introduction to his black pop history, briefly quoted above: 'Clearly, I am not trying to force the triadic concept. But what is true is that the white adaptation of the black original constitutes a synthesis, the word I employ in describing the transformation. I have chosen that word by way of trying to say that popular American music is neither white nor black, but a fusion, and the result of an interplay. That interplay has been in operation since at least the middle of the nineteenth century. Our popular American music is a blend whose designation should properly be Afro-American. Regardless of the social situation and the relations between black and white musicians, our popular music has always been integrated.' (Ibid.) In the foreword to 'Soul', Shaw sees the black contribution to the pop mixture as more considerable, but speaks of 'black musical innovators and white popularisers'. (SHAW, Arnold: Soul, p. 11)

277. The only alternative model to integration and adaptation in white America for George is deliberate separation and proud independence. 'Only a minority of blacks would openly agitate for more self-sufficiency. I find myself among that minority, not because I dislike whites or disdain the American dream – at least in both cases not entirely – but because I see the assimilationist's triumph, in the 1980s as it was in the 1920s, of little material value in improving the lives of most Afro-Americans.' GEORGE, Nelson: The Death..., p. 6.

kids, and sex. By breaking down the division between pulpit and bandstand, recharging blues concerns with transcendental fervor, unashamedly linking the spiritual and the sexual, Charles made pleasure (physical satisfaction) and joy (divine enlightenment) seem the same thing.'[278]

For white writer Nik Cohn, soul was

only updated rhythm'n'blues... and the only thing new about it was that it had been gingered with a big fat shot of gospel... Good-time music, loose and amiable, and, by comparison, gospel was purest poison. It was archaic, primitive, and it was determinedly down-home. It reminded Northern Negroes of everything they most wanted to forget. Older generations liked it all right but their kids, hip and sharp-shooting, got embarrassed about it and thought it was somehow Uncle Tom... So around the middle fifties, Negro pop started grafting gospel feel on to the existing R&B styles. The beat didn't change, neither did the subject matter, but everything dug deeper, more passionate and everyone sweated. That was soul.[279]

At any rate soul – as a slogan as well – became a symbol of black identification. The 60s were the decade of the civil rights movement, black nationalism and black pride.

Soul music and its most famous artists, led by James Brown, combined political struggle and art into a single unity: 'Say it loud, I'm black and I'm proud,' sang 'Godfather' James Brown in 1968, subsuming all the euphoria and pride the results of that aggressive decade. Black radio and its DJs helped to define soul as a style and an attitude of mind. The DJs acted as 'role models' to be followed as shining symbols of success.[280]

Among the record companies, two in particular made soul popular: Motown from Detroit and Stax from Memphis. While Motown (like some other labels, such as AFO records, Sue Records, Sar Records) was black, Stax stayed in white hands, and yet Stax records addressed black Americans even more strongly than those on the Motown label. Arnold Shaw compares the two labels in richly metaphorical terms: 'If Motown

278. Ibid. p. 70.

279. COHN, Nik: AwopBopaLooBop..., p. 104.

280. Cf. NEWMAN, Mark, op. cit., p. 164.

281. SHAW, Arnold: Soul, p. 185.

282. GEORGE, Nelson: The Death..., p. 87.

283. Ibid. p. 88.

284. In 1966 alone 75 per cent of all Motown releases made it into the Hot 100. (cf.: HÜNDGEN, Gerald: Hitsville U.S.A. – Tamla Motown in Detroit, in: Chasin' a Dream, p. 69f.)

285. COHN, Nik: Rock Dreams, unpaginated.

286. GEORGE, Nelson: op. cit., p. 98.

stands for the Northern ghetto, whose inhabitants are gradually moving into the world of high-class, plush clubs like the Mississippi overflowing the banks of the 60s. Because the Memphis Sound clearly has more mud and stones in it than the Detroit Sound.'[281] But both labels were characterized by their close collaboration with the black radio stations and their DJs.

Stax gave a contract to the famous black DJ Rufus Thomas from the radio station WDIA from Memphis, and turned him into a pop star. Thomas secured a recording contract for his daughter Carla. His good connections with DJ colleagues and radio stations meant that his songs, like those of other Stax productions, received an exceptional level of promotion. When black former civil rights activist and black star DJ Al Bell became manager of Stax in 1965, the airplays went on improving. For the black DJs Bell was – according to George – 'a blood'.[282] The black counterpart in Motown was Berry Gordy. As Motown didn't have as much money as Stax Records, which was sponsored and operated by Atlantic, Gordy appealed to 'racial solidarity to overcome an early lack of capital'[283] (George). His influence on black DJs was such that he went out drinking with them and wooed their goodwill. At one meeting he is even said to have served drinks and sandwiches for the card-playing DJs.

In addition, DJs who had to ensure their livelihood by organizing concerts were served with performances by Motown artists. The courting of black DJs quickly paid off. By 1961 Motown was able to climb to the top of the charts with artists like the Marvellettes, the Contours, the Miracles, Martha and the Vandellas, Little Stevie Wonder and Mary Wells. By 1969 Motown had managed to get a total of 78 records in the Top Ten.[284]

'Soul Brother Number One',[285] James Brown, who, during the 60s, demonstrated 'the possibilities for artistic and economic freedom that black music could provide if one constantly struggled against its limitations,[286] enjoyed the unbounded loyalty of the black DJs. Not just because his music remained authentic and unconformist despite his success, but because he involved the DJs in his shows and gave them an income from his performances. The DJs, in return, guaranteed him constant advertising and played every new song he made. 'In many cases these deejays became known in the market as "Mr. Brown's representatives" – a prestigious title in the black community.'[287] Brown recognized the power and importance of the black DJs,[288] and at the same time the necessity of the black radio stations in which the black DJs were not discriminated against or exploited. At the end of the 60s, two of the five black R&B radio stations (of a total of 528!) belonged to Brown, and he was considering buying another four.[289] But it wasn't to be; after his 1968 song 'I'm Black and Proud', which whites found menacing and militant, he was unable to get a record in the top ten until the 80s.

At the same time, he and many black radio DJs had saved America from a threatened race war. On the night of Martin Luther King's murder, Brown was going to call off his concert the following day in Boston, but the mayor asked him to stay and appear on television to keep the blacks from rioting. Brown agreed, and appeared on television that evening for six hours solid. His message was: 'Don't terrorize. Organize. Don't burn. Learn.'[290] At the same time black DJs throughout the US had set up special shifts – sometimes against the will of the (white) radio owners – and played music and talked to keep the blacks from rioting.

Del Shields, who was a radio DJ in New York at the time, tells of the night when black radio 'came of age': 'Up until that time, black radio had never been tested nationally. No one ever knew its power. You knew the popularity of black disc jockeys, the power to sell various products. But on the night Dr. King was killed, all across America every black station was tested and everybody who was on the air at that time, including myself, told people to cool it. We tried to do everything possible to keep the black people from just exploding even more than what they were.'[291] Although the DJs infringed all the conditions of the state Radio Commission with their lengthy broadcasts, they insisted on their responsibility and moral duty to use their authority in a sensible way.

There were no riots, and peace in American society was saved, at least for the time being. Both Brown and black

287. Ibid. p. 100.

288. 'We worked with disc jockeys because we knew they'd make sure the people heard about the show coming in, and it created good will with the jocks so they'd play our records before and after our arrival. I knew how little jocks got paid and co-promoting was a way to help them stay honest... I helped them make the kind of money they deserved – honestly.' (BROWN, James: The Godfather of Soul, p. 111.)

289. Cf. SHAW, Arnold: Soul, p. 254.

290. KARNIK, Olaf: The Godfather of Soul: James Brown, in: HÜNDGEN, Gerald (Ed.), op. cit., p. 62.

291. GEORGE, Nelson: The Death..., p. 111.

radio went unrewarded by the whites who had profited from their efforts. Del Shields explained the fact with reference to the fear of the whites: 'When America looked at black radio in that particular period, it suddenly hit them that this was a potent force. If, in every major city, a black disc jockey had said, "Rise up," there would have been pandemonium. And that night was also the beginning of the end of black radio. It was never allowed to rise up again.'[292]

Along with some of his colleagues, Shields managed to politicize the black DJ organization NATRA (National Association of Television and Radio Announcers), which up to now had been famous chiefly for its parties. A dialogue began between white radio owners and black DJs, to limit racist repression. The attempt to found a radio school belonging to NATRA failed because the organization had grown too powerful for many people. Shields and the other politically active representatives of the 'new breed'[293] were kept under surveillance, threatened, and some even beaten up. By 1969 the project of setting up NATRA as a real representative of political interests had failed – it turned back into a party machine.

A time was coming in which black DJs, hitherto the pioneers of all DJ ideas and styles, adapted and integrated. As a witness to this, Nelson George introduces the famous DJ Gary Byrd, who tells how the white radio managers told the DJs not to speak 'too ethnically' or to use too much slang, and made them go to work in a suit and tie. 'What it did was take jocks who were doing that and made them symbolic of all jocks. So even the jock who was doing a very hip personality thing in a hip way got wiped out.'[294]

The era of the personality DJs came to an end, and a new style in black radio was born, 'that emphasized a rigidly defined professionalism'.[295] Exceptions were DJs like Gary Byrd, Frankie Crocker and Dyanna Williams, but the black radio DJ as a cult figure, musical innovator, hipster, poet, politician and visionary was dead. At the same time, in the late 60s and early 70s, a new type of DJ was born in the black small, and gay clubs, one who would put the radio DJs in the shade and rewrite musical history: the underground club DJ.

292 . Ibid. p. 112.
293 . Ibid. p. 115.
294 . Ibid. p. 119.
295 . Ibid. p. 116.

DJS –
THE DEVELOPMENT IN EUROPE

America has always been the home of pop culture. The world domination of the Americans after the Second World War brought them not only a position of military and political power in relation to the rest of the western world, but also a position of cultural power. In cinema it was films from Hollywood that suppressed even the best European art films, in literature it was the works of J.D. Salinger, Thomas Pynchon and the authors of the Beat Generation who influenced the Europeans, and in painting New York replaced Paris as the world capital of art, dictating events from the Action Painting of the 40s and 50s to the Conceptual Art of the 70s.

But nowhere was the influence of the Americans on Europe so deep and lasting as in pop culture. Through to the early 60s, Europe remained a satellite continent of the USA where pop music was concerned. While England created its own sound in the 60s with the Beatles, the Rolling Stones, the Who and many other bands, the rest of Europe could only rework Anglo-American influences.

In Germany, independent developments only began with bands like Tangerine Dream, Can and Kraftwerk. No wonder, then, that for a long time DJs in Europe stumbled along behind their American models. The first European DJ of note came (of course) from England,[296] and his name was Jimmy Saville. For the British author Nik Cohn he was the best English DJ: 'To me, he was our only disc jockey.'[297]

Because while DJs in the US were selling fridges, inventing rock'n'roll or simply being superstars, in England (and the rest of Europe) they remained pallid figures who did nothing but spin records: 'Most of them sound like BBC announcers, neat, laundered, boring. They have nothing to do with pop. They aren't jockeys at all, in fact, they're only men who put on records.'[298]

In 1958 the first British radio programme devoted exclusively to pop music was set up. The two-hour

296. The first British DJ is Christopher Reynolds Stone (1882–1965), who played records for the BBC on 7 July 1927. At the time Stone was called an 'Announcer'. The term 'disc jockey' didn't appear until 1955, in the 'Times' (cf. OAKLEY, Nik/ GOTZ, Dave: The Music Spinners – Britain's Radio DJs, p. 123). The first DJ in Germany is considered to be Chris Howland, who presented the first DJ broadcasts with NWDR in 1952. In the early 60s DJ radio became successful on various other stations. (Cf. HANSBERGER, Joachim: Der Diskjockey, in: HELMS, S. (Ed.); Schlager in Deutschland, p. 279.)

297. COHN, Nik: AwopBopaLooBop..., p. 68.

298. Ibid.

299. MELLY, George: Revolt into Style, p. 212.

300. COHN, Nik: AwopBopaLooBop..., p. 68.

301. Ibid.

302. Ibid.

303. Ibid. p. 236.

304. MELLY, George, op. cit., p. 218f.

305. COHN, Nik: AwopBopaLooBop..., p. 236.

Saturday Club was presented by Brian Mathew, an ex-actor who came over as a friendly uncle. 'Pop was his job not his real life,'[299] wrote his friend, the pop writer George Melly.

But then, in 1963, came Jimmy Saville, a mixture of English eccentric and likely lad. A former Yorkshire miner, he had the working class background typical of British pop culture, and at the same time a conspicuously bizarre manner that quickly brought him to prominence. Cohn writes that his hair was a different colour every time he saw him: mostly peroxide blond, but sometimes pink or striped or tartan, as Nik Cohn fascinatedly observed. Saville wore weird shirts, shoes and suits – in short: he looked 'like something from space'.[300]

He was the first British DJ who clearly identified with the bright and exciting world of youth culture. Cohn describes Saville as a hero from a modern novel, full of contradictions, who earned a huge amount of money but lived in a council flat; who was shrewd and naïve, at once powerful and sentimental; who was a wrestler, organizing fights and charity balls: a man who had what it took to be a pop star.

His greatest talent as a radio programme-maker lay in the fact that he was 'a marvellous raconteur, truly original'.[301] He spoke in 'an exaggerated staccato Yorkshire accent',[302] waved his arms about, hammed it up and rolled his eyes. But for all his extravagance Saville remained conservative where subjects like sex or religion were concerned. And in the end Saville became part of the establishment: in the late 60s he interviewed leading politicians for the BBC.

After Saville, in Europe there was still Emperor Rosko, whose real name was Mike Pasternak and who began his career in the mid-60s. The American, who worked in Paris for Radio Luxemburg was – in Cohn's words – 'a greyhound spieler, one slippery mouth'.[303] For George Melly, Rosko was a 'near genius': ...his wild alliterative freewheeling punning ego creates before our very ears an extraordinary pop monster. What's more he plays good records... a true poet of pop-hype.'[304] Cohn stresses Rosko's knowledge of pop and his drive: 'He played amazing noise. Always and always, he was fast.'[305] At Radio Luxemburg Rosko got one hour's airtime every day and three hours on Saturdays, while on the British Radio 1 he was fobbed off with one hour per week.

John Peel was and remains the intellectual among British DJs. Born in 1936, he had worked as a DJ in America when he came back to Europe in the mid-60s and hosted a late-night show on Radio London called *The Perfumed Garden*. In this programme he played not only pop, but also classical and oriental music as well as songs from the 20s; there were even poetry readings on Peel's programmes. In the 70s he began his now legendary 'sessions', in which bands re-recorded a selection of their songs in his studio: first for the radio, then on record – most 'Peel Sessions' were released as their own series of records. Despite his age, Peel became an institution of punk music and the subsequent indie music movement.

Otherwise the European DJ market was dominated by tired mediocrity and pathetic copies of the US. A situation that was not to change until the 80s.

DJ CULTURE THE HISTORY

A. DISCO

DISCO – THE BEGINNINGS

Disco has two origins: musical and socio-topographical. In other words: disco was and is both the music and the place where the music was played. The word is an abbreviation of the term discothèque, originally French, which in turn derives from the Greek words dískos, a disc, and theke, a container. The word's French origin is due to the fact that the first discothèques were in France. During the German occupation of Paris in the Second World War, the jazz bands were driven out of the clubs, and with them the public that had danced to their music. But they escaped the prohibition and fled to dark cellars on the left bank of the Seine. They put down cables in the cellars and they installed simple sound systems which consisted of record-players and speakers. The Parisians came, they listened to the music and danced.

When the war was won and the occupiers had fled, many clubs reopened with bands, but some stayed with the concept of playing records. In the 50s, with the advent of rock'n'roll, the discothèques experienced a massive leap in popularity, because the live clubs found it difficult to get rock'n'roll bands or singers, while the records from America quickly made their way into

Europe. By the end of the 50s there were discothèques all over France. The example of the discothèques was accepted throughout Europe, and many of the club managers discovered that it was far more economical to engage a DJ than a full live band, let alone a swing orchestra.

So the origins of the discothèque were European, but the full scope of the concept was only discovered in America. In New York in 1960 'Le Club' was opened (the French name recalls the country of origin of the discothèque). Le Club was a former garage, which, funded by an illustrious circle of sponsors (including jet-setters like Henry Ford and the Duke of Bedford) was converted into the 'playboy's dream of the ultimate seduction pad'.[1] A tiny entrance, a kitsch romantic interior and a small dancefloor gave the club an appearance that was at once intimate and glamorous. The opening night on New Year's Eve 1960 was a triumph – the efforts and investments of the club manager, Olivier Coquelin, had paid off. There was just one problem: the music. At the beginning of every evening there was a mixture of meaningless cocktail music and gentle dance tunes, which gradually grew livelier and were supposed to lead to the twist. But rather than a constant crescendo that would have roused the guests and got them dancing, on the opening evening the DJ entertained the guests with an unharmonious stop-and-go mixture. So Coquelin decided to ask friends about an unemployed musician who might put on records in the club. Slim Hyatt was recommended, and after his first, catastrophic appearance as a DJ Coquelin asked him what instrument he had played before. The puzzled Hyatt answered that he had worked as a butler for Peter Duchin, a friend of Coquelin's. Coquelin then tried out some real musicians as DJs, but after a number of disappointments he returned to Hyatt, and a former butler became America's first disco DJ.[2]

Visitors to the club included the Duke and Duchess of Windsor and Ava Gardner. These and other VIPs popularized the idea of the discothèque. A handful of super-elegant kitsch and classy clubs were opened ('L'Interdit', 'Il Mio Club', 'Shepheard's'[3]), but it was not until the mid-60s that the disco concept became

1. GOLDMAN, Albert: Disco, p. 42.

2. Cf. Ibid. p. 43.

3. In this club, opened in 1964, half-naked girls danced in cages from as early as 1965, to get the guests dancing and provide an erotic charge in the club. A tradition unbroken until the present day. (Cf. Ibid.)

popular in New York.[4]

In its record 'hops', America had a tradition that disco could have built on. A hop was originally taken to be a dance, a ball or a show, but in the early years of rock'n'roll the hop stood for a particular kind of teen entertainment, monumentalized in many American films and television series. The Danny & the Juniors hit, 'At the Hop', euphorically sings of the joy that awaited teens at a hop: music, girls and the promise of sex. In his dancefloor almanac, Doug Shannon differentiates between sock hops, held without lighting effects and with the simplest sound systems in gymnasiums and halls, and the rather more refined, smaller 'platter parties' which were better equipped with light and sound.[5] One other influence on the development to the discothèque might be seen as the jukebox, which had successfully propagated the playing of records in America since the 1930s.

American Bandstand, a show broadcast from 1957, brought the hop to the remotest villages. It showed young people in the 'right' suits and dresses, with the 'right' shoes, dancing the latest steps to the latest music. Regional differences that had previously existed within youth culture were reduced to a homogeneous style that was identical across the country. Dick Clark, the moderator of *Bandstand*, turned the television DJ into a master of ceremonies. For most radio DJs the hops and platter parties were a good opportunity to top up their meagre salaries.

4. Cf. SHANNON, Doug: Off the Record, p. 8ff.

5. Cf. Ibid. p. 11.

THE TWIST

The twist was the first fashion dance to make a career for itself in the discothèques. In 1959 Hank Ballard & the Midnighters won few listeners with 'The Twist' (the B-side of their R&B hit 'Teardrops on Your Letter'). It became a massive hit only fifteen months later with the cover-version by Chubby Checker. The reasons for this lay not in its being musically refreshed, but in a new marketing strategy. Because of his appearance and his extraordinary dancing abilities, Checker's record company had originally conceived of him as a 'visual act'.[6] Parkway, a sub-label of Cameo Records in Philadelphia, had direct social links to Dick Clark, and consequently Checker was unusually well promoted in *American Bandstand*.[7] The concept of staking everything on the stylistic unity of music, dance and clothes was a successful one. Chubby Checker taught the whole of America how to dance, via television and drawn instructions in newspapers. Within a very short time America was in twist fever, and Chubby Checker was a rich man.

The twist, like the hula-hoop, should really have been a third-rate fashion with a life expectancy of six months at most. Nik Cohn, writing about the twist mania, called it a 'hype',[8] a classic pop euphoria intensified to hysteria by the media: '...1961 was parched, was really desperate. So first Chubby Checker had a hit record. Second, New York smart society decided that the Twist was cute and started to hang out in the Peppermint Lounge. Third, the gossip columnists jumped aboard. Fourth, the whole industry started hyping. And fifth, madness set in.'[9]

Greta Garbo, Judy Garland and Tennessee Williams danced in the Peppermint Lounge to the sounds of Joey Dee and the Starliters, and they played the twist all night long. For Cohn a new age was beginning; previously the world of the rich and beautiful had thought pop was uncool, and now Jean Cocteau, Jackie Kennedy and Margot Fonteyn were twisting. A 'superclass'[10] of opinion-leaders – artists, pop-stars, millionaires, intellectuals – devoted themselves to pop, night-life and dancing. In Europe the twist was only a discothèque dance, in America it was usually danced to live music. In any case, along with other, less successful fashionable dances[11] it represented a break with the conventional dance styles. The twist was an artistic product that made rock'n'roll chic,[12] and going out to dance became a major style issue. The Peppermint Lounge in New York, although it was a live club, became one of the origins of the New York club scene. The first generation of American discothèques in the mid-60s like Shepheard's, L'Interdit or the Hippopotamus, would have been hard to imagine without the success of the Peppermint Lounge. The Arthur replaced the Peppermint Lounge as the absolute

6. GILLETT, Charlie, loc. cit., p. 209.

7. Cf. SHAW, Arnold, Dictionary..., loc. cit., p. 394f.

8. Arnold Shaw's Dictionary defines hype as an abbreviation of 'hypodermic': 'It refers to an excited, enthusiastic superdrive to promote a record, song, or artist. Both as a noun and a verb, "hype" generally connotes that the enthusiasm is calculated if not fabricated. But "hypes" sometimes work, which then means that the thing hyped had enough appeal and quality to warrant the outlay of time, effort, and budget.' (SHAW, Arnold: Dictionary..., loc. cit., p. 180f.) Nik Cohn considers hype to be an abbreviation of 'hyperbole'. For him, hype 'means to promote by hustle, pressure, even honest effort if necessary, and the idea is that you leave nothing to chance. Simply, you do everything possible. Hype has become such an integral part of pop that one hardly notices it any more.' (COHN, Nik: AwopBopaLooBop..., loc. cit., p. 47.)

9. COHN, Nik: AwopBopaLooBop..., loc. cit., p. 82.

10. Ibid.

11. There was the Fish, the Drug, the Dip, the Jerk, the Stomp, the Boston Monkey, the Hully Gully and the Mashed Potato (cf. JOE, Radcliffe A.: This Business of Disco, p. 16.)

12. Cf. COHN, Nik: Rock Dreams, unpaginated.

in-place, and can be described as the first successful 'pure' discothèque where the music played was chiefly on record. The guests included stars like Lauren Bacall, John Wayne, the Stones and the Beatles, and the media organized a lot of noise about the place, as in the heyday of the Peppermint Lounge.

The music in the sophisticated discothèques remained indifferent and mainstream-oriented. The disco hype didn't last long, and by 1969 most discothèques that had spread throughout the whole country were turned back into live clubs. After the twist there was little new dance music; the leading youth culture, the hippie movement, listened mostly to folk and acid rock, and only the black minority seemed to have maintained their interest in dance music, with artists like James Brown, Isaac Hayes and Sly and the Family Stone.

The truly exciting musical developments were happening not in the elegant clubs of Manhattan, but at small parties and underground events. 'In the beginning was the rent party',[13] David Toop explains in his history of disco. Jimmy Castor, who 'put on shows' with DJs like Jocko Henderson at rent parties in the early days, claims to have been one of the first activists of the underground DJ scene: 'We had discos even before discos came into fashion. I'm now talking about 1962. We called them record hops.'[14] Through to the late 70s, rent or block parties remained a forum for new musical directions and DJ arts, from disco to hip-hop. In the early 80s these parties turned into garage sessions and illegal raves. The history of the innovative dancefloor remains closely connected with the development of those semi-public, semi-legal parties.

At the end of the 60s the only discothèques in existence were either high-society events or had been taken over by the black, Latino and/or gay communities. In the underground clubs and at the many parties and record hops the dominant musical mishmash of soul, Latin, funk and rock generated a new style that became the earliest form of disco music. It mostly consisted of fast soul songs, funk by James Brown and lasciviously rhythmic Latin tracks. This turned into a 'non-stop soundtrack for the whole night with peaks, pauses, letting go,'[15] with skilfully built-up tension and a

13. TOOP, David: Lost in Music: Zwanzig Jahre Disco-Produktionen, in: FREDERKING, Klaus (Ed.): Rock Session 8 – Sound und Vision, p. 149.

14. Ibid.

15. TOOP, David: Lost in Music, in: FREDERKING, Klaus (Ed.), op. cit., p. 150.

dramatic structure constructed by the DJ. For a long time DJs had faded music in and out, now the early disco DJs tried to guarantee a constant flow of beats. The pounding rhythm, where possible without major interruptions, was designed for the satisfaction of the dancers on the dancefloor. From the beginning, disco music had only one purpose: to make people dance. And once they were dancing, not to let them stop. The dancefloor had to bubble, as disco devotee Truman Capote put it: '...the whole place churning like a buttermilk machine.'[16]

The first famous underground club was 'Salvation', which started playing party music in 1969. Party music was so called because whenever the DJ turned down the music the people cried 'Paaarrtiiiiieee'. The Salvation's first DJ was Terry Noel, and he was soon replaced by Francis Grosso. After the Salvation closed, 'The Church' became the most important underground club in New York. A converted German Baptist church, it was in one of the gloomiest, most drug-ridden areas of Manhattan, known as 'Hell's Kitchen' and avoided by most New Yorkers. But it wasn't intimidating enough to keep away the high society that had previously tended to visit the clubs: Arnie Lord, who ran the place, decorated the former house of worship as if for a witches' sabbath. A massive picture of the devil was projected opposite the altar, its glowing eyes seeming to follow the clubbers wherever they went. Next to it was a flock of copulating putti. This blasphemous décor led to a ban from the Catholic Church, and meant that the club first had to take down the offending parts of the decoration and then change its name. The Church became the 'Sanctuary'. In the early days chic white heterosexuals flocked to the club, but this changed quickly when the club got new management. According to Albert Goldman, a drag queen called Shelley turned the Sanctuary into the first uninhibitedly gay discotheque.[17]

Fashionable gays, drag queens and a lot of good-looking young men were the Sanctuary's stock audience. The run-down area, the blasphemous interior decoration and the crazy atmosphere soon made the club the talk of the town. Parts of Alan J. Pakula's psycho-thriller *Klute,* starring Jane Fonda and Donald

16 . McCORMACK, Ed: No Sober Person Dances, in: PECK, Abe (Ed.): Dancing Madness, p. 11.

17 . Cf. GOLDMAN, Albert: Disco, p. 114.

Sutherland, were shot there. In the two scenes set in the Sanctuary you can see the opulence of the interior decoration, but the rock music being played and the predominantly white, strictly heterosexual crowd dancing are hardly a document of its early disco days.

Of the other venues, above all the black pre-disco clubs, there is little or no documentation. We only know of their existence because the first DJs producing disco and house music received their musical education in that environment.

FRANCIS GROSSO – THE FIRST DJ AUTHOR

Francis Grosso is often described as 'the first DJ-as-auteur/artist/idol',[18] and he was certainly one of the people who initiated the disco sound.[19] At a time when the hip-hop deejaying of Kool DJ Herc had not yet been invented, Grosso began to see the playing of records as a creative, musical process. Grosso had started out as a dancer, then as a part-time DJ. One evening when he stood in for Terry Noel at the Salvation, the novice was so good that the club manager took him on and Noel was fired. Francis played fast funk and soul records. Goldman describes his DJ style as a mixture of records by Aretha Franklin, Gladys Knight, Booker T. and the MGs, Chicago and Cat Mother. More original was the use of African folk choirs and rhythm sections that Grosso integrated within his party mix. He was the first not simply to spin records, but to manipulate and vary his material.

Grosso perfected the mixing of records. He invented 'slip-cueing', in which the record is held still on the rotating deck, and set off at exactly the moment the beat of the other piece ends. To prevent the belt of the record-player burning through, a felt disc ('slipmat') was placed between the deck and the vinyl to minimize the friction between the deck and the vinyl. When the thumb was removed from the record, the record started at exactly the right speed. Finally, when Grosso bought

18 . HARVEY, Steven/BATES, Patricia: Behind Groove, in: DJ, 3/1993, p. 4.

19 . Writing of the inventors of disco in an article for The Face, David Toop refers to Francis Grosso as 'the original DJ'. (TOOP, David: Disco, in: THE FACE, 9/1992, p. 54.)

two Thorens record-players with speed regulators called pitchers, he was able to assimilate the speeds of records with considerable precision, and mix them together. Thanks to the headphones and the pre-hear option on the mixing desk, which DJs had not yet got around to using, Grosso managed to connect the individual pieces harmonically. But mixing wasn't enough for him, so he started interpreting the pieces with the record-player and the mixing desk. He overlaid the drumbreak from 'I'm a Man' with the wild groans of Led Zeppelin vocalist Robert Plant from 'Whole Lotta Love', a mixture of drumbeats and orgiastic sounds that was to be popularized a good five years later by Donna Summer in 'Love To Love You Baby'. Thus Francis Grosso invented disco music before it was produced by the record industry.

In 1969 John Cage conceived an installation entitled *33¹/₃*, in which visitors were able to select records from a stand and play them on a number of record-players. Cage was fascinated by the record as a popular creative material: 'For that reason the only living thing that can happen with a record is for it to be used in such a way that something new comes out of it. If, for example, you could make a different piece of music using a record, by involving a record or other ambient sounds or other pieces of music, I would find that interesting.'[20] In this way Cage had developed the rough draft for a poetics of DJ culture before it had left the underground. Leaving aside the special examples of ska and reggae, disco represented the first instance in pop music of a new style being invented at the turntable. As with hip-hop and house music later on, a DJ's ideas represented the start of a kind of music that was first seen as dance music, and was later taken on board by the musical mainstream. But while almost all pioneers among hip-hop and house DJs were also the first to produce records of their particular style, most party and disco DJs remained true to their original profession, that of playing the tunes. Francis Grosso never saw himself as an artist, but only ever as someone who put on records and mixed them, thus realizing his own ideas.

Disco was born in the clubs, not studios, and the result was that disco the place defined disco the music. In the view of the American pop writer Tom Smucker it was

20. Quoted in: ZELLER, Hans Rudolf: Medienkomposition nach Cage, in: BLOCK, Ursula/ GLASMEIER, Michael (Ed.): Broken Music, p. 71.

the first pop music that was initiated by its consumers (via the DJs). If people danced to it in the clubs it was disco, if they didn't it wasn't.[21]

Van McCoy and producer–musicians like Giorgio Morodor took their impulses from the dancefloor, but it was their abilities as composers that gave DJs more than a vague idea of what the music was to sound like. DJs mixed their favourite soul and funk records and, like Francis Grosso, added African rhythms or rock'n'roll groaning, but they didn't think of taking it further, or even of producing the whole as music. They waited for records that worked in their club context and could be used in their mix. In retrospect, Joey Negro, a famous house DJ and musician of the 90s, sees one of the qualities of disco music as being that DJs wanted it but musicians made it, only for it to be remixed again by the DJs. For that reason Negro finds disco considerably more musical than house music, which is produced and remixed almost exclusively by DJs.[22]

21. Cf. SMUCKER, Tom: Disco, in: MILLER, Jim (Ed.): The Rolling Stone Illustrated History of Rock'n'Roll, p. 426.

22. Cf. SHARP, Elsa: Disco Dave, in: DJ, 3/1993, p. 12.

23. Cf. GOLDMAN, Albert: Disco, p. 117.

Francis Grosso was not only one of the first imaginative mixers at the turntables, but also one of the first superstars among the club DJs. His groupies were the few women who managed to get into the Sanctuary, and who made themselves available to satisfy any of Grosso's sexual needs while he worked. By his own account he had sex with a good 500 women during his work (but never on the altar, where the record-players stood!).[23] The small, muscular, long-haired boy from Brooklyn was having a good time. Club owners courted him, and he enjoyed his work. He loved the music and the crazy atmosphere in the Sanctuary. After a fight with a drug-dealer he also discovered the dark side of celebrity, when he was kicked and beaten until he was almost unrecognizable. The dealers' revenge meant that Grosso had to take a six-month break, in which his face was rebuilt with a series of operations.

There was an abundance of sex and drugs in the Sanctuary. The drug dealers supplied the frenzied dancers with speed, cocaine, hash and LSD as if in a 'supermarket' (Goldman). The exuberant drug consumption and bass-heavy, lascivious music turned the church into a sexual orgy. Sexual intercourse on the dancefloor was forbidden, so to the rhythms of James Brown, every imaginable sexual position was given a dry run on the dancefloor, to be brought to completion later in the cubicles of the men's toilets. In a time before Aids, the orgies were even such that the pews and choirstalls were used for copulation, as eye-witness Albert Goldman reported. 'The cute little angels on the walls staring down on some of the most outrageous behavior that has ever been clocked in a public place.'[24] The free expression of gay sexuality was celebrated in the Sanctuary. And that highly erotic, uninhibited celebration was the basis of disco. Donna Summer's yearning groans years later were merely a pale echo of the unbridled sexual practices in the first disco clubs. The Sanctuary acted as one of the first strongholds of gay militancy, because a strong sense of belonging, communal strength and power had formed among the dancers in the church. When the police started organizing raids with increasing frequency, this sense of communality turned into rebellion. At Grosso's demand to leave the club for the raid, the euphoric masses shouted, 'Fuck you! Let the cops carry us out!'[25] But the Sanctuary was finally closed down not because of drugs or blasphemous orgies, but because of the hundreds of men waiting in front of the church for entrance, flirting, laughing, shouting or – according to witnesses – having oral sex in house doorways. In April 1972 the city had the Sanctuary closed down. There was no place for Sodom and Gomorrah in the middle of Manhattan. After this Francis Grosso worked as a DJ in various other clubs, but his greatest time was past. As a teacher of DJs like Steven D'Aquisito and Michael Cappello he also had an influence on subsequent generations of DJs. His technique and his sound musical taste, his vision of the disco sound before disco existed, and his ability to realize that vision using old records made him one of the most important DJs in the history of pop music. He also provided the blueprint for the club DJ as a star, a hero (particularly to women), and the perfect master of the dancing crowds.

Thanks to the Sanctuary, disco won itself the attribute 'gay', at least in New York. There were other smaller clubs in which similar things happened to similar

24. Ibid.

25. Ibid. p. 118.

music. David Mancuso's 'Loft', for example, was one such place in which fewer drugs and hardly any alcohol were consumed, and less sex was practised, but which had still had an intimate atmosphere of absolute freedom from social taboos. The Loft was actually David Mancuso's apartment before he decided to throw weekly parties there. The Loft parties, entrance by invitation only, were at first only a meeting-place for Mancuso's friends, but crowds were soon jostling in front of the entrance to the apartment on Broadway, waiting to dance to the music that Mancuso played, and which was known as the 'gay sound' from 1972–3.[26] But Mancuso didn't mix – he had a sound taste for what drove the boys on the dancefloor to ecstasy, but he had no technique as a DJ. He just played one piece after another, as loud as possible, on his expensive equipment.[27] He was more interested in good acoustics than new sounds, but he still wrote DJ history. In 1975 he set up the first DJ record pool with Steven D'Aquisito and Vince Aletti. This common association of DJs had formed in order to be showered with promos from the record industry, and distribute those records to the relevant DJs according to taste. Mancuso's Loft parties remained classic events of New York nightlife through until the 80s.

The first disco clubs in the early 70s gave the gay community a place where, far from any social reprisals, they were able to express and experience their own sexuality. This liberation was particularly enthusiastic in the black and Latin American gay clubs. At the same time the kids – as young African-American homosexuals called themselves – were becoming more confident. In these clubs and at the parties, discriminating pleasure could be discovered as something exciting, stimulating and vital. 'It's a gay thing, you wouldn't understand,' black homosexuals said, adapting the well-known statement of black pride. Disco was the proud demonstration of types of behaviour, of fashion and make-up, language and drug consumption that were not tolerated by the dominant society. Disco was a truly free space at a time when Nixon was president, when the Vietnam War was still going on and American society yearned for peace and conservatism after the shake-ups of the student

26 . Cf. Ibid. p. 119.

27 . Cf. HARVEY, Steven/BATES, Patricia, op. cit., p. 7f.

rebellions and the Black Power movement. Disco as a minority music created a social niche within an otherwise hostile environment. Disco as a mass music, in the words of American sociologist Jim Curtis, celebrated the fact 'that we had survived Nixon'.[28] As evidence for his thesis, Curtis quoted (half seriously, half tongue in cheek) the first song from the film *Stayin' Alive* by the Bee Gees, and Gloria Gaynor's 'I Will Survive'. 'Nixon had gone and we should ignore politics for a while. It was a glorious, liberating feeling.'[29]

But this liberation was only accomplished by the gay communities in the American cities. Disco cannot be understood without realizing how far it was 'a gay thing'.

DISCO – A GAY THING

After the proletariat had become almost insignificant as a subject of political emancipation, new actors took the political stage in the 60s and 70s. Society fragmented into minorities. New groupings came into being which, according to Lyotard – 'have not yet been entered in the official registers: women, homosexuals, divorced people, prostitutes, the disappropriated, immigrants...'[30] The motivation and goals of the minorities were different – but what united them in their struggle was that it was a minority struggle.[31]

Historically, disco can be seen as part of the project of identifying 'homosexuals' as members of the gay minority, and giving them visibility. Disco became a token culture of the gay minority. For British music writer Richard Dyer, who wrote 'In Defense of Disco' in the magazine *Gay Left* in 1979, the gay conquest of disco culture is evidence of the possibilities of repression-free self-assertion within a flourishing culture industry in late capitalism. Although Dyer wrongly assumes that gays conquered rather than invented disco, he is correct in his thesis that 'the anarchy of capitalism' opens up opportunities for an oppressed minority, which need only take those opportunities in order to throw together a culture of

28. CURTIS, Jim: Rock Eras, p. 300.

29. Ibid.

30. LYOTARD, Jean-François: Kleine Perspektivierung der Dekadenz und einiger minoritärer Gefechte, die hier zu führen sind, in: idem: Das Patchwork der Minderheiten, p. 38.

31. Ibid. p. 8.

their own.[32] Within the context of the social space of entertainment, fun and style, a gay culture can establish itself while at the same time bringing fun and profit to society. Disco is camp in the sense that it amounts to a dissident use within the context of the dominant culture, and that at the same time it contributes to the formation and reinforcement of gay identity. Both disco and camp are spheres of domination which homosexuals rule as what Susan Sontag has called 'aristocrats of taste'.[33]

For Walter Hughes, gay identity chiefly relies on certain forms of behaviour that try to connect joy with self-chastisement. The subjection of the gay man to the beat is an act of pleasurable self-denial, rewarded with collective ecstasy and an unbounded, free and flowing eroticism. Gay identity as a mixture of celebration and pain can thus be repeated every evening in the disco. The tyranny of the beat is the underlying motif of disco culture. 'As Vicky Sue Robinson says in an early hit, disco turns the beat around, turns it upside down, making it the dominant element in the music and giving it the irresistibility that is disco's recurrent theme.'[34] Even the beginnings of disco in the gay clubs at the end of the 60s yearned for that constant beat. The challenge for the disco DJ was to keep the rhythm going as evenly as possible for as long as possible. The wonderfully ambiguous exclamation 'Don't stop! Don't stop!' has been one of the most frequently used samples in dance-floor music from the first days of disco to the house and hip-hop music of today. 'Don't stop!' the DJ commanded, keep going! Keep moving! 'As disco lyrics make clear, make obvious, make painfully redundant, the beat brooks no denial. It moves us, controls us, deprives us of our will. Dancing becomes a form of submission to the overmastering beat.'[35]

From the very first, disco was body music. For Michel Foucault, the body has always been the battle-ground of power, but the meaning of that occupation of the body has only entered (political) consciousness since 1968.[36] The needs, pleasures and desires of the body have always been controlled and suppressed. 'Mastery and awareness of one's own body can be acquired only through the effect of an investment of power in the body: gymnastics, exercises, muscle-building, nudism,

32. DYER, Richard: In Defense of Disco, in: FRITH, Simon/GOODWIN, Andrew: On Record, p. 413.

33. SONTAG, Susan: Notes on Camp, in: idem: A Susan Sontag Reader, p. 117.

34. HUGHES, Walter: Feeling Mighty Real, in: ROCK'N'ROLL QUARTERLY, Summer 1993, p. 10.

35. Ibid.

36. 'The emergence of the problem of the body and its growing urgency have come about through the unfolding of a political struggle. Whether this is a revolutionary struggle, I don't know. One can say that what has happened since 1968, and arguably what made 1968 possible, is something profoundly anti-Marxist... in this calling in question of the equation: Marxism = the revolutionary process, an equation that constituted a kind of dogma, the importance given to the body is one of the important, if not essential elements.' (FOUCAULT, Michel: Body/Power, in: idem: Power/Knowledge, p. 57.)

glorification of the body beautiful. All of this belongs to the pathway leading to the desire of one's own body, by way of the insistent, persistent, meticulous work of power on the bodies of children or soldiers, the healthy bodies.'[37] A reversal of the suppression and discipline desired by power comes into being. On the path towards the conquest of the body by power there emerge 'the responding claims and affirmations, those of one's own body against power, of health against the economic system, of pleasure against the moral norms of sexuality, marriage, decency. Suddenly, what had made power strong becomes used to attack it. Power, after investing itself in the body, finds itself exposed to a counter-attack in that same body.'[38] This reverse effect of the control and surveillance of the body is particularly strong in sexuality, engendering the 'intensification of each individual's desire, for, in and over his body'.[39]

Disco is a forum for liberated bodies. The revolt of the sexual body created, amongst other things, a protected zone for homosexuals in the clubs. The music speaks directly to the body. 'Set me free' or 'Set your body free' are typical lyrics in disco and house pieces. Like 'Release yourself' or 'Let your body go!', these commands appear in almost every other disco and house song. No story is told, the bodily emphasis of the music is simply underlined. The verbal function of the lyrics is purely performative. Walter Hughes stresses that the oft-lamented emptiness of disco lyrics is a part of the disco ideology that translates the rhetoric of the beat into simple imperatives.[40] Almost all traces of syntax and structure have been eliminated from the language. With frequent repetitions of the smallest linguistic units, words break down and become a helpless echo of the beat.

Everything points towards the body, and everything invites the body to let itself go and dance, to yield entirely to the rhythm. Everything disappears behind the force of the beat. The disco DJ assumes control, seducing and binding the clubbers with music until they follow him. The DJ boils down the individual elements of a disco until they adapt to the unbroken sequence of the music. The desire for rhythmic continuity is the

---

37. Ibid. p. 56.

38. Ibid.

39. Ibid. p. 57.

40. We might briefly list Hughes' examples of disco lyrics: 'Got to keep on dancing, got to keep on keeping me high'; 'My body, your body, everybody work your body'; 'Come on come on get busy do it I want to see you party.' Often these lyrics become little but counting, without teleology or terminus: '5, 4, 3, 2, 1, let's go' or '1, 2, 3, shake your body down.' (HUGHES, Walter, op. cit., p. 10.)

origin of the remixing of the song, which was to guarantee this evenness from the mid-70s. Without disco remixes and 12-inch singles, the early disco DJs had even greater difficulty making a non-stop soundtrack for the whole night without destroying the dramatic structure of the evening, and were thus thrown back on their talent for improvization. The right breaks and transitions could only be mastered with the greatest knowledge of the records, the speed and rhythms, and the most highly advanced treatment of primitive technology (two records and a slide-regulator for the transition). What was needed was a knowledge of music and an ability to freestyle.

From the beginning, the disco ideal was a kind of lascivious, tense monotony that was both constantly new and always the same – every second the same and yet completely different. The individual piece of music dissolves into a new whole without having to give itself up. It remains an individual piece, but at the same time it is placed within a larger frame of reference that can be called 'an evening in the club' or 'a non-stop soundtrack'.

For Walter Hughes the individual piece of music, and with it the artist and author, is lost in the infinite series of the beat. As evidence for the way in which disco mystifies its origins in individual authors, Hughes on the one hand introduces techno-group names like Hues Corporation, Machine, Change and Black Box, and on the other artists like the Village People or Shannon, who are clearly made-to-measure by their producers.[41]

Anonymity and artificiality are also among the fundamental experiences of the homosexual lifestyle. The disappearance of personal identity behind the force of bodily, purely physical seduction was – before Aids – a contemporary part of gay sexual behaviour.

The unity of bodies and liberated identities is produced by the tyranny of the beat. The clubber becomes a 'Slave to the Rhythm', as Grace Jones put it in a disco song in 1985. The heavy bass-line of the disco beat is not only heard but felt with the whole body. Every beat hits the stomach, is felt in the ribs and thus makes a (physical) reaction to the music inevitable: either dance or leave the club.

Hughes' analysis is interesting in that he sees the beat

41. HUGHES, Walter, op. cit., p. 10.

42. Ibid.

43. Ibid.

44. The corresponding passage in the Jones piece: 'Never stop the action/ Keep it up, keep it up/ Breathe to the rhythm/ Dance to the rhythm/ Work to the rhythm/ Live to the rhythm/ Love to the rhythm/ You slave to the rhythm!' (Quoted in HUGHES, Walter, op. cit., p. 11.)

45. TOOP, David: Disco, p. 56.

46. TOOP, David: Lost in Music, in: FREDERKING, Klaus (Ed.), op. cit., p. 145.

as the embodiment of longing. For Hughes, the compelling power of the beat to make people dance is just as great as the power of longing and desire that leads to sexual intercourse, and also to forbidden and supposedly unnatural forms of sexuality. 'Desire, according to this analogy, is more than a physical sensation or a psychological control over any number of individuals, drawing them into a community of submission.'[42] Love is described as slavery, madness, an addiction or a police state, 'as anything that rivals the despotism of the beat itself'.[43] For Hughes, the relinquishment of identity and the state of being penetrated and controlled by the beat lead to the abandonment of one's sense of oneself as a human being or a citizen. Deliberate self-enslavement as the most radical counterblow to the repression of society as a whole. Submission as the realm of freedom, in which one breathes, dances, works, lives and loves to the beat, and in which one becomes a slave to the rhythm.[44]

THE ROOTS OF DISCO MUSIC

David Toop begins the story of disco music with James Brown's records 'Out of Sight' and 'Papa's Got a Brand New Bag'.[45] With these records from 1964–5, Brown's music outgrew the old concept of R&B and developed into a powerful soul sound with a heavy groove. The arrangements were more bass-heavy, the bass drum and the bass guitar forced themselves acoustically into the foreground. The horn sections were – says Toop – also 'tight, and no longer used for melodic fills. Now they crash in rhythmically on the beat, their sweet tone was removed by hard, incisive tones and an "underlaid" baritone saxophone.'[46] The endless loops of the rhythm units were the first to take pop music to the brink of non-melody. The eternal recurrence of the same figures, accentuated by the groaning, shouting and cheering, rapping and singing of the voice, bursting with power, hypnotized every form of linear perception of music. Each element in Brown's arrangement was subordinated to the predominance of the rhythm. In this sense Brown can easily be identified as an ancestor of the disco sound, even if his hot-blooded, warm 'funkiness' was not rediscovered until the loving funk reconstructions of hip-hop. As the blueprint of a repetitiveness operating on the borderline of monotony, the nearly nine-minute-long pieces like 'Hot Pants' or 'Sex Machine' are direct predecessors of the dance remixes that would only be invented for disco years later. In addition, the groundwork was laid for the idea of the remix, in Brown's recording of songs in two parts, the second part usually being an instrumental version, the idea of a variation.

The Godfather of Soul himself dismissively referred to disco as a simplification of what he had done himself: 'Disco is a very small part of funk. It's the end of the song, the repetitious part, like a vamp. The difference is that in funk you dig into a groove, you don't stay on the surface. Disco stayed on the surface. See, I taught 'em everything *they* know, but not everything *I* know.'[47]

It is true that disco stopped at the surface of groove, though it is less true that disco producers owe everything they know to Brown. Because of the loss of soul that Brown complains of, and the swapping of raw funkiness, however it might be defined, for sweet monotony, there was the autonomous new creation of dance music as made by disco producers in the mid-70s. It is understandable that the 'Sex Machine' himself should have felt more than detached in response to the functionalist transformation of his soul and his eroticism. Brown's despairing accusation that disco is chiefly machine-made makes it plain the extent to which he felt alienated from these increasingly cold constructions.

When disco was put together from numerous black forerunners into a new and white sound, the representatives of the old soul and funk music could only hear those things that had been lost. One interesting transitional phenomenon from soul to disco is the Philadelphia Sound, which peaked between 1970 and 1973. The Philadelphia record label, founded by the two producers Kenny Gamble and Leon Huff in 1971, had artists like the O'Jays, the Blue Notes and Harold Melvin under contract. Perhaps the purest

47. BROWN, James, op. cit., p. 242f.

example of the Philadelphia Sound was the MFSB Orchestra, a collection of studio musicians who had worked on other Philadelphia International productions, and who were able to keep their success going into the disco age. As part of the soundtrack to *Saturday Night Fever*, their polished and elegant arrangements, with opulent strings and horn sections, document their influence on all subsequent disco productions after the MFSB number-one hit 'TSOP' (The Sound Of Philadelphia). All of Gamble and Huff's productions came out of studio sessions, beginning with the construction of a 'rhythm track'. Everything else was then handed over to the studio musicians of the MFSB family, who had developed a fine sense for the Philadelphia Sound, as Leon Huff observed: 'Our sound stems from the feeling of the musicians; you know everybody down there is in a relaxed atmosphere ... the warmness shows in the grooves, the mechanical feeling is not there, it's more a free type of thing.'[48] But this relaxed freedom, under the direction of Huff and Gamble, always led to precise, perfect arrangements whose elegance was often more important than their soul. In 1974 three producers from Philadelphia dominated the Billboard Awards for best-selling records and records with the most airplay. Thom Bell, who produced the Spinners and the Stylistics, won awards for eleven hit singles, Gamble and Huff ten each. The Sound of Philadelphia had become the sound of America, and the same year saw the outbreak of the 'Disco Inferno' (the title of a piece by the Trammps from Philadelphia).

Drawing up family trees is always one of the most important, and one of the most questionable elements of historiography, in pop music as elsewhere. But perhaps the playlists of DJs like Francis Grosso could be adduced as testimony and perhaps as a more legitimate way of reconstructing history and style. The pre-disco disco DJ mixed the fast pieces by Curtis Mayfield and Isaac Hayes, Jimmy Castor and the Persuaders with the sounds of Nigerian percussionists, and played Motown sound as well as the Street Funk of the Ohio Players. Any kind of music focusing on rhythm rather than melody could be used. Equally telling are the charts which, in 1972–3, put the

48. MILLER, Jim: The Sound of Philadelphia, in: idem: (Ed.), op. cit., p. 371.

percussive 'Soul Makossa' by the Paris-based African musician Manu Dibango at the top, revealing that this kind of 'ethnic' music had been rendered comprehensible and enjoyable for Europeans and white Americans by being further developed and treated by African-Americans in the USA. On the other hand, the sound of Manu Dibango was itself so highly influenced by European and American pop music that non-Africans could easily taste the 'ethnic' elements and embellishments within it.

49. COHN, Nik: Another Saturday Night, in: Ball the Wall, p. 330.

DISCO FEVER – INCUBATION PERIOD

In 1975 the minority culture 'disco' became DISCO, the pop culture of the mid-70s. A new dance form had established itself in New York's 'Adam's Apple' club. The public, particularly young people and/or gays, danced the Hustle, a synthetic, fast version of 40s swing connected up with various Latin elements. The club's DJ, David Todd, took the creative dancing frenzy of the public as enthusiasm for his sound, and saw himself as the actual creator of the new dance fashion, which rapidly spread throughout New York. In his story 'Another Saturday Night', Nik Cohn describes how the Hustle is studied by a hip gang-leader called Vincent and his friends, called the 'Faces', and then taught to the rest of the club audience: 'Vincent was already at work on the floor. By now the Faces had gathered in force, his troops, and he worked them like a quarterback, calling out plays. He set the formations, dictated every move. If a pattern grew ragged and disorder threatened, it was he who set things straight... Sweeping back and forth across the floor in perfect unity, fifty bodies made one, while Vincent barked out orders, crying out orders, crying One, and Two, and One, and Tap. And Turn, and One, and Tap. And Turn. And Tap. And One.'[49] And in this way, as Cohn observed in his New York odyssey, the Hustle was danced in the mid-70s in all the clubs as if in response to a secret command.

50. HANSON, Kitty: Disco Fever, p. 97.

51. Ibid. p. 96.

Club DJ Todd used his contacts with the record industry and told the song-writer and producer Van McCoy and his partner Charlie Kipps about the enthusiasm for the Hustle in the Apple Club. Like the legend of Alan Freed, who was inspired by dancing teenagers in his sponsors' record-shop to become a pioneer of black R&B, it was now the euphoric tales of a club DJ that prompted Van McCoy to produce one of the earliest disco hits. A subcultural phenomenon gradually turned into pop. Van McCoy, who produced Aretha Franklin and other soul greats, was working on his new album. Ten songs were finished, and waiting for arrangements. Because he was short of time, McCoy sent his partner Charlie Kipps to the Adam's Apple to watch the new fashionable dance. Kipps climbed into the DJ's cockpit and stared in astonishment at the dancing crowd: 'I noticed the steps were regimented and not random, and I thought, how did these kids choreograph themselves before they came to a disco?'[50] Confronted with a strictly coded subculture, whose style, rules and rites were strange to him, Kipps came back to the studio and told McCoy about his experience of the new youth style. Despite his great interest, McCoy still had no time to visit the club, but had one of the secretaries at the record company dance the Hustle for him. McCoy took a good look, went into the studio and produced an eleventh track for his album, entitled 'The Hustle'.

A pumping bass line, a simple melody and rousing vocals, calling: 'Do it! Do the Hustle!' turned 'The Hustle' into the prototype of the new disco wave. In her book *Disco Fever*, Kitty Hanson points out that the seductive mixture of Latin and R&B elements was nothing but 'a rendition in music of a dance beat that, up until then, was known only in a few Latin clubs in the South Bronx'.[51] She was referring particularly to the clubs which had been playing pre-disco party music since the late 60s and early 70s. Van McCoy, who didn't belong to this predominantly gay subculture, picked up its musical and stylistic impulse and got it heard and famous throughout America for the first time. The single version of 'The Hustle' sold about eight million copies by 1978, and became one of the biggest dancefloor hits of the 70s.

At about the same time as McCoy was composing his Hustle, Donna Summer recorded 'Love to Love You Baby' in Munich with the two producers Giorgio Moroder and Pete Bellote. Summer, who had begun her career with gospels and come to Europe as a singer in the hippie musical *Hair*, had used a traditional singing style in the original version of the song and Moroder thought it was unsuitable to the theme of the song. He asked Donna Summer to be more dramatic: 'Don't sing... whisper and groan.'[52] The trained singer stripped down her musical abilities to the basics and endlessly groaned the refrain and title of the song to a monotonously driving synth beat. The fake sensuality turned 'Love to Love You Baby' into a standard work of erotic pop music. But the three artists involved in the production were not sure how good the product of their studio session was, so they sent Neil Bogart, the owner of Casablanca Records, a promo tape. He in turn tested the tape out at a party to see how people reacted. The party audience was so enthusiastic that the piece had to be played over and over again. Bogart saw the chance of a hit and the next day he called Moroder to discuss the further production of the piece, and asked him to extend the song to twenty minutes.[53] A song on the subject of sexual intercourse with that lascivious monotony could hardly be long enough.

In its original form the song was the usual length of a single, three to five minutes. One fundamental rule of the disco DJ, monotony plus excitement, was now understood and co-opted for the first time by a representative of the record industry. Moroder and Bellote stretched the song to the then absolutely sensational length of sixteen minutes and fifteen seconds, a format that was later outdone only by the most lengthy remixes. The lyrics were nothing but the apparently endless repetition of the title, and were repeatedly interrupted by faked orgasms. The repetitiveness which, in its consistency, recalled the most 'stubborn' pieces by James Brown, created the illusion of an endless – albeit artificial – passion. Bogart tried to persuade radio DJs to play the piece 'once, on one station, at midnight'.[54] The strategy was successful, and the many radio bans, and the harsh criticism of

52. USLAN, Michael/ SOLOMON, Bruce, op. cit., p. 446.

53. Cf. SHAW, Arnold: Black Popular Music in America, p. 249.

54. Cf. HANSON, Kitty, op. cit., p. 107.

several cultural moralists encouraged the incredible success of 'Love to Love You Baby'. The music of a small minority left the underground without having to betray it, because both hits, uncompromising and daring as they were, had absorbed all the virtues of the party music scene and emerged into the glaring light of the public.

The hammering bass and the over-lush orchestration marked a clear break from the sounds of electric guitars that had predominated since the mid-50s. But what was most important was that these first disco songs had been composed only to get people dancing, ideally in clubs. For Joey Negro, the famous DJ and remixer, this is also the definition of disco: 'Disco music was the first music that was engineered specifically for clubs – it was made with dancefloors in mind.'[55] The needs of the audience and those of the DJ as a mediator between the producer and the listeners became the most important criterion in the evaluation of a song. Almost seventeen minutes for one number was a dream in a dance-track for DJs, and also for manic clubbers, and now the industry was producing it – glorious times for the DJ.

55. SHARP, Elsa, op. cit., p. 12.

THE REMIX AND THE ETERNAL RETURN OF THE SAME

The first media product of DJ culture was a new record form: the maxi single. It had been prompted by the DJs' constantly growing need of records in which the passages of pure rhythm that they loved so much were infinitely extended. The first disco DJs had constantly switched from record to record, to set the 'clean' percussion points of the songs side by side and thus create a form of their own. But in the long run these experiments were unsatisfying, and many DJs helped themselves by making tapes to avoid the constant, hectic switch of the little three-minute singles. But if you worked with tapes you couldn't react directly to the requests and moods of the audience, so many DJs longed for singles that would satisfy their needs – and of course those of the clubbers.

The first people to recognize this were the DJs Tom Moulton and Walter Gibbons. The idea of remixing came to Moulton, a former advertising manager at United Artists, in the clubs he visited. 'I was going to a few discotheques in those days and I was struck by how people went for the music, and it was quite unlike what I'd always imagined. I noticed how people were totally into the music towards the end of a record, and all of sudden they were back down for some reason. Then another record would be played, or two records were played at the same time. God, I thought, if people can be turned off from music like that there must be a way to take them at that peak at the end of a record and keep them there and lift them to a higher level.'[56]

As early as 1972 Moulton mixed his first disco remixes for the Trammps, but it was two or three years before remixing became a highly successful DJ device. Moulton's first remixes show a very chaste treatment of the original song. Moulton sought above all a different weighting of the various soundtracks, and worked the rhythmic elements of the disco songs even more clearly and powerfully. The power of the song was 'tuned' to the wishes of DJs and clubbers. Moulton used the various elements of the sixteen or twenty-four track master tapes and remixed them. Only very rarely did he add new tracks, so his remixes remained close to the original[57] and usually appeared as their B-sides.

But despite this fidelity to the original, Moulton achieved some interesting reinterpretations. 'A monotonous piece with few breaks or melodic hooks could, for example, be reconstructed in such a way that you lengthened the breaks or incorporated catchy tunes at the right places. Behind this was the idea to produce the best possible relation between tension and relaxation.'[58] Moulton's work for the Philly Sound labels in Philadelphia and New York (P.I.R., Salsoul, Scepter, Buddah) was very successful, and the booming disco market demanded more remixes.

Walter Gibbons, a practising DJ, was more prepared to take risks than Moulton. He completely took apart the pieces offered to him for remixing, and then completely rebuilt them. What Gibbons lacked – as Moulton did too – was the possibility of pressing longer remixes on record than the usual three-minute singles allowed. The

56. Quoted in: TOOP, David: Lost in Music, in: FREDERKING, Klaus (Ed.), op. cit., p. 157.

57. Ibid.

58. Ibid.

solution was called the maxi or 12-inch single. It was the size of an LP, but had to be played at 45 rpm like a single and had room for fifteen-minute-long tracks – a paradise for DJs and remixers.

1976 saw the pressing of the first maxi-single to be sold in record-shops.[59] It was 'Ten Percent' by Double Exposure, and appeared on the New York Salsoul label, whose company motto 'Dance Your Ass Off' was an incitement to produce particularly addictive dance remixes. Walter Gibbons extended the three-minute song by Double Exposure to over nine minutes, 'making the record start with a few percussion instruments, then increasing the tension from beat to beat with the introduction of more instruments, finally extending the string melody with a catchy motif'.[60] Break on break, a revolution, produced 'specifically for the underground clubscene in New York'.[61]

Many of the remixes used the very same stylistic devices that DJs had developed before the era of 12-inch records. David Toop describes this by referring to the example of the Gloria Gaynor productions in which only the vocals are taken from the original version, and then all other tracks are re-produced with a disco audience in mind. Gloria Gaynor's voice was reduced more or less to a marketable irrelevance. The main concern was to transform the track into a magical dance number with an even, rhythmically monotonous pattern of melody and beats. This procedure was, for Toop, 'quite clearly a return to the technique of segue or slipping, a discothèque invention by DJs like Francis Grosso'.[62] And while singers profited from the disco fever and were stylized into divas (earning plenty of money in the process), musicians like James Brown were exploited and musically misunderstood. In his view, disco was a soulless machine music for artists who didn't know how to do anything but use sequencers and count the beats per minute. Even more than this, for him disco productions endangered the work of many artists who didn't want to be replaced by producers. 'Disco hurt me in a lot of ways,' Brown complained. 'I was trying to make good hard funk records that Polydor was trying to soften up, while the people were buying records that had no substance.'[63]

Nelson George voiced similarly bitter views about

59. Karnik points out that the inventor of the maxi-single was Mel Cheren, who worked for Specter Records in New York, where he had the first maxis pressed (cf. KARNIK, Olaf: Zwischen Underground und Pop-Charts, in: HÜNDGEN, Gerald (Ed.), op. cit., p. 169). Radcliffe A. Joe, an editor at *Billboard*, describes Tom Moulton as the inventor of the maxi because he prompted the need for longer singles with his remixes, and then introduced them. (JOW, Radcliffe A., op. cit., p. 63.) Cheren and Moulton must have been very close together in time.

60. KARNIK, Olaf: Zwischen Underground und Pop-Charts, in: HÜNDGEN, Gerald (Ed.), op. cit., p. 173. This song and many others on the legendary Salsoul label are highly popular with remixers even today. Thus Salsoul, now with the subtitle 'The New Generation', brought out a double maxi compilation in 1992 with the title 'Synergy', on which the star remixers of the 90s reinterpret the classics of the 70s. It includes Steve 'Silk' Hurley, Junior Vasquez, Tommy Musto, Little 'Louie' Vega, Kenny 'Dope' Gonzales, Todd Terry and Tony Humphries – a list that reads like a Who's Who of the best DJs and remixers. A compilation that proves how close today's house and club music is to the early disco songs.

61. HARVEY, Steven/BATES, Patricia, op. cit., p. 5.

62. TOOP, David: Lost in Music, in: FREDERKING, Klaus (Ed.), op. cit., p. 160.

63. BROWN, James: op. cit., p. 243.

disco. For him, disco was a betrayal of black dance music. It was inhuman, particularly when it came from Europe, it was passionless and monotonous. And George quickly identified the culprits of this betrayal as the DJs who had dictated this sound: 'Most were gay men with a singular attitude toward American culture, black as well as white.'[64] The products of this gay conspiracy were hedonism and bisexuality, as well as a pseudo-intellectualism that George does not further explain. George's attacks on disco peak in accusations against the famous disco DJ Frankie Crocker, who turned the black radio station WBLD into the most important disco station. Even in this George saw betrayal and corruption – Crocker only wanted to become a regular at Studio 54 and forget the interests of his community. Crocker was hip, but he was also beige.[65] George couldn't understand a real black person playing beige music like disco. What is interesting is that both Brown and George see the ways in which the songs are produced as lifeless, a sellout, rather than the songs themselves. The phenomenon of remixers and producers preparing songs by artists for a new context destroyed ideas of autonomous artistic creation.

The tendency of disco remixes to use rigidly monotonous repetitions of tiny rhythmic patterns meant trance-like states of happiness for the audience, and, for the recipients of an old idea of music, a state of anxiety about the preservation of value. Could the soul of music survive the long disco remixes, or was the spirit of funk and soul perverted by the high-tech producers? Brown resisted when the record company told him of its project to have his songs reworked by the – in Brown's terms – 'outside' producer Brad Shapiro. But in the end he gave up. The album *The Original Disco Man* was not entirely disco, but Brown was desperately unhappy: 'Disco had no groove, had no sophistication, it had nothing.'[66]

Disco productions weren't for everyone, but at any rate they were a thing of the future. The remix on the maxi-single became an integral component of DJ culture that also reached broad sectors of buyers, attaining higher sales figures. The 12-inch single meant not only the possibility of pressing longer remixes, but also an improvement in the sound over the narrowly pressed

64. GEORGE, Nelson: The Death..., p. 154.

65. Ibid. p. 159.

66. BROWN, James: op. cit., p. 253.

7-inch singles. The basses sounded fatter, the hi-hats sharper, the vocals clearer. The fine finish of the producers now had a medium that made the tiniest differences audible, and the experience of music in the clubs even more impressive.

SATURDAY NIGHT FEVER – NIK COHN AND THE FACES AND A NUMBER OF ATTEMPTS TO DISCOVER THE HIPSTER ON THE DANCEFLOOR

67 . WOLFE, Tom: The Noonday Underground, in: The Pump House Gang, p. 101.

In 1975, when Nik Cohn recognized and described the disco phenomenon, it was just starting to leave the gay ghetto. Disco wasn't yet mainstream, but still a pleasure for people who lived on the margin of society. Vincent, the hero of 'Another Saturday Night', is an 18-year-old Italian. He sells paints in a warehouse; his father, a thief, is in jail, his oldest brother has been killed in Vietnam. Vincent has nothing but the love of his family and the great feeling he gets when he goes dancing on Saturday night. The club 2001 Odyssey turns him into a star, dancing and being cool give a meaning to his whole life. The discothèque is the centre of his life.

15-year-old Larry Lynch is an ancestor of Vincent. He's the hero of Tom Wolfe's 'The Noonday Underground'. Larry lives, works and dances in the London of the 60s. He is a mod and thus part of a youth culture recruited from the working class. He works in an office, and every lunchtime he goes – in expensive suits and with freshly cut hair – to a discotheque. 'Tiles' is life, 'underground at noon – a vast black room heaving with music and human bodies'.[67] 250 mod boys and girls enjoy the lunch-breaks from their jobs as secretaries, shoe-salesgirls, shop assistants, messengers. The loud beat music, played by a DJ, spoils them like a 'vibro-massage'. Each of them has his own dance style, the Spasm, the Hump, the Marcel, the 'Two-backed Beast'.

For Wolfe this midday 'night-club' embodies 'the life of working-class teenagers in England.'[68] The mod lifestyle, which had existed since 1960, had turned into something new, a 'life totality': 'It all goes within a very set style of life, based largely on clothes, music, hairdos and a... super-cool outlook on the world. It is the style of life that makes them unique, not money, power, position, talent, intelligence.'[69] Clothes are the most important thing for the mods. They are signs of their independence from all traditional lifestyles. Half of their money, earned in completely alienated ways, they take to the tailor or the fashion boutique. At lunchtime in the club they display the new suits and shoes, the skirts and make-up, and lunchtime becomes the glamorous celebration of their own youthful style.

It is the dream of all mod boys and girls to find a job that lets them live in this glamorous world all day. Girls become fashion salesgirls in hip shops near the clubs, which they slip into during their lunch-breaks, and whose music they can still hear in the shop. For the boys, being a DJ is a dream job: 'Oh God, if only you could somehow make money without leaving The Life at all, the way Clem does, being a DJ, playing the records at Tiles, coming on with some swift American-style talk, having these great performers hanging around all the time... A DJ? So all these boys want to be DJs and they will do anything for a break.'[70] Wolfe ends Larry Lynch's story as it began: the perfectly styled 15-year-old full of dreams and longings has to creep back to his office. Lunchtime in the discothèque has given him strength, and tomorrow, tomorrow there's another lunchtime.

Wolfe's Larry Lynch is a prototype for all the kids who have devoted their life to the dancefloor. Ravers of today think, feel and speak similarly. They spend their money on Stüssy and Fuct T-shirts, they buy drugs (as mods did), they style themselves perfectly and meet each other when hanging out. At the centre of their world-view is the club, the dancefloor as theatre and catwalk. And enthroned above them all is the DJ. With a very few changes Wolfe's scenario could be transferred to the present day. Much the same could be said of Cohn's Vincent.

68. Ibid. p. 103.

69. Ibid. p. 103f.

70. Ibid. p. 108.

71. COHN, Nik: Another Saturday Night, in: Ball the Wall, p. 321.

72. Ibid.

73. Ibid. p. 322.

74. Ibid. p. 323.

75. Ibid. p. 325.

'Vincent was the best dancer in Bay Ridge – the ultimate Face.'[71] With these words Cohn opens his story (or is it a reportage?). Vincent had fourteen flower-patterned shirts, five suits, eight pairs of shoes, three coats, and had once appeared in Dick Clark's *American Bandstand*. People from the music industry have offered him contracts as a dancer, and come specially from Manhattan to see him. Everyone knows him in the club, and all the other Faces hold him in high regard and imitate him. 'Gracious as a medieval seigneur accepting tributes, Vincent waved and nodded at random. Then his face grew stern, his body turned to the music. Solemn, he danced, and all the Faces followed. In this sphere his rule was absolute.'[72]

The only problem is his age. At eighteen and a half Vincent already feels old and thinks his time had come. At some point someone else will assume his sovereign position. The end of great hipsterdom.

During the week Vincent is a smiling, helpful person. On Saturday he is a hero. Concentrated, attentive, completely sharp. Saturdays follow a strict ritual: 'Promptly at five the manager reversed the "Open" sign and Vincent would turn away, take off his grin. When the last of the customers had gone, he went out through the back, down the corridor, directly into the bathroom. He locked the door and took a deep breath. Here he was safe. So he turned toward the mirror and began to study his image.'[73]

Arriving home, Vincent takes a bath, shaves and gets dressed. It takes four hours, and when he's finished he feels newborn. He kisses his mother goodbye and then marches into the street. 'He wore an open-necked shirt, ablaze with reds and golds, and he moved through the night with shoulders hunched tight, his neck rammed deep between his shoulder blades in the manner of a miniature bull. A bull in Gucci-style loafers, complete with gilded buckle, and high black pants tight as sausage skins.'[74] Two blocks from his apartment four boys from his posse, the Faces, are waiting in a '65 Dodge. None of the five in the car is laughing, and none is speaking, 'they all held their distance, conserved their strength, like prize-fighters before a crucial bout'.[75]

For Vincent the Faces are the elite. The rest of America is 'a vast faceless blob. And then there were the Faces.

The Vincents and Eugenes and Joeys. A tiny minority, maybe two in every hundred, who knew how to dress and how to move, how to float, how to fly. Sharpness, grace, a certain distinction in every gesture. And some strange instinct for rightness, beyond words, deep down in the blood: "The way I feel," Vincent said, "it's like we have been chosen."[76]

THE HIPSTER IN CHANGING TIMES

76. Ibid. p. 326.

77. Cf. HEBDIGE, Dick: Subculture, p. 48.

Where Wolfe stays at the level of the phenomenology of the hipster, the gestures, the clothes and the most urgent desires, Cohn manages to describe the whole disposition of a hipster. The word 'hipster' made its first appearance in the early 50s in connection with the birth of bebop, existentialism and the beatnik. The hipster was usually white and had black idols like the jazz musicians Dizzy Gillespie and Slim Gaillard. Dizzy Gillespie's goatee, his beret and his sound have remained definitions of absolute hipsterdom. Whatever Dizzy wore, the 'White Negroes', as Norman Mailer called them, followed him in his style. Jack Kerouac described Slim Gaillard as a god in *On the Road*. The ease and cool of the hipsters became a model for white dropouts and bohemians. For Hebdige the hipster style and the gestures of these liberal whites is simply a copy of the black hero in the ghetto.[77] Aestheticized self-humiliation is carried out as an act of rebellion against the hidebound America of the 50s.

The first generation of hipsters grew up in the white mishmash of jazz, existentialism and beat literature. That was before pop. Hipsterdom changed with the beginning of pop music. The youth subcultures became more and more elaborate and refined. The hipster lived in a rigid world full of orders and hierarchies of clothes, records and ideas. The mods described by Wolfe were like that, as were the Faces, the first non-gay disco hipsters who built their life around the nightclub.

It isn't hip to provide a definition of a hipster, so no hipster has tried to define his hipsterdom. 'HIP is hard to nail,' says a 1986 book entitled 'The Hip'. And later:

It no more responds to definition than it does to the common light of day, which is little... HIP lives along the rising smoke from a cigarette parked under the rods of a Selmer Mark VI during the saxophone solo, rides a fingersnap on the offbeat, claps only triplets. It hints at its presence in the rake of a hat and the wristly dismissal. Hip has a great ear and a great eye and a greater instinct, but is easy-over on the words. It communicates with itself. Hip has shifted more shades than any other philosophy throughout history, but fewer manuals and no pyjama cases.[78]

Norman Mailer's 'The White Negro' was the reaction to an article on the hipster published in 1957 in *Harper's Bazaar*. For Mailer, the hipster is the American version of the existentialist who, confronted by the existence of the atom bomb with the omnipresence of death, chooses a life at the edge of society. A society with the power to extinguish millions of people can only be ignored or resisted. He chooses a new lifestyle and everyday life that distinguishes him completely from that of the normal American. He consumes sex and drugs to excess, and through a morally justified hedonism (a kind of ethics of resistance) he achieves a new kind of fun. 'The unstated essence of Hip, its psychopathic brilliance, quivers with the knowledge that new kinds of victories increase one's power for new kinds of perception',[79] wrote Mailer, referring to the enticements of an autonomous world-view not dictated by society. The white hipster's model is the 'Negro', faced because of his minority existence with the choice of a life in constant humiliation or in the constant presence of danger. From this existential situation the 'Negro' develops a refined strategy for enjoying life anyway:

Knowing in the cells of his existence that life was war, nothing but war, the Negro (all exceptions admitted) could rarely afford the sophisticated inhibitions of civilizations, and so kept for his survival the art of the primitive, he lived in the enormous present, he subsisted for his Saturday night kicks, relinquishing the

78 . CARR, Roy, et al: The Hip, p. 11.

79 . MAILER, Norman: The White Negro, in: The Long Patrol, p. 211.

pleasures of the mind for the more obligatory pleasures of the body, and in his music he gave voice to the character and quality of his existence, to his rage and the infinite variations of joy, lust, languor, growl, cramp, pinch, scream and despair of his orgasm.[80]

The hipster made this mixture of primitivism and refinement – what Mailer called 'the existentialist synapses of the Negro' – his programme, and thus became a 'white Negro'.

Mailer's hipster is a reflective psychopath, at once a philosopher, a rebel and a narcissist who creates himself (away from the dominant world). He sees himself as part of an elite that possesses not only its own values and norms, but also its own language, which can only be understood by other members of the elite. And what is more, like all psychopaths the hipster tries to create a nervous system of his own: to escape all forms of determination by biology or the family. The hipster rebels against his genes, his birth. His private war keeps him alert and moving:

In motion a man has a chance, his body is warm, his instincts are quick, and when the crisis comes, whether of love or violence, he can make it, he can win, he can release a little more energy for himself since he hates himself a little less, he can make a little better nervous system, make it a little more possible to go again, to go faster next time and so make more and thus find more people with whom he can swing... To swing with the rhythms of another is to enrich oneself – the conception of the learning process as dug by hip is that one cannot really learn until one contains within oneself the implicit rhythm of the subject or the person.[81]

To swing is to be in motion, and thus in a position to learn. And whoever learns comes closer to what might be called self-creation, self-dramatization. Anyone who wants to be cool must know and control his life. If life is seen as a struggle, every act of learning is a victory, and every victory a strengthening of one's own position, which makes it more difficult for others to defeat the hipster. More important than the character and the context in which the hipster acts is the energy

80. Ibid. p. 212.

81. Ibid. p. 220f.

with which he carries out his actions. Intensity is the only quality that really interests the hipster. And nothing is more intense than the present. The future and the past can wait.

Vincent and his Faces are instinctual hipsters. Their life is entirely subject to a symbolic order, they move in a world filled with cinematic images (Al Pacino and gangster movies), fashion extravaganzas and the best music for dancing and posing to. Things might be different in a few weeks, but while they were as they were, the Odyssey was the Faces' club.

It was a true sanctuary. Once inside, the Faces were unreachable. Nothing could molest them. They were no longer the oppressed, wretched teen menials who must take orders, toe the line. Here they took command, they reigned.

The basic commandments were simple. To qualify as an Odyssey Face, an aspirant need only be Italian, between the ages of eighteen and twenty-one, with a minimum stock of six floral shirts, four pairs of tight trousers, two pairs of Gucci-style loafers, two pairs of platforms, either a pendant or a ring, and one item in gold. In addition, he must know how to dance, how to drive, how to handle himself in a fight. He must have respect, even reverence, for Facehood, and contempt for everything else. He must also be fluent in obscenity, offhand in sex. Most important of all, he must play tough.[82]

Cohn's description of hipsterdom is precise and analytical. Positioning himself within the text as an anonymous man in a tweed suit (while Wolfe presents himself as a man from America), he seriously and attentively jots down all the fine points of the rites and ideals within the disco hipster community. The clothes, the movements and postures, everything is documented. Like Wolfe, Cohn demonstrates a passionate fascination with his characters. In the introduction to his early works Wolfe speaks of the esoteric rules that young people create to escape the everyday, while Cohn rejects the idea of detachment. His snapshots are close-ups, recordings of the streams

82 . COHN, Nik: Another Saturday Night, loc. cit., p. 326.

of consciousness of his heroes. Vincent comes close to the reader, while Larry Lynch remains an abstraction of a mod.

Wolfe's amazement at the many subcultures in America and Britain gives his text a certain detachment. For Wolfe these people have found new ways of enjoying, 'extending their egos way out on the best terms available, namely, their own'.[83] For Wolfe this enjoyment is too limited, while Cohn sees the glittering gleam of pop in this extension of the ego: self-expression as stylistic rebellion. And as in his history of pop, *AwopBopaLooBop AlopBamBoom*, Cohn likes it. Although Cohn has now become the guy in the tweed suit, age remains the only clue to his detachment – and that detachment is involuntary and biological.

Within the disco subculture there were various ideals, styles and 'Faces', those of the Italians, the Latinos, the Jews and the Blacks. There was no contact between the groups, and fights were guaranteed if one strayed on to foreign territory. Somewhere in between were the girls, who were at best accessories of the Faces. 'In general, the female function was simply to be available. To decorate the doorways and booths, to fill up the dance floor. Speak when spoken to, to put out as required, and then go away. In short, to obey, and not to fuss.'[84] The hipsters rejected all kinds of fuss and excitement. Vincent turns away if anyone starts leaping around and gesticulating. Cool is what counts for the Faces as for all hipsters. Anyone who failed to demonstrate cool for a moment was out the door. If Vincent sees someone waggling his butt, he feels unwell. Waggling is impure.

That was why he loved to dance, not talk. In conversation, everything always came out wrong, confused. But out on the floor it all somehow fell into place. There was no muddle, nothing that could not be conveyed. Just so long as your feet made the right moves, kept hitting the right angles, you were foolproof. There were certain rules, watertight. Only obey them, and nothing could go wrong.[85]

One false move, one of last month's dance steps could ruin you. 'Absolutely disastrous. Because the whole magic of the night, and of Odyssey, was that

83. WOLFE, Tom: Introduction, in: The Pump House Gang, p. 13.

84. COHN, Nik: Ball the Wall, p. 327.

85. Ibid.

everything, everyone, was immaculate. No detail was botched, not one motion unconsidered. Purity. A sacrament. In their own style, the Faces were true ascetics: stern, devoted, incorruptible.'[86] Hipsters are always ascetics, not for fear of the temptations of the world, but in their knowledge of them. Even if the rest of humanity falls into indifference and ennui, the hipster fights, strictly and seriously, for his rules. Passion is the greatest enemy of liberality. If you feel passionate, you are either attracted or repelled by things, there is no 'perhaps' or 'possibly'. To be passionate is not to be cynical, and that can only be achieved in a good world.[87]

At about the same time, in the mid-70s, and a few miles away by air, the first homeboy generation of break-dancers, DJs and graffiti-artists was forming, and founding the most important dancefloor subculture after disco. The ritual strictness and precision within the subcultures was comparable, except that amongst the black homeboys the creative element had grown in importance over the style element. The disco hipsters can be described as the first representatives of a fully formed dancefloor subculture who managed to escape the underground for the forefront of pop culture: to enter the ranks of the makers of meaning and image.

In Cohn's work the music is a side-issue, and completely subordinated to the sociologically precise description of the dancefloor hipster. It was of secondary importance to Cohn whether the music was supplied by a band or a DJ. For Wolfe, who seems from the start to have taken a greater interest in the DJ as a pop phenomenon (see Murray the K), the DJ had made his appearance in the mid-60s as a significant youth idol.

There is no literary description of what the pre-disco clubs of the gay blacks and chicanos looked like and how people lived and danced in them. The few documents about that underground reveal that a wilder and more unbridled life was played out there, informed by the desire and the will to wig out and live it up, less by the desire to erect an imaginary world order, as the Faces and the mods were driven to do. What was certain, at any rate, was that the hipster had finally crossed over from jazz to the ranks of pop

86. Ibid.

87. Cf. POSCHARDT, Ulf: Die beste aller Welten, in: SPIEGEL SPEZIAL 'Pop und Politik', pp. 117–20.

music, and that they liked being close to the dancefloor and recognized that the clubs provided the ideal conditions for the construction of their power. The hipster became the crony of the DJ, and more and more often it was the DJs themselves who, like Vincent in the Odyssey, laid out the rules and norms. But more of that later.

WELCOME TO THE DISCO – STUDIO 54 AND THE REST

88. Cf. SHAW, Arnold: Dictionary..., loc. cit., p. 107.

In 1975 radio stations started playing disco songs, and after the successes of Donna Summer and Van McCoy many musicians wanted to compose disco music. Hits like 'Get Down Tonight' and 'That's the Way (I Like It)' by K.C. & the Sunshine Band, 'Fly, Robin, Fly', by Munich band Silver Convention, or 'I Love Music' stormed the charts. The first clubs outside of the underground and scarier parts of town began to organize disco evenings.

Disco fever rose from 1975 until 1977, and between 1977 and 1979 there were more than ten thousand discothèques in the United States.[88] After the first hits and the invention of the maxi-single there was relatively little musical innovation. Records of the quality of Sister Sledge's 'We Are Family', Sylvester's 'Dance (Disco Heat)' or Patrick Hernandez' 'Born to Be Alive' were reproduced by the dozen, but there was no real development of the disco sound. Disco remained exciting above all because of its mass effect. Bookstores were stacked high with picture-books showing how to perfect your disco-dancing. Every disco style was illustrated with dance steps and even with style hints. The funniest and most informative of these books is the *Official Guide to Disco Dance Steps*, identified by its authors, a pair of Chicago dancing teachers, as the result of four years (!) of research. Dancing was supposed, despite rigorous prescriptions and strictly enumerated movements, to be a route to self-discovery. 'This easy-to-follow guide will help you develop an individualized dance style and the self-confidence that will put *you* in the spotlight.'[89] As always, in the heady phase of pop hysteria, it was a matter of conformity, and as always it was sold as absolute self-discovery. 'Discover Yourself Through Disco' is the heading to the foreword of the disco guide. If this imperative had meant something in the underground clubs, during the period of disco hype in the mainstream discos it got out of control.

Studio 54 in New York was the most famous discothèque of all. Dancers in Studio 54 included Truman Capote and Bianca Jagger, Mikhail Baryshnikov, Jacqueline Bisset and Grace Jones. As with the twist, going to the discothèque became a social event. The glamorous world of the stars and starlets, the models and photographers, the rich and powerful, quickly united, from 1976 onwards, in taking its greatest delight in the 'biggest, boldest, and brassiest'[90] disco, to let go with as much decadence, wantonness and generosity as possible. What had been an existential act of self-liberation and self-creation in the gay clubs, became, for high society, a way of improving the quality of one's life. Repressive social attitudes even within the supposedly liberal jet-set life could be set aside in the discothèque, and before the eyes of the public. For Truman Capote it was a form of absolute democracy: 'Boys with boys, girls with girls, girls with boys, blacks and whites, capitalists and Marxists, Chinese and everything else, all in one big mix.'[91]

But the mix of people was pre-programmed, and the supposed democracy was the result of a strict selection process. 'Painting the picture'[92] was identified as the job of the doorman, and the resulting picture was supposed to be as similar as possible every evening. For Studio 54 this meant that only a small number of gays and blacks were allowed into the club, for reasons of proportion and decoration. In her euphoric book *Disco Fever*, Kitty Hanson saw that as a masterly creative achievement: 'The door people are like chefs preparing an exotic dish, like chemists choosing solutions, like painters very carefully mixing colors – all of them working to produce the magic combination that will keep the floor "hot" or the ambience "cool", that will make the setting exciting and keep the mystique going.'[93]

89 . VILARI, Jack/ VILARI, Kathleen Sims: Disco Dance Steps, p. v.

90 . HANSON, Kitty, loc. cit., p. 16.

91 . Ibid. p. 18.

92 . GOLDMAN, Albert: Studio 54, Driver, in: Sound Bites, p. 278.

93 . HANSON, Kitty, loc. cit., p. 11.

By now disco was mainstream, and the mystical thing about it was that it was *hip* at the same time.[94] August Darnell, the musical brains behind Kid Creole & The Coconuts, went to Studio 54 because at the time it was so decadent and exciting to be part of a world movement. For the first time dancefloors defined what was up and what was down. Disco meant global domination, and anyone who took part could see themselves as part of that global domination. Particularly easy in clubs like Studio 54, where Canadian Prime Minister Trudeau danced with his wife, and where you might sometimes even see a former US Foreign Minister.

Disco was at once domination and mainstream, and yet it was undeniably a gay thing. Bands like the Village People, who dressed up like caricatures of homosexuals in leather, moustached and with the physique of body-builders, marched world-wide to the top of the charts, with songs that paid open homage to their sexual orientation.

Their first hit was called 'San Francisco', the second 'Macho Man', the third 'Y.M.C.A.' All of these songs were 'gay goofs to those who got the joke, and disco novelties to those who didn't'.[95] As if nothing could be more natural, all kinds of homosexual images were consumed by the masses throughout this period of disco fever, under the heading of 'nightlife exotica'. Sylvester sang his way into the hearts of all Americans

94. Cf. ALETTI, Vince: Lost In Music, in: ROCK'N'ROLL QUARTERLY, Summer 1993, p. 17.

95. SMUCKER, Tom: Disco, in: MILLER, Jim (Ed.), op. cit., p. 428.

Village People

with 'You Make Me Feel (Mighty Real)'. Two years before disco the black man with the plucked eyebrows, full, made-up lips, long ear-rings and eyeliner would have been mercilessly discriminated against, but now he was the darling of the mainstream. Sylvester's 'Oh! You make me feel/Mighty real' applied entirely to his self-assertion as a homosexual. The black homosexual only felt 'mighty real' when he was being touched, held, kissed – when he was having homosexual contact.

The heterosexual majority simply ignored the passionate seriousness underlying disco. Only those familiar with its roots could understand disco, for the consuming masses it was just a good night out. Of course that didn't mean that only gays could really understand it. It was more that the decontextualization of the music implied the kind of shift in perception and meaning that has constantly run through the history of pop. Rock'n'roll was the decontextualization of R&B, white soul was the decontextualization of black soul, Kraftwerk was the decontextualization of Malevich and James Brown. With one difference, that in disco the decontextualization only occurred in the perception of the consumer, and was not composed within the songs themselves. Many of the great disco hits came out of 'gay disco' culture, and made no secret of the fact. They made no pretence of normality and heterosexuality, but relied on the average member of the public bringing their own longing and passion to that of a black man or woman. The crossover to the mainstream didn't require any great efforts of adaption. Whether you were gay or straight, Liza Minnelli or a lovesick shop assistant, everyone understood what it was to feel 'mighty real' when it came to sex.

Style was another part of the gay identity which now made its way back into the wardrobe of the general population thanks to the hype of pop. 'The meaning of subculture is always in dispute,' wrote Dick Hebdige and style is the area in which the opposing definitions clash with most dramatic force.'[96] Fashion had been a gay trademark since the 19th century at the latest. Fetish wear was the eloquent sign of sexual orientation for members of the subculture. The dominance of gay subcultures in the areas of style and fashion ran through romanticism, the decadents, the dandies and

96. HEBDIGE, Dick: op. cit., p. 3.

camp to the first disco dancers. It is no coincidence that Hebdige begins his book with a quote from Genet and a tube of Vaseline, dramatically presenting the meaning of 'style' as the absolute symbol of homosexuality. The lack of ambiguity in the clothing of the Village People or Sylvester was outdone only by the tube of Vaseline. And yet many of the unambiguous accessories effortlessly crossed over into the mainstream. Most books about disco dance steps had at least one chapter about the correct outfit to wear, and challenged trainee clubbers to be brave and committed in their style of dress. Under the heading 'If My Friend Could See Me Now', Kitty Hanson celebrated the fact that more and more people were using the opportunity to change not only their clothes for an evening in the discothèque, but their personalities as well: 'Discos are flights into fantasy, and disco fashion is the boarding pass.'[97] For many 'evening' gays who had to spend the day in suits and overalls, putting on leather trousers and tight T-shirts represented an intensification of their gay identity every day or every weekend. Personality transformation was a reaction to and protection against everyday repression. Clubbers also discovered that fantasy and liberation through style and fashion was a huge source of enjoyment that didn't belong to any particular minority. If, for homosexuals, dressing up represented an existential necessity in a repressive society, for the WASP mass audience it became a refined piece of Saturday night theatre.

It became easier for gays to dress up to the nines even outside their own bars and clubs. At parties and dances, and even in the street, extravagant displays of fashion no longer attracted as much attention as they might have done as little as two years previously. American pop writer Tom Smucker even went so far as to claim that the old American clichés were being undermined: 'It was as if a journey to the heartland now started out on Christopher Street in Greenwich Village.'[98] Although Christopher Street in New York remained a gay ghetto, large parts of the gay subculture had influenced pop culture, and thus achieved a new level of tolerance, although to a much more modest extent than the general reception of disco might encourage us to believe.

97. HANSON, Kitty, op. cit., p. 35.

98. SMUCKER, Tom: Disco, in: MILLER, Jim (Ed.), op. cit., p. 429.

The initial harmonious commingling of homosexuals and heterosexuals, whites and non-whites, retrospectively remembered by Filipe Rose of the Village People,[99] only happened in a few places. The clubs kept to their own clientele, and minorities were fitted proportionally into the picture they wanted to create. The only advantage for minorities was that they weren't absolutely certain the doorman would turn them away. There was at least a theoretical chance of getting into a club. The conscious debate about the gay roots of disco didn't occur in the media. Some more recent DJ magazines tried to make up for this in the wake of a disco revival in the early 90s, and interviewed the old DJs. By that time, though, the prehistory was completely unknown. For most people disco started with the Bee Gees and John Travolta.

99. Cf. ALETTI, Vince: Lost in Music, in: ROCK'N'ROLL QUARTERLY, loc. cit., p. 15.

SATURDAY NIGHT FEVER – THE FILM

Everyone was a star. John Travolta played the Face Vincent in the disco film *Saturday Night Fever* as the definitive democratization of narcissism. In his film version – much of it deliberately superficial and clichéd – of Nik Cohn's original story the director, John Badham, managed to keep an amazing amount of Nik Cohn's subtle, original and sociologically refined observations. Badham's leading concept was the combination of realistic details with gleamingly polished props from the world of pop and glamour. This connection was designed to reproduce the living conditions of the main character, Tony Manero, as precisely as possible. The scriptwriter, Norman Wexler, turned Cohn's document about a nightlife hero into a touching story full of poverty, love, hard work, success. Vincent became Tony Manero, and Tony Manero became John Travolta. Tony Manero was Travolta's first major role, so he worked on it like a man possessed. On Nik Cohn's trail, he visited the original scenes and tried to study his models' movements and behaviour as precisely as possible. The aura that

Vincent and his Faces had emanated was now to enchant the cameras as well.

The transfer worked. Travolta had learned a great deal, from his dance interludes and his body language down to his smallest gestures, in the Odyssey in Brooklyn. Travolta's acting was particularly compelling when it tipped into naked self-display. In the almost theatrical dance interludes, the narcissism and exhibitionism of the actor Travolta merged with that of the character Tony. As if given wings by the music, Travolta's wiry body flies over the dancefloor and shows the spectators in the club, stand-ins for the viewers in the cinema, that this is not just about dancing, but about everything else as well – that with every movement to the gangling beats of the Bee Gees the ego becomes more aware of itself, more confident. The pride and dignity of Tony Manero and John Travolta emerge primarily from the character's supreme ease on the dancefloor. That is the source of Tony's power, making women desire him and men admire him.

In Badham's coarsely outlined dramatization, the club, as a centre of sensuality and life, casts its rays into the gloomiest corners of Brooklyn working-class life. The dignity that Travolta, as Manero, has fought for in the Odyssey is only partially to be found in everyday life. The ritual power with which, in the club, Manero conducts dozens of dancers with the fluid movements of his body, seems to fall away once he can no longer see the glittering lights or hear the rumbling music.

John Travolta in Saturday Night Fever

In its oscillation between escapism and the reality of everyday life, Manero's character becomes comprehensible. The discrepancy between Tony Manero/John Travolta as a shining king of nightlife and the same person as a humiliated young man at the family dinner table, also chimes tellingly with the Hollywood hype about Travolta. The myth of the star no longer counts for anything without the environment that allows the aura to shine.

The film was one of the sensations of 1978, the soundtrack dominated by the Bee Gees one of the most successful records of pop history.

YOUNG SOUL REBELS – ANOTHER SATURDAY NIGHT FEVER

In 1990 the young British director Isaac Julien made a film about disco and punk in 1977. *Young Soul Rebels* brought together the two most important youth cultures of the 70s, which shook the pop world at about the same time. Punk and disco were presented as two sides of one youth culture: anarchy and hedonism, rebellion and celebration. 'The real starting point for *Young Soul Rebels* was the desire to make a film about 1977',[100] Isaac Julien explained. For Julien as a black, left-wing homosexual it was also an attempt to torpedo the current left-wing perception of 1977. For him, disco was just as oppositional as punk. 'There was another counter narrative, much disdained by the left, which was the growth of a black popular culture in terms of disco music – soul music. All the left had to say was that disco music was part of the capitalist music industry and that one should adopt the punk ethic of dismantling it. But what the left didn't realize was that their formulaic slogan "black and white unite and fight" actually had some reality in this black popular culture.'[101]

For Julien, who enjoyed both left-wing agitation and the excitement of disco during this period, the black soul boys and soul girls were the equivalents of the white punks. Without explicitly mentioning the background of disco as a black, gay, underground culture, Julien recontextualizes disco as a minority music.

The heroes of the film are Chris and Caz, two black DJs who run a pirate station as the 'Soul Patrol' and play records in clubs. For Julien the soul boys, as well as the white punks, embody both the elite of style-makers and rebels. Julien is particularly interested in 'how black culture remakes itself wherever it is placed'.[102] For Julien this constant reinvention of his own culture is the precondition for its survival. In the case of the Young Soul Rebels, within a powerful, white youth culture (and youth rebellion) this meant finding one's own direction and, if one was a DJ, playing not the Sex

100. JULIEN, Isaac: Introduction, in: idem/ MacCABE, Colin: Diary of a Young Soul Rebel, p. 1.

101. Ibid.

102. Ibid. p. 2.

Pistols but soul, disco or P-funk by George Clinton and Parliament.

'1977 was a very important moment of reinvention. Because there were no real examples of the signifying practices of black British culture in the dominant media, the youth movement had to do it by connection with the soul music from America often through the medium of pirate radio.'[103] The radio stations and the clubs where the Soul Patrol play their records are places where social barriers are crossed. The separation between white and black, heterosexual and homosexual young people is perforated. And Julien wanted to make the enthusiasm of this moment comprehensible in the film, because it had been completely ignored in the historiography of the mass media.

103. Ibid.

The Soul Patrol are the first DJs to appear as protagonists in a film. They are part of a 'cultural resistance' (Julien), and fight for their music, their lifestyle, their happiness. Chris and Caz ally themselves with the punks and tie together the various strands of resistance. The film begins with 'P–Funk Wants to Get Funked Up' by Parliament as background music to a silhouette of London at sunset. We hear a DJ greeting his audience and putting on a new record. In the second scene of the film the Soul Patrol's radio broadcast is on in the background as well, and in the third we see Chris and Caz standing by their turntables in a garage. The T-shirts and very short haircuts reveal both DJs as soul boys. By the end of the film all the elements of a DJ lifestyle have made an appearance, from record buying to playing records in the club to the amorous adventures in their night-life. Chris and Caz are not only soul and funk fanatics but also fashion victims who spend their money either on records or fashion. The film ends with two hipsters spinning records in the crypt of an old church. One of the most beautiful scenes in the film shows white punks and black soul boys dancing between the columns of the dark stonework, to the heavy punk number 'Oh Bondage Up Yours!' by X-Ray Spex, and you can practically feel the euphoria of loud music and hip people. Chris and Caz climb on to the DJ's desk and push the two punk girls away. Chris takes 'I Like It' by Players Association out of his

Young Soul Rebels: *Chris and Caz as pirate DJs (top) and in the club*

104. ALLAM, Paul et al: Film Script, in: JULIEN, Isaac/ MacCabe, Colin: op. cit., p. 161.

105. Also notable, however, is the role of a good-natured Hip-Hop DJ in Ernest Dickerson's 1992 American film *Juice*. The film about the self-destruction of teenagers in a black ghetto contains an authentic DJ battle, as well as the DJ going to the record-shop and working on a mix-tape.

record box. He slowly fades out the X-Ray Spex number and starts the Soul Patrol programme. The first sounds of the black music organize the soul boys and girls on the dancefloor and some punks slope off to the bar with their heads hung low, but most of them switch from pogoing to the soul groove. Everyone dances to everything with everyone else, prejudices are abandoned. The camera lingers on the dancing people. Chris and Caz are happy, the dancefloor vibrates, and the dancers whistle and shout. The script puts it concisely: 'They're at their closest in creating the club atmosphere.'[104] It isn't just the two Soul Patrol DJs who get close to the ideal club atmosphere, Julien's film does as well. The work is autobiographical, as the director reveals in an interview. Julien's precise memory of this period and his unconditional passion for the music, fashion and life of his characters made *Young Soul Rebels* into a cinematic masterpiece about youth cultures. Along with Charlie Ahearn's semi-documentary hip-hop film *Wild*, Julien's work is the only good, beautiful and authentic film about dancefloor subculture, and DJ culture in particular. Since Ahearn's film concentrates primarily on graffiti-sprayers, we may legitimately call *Young Soul Rebels* the first real DJ film so far.[105] The film ends as it began: with the Soul Patrol's music. And with Chris and Caz dancing beside their turntables.

DON'T BELIEVE THE HYPE – DJS, CLUBS AND THE RECORD INDUSTRY

Sales of disco records soared from 1975 onwards, and the music industry quickly recognized that the discos were full of potential record-buyers, and that the people who danced to disco would also buy the records for home listening. The DJ didn't just play for his clientele, he also influenced their taste. At the time of the great disco hype, the record industry started showering DJs with new products that seemed club-compatible, in borderline cases bribing them with payola payments. For the British pop sociologist Simon Frith, the relationship between disco music and the disco market is a prime example of the dialectic of 'give the people what they want'. The DJ was the hugely important gatekeeper who conveyed the taste of the public to the record industry, selected the records that emerged from that feedback and 'sold' them to the public. The DJ moderated the communication between the industry and the public.[106] Frith considers the position of the consumer in this dialectical process to be just as strong as that of the industry, in all likelihood because of the complete occupation of the individual by disco when dancing. The question was: to what extent could this profound will to dissolve in the music be manipulated? Disco hype and its development would lead one to suspect that even the passion for dancing can be encouraged artificially.

In the underground there are no dialectical processes arising out of differences in power. In the underground, producers and consumers always see themselves as a unit. Here the producer, whether he is a DJ or a musician, is primarily interested in realizing himself in the music with as little alienation as possible, and not, as in the pop mainstream, in selling himself as well as possible. Both consumer and producer derive their supreme ease from this. Their community of interest solders the underground together.

106. Cf. FRITH, Simon: Sound Effects, p. 129.

BACK IN THE UNDERGROUND

The disco chapter should end where it began: in the underground. If Studio 54 was the most famous disco of the hype, the Paradise Garage was the most influential and effective club of the disco age. The Paradise Garage survived the period of disco frenzy unscathed. The Garage, as it was known, never succumbed to the temptation of being everyone's club or one of the top ten thousand, but remained true to the roots of disco music and above all the disco spirit: disco was underground, and nothing in the Paradise Garage suggested that it had ever been otherwise. The Garage was a gay club, with a mostly black clientele on Fridays, and a lot of women and whites on Saturdays. It came very close to what Isaac Julien wanted to show as the ideal disco in his film.

Everywhere in the enormous, dark, cavernous space you could physically feel the music. The bass line was heavier than in any other club: 'You can hear the music through your feet, through your hands,' one disco guide had it, 'you can smell the music here, it is so overpowering.'[107] The records were played by Larry Levan, who died in 1992 and was one of the most influential disco DJs of all time. Levan played a style that most other discos avoided. He left gaps between the songs to give the people time to get into the music; he played slow pieces when his audience seemed to be serious-minded; he showed videos when he didn't want his audience to dance. Levan had started out as a dancer; then he worked as a lighting man at the club 'Continental Baths'. When the DJ there didn't show up, the club manager asked him to step in. Levan borrowed records from a friend and became a DJ. To improve the sound and give it a better mix, Levan used three record decks in the Garage. He also used various different pickups: he began the evening with cheap, average systems, and boosted the sound until he was using the best and most expensive systems at the climax of the evening. Since Levan thought the sound was one of the crucial criteria for a good club, he experimented with various speakers and amplifiers.[108] With the air conditioning system he regulated the temperature according to the music, and for some songs he had selected perfumes wafted through the Garage. 'It was total hypnosis,'[109] recalls hip-hop DJ and producer Africa Islam. The Paradise Garage had not only the best sound system at that time, and an excellent air conditioning system, but also a relaxation room with film showings and a buffet with fresh fruits, ice-cream, nuts and chocolate. No alcohol was sold, and levels of drug consumption were less dramatic than in other underground clubs. The drug of the people who went to the Garage was the music. Torsos bare, sweat-drenched and with a handkerchief around their necks or in their pockets, they devoted themselves totally to the sound and danced until they were completely

107. MIEZITIS, Vita/ BERNSTEIN, Bill: Night-Dancin', p. 67.

108. Cf. HARVEY, Steven/ BATES, Patricia, op. cit., p. 7.

109. DIEDERICHSEN, Diedrich: Präsident Bush's Most Wanted – Unterwegs mit Ice T, in: Freiheit macht arm, p. 221.

exhausted. The perfect disco, which influenced the origins of house music and kept the old spirit of disco as a club music alive until 1987.

DISCO – THE END, NOT AN END

When the disco hype slowly subsided in 1979, clubs like the Garage and a huge number of pop bands assumed the mantle of disco and kept it alive. Disco no longer looked like the Village People and no longer sounded like a maxi-single by Cerrone, but almost all of dancefloor music, from hip-hop to techno, incorporated all its favourite disco songs into its own creations. Disco lived on, and many records by the Pet Shop Boys, New Order, Deee-Lite and Madonna can be seen as a direct continuation of disco music. All of house music can be heard as a technologically advanced form of disco. 'Garage House' was the further, heavier development of the sound of the Paradise Garage. In the context of house music, there was a disco revival in the early 1990s in which many of the sounds and above all the funky bass-line of disco songs were dubbed over the driving house beat.

So the story of disco is far from over in 1979. In this book disco will appear both in the chapter on hip-hop and in the chapters about house and the contemporary dancefloor scene. Disco – 'Born to Be Alive'.

B. HIP-HOP

WORD UP

More than any other kinds of dancefloor music, rap and hip-hop have taken their historiography into their own hands. First of all in the songs, whose self-reflexiveness is one of the central characteristics of hip-hop, and then in the handful of books written by curious and passionate devotees of the music. There are also a number of magazines on the market which anticipate or propagate ideologies in the context of hip-hop culture, and tell its history. Magazines like *The Source*, *Urb* and *Rap Sheets* act as a forum for all the rap artists who want to use interviews to explain their music and their view of the world. In comparison to the two other kinds of DJ music, disco and house, hip-hop has had ample documentation in terms of publicity, although David Toop's *Rap Attack* is so far the only detailed standard work on the history of hip-hop. The most intimate knowledge of rap and hip-hop comes from the lyrics of the songs which, as rarely before in pop music, engage with the origin, the understanding and the purpose of their own music. Hip-hop takes language and music equally seriously.

Black history has mostly been handed down as oral history – 'oral' often meaning 'sung'. Rap musicians follow on from this tradition and see themselves – like teachers, pastors and politicians – as the creators of meaning and knowledge in the black community. Against this background the song lyrics assume a central importance. Answering the question, what is a good rap, Kid Frost gave the firm answer: 'Lyrics. That's the most important thing. You can't just be talking out of the side of your neck. "I'm this. I'm that. I can get that girl. I can screw him." It's got to be intellectual enough to make somebody sit back and say, "Dang, that shit makes some sense."'[1] In hip-hop this 'making sense' often means explaining to the audience the mode and conditions of production of the music itself. Anyone who writes about hip-hop has to listen to every major record of both the old and new schools to hear their message. There are no clearer and more direct messages in any book, interview or fanzine essay. 'Rap music is history in a literal sense: an account, a body of language that tells what happened and why, a combination of information and interpretation that summarizes, dramatizes and makes comprehensible what African-Americans were doing from the late 1970s to the early 1990s,'[2] wrote Jefferson Morley as an introduction to his 1992 book of rap lyrics. Rap was, and remains, a linguistic liberation for not only the black minority, but also for the many Puerto Ricans, Chicanos and Asians who produce rap in America. In this essay, the focus will stay on African-American hip-hop. The need to find a language of their own has been the chief concern of almost every African-American cultural position. Jazz, R&B, soul and funk tried to do it, but it was hip-hop that picked up all these attempts and packed their energies together. The radical nature of rap lyrics was the expression of the new aggressive consciousness of the children who had grown up with the struggles of the Civil Rights movement and Black Power in the 60s and 70s.

Rapping in one's own language, and the search for one's own semantics also involved paying increased attention to the language of one's opponents and enemies. The linguistic critique, and thus the historical critique, of ruling white America, was a new challenge once one's own words had found a medium of agitation. 'The power of words/ Don't take it for granted/ When you hear a man ranting/ Don't just read

1. SMALL, Michael: Break it Down, p. 41.

2. MORLEY, Jefferson: Rap Music as American History, in: STANLEY, Lawrence A.: Rap – The Lyrics, p. xxxi.

the lips/ Be more sublime than this/ Put everything in context,'[3] recommend the Disposable Heroes of Hiphoprisy in the song 'Language of Violence'. A revolution, a revolt, even reforms have to find their own language. For Foucault, truth-telling is an endless task, and a duty that every power must take on board.[4] The black minority, as a dissident force, takes the task very seriously. 'But when it comes to speakin' the real, I won't be silent/ Speak all reality when I'm on the mike,'[5] rapped Above the Law in 'Livin' Like Hustlers'. The 'mike' becomes a 'weapon' in many hip-hop lyrics, the MCs (masters of ceremony) fire off 'lyrics like a harpoon',[6] and become champions of free speech so as not to succumb to the 'silence of slavery'[7] (Foucault).

WORD SOUND POWER is the title of an LP by British rapper Rebel MC. On the cover the three words are printed in enormous black letters. The O of 'word' shows a shouting mouth, the O of 'sound' a loudspeaker, the O of 'power' a black fist. The triumvirate of hip-hop: all three belong together, one isn't thinkable or imaginable without the other. 'Word' or 'Word up', placed like an exclamation mark after important statements, means, in hip-hop slang, something like 'that's absolutely true', the abbreviation of the saying 'My word is my bond'[8] – 'bond' with the twin meanings of obligation and fetter. From this tension emerge both hip-hop and the knowledge of hip-hop.

3. DISPOSABLE HEROES OF HIPHOPRISY: Language of Violence, in: STANLEY, Lawrence A., loc. cit., p. 90.

4. EWALD, François: Michel Foucault oder Die Sorge um die Wahrheit, in: Pariser Gespräche, p. 30.

5. ABOVE THE LAW: Livin' Like Hustlers, in: STANLEY, Lawrence A., loc. cit., p. 3

6. BIG DADDY KANE: Smooth Operator, in: STANLEY, Lawrence A., loc. cit., p. 22.

7. EWALD, François, loc. cit., p. 30.

8. Cf. FAB 5 FREDDY: Fresh Fly Flavor, p. 63.

9. Cf. MAJOR, Clarence: Juba to Jive, p. 376f.

ROOTS OF RAP

The word 'rap' comes from the English verb 'to rap', as in knocking or beating. In African-American usage, the word appeared as early as the 17th century, and was given various different meanings. Since 1870, it has been used to refer to a form of speaking or conversing. In 1916 a 'rapper' was a police informer; only in the 40s and 50s did 'rap' come to mean rhythmic speaking with or without music.[9] Someone who rapped 'opened his mouth wide', and tried to 'rap down' someone else with words. Jazz musicians rapped, radio DJs rapped, and politicians did it too. But rap only became an autonomous, artistic genre after the invention of the breakbeat. By the end of the 80s, the term was used as a synonym for music consisting of rapping and beats. The term stresses the hegemony of the rhythmic speech act over all the other elements of hip-hop music. In the late 70s, DJs still liked to speak of 'scratch' or 'breakbeat' music, to foreground their own contribution to the music, although in this they were unsuccessful. The term 'rap' found its way into the linguistic mainstream. Today, the term 'rap' is used more for the 'poetry' and 'rhymes', or as a description of the 'old school' bands, musicians and songs. Particularly in America, many writers and musicians stuck with the term 'rap music' to describe hip-hop music.

The history of the term 'hip-hop' is much disputed. Fab 5 Freddy, one of the first homeboys and experts on the subject, explains in his dictionary that the expression was used by DJ Hollywood in the mid-70s to comment on the playing of records. He liked shouting into the microphone: 'To the *hip-hop* the hippy hippy hippy hop and you don't stop.'[10] S.H. Fernando, on the other hand, claims in his book *The New Beats*, that the expression 'hip-hop' has been used since the days of Malcolm X to describe young people's dance parties; only DJ Afrika Bambaataa redefined it to include the whole of hip-hop culture.[11] Bambaataa also sees himself as a creator of the term, which, according to him, he invented in 1974.[12] The expression was quickly taken up by other DJs and first flowed into the vocabulary of all rappers, then all fans of the subculture, and finally into general linguistic usage. Today the word refers to the current form of rap music (not old, but new school), which remains both 'close and true' to the original and its attitude, and to the 'style and state of mind as established by the originators of hip-hop music and culture'.[13] Hip-hop doesn't just mean the music, but refers to the whole cultural environment: style, fashion, breakdancing, graffiti, ideologies, performance and attitudes of mind. Hip-hop covers all spheres of the subculture with music at its centre.

Rap has many ancestors. In *Rap Attack*, David Toop reveals the extent to which rap has its roots in African and Afro-American cultural forms. At the beginning of

10. FAB 5 FREDDY, loc. cit., p. 32.

11. Cf. FERNANDO, S.H.: The New Beats, p. ix.

12. SMALL, Michael, loc. cit., p. 218.

13. FAB 5 FREDDY, loc. cit., p. 32.

rap's gallery of ancestors are the 'griots' of West Africa's savannah bands, who combined, and continue to combine, the function of a living history book and a newspaper with those of a musician.[14] Chuck D., Public Enemy's thinker-in-chief, has this tradition in mind when he describes rap as the black ghetto version of CNN.[15] The griots have biting scorn as well as a profound knowledge of history and the contemporary situation of their audience.

A new form of this verbal historiography came with Afro-American 'toasting', which generally reflected a male world of violence, obscenities and misogyny (the tradition also continues in rap) and with the minstrel shows. This form of 19th century entertainment combined dance, song, theatre and comedy, and was originally practised by whites, but then increasingly by blacks as well. In the second half of the 20th century 'verbal contests' became an important phenomenon in black communities: when men met up they fought not just with fists but with words, and the older (in the sense of linguistically experienced) the participants in these verbal fighting displays, the more weight they carried. The purpose of the confrontation was to finish off and/or demoralize one's opponent with language. This tradition recurs today in the MC battles and dis campaigns within the hip-hop community. 'To dis' is an abbreviated form of 'to disrespect', and means: to bring someone down and defeat them verbally. Dissing is a real battle for pride and honour, because 'nobody disses me and gets away with it'.[16] Even today fighting continues in the 'war of words', to see who's the cleverer, the quicker, cooler and harder. The boundaries of good taste, traditional verbal usages or politeness are all distinguished by their absence. What counts is winning.

David Toop refers to another branch in rap's family tree, dealing not with the function of the spoken word but with the act of speaking. Scat is an art form in which the voice is used as an instrument. Earlier forms of scat appear in the spirituals of the 19th century and then in New Orleans jazz. It is interesting is that scat should have appeared as a musical distortion of speech in a city whose linguistic mishmash was a unique combination of French, African, English, Spanish, West

14. Cf. TOOP, David: Rap Attack, p. 31f.

15. Cf. FAB 5 FREDDY, loc. cit., p. 50.

16. FAB 5 FREDDY, loc. cit., p. 18.

Indian, Cajun and Creole.[17] In bebop, scat singing became the central stylistic element. Jazz legends like Louis Armstrong, Ella Fitzgerald and Betty Carter are held up as the masters of scat. Cab Calloway delivered his own version with jive scat, the secret language that mixed scat and chattering. Because of the delight he took in juggling with nonsense syllables, Calloway was called the 'hi-do-ho man'.[18] He used jive scat to introduce guest artistes at his performances, and introduced (or ridiculed) the members of his own ensemble, as hip-hop MCs would later do with DJs.

The tradition of jive and scat was taken up and developed by black radio DJs in the 40s and 50s (see the chapter on the black radio DJs, pp.83–94). Further influences identified by Toop were black comedians, the self-adulation of Cassius Clay and the many funk and disco records in which street slang, the jive of the radio DJs and supposedly grotesque verbal distortions appeared in the lyrics.

The last branch of the hip-hop family tree as drawn up by Toop belongs to gospel and soul. Religious services in black communities were a major pillar of black socialization and identity-formation. The combination of prayer, preaching and a great deal of music had, since the days of slavery, had nothing of the liturgical rigidity that prevailed in Europe. As Arnold Shaw sees it, the churches of the poor, in all that misery, had to serve not only as instruction but also entertainment. A passage from James Baldwin, who had worked as a preacher in a street church in Harlem, lends credence to the thesis:

There is no music like that music, no drama like the drama of the saints rejoicing, the sinners moaning, the tambourines racing, and all those voices coming together and crying holy unto the Lord. I have never seen anything to equal the fire and excitement that sometimes, without warning, fill a church... to 'rock'. Nothing that has happened to me since, equals the power and the glory that I sometimes felt when, in the middle of a sermon, I knew that I was somehow, by some miracle, really carrying, as they said, 'the Word' – when the church and I were one. Their pain and their joy was mine, and mine were theirs – they

17. Cf. WINNER, Langdon: The New Orleans Sound, in: MILLER, Jim (Ed.), loc. cit., p. 72.

18. Cf. SHAW, Arnold: Soul, p. 65.

surrendered their pain and joy to me, I surrendered mine to them – and their cries of 'Amen!' and 'Hallelujah!' and 'Yes, Lord!' and 'Praise His name!' and 'Preach it, brother!' sustained and whipped wet, singing and dancing, in anguish and rejoicing, at the foot of the altar.[19]

Among the audiences of the griots in Africa it was deemed impolite to listen to the stories in silence, so the performances were commented upon in echoes, repetitions and interpolations. This custom continues until the present day in religious services and hip-hop concerts. With song, cries and hysteria, the priest and the community shriek themselves into a state of blissful euphoria. Gospel arose from the alternation of singing between the congregation and the preacher, and became an art form of its own, borne by deep piety and the desire to give pious feelings free rein. Nothing of the powers of negation, of prohibition and slavery, such as that which Nietzsche identified in white Christianity, was present in the black churches. The religious service was a festival of liberation, of affirmation and euphoria. The power of these spiritual experiences flowed from the religious sphere into every cranny of black culture.

Gospel stands at the beginning of a line of development stretching from church-song via soul and funk to house music and hip-hop. The secularization of music that was originally liturgical did not deprive it of its spirituality and emotion. No matter what form Gospel reappears in, whether in soul or in deep house: its sacred origins are always apparent. Faith in God became faith in the good in man, and this message was easily carried over into every other form, including pop music. And just as the 'power of oratory' (Toop) dominated culture and historiography, it also predominated in every form of Afro-American religion and continued in almost all (secular) verbal art forms, particularly in soul rap.

Soul rap was the speaking of a song, usually in a religious context. Soul raps were as effective as they were because they set out to erase any distance between musician and audience. This form of speech-song was built into soul pieces as a break element, to intensify the

19 . BALDWIN, James: The Fire Next Time, p. 33f.

emotionality of the pieces, or to give particular emphasis to certain parts of the lyric. In deep soul, monologues and speech became a major component of the song. Barry White, Isaac Hayes and Millie Jackson made the rapping of deep soul world famous. The divas of the disco age took their bearings chiefly from the erotic variants of the soul monologue, and tried to shift the spirituality of prayer for salvation to a sexual level. After disco, 'release me', and 'set me free' became a central motif of house music. In hip-hop release often had less to do with sex and more with violence. Rapping was always a form of threat and at the same time the expression of being threatened.

ROOTS OF RAP – ROOTS OF REGGAE: THE JAMAICAN SOUND SYSTEM

American pop culture has many different echo chambers. One of the most interesting of them must surely be the pop music of the Caribbean island of Jamaica, three quarters of whose population consists of the descendants of black African slaves. During the Second World War, the US sailors based on Jamaica gave the islanders their first contact with jazz and blues. Interest in the music was so great that there was soon a flourishing business in second-hand gramophone records. After the end of the war, a US military base was set up, American companies invested capital and tourists discovered the delights of the Caribbean island. The influence of the American way of life, and particularly of American pop music, grew. The radio stations WINS and WMBM, operating out of Miami, ran R&B shows that could be picked up in Jamaica, and which were enthusiastically received there. At that time Jamaica's pop music was a mixture of Caribbean calypso and mento sounds, loosened up with catchy samba rhythms. Black R&B from the states, on the other hand, was hard, loud, rebellious and yet, in its rhythms, not entirely unfamiliar to the Jamaicans. Dick

Hebdige points out that R&B songs from the southern states, particularly from New Orleans, were Caribbean in tone.[20] So in discovering R&B, people were also rediscovering a part of their own musical culture. But the R&B songs produced outside New Orleans soon won a large following, particularly in the slums of the cities.

As most musicians played kitsch for the tourists and there were no local bands capable of playing good R&B, people hit on the idea of putting big speakers and a record-player (later two of them) – on a truck and touring around the cities with it. The idea of the sound system was born – a Jamaican form of mobile disco that quickly became an important part of life in the slums and ghettos. From the start, the bass-line of the sound system was the most important criterion for its quality. The shuffle rhythm was supposed to reach everyone, and the louder the sound systems, the more people came and danced. Soon the bass boxes were over a foot and a half across, and every beat of the bass-line could be felt physically. The various sound systems rivalled one another. The winner was the loudest one with the best and rarest records. To avoid telling possible competitors what record company or interpreter the single was by, the DJs often scratched off the labels.[21] Hip-hop DJs like Grandmaster Flash would later wash off the labels of their vinyl records in bathtubs.

To heat up the competition between DJs, at least two sound systems were invited to parties and events, and these then fought it out in the disciplines of taste, selection and loudness. Because of the incredible popularity of these battles, the most successful DJs were Jamaica's first pop stars. Their names were Duke Reid, Sir Coxsone and Prince Buster, and they had troops of roadies, engineers and bouncers. These DJs had imaginatively loud-mouthed names, and dressed up as criminals and gangsters. Duke Reid turned up in an ermine gown with a gold crown on his head and two Colt 45s at his hips, a rifle over his shoulder and a cartridge-belt. He often had his fans carry him to the decks to put on new and old R&B rarities. As he played them he shouted and yelled along with the music, particularly rhythmic passages with few vocals. At the

20. Cf. HEBDIGE, Dick: Cut'N'Mix, p. 62.

21. SCHWANER, Teja: Reggae, Volksmusik aus Babylon, in: GÜLDEN, Jörg/ HUMANN, Klaus (Ed.), Rock Session 1, p. 77.

peak of his ecstasy, Reid is even supposed to have shot his rifle over the heads of the dancers. At any rate, Reid and the other star DJs became the role models of the 'rude boys', the slum hipsters of the fifties. Everyone wanted to be a DJ or at least work for a sound system. The sound systems brought together everyone who was interested in music, dancing and having fun. By the late 50s, the call for records for the sound systems was so great, and taste in music so highly developed, that it could no longer be satisfied by American productions. There were even troops of people who went around the USA looking for more and more new and exclusive records. Nonetheless, the three most famous DJs felt the desire to produce their own music – initially for their own needs. This brought into being 'rudie blues', a raw Jamaican version of R&B played by local bands. The pieces were mostly instrumental versions of old R&B standards, or New Orleans compositions, heavy on the rhythm section for use with the sound systems. The DJs rhymed live to the music in a style copied from black radio DJs of the USA. But with the development of a musical style of their own, they also grew more independent in their scat rap, and toasting came into being. Alongside typical encouragements to dance, such as 'Work it! Work it!' or 'Move it up!', toasting became a poetic secret language that blossomed with the development of ska and reggae. On some of the early 'rudie blues' records the toasts of the DJs were pressed on vinyl, becoming the basis for two types of reggae music: 'talk over' and 'dub'. Dub is the version of a piece almost entirely reduced to drum and bass,[22] which can be defamiliarized with every technique the studio has to offer. The DJ magazine *Mixmag* speaks of dub as Jamaica's gift to all kinds of modern dance music: 'This isn't remixing. This is art, altering the perspective of the existing music to create an unrecognizable offering on the higher altar of the God Bass.'[23] Talk-over is a form of toasting over the music. Thanks to artists like Linton Kwesi Johnson, toasting has become literature read over reggae music,[24] – a poetry that had its origins in the shouting of DJs.

The sound system DJs began to create a style directed towards the needs of the dancers – and of course those of the DJs. According to personal taste, the R&B roots

22 . Cf. SHAW, Arnold: Dictionary..., loc. cit., p. 113.

23 . JOHNSON, Dean: Dub, in: MIXMAG 3/1993.

24 . Cf. HALBSCHEFFEL, Bernward/KNEIF, Tibor, loc. cit., p. 392f.

were recontextualised. The characteristic shuffle rhythm was almost always retained, although in a more quiet and stately form. All the instruments seem to stay on the offbeat for a long time.[25] In the early 60s 'rudie blues' broke away from its American predecessors, and became a musical form in its own right – ska. This also incorporated elements of Jamaican tradition, particularly the drumming of the cult of Rastafari. In the process, within a decade or so a completely new style had come into being, one which, under the influence of the sound systems and DJs, copied R&B – and was almost entirely produced, arranged and composed by DJs.

Duke Reid and Sir Coxsone helped to initiate all types of Jamaican pop music: rudie blues, ska and reggae. Sir Coxsone's sound system launched the careers of such famous musicians as Toots And The Maytals, Dennis Brown, Burning Spear, Johnny Osbourne, Dennis Alcapone, Dillinger, Michigan And Smiley, The Wailing Souls, Marcia Griffiths and Bob Andy, Delroy Wilson, Don Drummond, The Skatalites, The Heptones, Lee 'Scratch' Perry and Bob Marley's Wailers.[26] Coxsone (whose real name was Clement Dodd) earned the money for his first sound system in the cane-fields of Florida and became one of the most important music producers in Jamaica, turning fans of his sound systems into celebrities.

One example is the story of Lee 'Scratch' Perry, who began as a runner for Coxsone in the mid-50s, and is now one of the greatest interpreters, poets, composers and producers of reggae. Employed as a messenger-boy, Perry quickly became a record-seeker, trying to turn up American R&B rarities. His industry and skill turned him into a 'top sounds searcher'[27] and in 1959 he became a talent-seeker for the first record productions of the 'Sir Coxsone Downbeat Sound System'. By 1960 the DJs had stopped only pressing for their own needs, and sold thousands of records. The battles between the sound systems were no longer fought only over loudness and exquisiteness of taste, but also over their own hits and their sales figures. Perry began writing words for songs, and quickly became successful. His own songs, arrangements and productions followed. The sound system of Sir Coxsone and Lee Perry was the

25. Cf. HEBDIGE, Dick: Cut'N'Mix, p. 62.

26. Cf. WEISS, Karl-Erich: Lee Perry – Music Is Madness, in: FREDERKING, Klaus (Ed.), loc. cit., p. 118.

27. Ibid., p. 119.

biggest on the island by 1965. Perry was now the chief sound system DJ. He usually began his show with his own songs and his signature tune, the 'Chicken Scratch'. Perry's nickname 'Scratch' comes from the same song; he was also called Lee King Perry. In the mid-60s the style of ska changed, the rhythm became more complicated, the instrumentation more loaded towards the bass and the rhythm, the brass sections disappeared. Ska became rock steady, and rock steady became reggae. But all the Jamaican musical styles shared their origins in the DJs' sound systems.

The DJ was originally called the sound system operator, and then the DJ. Later, in reggae and dancehall raggamuffin – a mixture of hip-hop and reggae that came into being in the mid-80s – he was called a 'selector', a term that stressed taste and discretion. Because the DJ in Jamaica also shouted, sang and toasted, the rapper in dancehall raggamuffin is still called a DJ today.[28] But even before the bastard son of dancehall raggamuffin appeared, reggae and the sound systems in particular exerted an influence on the birth of hip-hop in the 70s.

28 . Cf. FAB 5 FREDDY, loc. cit., p. 20.

29 . GEORGE, Nelson: Hip-Hop's Founding Fathers..., loc. cit., p. 44.

THE FIRST RAP DJS

Historiography becomes difficult when the history being described took place in the cellars, apartments or backyards of the Bronx. In the lifetime of rap and hip-hop, a number of DJs have fought over the honour of being the first true hip-hop DJ. In autumn 1993 this found expression in the 'Founding Fathers'[29] of hip-hop meeting in the editorial offices of *The Source* in New York. Kool DJ Herc, Afrika Bambaataa and Grandmaster Flash elaborate, in a discussion moderated by Nelson George, who had first started doing what when with turntables. The state of knowledge prior to the discussion was confused, contradictory and distorted by vanities. The books and articles that had been published about the beginnings of hip-hop were contradictory on many points: the three DJs had repeatedly come up with new versions of their own legends in interviews and statements. This meeting

Cover of The Source 11/1993

meant that the improvisers of myths and legends were able to agree on a consistent and internally coherent 'historiography' – even if some years and precise dates will probably always differ to some extent. The desires of the western sense of history cannot be satisfied here, but the African-American tradition of oral history permits imprecision, as long as there are no crass untruths. Grandmaster Flash imposes one rule on all attempts by outsiders (people outside the original culture) to write hip-hop:

I think the only ones that can really tell you the story are Herc, Bam, Breakout and myself. Either you can hear this story, or history, and the only way you gonna hear the real historical views on it is by the people who were actually there – who actually took it from nothing and built into whatever it became to be. Some people don't dig deep enough to find out what happened back then. They just fix it so it's comfortable for the reader, which is really dangerous.[30]

That's why in this book we are trying to bring as much of the original tone of the hip-hop musicians and their authentic environment into our historiography.

KOOL DJ HERC AND THE BREAKS

The first hip-hop DJ and the 'godfather of hip-hop culture'[31] was Kool DJ Herc. Born in Kingston, Jamaica, as Clive Campbell, at the age of 12 he moved with his parents – his father was a musician – to the USA, and brought the tradition of the Jamaican sound system to New York. Because of his great stature and his accomplishments in basketball, Clive was given the nickname 'Hercules', which graffiti-sprayers[32] abbreviated to 'Herc', later adding the predicate 'Kool'. Herc was influenced by Disco DJs from the Bronx like Grandmaster Flowers, Pete Jones, Amazing Birth[33] and John Brown, in whose club 'Plaza Tunnel' he first heard James Brown's 'Give It Up or Turn It Loose' and Rare Earth's 'Get Ready'.[34] But at least equally important for Herc were his memories of the rolling sound systems in

30. Ibid. p. 50.

31. HOLMAN, Michael: Breaking and the New York City Breakers, p. 61.

32. Herc became his *tag*, in graffiti slang, to leave the name of the artist as a stylized signature: to be sprayed under a picture or scrawled on every imaginable surface with a magic marker. Tagging is also used as a weapon in the battle between sprayers. The tags of outsiders on one's own patch are overtagged (crossed over with one's own tag) or crossed out and one's own tag set next to it. In Steven Hager's book Herc relates that he was annoyed with the nickname Hercules and shortened it to Herc: 'That sounded rare, so I kept it.' (HAGER, Steven: Hip Hop; The Illustrated History of Break Dancing, Rap Music, and Graffiti, p. 31.)

33. Cf. OWEN, Frank: Hip-Hop's Original DJ Is Back at the Turntables, in: NEW YORK NEWSDAY, 11 October 1993.

34. Cf. HAGER, Steven, loc. cit., p. 31.

Jamaica, which set whole blocks dancing with their massive bass boxes.

In 1973 Herc's sister Cindy celebrated her birthday, and asked her brother to take care of the music. He bought a few new records and installed a DJ system with two turntables. The Campbells' friends came to the party in a gymnasium, and Herc played all his favourite records. Everyone was so enthusiastic that Herc was immediately engaged to put on records at more parties and events. By the end of the year Herc was already able to charge admission (at the beginning 25 cents) when he deejayed, and he proudly called his sound system the 'Herculoids'. The turntable, mixer, amplifier and boxes now – just like musicians – had their own artistic names.

Herc had borrowed the sound system from friends, but when he became successful he began working on a system of his own. At first Herc still played Reggae records from his home, but when he noticed that this music left the inhabitants of the Bronx somewhat unmoved,[35] he mixed them with Funk and Latino pieces. Herc's sound was louder and harder than all the disco DJ's whose style he found too gentle, their record collections too limited.[36] With block parties, in schools or parks, Herc was soon well known in the Bronx.

Afrika Bambaataa[37] and Grandmaster Flash[38] were among Herc's first admirers. Herc's signature tune was 'Apache' by the Incredible Bongo Band, a highly rhythmical form of the classic by the Shadows that Nelson George called a 'pioneering hip-hop record',[39] and named as an important event of the year 1973 in his chronicle 'of Post-Soul Black Culture'.[40] Herc generally began his evenings with the tune. What followed was a series of rap-like speeches praising Herc and his 'Herculoids'. These speeches were in the tradition of black American radio DJs and Jamaican sound system DJs, and were later taken up by all the other DJs and MCs.

Yes, yes, y'all
It's the serious, serio-so jointski
You're listening to the sound system:
The Herculords… cu-lords… lords…
And I just want to say to all my b-boys… boys…
boys… boys:

35. 'I couldn't play reggae in the Bronx. People wouldn't accept it.' (Ibid. p. 45.)

36. Cf. OWEN, Frank, loc. cit.

37. Bambaataa puts Herc at the start of hip-hop in 1992. In his list of 'Major Moments in Hip-Hop History' the first entry is: '1969: Kool Herc moves to the Bronx [in fact this had happened two years previously] from Jamaica and introduces a new DJ style; in live shows he mixes excerpts from several records to create new versions of R&B and funk songs (a technique that originated in Jamaica with reggae).' (In: SMALL, Michael, loc. cit., p. 218.)

38. In conversation with Herc and Bambaataa, Grandmaster Flash relates: 'I didn't really hear a real heavy, heavy, heavy system until I heard this man (Herc) out in the park. It was incredible.' (GEORGE, Nelson: Hip-Hop's Founding Fathers…, loc. cit., p. 47.)

39. GEORGE, Nelson: Buppies, B-Boys, Baps & Bohos, p. 11.

40. Steven Hager writes that Herc could only have used 'Apache' from 1974 because it was not produced until that year (cf. HAGER, Steven, loc. cit., p. 33.)

Rock on!
Time to get down to the a.m.
But please remember:
Respect my system and I'll respect you and yours[41]

41. Quoted in: BECKMAN, Janette/ ADLER, B.: Rap, p. 15. The same quotation is found in Hager. (HAGER, Steven, op. cit., p. 33.)

42. HAGER, Steven, op. cit., p. 32.

43. Afrika Bambaataa defines the break as the part of a hip-hop song 'that grabs you and makes you get emotional and wild'. (SMALL, Michael, loc. cit., p. 11.)

44. Cf. GEORGE, Nelson: Hip-Hop's Founding Fathers..., op. cit., p. 47. Herc later used a powerful Macintosh amplifier and two massive Shure speaker stacks (cf. HAGER, Steven, op. cit, p. 33).

45. TOOP, David: Rap Attack, p. 60.

46. Ibid.

One of the first fans and early homeboys relates how going to a Herc party as a twelve-year-old changed his life. 'The thing I mostly remember was how loud the music was. The sound overtook you. The place was packed – a real sweatbox. Herc was on the mike. He'd say things like "Rock the house"and call out the names of people at the party... After the first time, we didn't want to go anywhere else. It was Kool Herc's, Kool Herc's, Kool Herc's. Every weekend.'[42] He went on to become one of the first breakdancers to dance to Herc's music, in a completely new form that was the optimistic and athletic equivalent of the first breakbeats put out by the 'Herculoids'.

Herc had noticed that sparsely instrumented rhythmic passages sounded particularly good with the sound system, and got the audience dancing. To preserve the intensity and power of these passages, or at least to extend them, Herc worked with two copies of the same record, playing the desired passage, the break[43] alternately on one or other turntable. Or else he would simply switch from the break passage in one piece to the break in another piece.

The sound system became an instrument, the basis of a new music. The technology that Herc used was very primitive. Two old Gerard turntables, a pre-amp with two buttons to mix the two turntables and enormous bass boxes.[44] With this technology, Herc invented breakbeats and thus laid down the roots of hip-hop music.

'He just kept that beat *going*,'[45] Bambaataa remembers. 'He took the music of like Mandrill, like "Fencewalk", certain disco records that had funky percussion breaks like The Incredible Bongo Band when they came out with "Apache", and he just kept that beat *going*. It might be that certain part of the record that everybody waits for – they just let their inner self go and get wild. The next thing you know, the singer comes back in and you'd be mad.'[46] Various pieces of music merged into the 'endless peak of dance beats' (Hager). All of a sudden the DJ had become a musician and an author in his own right, but no one could have foreseen the extent of that transformation at the time. Bambaataa, Flash and many other DJ's copied the style and made it the basis of hip-hop music and hip-hop culture.

The underlying idea of the breakbeat was as simple as it was groundbreaking. Up to now most DJs, apart from the pioneers of disco, had seen a piece as a unit and revered it accordingly. Herc and his successors saw songs as quarries from which they could knock out stones to build their own works. The old music became material for the new music, which transcended in the Hegelian sense the old music – at once negating, conserving and elevating it. Simply by being so bold as to make previous musical history the material of his own creation, Herc made the DJ an author, the originator, creator and founder of something that was new and his own. With his breakbeats, he freed music from its old context and integrated it within 'the process of composition'. What was crucial was not how the pieces could be perceived as a unified work, but how they or their parts worked as dance-tracks in the context of a party.

One of the most important contemporary forms of composition, collage, moved into pop music. But where Dada attempted the 'destruction of all meaning to absolute nonsense',[47] and where collage, through to the punk dada revival, was used principally for the destruction of old structures of meaning, hip-hop and the early disco DJ worked with sound clips without any destructive impulse. The old song is taken to pieces because parts of itself can be better used in the context of the DJ's creation, not because the original song is not valued or has to be destroyed. While collage defines itself through the fragmentation and heterogeneity of its composition, the constitutive element of DJ composition is the interpretation and reconstruction of something that has been deconstructed at the turntable. To that extent it may make more sense to speak in terms of a technique of montage rather than collage.[48]

As in the films (and the film criticism) of the *nouvelle vague*, what is at work is a critique of love, which is guided almost entirely by passionate affirmation, never by a nihilistic lack of respect. Just as Godard and Rivette dotted their first films with samples from their favourite films, borrowing from them some of their fundamental

47. HAUSMANN, Raoul: Alitterel Delitterel Sublitterel, in: RIHA, Karl (Ed.): Dada Berlin: Texte Manifeste Aktionen, p. 54.

48. Diederichsen refers to the different ways in which the use of collage can be understood: collages were used in classical Modernism to attack and destroy history. 'In hip-hop... collage is supposed to be used to produce meaning, to construct history, and hence to do the opposite. And yet the symptoms are structurally similar. On the one hand we have hip-hop as a movement that speaks, you might say, for an excluded ethnic group. And on the other side we have the people who want out of what exists, who want to destroy what exists.' (DREYER, Michael: Hey hey, we are not the monkeys – Interview with Diedrich Diederichsen, in: BEERMANN, Wilhelm et al (Ed.): 5 Interviews, p. 113.

Breakdancers from the film Wild Style

B-Boy from the film Wild Style

motifs and characters, so the DJ uses the favourite moments from his record collection to bring them into his own compositions. 'Positivity' is one of the central concepts of hip-hop, and in the declaration of faith in the Zulu nation by Afrika Bambaataa, 'Overcoming the Negative to the Positive'[49] becomes a task and a goal.

The actual history of hip-hop begins in the mid-70s, at around the same time disco leaves the underground. In a newspaper interview Herc admits that he was influenced by the early disco DJs, but that he also wanted to do something quite different.[50] Grandmaster Flash and Afrika Bambaataa also said that the disco and party music DJs were their models in mixing techniques and the use of records.

By 1975 the DJ had become an independent entrepreneur with a portable sound system and an enormous collection of records, and a 'new cultural hero',[51] at least in the Bronx.

The fans of this new culture were called B-Boys. Originally the B-Boys were the boys who would 'break' – breakdance to breakbeat music.[52] The B-Boys usually started their acrobatic dancing when the DJ played an especially pure passage of breakbeat. Just as language and music were re-ordered in hip-hop, the same thing happened with the dancers' body language. In the typical hip-hop combination of tradition and innovation, some old dance elements were appropriated from bebop, soul train dancers and funkateers, and a series of new elements were introduced: most notable among them were the 'helicopter' – rapid rotation on the head – and the 'electric boogie', which made the dancer's body look as if it was moulded out of plasticine. Body language had found a new jive-scat. Just as disco supported the revolts of the sexual body, it was now the revolts of Afro-Americans which, in this form of ghetto culture, reasserted their supremacy over their body and its poetics. The advance of power over the body, as diagnosed by Foucault, was repelled in the highly-trained dance steps, and hegemonic ideas of the use of the body and body language were replaced by original ideas. Similar things were later to happen in house culture, with Vogueing.

49. THE BELIEFS OF UNIVERSAL ZULU NATION, in: THE SOURCE 11/1993, p. 49.

50. OWEN, Frank, op. cit.

51. HAGER, Steven, op. cit., p. 33

52. Kool DJ Herc, who invented the term, explains in an interview: 'B-boys, these are the boys, these are the boys that break. So we call 'em B-boys.' (GEORGE, Nelson: Hip-Hop's Founding Fathers..., op. cit, p. 46.)

In the second half of the 80s the term B-Boy or B-Girl was used for all 'totally devoted' hip-hop fans, whether anyone was actually dancing or not. What mattered was that the new music invented by a DJ immediately encompassed a cultural environment in which there had been graffiti spraying even before breakbeats; in the wake of the DJ and the rapper, whose prototype came into being at around the same time, the horde of fans appeared, to turn a new dance style into a new musical form. All of a sudden all the forms of hip-hop culture existed side by side and jumbled together: graffiti, breakdance, deejaying and rapping.

GRANDMASTER FLASH: MIX, SCRATCH AND BEATBOX

Grandmaster Flash

53 . Quoted in: BECKMAN, Janette/ ADLER, B.: op. cit, p. 19.

54 . TOOP, David: Rap Attack, p. 60.

55 . Ibid.

Grandmaster Flash at work

Herc had invented the underlying principle of the breakbeat, but it was Grandmaster Flash who turned the DJ into a filigree technician and turntable virtuoso. 'Life' magazine was later to call Grandmaster Flash the 'Toscanini of the turntables'.[53] Flash was fascinated by Herc's sound systems, and impressed by his breakbeats, but he also recognized his limitations: 'Herc really slipped up. With the monstrous power he had he couldn't mix too well. He was playing little breaks but it would sound sloppy.'[54] Flash started spinning records at small parties himself, and Herc kept dissing him afterwards, because his system was a lot better than Flash's home-made sound system. Flash, who had grown up with his father's vast record collection, had been sent by his mother to a college of electrical engineering, where he had acquired the ability to repair broken systems and use them for his own purposes. This technical know-how helped Flash not only in the construction of his sound system, but also in the solution of a difficult problem encountered in the mixing of one record with another. Flash's model was disco DJ Pete Jones, who mixed his records together perfectly, never making a mistake. Flash asked Jones permission to use his mixing desk, but he refused twice before letting Flash on to the sound system. 'He told me what to do and to my amazement, wow, you can actually hear the other turntable before you play it out to the people. I knew what it was because I was going to the technical school for electronics. I knew that inside the unit it was a single pole double throw switch, meaning that when it's in the center it's off. When it's to the left you're listening to the left turntable and when it's to the right you're listening to the right turntable.'[55] The pre-hear possibility over the headphones made more precise mixing possible. Flash was beside himself with joy, he had finally solved the problem of merging one record into another.

Flash went to the electrical goods store to buy 'a single pole double throw switch', and installed it in his system.[56] After three years of searching, Flash had finally found a way of anticipating records. After this Flash began mixing short breakbeat passages of less than a minute so that they could be extended to five minutes. Flash quickly perfected the mixing of breakbeats to the point where the dancers couldn't hear the transitions.

The next step in the development of mixing technique was 'punch phasing'. This method didn't add beats, but brought the breakbeat of a piece together with the 'naked' instrumentation of another piece. And while the piece went on running on one turntable, the second turntable could be used to enrich and reinterpret the original version of the song. At the same time as the remix was being pressed on vinyl in disco music, a live version of remixing was emerging in the Bronx. Using the second record-player, the DJ could keep taking the piece apart and putting it back together again. According to what was happening on the dance floor, the tension was intensified or relaxed, the beats were made heavier or quieter, the orchestration rendered more opulent or kept simple. To find the right passages on the records and quickly insert them, Flash had to be very familiar with his records, and particularly with the crucial points in them. To find the important passages in the black-on-black vinyl, Flash invented 'clock theory'.[57] He used the record label like the face of a clock, dividing it up accordingly. He noted where which passages were to be found, and was thus able to mix breaks quickly and precisely. Later DJs would mark their favourite passages on the records with sticky tape and coloured labels.

One other technical innovation of Flash's was backspinning, quickly pulling back a passage without losing the beats. Exclamations like 'let's dance' or 'rock it' could now be repeated an infinite number of times and placed between the breakbeats. This was done in two ways: either using the rapid backspin as a sound effect (loud squeaking), or silently reversing the record, the throw switch being pushed aside and, only after the needle had been turned back, pushed back again. The more perfect Flash's mastery of this technique, the more elegantly and delicately he was able to incorporate parts of a song into another song – without a trace of the sticky tape and glue of the collage process. Although Flash was initially unpopular with the public because of the experimental nature of his music, by 1979 he was a celebrity.

Flash kept his system at the home of family friends.

56. Ibid. He told Steven Hager the story exactly like that. (Cf. HAGER, Steven, loc. cit., p. 36.)

57. HAGER, Steven, op. cit., p. 36.

Grandmaster Flash at work

The Livingstons had one young son, Theodore, and an elder son called Gene. Gene was friends with Flash, and told his little brother not to play with his friend's system. But the little boy was too keen, so Flash let him have a go when Gene had gone to work. Flash encouraged Theodore to show him what he could do. After a short time, Flash was very impressed: 'He had an ability to take the needle and drop it and just keep it going. He had such a rhythm that was incredible.'[58] Flash had to beg big brother Gene for a year and half before Theodore was allowed to go with them to the park to play records.[59] Within a short time Theodore had put his big brother in the shade. For Flash, Theodore was the first DJ who could really scratch – there was no shortage of DJs who had used the needle on records.[60] 'What Theodore did for scratchin' is this – where I had expertise on the backspin or fakin' the faze, what Theodore would do with a scratch is make it more rhythmical. He had a way of rhythmically taking a scratch and making that shit sound musical. He just took it to another level.'[61]

At exactly the same time as Flash and DJ Theodore were discovering scratching, Laurie Anderson was playing on her viophonograph, a violin with a 7-inch single mounted on its belly. The performance musician scratched around over the vinyl surface with an electrically amplified violin bow. The horse hair of the bow thus became an analogue of the record needle that the DJ scratches back and forth in the record grooves.

Hans Keller was the first German music journalist to investigate hip-hop and do research in Harlem and the Bronx. In his big rap article for the magazine *Sounds* in November 1981 he describes the skill of DJ Theodore, whom he had seen 'at the closest quarters':

On the left, for example, 'Heartbeat' is running, and on the right he's just put on a particular record, he accurately puts the needle somewhere near the centre, and, with brief jerks to the rim of the record, he introduces a syncopated, rapid machine-gun rhythm. He pushes the switch on the mixing box to the left, says something to his assistant, who reaches into a box to take out another record. Same again, only that this time

58. Ibid.

59. Previously, Theodore had always bought records for Flash, and George points out that he also purchased white rock records like 'Walk This Way' by Aerosmith, and that these – before any kind of crossover, and years before Run DMC's cover-version – were used by Flash and Theodore. (Cf. GEORGE, Nelson: Buppies..., loc. cit, p. 13.)

60. Kittler suggests that New York DJs 'take the esoteric graphic work of an artist like Moholy-Nagy and turn it into the everyday of Scratch Music', and thus puts scratching in the context of an artistic engagement with records. (KITTLER, Grammophon..., loc. cit., p. 79.)

61. GEORGE, Nelson: Hip-Hop's Founding Fathers..., loc. cit., p. 47. In Dufresne's *Yo! Rap Revolution*, Lil Rodney Cee is credited with the invention of scratch, along with DJ Grand Wizards Theodore. (Cf. DUFRESNE, David: Yo! Rap Revolution, p. 20.)

Laurie Anderson (1976)

62. KELLER, Hans: Rap, in: SOUNDS, November 1981, p. 47f.

63. Ibid., p. 48.

what comes out is a choppy bass run. At the same time he might have turned up the bass of 'Heartbeat' and gives the whole thing a dub-like reverb, and the imagination is given free rein. There's no rapping, but the guy on the left says a few words in rhythm, commenting on what's happening.[62]

DJ Theodore belonged, after Flash, to the second generation of hip-hop DJs, and he too had pupils, after 1981, who embodied the third generation. Flash saw the passing on of knowledge – in the form of records, live deejaying and explanations – as part of his mission: 'I still teach kids who want to become DJs themselves. They look at me and ask, Flash, how do you do this and how do you do that.'[63]

Flash's masterpiece 'The Adventures of Grandmaster Flash on the Wheels of Steel' in 1981 was the primer for all later DJs. This record contained all the possibilities, finer points and refinements of mixing and scratching on vinyl. The 'Wheels of Steel' as the affectionate synonym for the turntables, which became instruments beneath the hands of the DJ. Flash's turntable jazz on the 'Adventures' was the first inventory of everything a DJ could do with his records and turntables. For *The Source* this record marks the birth of the DJ cut: 'In this [record], the first and probably the best of its kind, Flash wove musical snippets and spoken phrases into an enduring tapestry of sonic art.'[64]

To weave this sonic tapestry to complete perfection, Flash used a third turntable. While the drumbeats ran on the two turntables connected by the crossfader, on the third there was a record with which – according to Flash – 'the holes' could be filled in: 'It can be anything. I've got four records here, they're all shit, but I can use a particular twelve seconds from them, sometimes just a word, "Shoot", or "Pow", and stuff like that. Or I can take a comedy record as a background (like the extract from a Richard Pryor record on "Adventures"). Or a phone ringing, or a police siren. I mix that in.'[65]

So as not to lose sight of his material when mixing, Grandmaster Flash distributed his records among five boxes. The first box was for slow pieces like 'Heartbeat', the second box for semi-slow songs like 'Good Times', the third for medium-speed numbers like the ones by Kurtis Blow, and the fourth, finally, was for all faster pieces like Rick James' 'Give It to Me Baby'. The fifth box contained all kinds of special effects, above all Kraftwerk's 'Trans Europa Express', which were used as a break, a hole-filler or for disturbing effect. From these five boxes Flash was able to compose his pieces. And Flash worked on his music like a composer and performer. 'I study theories, I sleep and I dream about the things I want to do at the turntables. Then I get up the next day, try it out, try it and try it and record everything on tape. I give the tapes to my driver friends and the people I know who carry the radios around, and they play these tapes.'

With scratching and mixing the basic forms of deejaying had been invented. After this the mastery and refinement of these DJ techniques were developed to absolute perfection. For Flash this meant working on his show technique as well. For the DJ as star it was impossible to look good when mixing and scratching. Fab 5 Freddy told Hans Keller what acrobatic achievements Flash was capable of. 'Shit and he did it with his elbows, his feet, man, shit, and with his head, and the people stood there with their mouths hanging open. And then they went out, shit, and said, yo man, and he did it with his feet. And of course no one believed it. And the next Flash Party, it was full to

64. DENNIS, Reginald C.: 25 Old School Turning Points, in: THE SOURCE, 11/1993, p. 55.

65. KELLER, Hans, loc. cit., p. 47.

bursting, he cut with his feet, man, tell you, fucking unbelievable. He took off his shoes and socks and went to the record with his bare toes.'[66]

By the time Flash, Herc and Theodore had developed all the technical disciplines of deejaying (1977–79), no one could ignore the unexpected possibilities of this new music. The birth of rap music happened unnoticed,[67] wrote Jefferson Morley in 1992, stressing that hip-hop was originally a local affair: the culture of a few black districts of New York. The socially marginal position of the culture and its remoteness from the entertainment industry forced it to go its own way from the very beginning. As Herc and Flash often stressed, they hammered and soldered their first systems together themselves. Poverty forced them to make their own technology to measure. The saying about necessity being the mother of invention seems to have hit the mark in the origins of hip-hop. Like children on a scrapheap, they taught themselves about turntables, mixers and boxes. 'Break up plenty equipment to get what it was,' was how Flash summed up this experimental phase in 1993.

Flash, the only one of the original DJs to have had a training in electronics, invented the Beatbox: 'The beat box was an attempt to come up with something other than the techniques I created on the turntables to please the crowd.'[68] The basic DJ unit of turntable and mixer was extended by an analogue drum machine that had stored a few current rhythm patterns and repeated them endlessly – like a metronome – at the touch of a button. Flash had been shown the machine by a drummer friend, who used a drum machine as a control instrument for his sense of beat and precision. He bought it, connected it up to his system and called it a beatbox. 'The drummer taught me how to use it. When my partner Disco Bee would shut the music off, I would segue into it, so you couldn't tell where the music stopped and I started.'[69] For the first time, the beatbox took the DJ over the edge of his own turntable and into the sphere of playing music and free composition. The basis of his own creation was no longer his own record collection, but an electronically amplified beatbox that could 'beat' the transitions

66. Ibid.

67. MORLEY, Jefferson: Rap Music as American History, in: STANLEY, Lawrence A., loc. cit., p. xv.

68. GEORGE, Nelson: Hip-Hop's Founding Fathers..., loc. cit., p. 48.

69. Ibid.

between two songs. The beatbox was Flash's second important step towards making his own music. While the manipulation of records referred only to past musical history, the beatbox – even if it was restricted to a few rhythmical patterns – added his own, contemporary sound to the montage of 'old' pieces of music.

But towards the end of the 70s hip-hop was far from being taken seriously as a musical style. It was the interest of the B-Boys in the Bronx and in Harlem, and existed only at parties and on a few cassettes that were treated like gold dust in the ghetto. According to Afrika Bambaataa, the cassettes were actually the first hip-hop albums, and Grandmaster Flash emphasizes this: recording cassettes in those days was the same as making records is now: they were not just bought by many fans, but also – and the three DJs repeat the legend in the *Source* magazine interview – by taxi-drivers and chauffeurs who used them to persuade their clients to take longer journeys. 'How it worked was people would call for a car, and if they had a dope Herc tape, or a dope Bam tape, or a dope Flash tape, that particular customer might stay in the cab all day long. So these cab drivers were making extra money and at the same time they were advertising us.'[70]

Michael A. Gonzales, in his introduction to *Bring the Noise*, describes how hip-hop left its influence on Harlem in 1977. There were heavy beats everywhere, in the streets, in the parks and in the taxis. The tapes were treated like drugs:

Hiding out in front of Jose's, the local candy store/pinball arcade, with my homebody Darryl, both us just shootin' the breeze, a guy dressed in Lee jeans and unlaced black Pumas approaches us and says, 'Yo. You brothers interested in buyin' some music?"Darryl and I look at each other and smile. 'What kinda music?' I ask. Silently the brother glares as though searching for the right words to express himself. Then he mumbles, 'Check it B, I'm selling tapes of that new shit, that rap shit... know what I'm sayin', B? I got tapes of them brothers from the Bronx – ya know, Flash and Herc and Bambaataa? Even got some of them uptown niggas like Kurtis Blow and Spoonie G.'

70. Ibid.

The same way drug dealers whisper and gesture when attempting to make a sale, that's the way this brother was hawking tapes.[71]

Its remoteness from the record industry enabled hip-hop culture, free of any temptation to be marketed or to conform, to develop and mature in its own subcultural environment. 'New music,' the pioneer of electronic music, Karlheinz Stockhausen, declared in 1965, 'is actually less the consequence, the sonic result of the thoughts and emotions of modern composers, less the composer's self-expression (although it is that as well), and more a music that is, even to those who find it, who bring it into being, weird, new, unknown... The process of renewal is constant; an unpredictable process with the unknown comes to light thanks to a few creative people who have a sixth sense for where and how the unknown can be sensed; who haven't just made it their task to create something new, but to enable this to happen.'[72] From this point of view, hip-hop, as a new music, had a lot of time to 'happen'. DJs like Grandmaster Flash and Kool DJ Herc were given free and playful rein to allow the music to 'come into being'. Undiscovered by the rest of the world, hip-hop, rap, breakdancing and graffiti art existed only for their fans, from their beginnings in 1973 to 1979–80. During that period all the fundamental definitions of hip-hop culture were set out and promulgated within it. By the time rest of the world began to take an interest in the 'black new thing' from the Bronx and Harlem, it had already established and strengthened itself so much that this interest could take away nothing of its original power and intention. The culture of the 80s had thus discovered its sole authentic and, in this sense, un-postmodern position.

71. NELSON, Havelock/ GONZALES, Michael A.: Bring the Noise, p. xvii.

72. STOCKHAUSEN, Karlheinz: Elektronische Musik und Automatik, in: Texte zur Musik 1963–1970, p. 234.

AFRIKA BAMBAATAA AND THE ZULU NATION

In his own list of the most important moments in the history of hip-hop, Afrika Bambaataa puts himself in second place as inventor of the term hip-hop, after Herc, the inventor of the breakbeat.[73] There are good reasons for this self-appraisal. Apart from his musical and technical ideas, it was primarily down to Bambaataa that hip-hop won a political and social consciousness. Having grown up in the late 60s and been influenced by the actions and ideas of the Black Panther movement, even as a young boy Bambaataa was a member of the notorious gang 'The Black Spades', which engaged in bloody battles with rival bands. For Bambaataa the gang represented security and home. It was a substitute family for all the young people from broken homes in the ghetto. Black Spade members also learned how to survive on the street. The 60s saw the transition from the sense of 'being a nigger' to 'being Black and proud'. Like other young people who grew up during this period and experienced black nationalism as a liberation, Bambaataa also developed ideas of what a black community would look like, and how it might work.

Whipped up by excessive drug consumption and challenged by repressive local policies, gang violence escalated between 1968–73. Bambaataa often witnessed black-on-black violence.

In 1975, when he saw his friend Soulski mown down and killed by nine bullets he turned his back on the gangs.[74] Bambaataa was very interested in music even during his time with the gang, particularly early disco DJs like Pete Flowers and Kool DJ Jones. Then, the first time he heard Kool DJ Herc, another member of the Black Spades, mixing breakbeats, he was deeply impressed and started paying more attention to the new Bronx culture than to the gang. Other factors led to a cooling in his attitude towards gang-banging – the Lysistrata-like hatred women had for the violent lives of their men,[75] the frenzy of marauding cops who were allowed to turn their attention to gang members after they got back from Vietnam, and the many gang members dying from the consumption of hard drugs.

Bambaataa became increasingly fascinated by the idea of a well-organized black community, offering intellectual as well as social security. This longing prompted Bambaataa to become a member of the Nation of Islam. But Bambaataa wanted a form of

73 . Cf. SMALL, Michael, loc. cit., p. 218.

74 . One legend has it that Bambaataa takes the witness stand in the murder trial, hangs a copy of the death certificate in his room and leaves the gang. (Cf. DUFRESNE, David, loc. cit., p. 25.)

75 . This Lysistrata thesis is also put forward by Holman, a close friend of Bambaataa's (as he himself says) in his book about Hip-Hop: 'Realizing that the police were not useful in stopping the gang wars, the families and the girlfriends, who were desperate to see the senseless violence put to a halt, started taking action into their own hands. Through withholding of love, affection and a home life.' (HOLMAN, Michael, op.cit., p. 61.)

community other than the strictly organized Nation of Islam, and remembered a British film entitled *Zulu* with Michael Caine in the leading role, which he had seen as a child. In it the blacks were shown – 'for the first time', according to Bambaataa, not as bad guys but at courageous fighters defending their land against the British army. Since seeing this film, Bambaataa had had the desire to re-establish the Zulu Nation and become the chief of the organization. In his youth he took the name of Bambaataa, in memory of a 19th century Zulu chief. Bambaataa means something along the lines of 'benevolent leader'.[76] Despite the Civil Rights Movement, the Black Panthers and the Hippie Resistance, Bambaataa remained true to the idea of a Zulu Nation.[77]

While still in high school he founded a group which he called 'The Organization', and which turned into the 'Zulu Nation' in 1975. 12 November 1975[78] was the date of the 'First Annual Universal Zulu Tribute to James Brown, Sly and the Family Stone and the Pioneers of Hip-Hop'[79], which brought sudden fame to the Zulu Nation, at that time consisting of five breakdancers. The career of the 'longest-lasting institution of hip-hop' (George) was beginning. Twenty years later, the Zulu Nation had 'embassies' and 'consulates' in every large city in America, and in many countries in Europe, Asia and Africa. Many famous rappers, DJs and producers are members or sympathizers of the Zulu Nation, and Bambaataa is still its king and president. For white European and American intellectuals, the quasi-religious, quasi-mythical, quasi-political association[80] of young breakdancers and a DJ might look trivial or ridiculous. For inhabitants of black ghettos in the mid-70s it was the only chance to escape the vicious circle of domination by criminal gangs, without losing the protection and security of a group. Rather than shooting, beating, dealing and stealing, the young people danced, sprayed, scratched and rapped as 'gangs'. Criminal action made way for cultural actionism. The gangs no longer fought out their arguments with weapons, but in DJ or breakdance battles, at which Bambaataa and the Zulu Nation were often employed as security.

76. Ibid.

77. Cf. WICKE, Peter: Bigger than Life.

78. Both Dufresne (cf. DUFRESNE, David, loc. cit., p. 26) and George (cf. GEORGE, Nelson: Buppies..., loc. cit., p. 14) put the date of this first big public party a year later, in 1976.

79. SMALL, Michael, loc. cit., p. 218.

80. The Zulu Nation stands for 'Knowledge, Justice, Equality, Peace, Unity, Love, Respect, Work, Fun, Overcoming the negative to the positive, Economics, Mathematics, Science, Life, Truth, Facts, Faith and the Oneness of God.' (Cf. THE BELIEFS OF UNIVERSAL ZULU NATION, p. 49.)

81. Cf. PERKINS, William Eric: Nation of Islam Ideology in the Rap of Public Enemy, in: BLACK SACRED MUSIC 1/1991, p. 42.

Afrika Bambaataa in the 'Roxy' in New York

But the Zulu Nation, as an association of B-Boys, not only looked after and protected the emerging hip-hop culture, but also strengthened the new black nationalism, which was to influence the ideology of hip-hop and of many young blacks in the 80s. Linked with a revival of early forms of black radicalism and nationalism, they resumed a black tradition of rhythmical agit-pop which led via the griots, the 'rhythmic boasts' of Muhammad Ali and the 'message rap' of Gil Scott-Heron to the first rap pieces. Gil Scott-Heron tried to preserve the Black Power idea in the 'do your own thing' 70s.[81] Diedrich Diederichsen (a white intellectual) interprets black nationalism as a tribalistic attempt to assume power for oneself: 'It isn't this position that life in capitalism is only possible as an illness, but more of an attempt actually to overcome the illness and produce a healthy state. It has utopias, it knows universalisms, namely a universal black quality, a universal black nation. Despite or because of its necessarily particularist strategies in contemporary America.'[82] Afrika Bambaataa added this black utopia to the inheritance of hip-hop culture, and thus supplied one of the philosophical constants for many hip-hop artists and devotees. Hip-hop was, from the beginning, a medium of agitation for Black Nationalism.

Pop theorist Jeremy J. Beadle suggests that hip-hop was the equivalent to punk for black youth. The decline of the big urban factories in the late 50s and the 60s created a new class – the urban poor, people who were predominantly black and had been enticed to the cities by the promise of money. At the same time Martin Luther King and Malcolm X were teaching these blacks to fight for their civil rights. Beadle: 'At the precise moment they seemed to fall into a new poverty trap, the black community was learning about pride, about rights, about the denial of rights, and thus about justifiable anger. It was unlikely that any future black subculture would be particularly quiet or restrained.'[83] For Beadle, rap is from the very first a vehicle for hate, rage and frustration, and in the process the white left-wing pop intellectual entirely forgets that the beginnings of hip-hop have everything to do with the music, and little to do with rage. There is more a sense of pride in conjuring great music from old records, in redirecting violence of the gangs to something more positive. But where Beadle is right is that the clash between the claims of the Civil Rights Movement and progressive impoverishment was a great influence on young people. Afrika Bambaataa is a good illustration of this thesis. But even in Bambaataa, the driving forces were not hatred and rage, but the love of music and only secondarily an intellectual debate about the situation of black youth and the 'Black Nation' in general.

Typical of the central importance of the DJ in hip-hop is the fact that the most important philosophical hip-hop association was founded and run by a DJ. Afrika Bambaataa principally used his influence over a growing number of young blacks to give them a black historical awareness of their own and a world-view

82 . Quoted in DREYER, Michael; Hey hey, we are not the monkeys, loc. cit., p. 121.

83 . BEADLE, Jeremy J.: Will Pop Eat Itself? p. 77.

which seems in many ways extremely esoteric to a white materialist intellectual. To the present day, Bambaataa has remained an important ideologue and historian of hip-hop.

But Bambaataa also gave a crucial influence to young hip-hop culture as a DJ and musician. His love of music, not only black music, but any kind of music including classical, extended the spectrum of the hip-hop sound archive. When he was growing up he heard not only records on Motown and Stax by James Brown, Isaac Hayes and other Black musicians, but also Edith Piaf, Barbra Streisand, the Beatles, The Who and Led Zeppelin. A little later he started to take an interest in African music such as that of Miriam Makeba. Bambaataa was known for mixing the most absurd records into his sound collages, whether they were by the Monkees, the Rolling Stones or Grand Funk Railroad. In one of his first DJ battles he astonished everyone with his choice of music. The young Bambaataa had to appear against the renowned Disco King Mario, and it was his exotic collection of sounds that brought the Zulu King his eventual victory. Bambaataa opened his show with the signature tune of a television show that he had recorded on tape at home, and mixed the ditty with a hard drumbeat. After this came the signature tune of the television series *The Munsters*, and a transition to James Brown's 'I Got the Feeling'.[84] Four songs, three transitions and the young Bambaataa was respected as a grandmaster DJ.

Bambaataa turned looking for and buying records into regal disciplines. He listened to everything, without taboos and prejudices. His vast knowledge and his archive soon brought him the title 'master of records'.[85] The other DJs were so curious about where Bambaataa bought his records that they – including Grandmaster Flash disguised in dark glasses – followed him on Saturdays when he went shopping. The B-Boys would wait for Bambaataa in the record-shop to see what kind of records he would choose. Bambaataa: 'So I pulled some Hare Krishna records... It had beats but...'[86] The secretiveness about the records, every DJ's raw material, was taken so far that Flash started washing the labels off the records in the bathtub. And even then DJs like Bambaataa could still guess what the record

84. Cf. HAGER, Steven, loc. cit., p. 34.

85. Cf. TOOP, David: Rap Attack, p. 65. In *The Source* interview both Flash and Herc admit that Bambaataa's record collection was unbeatable. Herc: 'When I go to his party, I'm guaranteed to be entertained by some shit I don't hear other people play. Then I step to Mr. Bam, "What's that one?"' (GEORGE, Nelson: Hip-Hop's Founding Fathers..., loc. cit., p. 47.)

86. Ibid.

was: 'I had a way of telling things from the color of the album. I could know if it was Mercury or PolyGram.'[87]

THE MAN FROM HARLEM — DJ HOLLYWOOD

When the great DJs agreed on the basic lines of the history of hip-hop, a man turned up who became famous in the mid-70s and then disappeared into oblivion: DJ Hollywood. According to Fab 5 Freddy he was even the inventor of the word hip-hop,[88] but Herc, Bambaataa and Grandmaster Flash go monosyllabic when Nelson George reminds them of DJ Hollywood and his club 371. For Bambaataa, Hollywood wasn't a true rapper, because he was too disco-oriented. And when George claims that DJ Hollywood was the first hip-hop rapper, Flash answers with a curt 'No'.[89]

DJ Hollywood grew up in Harlem, not the Bronx, so he was only on the periphery of actual hip-hop culture. By his own account, DJ Hollywood started rapping in 1970, at the age of 14. 'One day I was just sitting around at home with my microphone and my guitar. I looked in the mirror and the radio was on. The DJ said, "Hi, here's WBLS and so on." He was rapping! And I thought, "Hey that's what you've been looking for all the time." I grabbed my microphone and just started: "Hi, I'm DJ Hollywood. Listen to this sound. And it's going on." It was short and simple sentences. Then I took it around little clubs in Harlem, taking the whole thing further.'[90] The music Hollywood rapped to was the sounds that disco music was growing out of at the same time: fast soul and funk songs. As early as 1973 DJ Hollywood started spinning records, mixing and rapping in the famous Charles Gallery disco. 'I rapped along with the audience. I said "partytime" and they said "anytime". It went back and forth like that.'[91] In the mid-70s he turned up at the 371 club in the Bronx and played records on Fridays and Saturdays. Those evenings were to establish his fame. For Kurtis Blow,

87. Ibid.

88. Cf. FAB 5 FREDDY, loc. cit., p. 32.

89. GEORGE, Nelson: Hip-Hop's Founding Fathers..., loc. cit., p. 48.

90. OSSI, Rapneck/ MOONDUST, Ziggie, Hip-Hop, p. 11.

91. Ibid.

Hollywood was 'the first king of rap'.[92] But for hip-hop purists – like David Toop – Kool DJ Herc remains the first 'real rapper'. Bambaataa doesn't even mention DJ Hollywood in his history of hip-hop.[93] Nelson George's 1980 article on 'rapping Deejays' presents DJ Hollywood as a charming entertainer who combined black (African-American) humour and the qualities of the true DJ with a keen ability to choose the latest dance hits. George had first seen him at a concert in Harlem in 1977, when Hollywood tapes were already being exchanged at high prices and the club evenings in 371 were legendary. His job was to fill the gaps between the sets of various bands as entertainingly as possible. But the DJ breaks gradually became the main attraction, and the headline bands became interludes for Hollywood's performances. The two thousand blacks and Hispanics gave him their full attention. 'With MFSB's "Sexy" grooving underneath him, Hollywood scat-rapped à la Eddie Jefferson. "Hip, hop de hip be de hop, de hip hop, hip de hop. On and on and on and on. Like hot butter on what...?"Hollywood then cut the music, leaving the crowded room to shout "Popcorn?" right on time. The huge college gym had become a gigantic disco, and people were dancing everywhere.'[94] DJ Hollywood was a populist, and a very successful one; but he only appears on the margins of hip-hop history.

WORDS TO THE BEAT: THE BEGINNING OF RAP

Rap existed long before rap music. As we have already shown, the playful and artistic use of language and words has a long tradition in African and African American culture.[95] The first rappers of the emerging hip-hop culture were 'co-workers' of the DJs. The first hip-hop DJ, however, rapped himself. Kool DJ Herc, who, as a Jamaican, took the toasting DJs as a model, hooked up a microphone to his mixing desk and, to breakbeats, praised himself, his sound system and whichever party that happened to be going on. His

92. Ibid.

93. Cf. SMALL, Michael, loc. cit., p. 218.

94. GEORGE, Nelson: Buppies..., loc. cit., p. 45.

95. Beadle points out that the spoken word also plays a major role in white pop music, with reference to examples by Elvis Presley, Al Jolson and Red Sovine. (Cf. BEADLE, Jeremy J., op. cit., p. 86f.)

penetrating voice attracted attention, loud though the music was. Herc rapped until he had a complete hold on his audience. But his rapping was merely an addition to what he was doing on the deck with vinyl and a mixing desk.

According to the three founding fathers of hip-hop, rap as an autonomous expression – in the context of the music, but no longer as an accessory to it – started with one of 'Herc's People', Coke La Rock, who simply chattered and talked while Herc mixed his records. Herc: 'Little phrases and words from the neighborhood that we used on the corner, is what we would use on the mic. Like we talking to a friend of ours out there in the crowd.'[96] The words, rhymes and stories were improvised to the music from the feeling.

Grandmaster Flash's posse, later to be members of the Furious Five, are seen as the first rappers who turned these words to music into words as music. 'They got into rhymin''[97] as Bambaataa loosely put it. Flash's friend Keith Wiggins, later known under the name of Cowboy, addressed the dancers directly and involved them in his rhymes. Flash: 'He'd say stuff like, "Throw your hands in the air. Wave 'em like you just don't care! If you like the sounds that are goin' down, somebody say Oh, yeah!" And he'd get a tremendous OH YEAH back, so I know this guy could help me.'[98] Other sayings were 'Clap to the beat!' or 'Somebody scream!'[99] Cowboy had a powerful voice that made the audience listen and shout along. Soon he was always there if Flash was playing records somewhere.

It is interesting that Flash saw the necessity of an MC as lying principally in the fact that the audience was so fascinated by the DJ's mixing and scratching virtuosity that they would stop dancing. 'The crowd would stop dancing and just gather round, as if it was a seminar. This wasn't what I wanted.'[100] Flash needed an entertainer who could turn his virtuosity as a DJ into dancing fun. But the challenges went beyond the work of a mere host. What was needed was an MC who not only knew the DJ music but really understood it. 'This person had to be able to talk with all the obscure scratching I was doing. I'm doing all this but I'm doing it all on time so you have to have an ear to really know. Even now, I might walk into a club and if I'm cutting

96. GEORGE, Nelson: Hip-Hop's Founding Fathers..., loc. cit., p. 48.

97. Ibid.

98. NOBLE, Peter L.; Future Pop, p. 44.

99. GEORGE, Nelson: Hip-Hop's Founding Fathers..., loc. cit., p. 48.

100. TOOP, David: Rap Attack, p. 72.

and keeping it going they rap, but if I stop on time to the beat they get lost. There's some that can't really catch on to it when the music's being phased in and out to the beat.'[101] Cowboy could do all that, and brilliantly. Cowboy invented dozens of sayings to praise Grandmaster Flash and make the music more accessible. The talk fulfilled its purpose and volubly distracted from the DJ's virtuosity, while hymnically transfiguring it.

Apart from the party-maker Cowboy, Kid Creole and his brother Melle Mel soon joined the posse around Grandmaster Flash. These two 'were the first to really flow and have a poetic feel to their rhymes. They were the first rhyme technicians. They were the first to toss a sentence back and forth.'[102] Mel and Creole soon developed a rap style of their own and introduced lengthy vocal passages which were then performed to the breakbeats of Grandmaster Flash. Apart from rap passages there were also song and choral elements. The MCs started to assume the profile of stars alongside the DJs. This new confidence was also reflected in their lyrics, as in 'Supperrappin'' by Grandmaster Flash & the Furious Five:

M.C.s, disc jockeys to all the fly kids and the young ladies
Introducin' the crew ya got to see to believe
We're one, two, three, four, five M.C.s
I'm Melle Mel and I rock so well
And I'm Mr Ness because I rock the best
Rahiem in all the ladies dreams
And I'm Cowboy to make ya jump for joy
I'm Creole – solid gold
The Kid Creole playin' the role
Dig this

We're the Furious Five plus Grandmaster Flash
Givin' you a blast and sho' 'nuff glass
So to prove to ya all that we're second to none
We're gonna make five M.C.s sound like one
...
We're five M.C.s and we're on our own
And we're the most well known on the microphone
And we throw down hard and we aim to please

101. Ibid.

102. GEORGE, Nelson: Hip-Hop's Founding Fathers..., p. 48.

With finesse to impress all the young ladies
We got rhymes galore and that's a fact
And if the satisfaction's guaranteed
to cause a heart attack
We are the best as you can see
So eliminate the possibility
That to be an E-M-C-E-E
Is not a threat to society
...
To the hip hop, hip hop, don't stop,
don't stop that body rock
Just get with the beat, get ready to clap
Because Melle Mel is startin' here to rap
Ever since the time at my very first party
I felt I could make myself somebody
It was something in my heart from the very start
I could see myself at the top of the charts
Rappin' on the mike, makin' cold cold cash
With a jock spinnin' for me called DJ Flash.[103]

103 . GRANDMASTER FLASH and the FURIOUS FIVE: Superrappin', in: STANLEY, Lawrence A., op. cit., p. 145–148.

For Steven Hager 1978 was the year in which the emphasis was shifted within hip-hop music from the DJ to the MC. Where young people had previously revered the DJ as a hero, rappers now became the new idols. The DJ had invented hip-hop music, but the rappers and MCs contoured the flow of the breakbeats into a classic song structure with vocal passages, refrains and themes that made the abstract music more accessible and comprehensible.

Despite the shift in popularity and growing disagreements over the gap in income between DJs and MCs, the rapper respected the DJ. In 'Superrappin' Grandmaster Flash is praised:

Clean out your ears then open your eyes
And then pay at the door as a donation
To hear the best sound in creation
He's a disco dream of a mean machine
And when it comes to size, ya see what we mean

Ya see his name is not found in the hall of fame
but he'll shock
And amaze ya and make ya feel shame
He takes a lime from a lemon

From a lemon to lime
He cuts the beat in half the time
And as sure as three times two is six
Ya say Flash is the King of the quick mix[104]

But these genuflections of MCs to DJs could not conceal the fact that after 1978–9 hip-hop was mostly rap music, which was dominated by the MCs rather than the innovative thrusts of the DJs. This may also be one of the reasons why hip-hop fell into such serious doldrums in the mid-80s that many people thought it would never survive. Extraordinary things were achieved during the regency of the MCs, however, you just have to listen more closely to the rhymes and lyrics.

WORD UP – WHAT CAN LANGUAGE DO FOR THE DJ?

'Word' in African-American slang is an interjection, an exclamation and interpolation that is supposed to express absolute agreement.[105] 'Word' thus becomes a synonym for truth. The truth lies in the 'word'. The agreement is perfect if the other party is taken at his word, and one can agree completely with that same word – meaning: that speech. The truth comes into being every time the exclamation 'word' announces a consensus between the communicating parties. At hip-hop concerts these are moments of the greatest unity and euphoria, when the DJ raps and the audience agrees with 'word' or 'word up'.

In order for language as speech to become so capable of consensus and truth, all the hegemonies of the dominant discourse must be excluded. This exclusion is the central motif of African-American verbal art, which is primarily not a written but an oral culture. The battle against the ruling signifiers, as Lacan would put it, occurs in a displaced form because blacks have never acknowledged white language and thus the white 'masters', but have always felt alien within the ruling symbolic order.

104. Ibid. p. 146.

105. Cf. MAJOR, Clarence, op. cit., p. 514.

'The word [is the] ideological sign par excellence'[106] wrote Volosinov in the first Marxist theory of language to abandon the 'mechanistic causality' of reflection theory. Hitherto, Marxist semiotics and linguistics was still 'in the stage of pre-dialectical, mechanistic materialism'.[107] The sign and, above all, the ideological sign par excellence, the word, becomes 'an arena of the class struggle'.[108]

Class struggle is an old phrase and itself an ideological sign that seems almost to have vanished. It can no longer be used innocently today. The classes are still at war, but the class struggle has turned into small, particularist scuffles between social factions and minorities. Language in pop music, particularly in rap, is the product of those conflicts and must be examined for the traces of them. 'Real rap comes from the soul and the mind, from the inner self',[109] explained Chuck D. of Public Enemy, meaning above all the consciousness of the black minority in America, which first wrote itself into the wider public consciousness of white-run America with rap. Because of rap music's dissemination throughout the media, rap has endangered the linguistic supremacy of white America. One characteristic of verbal violence by the ruling class is the attempt – according to Volosinov – 'to impart a supraclass, eternal character to the ideological sign, to extinguish or drive inward the struggle between social value judgments which occurs in it, to make the sign uniaccentual'.[110] The black use of language seeks from the start to undermine that eternal character and set language vibrating. Black 'signifying' tries to rescue language from the unambiguity of white dominance and throw words into a new context to see what survives. Signifying is play and at the same time self-assertion, creating self-confidence through the gaining of one's own language. The Signifying Monkey is a 'folk figure' (Diederichsen) and appears in a myth representing the foreignness of the black person in the white linguistic body of 'English'. The copying monkey using linguistic distortions, repetitions and wordplay, ignores the meaning of the words and uses the signifiers of the words as play material. This produces – according to Diederichsen – a speech 'of strangeness, division and fissure', whose subjects 'precisely don't

106. VOLOSINOV, Valentin N.: Marxism and the Philosophy of Language, p. 9.

107. Ibid. p. 1.

108. Ibid. p. 23.

109. SMALL, Michael, op. cit., p. 41.

110. VOLOSINOV, Valentin N.: op. cit., p. 23.

mean what they say'.[111] That strangeness has given rise to a lively verbal culture, which has ensured itself independence and autonomy with a form of semantic dissidence.

The black cultural critic Greg Tate, in the context of a discussion of black linguistic theory (under the title 'Yo! Hermeneutics!') makes the ironic observation that typically black verbal distortion is a sign that the blacks are not primitivists (as whites assume), but born deconstructionists.[112] Lest black language be mystified any further, Tate dreams of a clever theorist who could bring all the studies and considerations of black talk together in a theory. 'Yo Greg, black people need our own Roland Barthes, man. Black Deconstruction in America? I'm way ahead of the brother, or so I think when I tell him about my dream magazine: "I signify – the Journal of Afro-American Semiotics".'[113]

In 'Rap Attack' David Toop has told a story of black verbal distortion and verbal creation in pop music. Hip-hop brings the poetry of the street and the poetry of pop music back together and gives it a new, concentrated power. Without a true understanding of this verbal practice misunderstandings are inevitable. Ice T traces the greatest misinterpretations of rap back to the incomprehensibility of 'shit talkin''. Rap is the art of shit talkin'. For Ice T, shit talkin' is found 'in the ghetto talk and machismo, even in the basic body language'.[114] The history of rap as shit talkin' extends from the Stagolee stories[115] to the writings of H. Rap Brown, the former justice minister of the Black Panthers. Taken together these raps are 'nothing more than straight-up black bravado'.[116] As a typical example of this macho, heterosexual bragging, Ice T suggests the saying 'I'll take my dick and wrap it around this room three times and fuck yo' mama'. That the man could not wrap his member three times around the room is just as obvious as the fact that he cannot be especially interested in sleeping with the mother of the man he is rapping to. But that is irrelevant: 'It's a black thang. It's machismo. It doesn't mean anything.'[117]

Ice T is amazed by feminist criticism of raps. For him the exaggerations, and in hip-hop they are incredible, are indications that shit talkin' is not the same thing as the traditional (white) way of using language. Among

111. DIEDERICHSEN, Diedrich: Schwarze Musik und weisse Hörer, in: Freiheit macht arm, p. 75.

112. Cf. TATE, Greg: Yo! Hermeneutics!, in: Flyboy in the Buttermilk, p. 147.

113. Ibid. p. 145.

114. ICE T: The Ice Opinion, p. 94.

115. One story from the Stagolee myth occurs in Greil Marcus' article on Sly Stone in 'Mystery Train'. (MARCUS, Greil: Mystery Train, pp. 86–122.)

116. ICE T, op. cit., p. 94.

117. Ibid.

non-ghetto-dwellers unfamiliar with referential semantics, shit talkin' must be understood as an artificial language. On no account must it be taken seriously in the literal sense (of those unfamiliar with the codes).

Insistence on the meanings that were fixed in the ruling symbolic order, in the 'reading' and understanding of Afro-American slang, itself constitutes an imperial act. Black talk is language that lives and is not fixed in any way influenced by writing. For Volosinov the existence of language is constituted above all in dialogue: 'The word is oriented toward an addressee, toward who that addressee might be: a fellow-member or not of the same social group... Each person's inner world and thought has its stabilized social audience...'[118] The reality and thus also the meaning of language is always determined by communication. Understanding is dialogical. 'The immediate social situation and its immediate social participants determine the "occasional" form and style of an utterance'.[119] And that is precisely what Ice T means when he refers to the particularity of shit talkin'. 'Rapping is just something you pick up growing up in the ghetto. I knew how to write rhymes, because I used to recite rhymes for the gangs.'[120]

The response to the apparently misogynist expressions of rapping men can only come from rapping women. Then female strength is set against machismo. 'Shit talkin' doesn't piss off ghetto women, 'cause anything I can issue to a ghetto girl she's got an answer for. They'll answer all the shit we talk with a "Fuck you, Ice". And that's it. They don't say "You're sexist". They respond with their own rap.'[121] All other observations on shit talkin' involuntarily become shit talkin' in their own right.

Signifying is work on language as a living organism. Oppression through language is relativized in play with language. The true reality of language as speech is – according to Volosinov – 'the social event of verbal interaction implemented in an utterance or utterances. Thus, verbal interaction is the basic reality of language.' In a writing-centred culture such as that which predominates in the First World, this is easily forgotten. If it is ignored in the interpretation of rap lyrics, what one ends up with (as in most

118. VOLOSINOV, V.N., op. cit., p. 86.

119. Ibid. p. 87.

120. ICE T, op. cit., p. 95.

121. Ibid. p. 105.

interpretations) is only a dub version of one's own thoughts. Minority languages are not simply sub-languages, idiolects or dialects, Gilles Deleuze explains, 'but a potential means to take the majority language and make it minority with all its dimensions and elements'.[122] The example that Deleuze uses is the Afro-American treatment of the English linguistic body.

Black verbal mastery is aimed against the language of the rulers. In 'Fight the Power' Public Enemy programmatically declared their rhymes the arena of a minority struggle:

122 . DELEUZE, Gilles: Philosophie und Minderheit, in: idem: Kleine Schriften, p. 29.

123 . PUBLIC ENEMY: Fight the Power, in: STANLEY, Lawrence A., op. cit., p. 258f.

124 . VOLOSINOV, V.N, op. cit., p. 23.

As the rhythm's designed to bounce
What count's is that the rhyme's
Designed to fill your mind
Now that you've realized the pride's arrived
We got to pump the stuff to make us tough
From the heart
It's a star, a work of art
To revolutionize, make a change, nothin' strange[123]

Language is used by both sides. By the rulers as a means of ruling, by the oppressed as a means of rejection. Every ideological sign, even and especially the word, has two faces. For Marx there were two separate class languages. Volosinov sees only one language, and it presents itself as ambivalent in its practical use. 'Any current curse word can become a word of praise, any current truth must inevitably sound to many other people as the greatest lie. This inner dialectic quality of the sign comes out fully in the open only in times of social crises or revolutionary changes.'[124] The overwhelming majority of rap rhymes are the expression of a social crisis. In rap, the fracture of being in the word has become an aesthetic. Signifying is the expression of enjoyment in that fracture. The social contract concerning the unity of language and its use is heralded in an act of creative self-assertion. The black speech act sees itself as autonomous. Verbal force is, like physical force, a source of pride. In one of the first rap songs, 'Rapper's Delight' by the Sugar Hill Gang, this is made clear:

Ice T

So when the sucker M.C.s try to chump my style
I let them know that I'm versatile
I got style, finesse, and a little black book
That's filled with rhymes and I know yo wonna look
But the thing that separates you from me
And that's called originality[125]

Breaking becomes a creative act and the expression of creativity. By virtue of the fact that rap rhymes must function in a rhythmical context, they move even further away from the old (ruling) contexts of language. Language becomes irregularly heterogeneous and thus difficult to master. Burroughs saw language as an extraterrestrial virus. Signifying, on the other hand, considers it its task to set language alight with double and multiple meanings, and weaken it as a unified system of power. This use of language as a destroyer of imperial unambiguities is only a transitional stage.

Black verbal poetry now seeks a new unity: a unified language of black power. Rap. Rap is both a witness and a main activist of that transition from signifying to truth-telling, as undertaken by the new black historiography. KRS One is the head of the hip-hop band BoogieDown Productions and, along with Bambaataa and Public Enemy, he is one of the advanced thinkers of black consciousness. Like many rappers he also feels the power to utter truths:

So all the racist codes I'll decode, explode...
My words are subliminal
Sometimes metaphysical
I teach, not preach...
rap needed a teacher, so I became it
Rough and ready, the beats are very steady
With lyrics sharp as a machete[126]

KRS One sees himself not only as a 'rap missionary', as a 'walking dictionary' or as 'truly legendary', but as a 'black revolutionary'[127] who embodies the intellectual avant-garde of black resistance. Rap is art and politics, the coup's first front line is language. Truth-telling as the first step to a new world.

125. SUGAR HILL GANG: Rapper's Delight, in: STANLEY, Lawrence A., op. cit., p. 325.

126. BOOGIEDOWN PRODUCTIONS: House Niggas, in: STANLEY, Lawrence A., op. cit., p. 38ff.

127. Cf. Ibid. p. 38.

THE ROAD TO SUCCESS

Until 1979 hip-hop was a local phenomenon that existed in two New York ghettos unnoticed by the rest of the world. Over a period of five years, without contacts with the culture industry, an autonomous subculture had developed with its own aesthetic, its own style and its own infrastructure. The marginalized profited from their socially marginal status, which achieved an organic, authentic development of the subculture. When the first tapes left the ghetto, quasi-idyllic isolation was shattered. Young hip-hop culture went out into the world.

In leaving its supportive environment, hip-hop culture lost its autonomy over its own aesthetic and production. All of a sudden other rules came into play. The hegemonic culture and the entertainment industry used their own rules to define their own form of rap music, without taking any interest in an authentic documentation of its culture of origin.

Co-option as fake began in hip-hop with the first record. Until 1979 rap and breakbeat music were only ever played live as party or concert music, or in the form of tape recordings. Of course, in a city like New York a cultural explosion in one part of the city could not remain undiscovered indefinitely. But it was still surprising that a declining funk band called the Fatback Band should have brought out the first rap record of all time. On the B-side of their single 'You're My Candy Sweet' was a rap with the title 'King Tim III (Personality Jock)'. The rapper, like the band, was not a part of the original hip-hop culture. After the band had heard DJ Hollywood rapping in a concert in the Apollo it had gone in search of an artist who was even moderately capable of reproducing that kind of rhythmical verbal agility in the studio for their latest record, and ended up with the conférencier King Tim III. On vinyl this copy of the original sounded like just that, a copy of the original. David Toop sees the first rap on vinyl as a stilted mixture of the raps of the radio DJs and the first party MCs, garnished with a few tired B-Boy expressions,[128] for Nelson George 'King Tim III' is nothing but an enormous 'goof'.[129] By no means was

128. TOOP, David: Rap Attack, p. 82.

129. GEORGE, Nelson: Buppies..., p. 16.

'King Tim III' a successful recording debut for a new music. But this failure was to be the first succès d'estime for rap music: the record shops in New York turned the B-side into the A-side, and both the single and the subsequent album by the Fatback Band sold well.

Hardly had hip-hop left the ghetto than the music lost its innocence. The Sugar Hill Gang was assembled specifically for the making of the record 'Rapper's Delight', and was a synthetic construction of random rappers and part-time B-Boys. They were brought together by Sylvia Robinson, who owned a number of small record labels, and who had herself enjoyed a succès d'estime in the 60s as a starlet with a little soul rap. The All Platinum label was Sylvia Robinson's most important label, featuring a varied mixture of black music from soul and funk via disco to all kinds of bizarre singing artists. Its success was average, and there was nothing to indicate that things were going to change so quickly.

According to legend, Sylvia Robinson discovered rap music either through her children[130] or by visiting the Harlem World Disco. In Toop's *Rap Attack* Lil Rodney Cee, a member of the rap band Double Trouble, tells his own version, in which cassettes circulated via relations in New York to the inhabitants of New Jersey and finally to Mrs Robinson. It was her children who brought her the tapes and thus gave her some insight into the wild activity going on in the Bronx. Her children's enthusiasm made her sense business, and she decided to make a record. Just as illustrious is the story of how she put together what was to be the Sugar Hill Gang. She first discovered a rapping doorman in a pizzeria, and then she hired a friend of her eldest son. A third rapper sold himself to Mrs Robinson and became a Gang member.[131] In tandem with the foundation of the Sugar Hill Gang came the foundation of the Sugar Hill label, which became the first rap label. Thanks to the catchy bass-line of Chic's 'Good Times' and a clever copy of the Bronx rappers, 'Rapper's Delight' sounded incredibly good. But it had no 'street credibility'[132] among the B-Boys, since they knew that their rhymes[133] had been stolen from elsewhere: 'To the hip hip hop, and you don't stop to rock/ To the bang bang boogie, say up jumped the

130. Cf. DUFRESNE, David, op. cit., p. 21, and TOOP, David: Rap Attack, p. 80.

131. Cf. TOOP, David: Rap Attack, p. 80f.

132. Cf. NELSON, Havelock/ GONZALES, Michael A., op. cit., p. xviii.

133. And this when using lines like: 'But the thing that separates you from me/ And that's called originality'. (SUGAR HILL GANG: Rapper's Delight, in: STANLEY, Lawrence A., op. cit., p. 325.)

134. Ibid. p. 318.

135. HAGER, Steven, op. cit., p. 49f.

136. Ibid. p. 49.

137. GEORGE, Nelson: Hip-Hop's Founding Fathers..., loc. cit., p. 49f.

138. Ibid. p. 49.

139. Bambaataa considered it particularly unpleasant that Hank Grandmaster Caz never got a 'credit' for his rhymes. (Cf. Ibid.)

140. Cf. BEADLE, Jeremy J., loc. cit., p. 86.

boogie/ To the rhythm of the boogie, the beat.'[134] All of these rhymes came from the repertoire of the real old school MCs, from the Cold Crush Brothers, DJ Hollywood or the Furious Five. Grandmaster Caz of the Cold Crush Brothers felt particularly betrayed. Hank, the man who was supposedly discovered in the pizzeria, wasn't playing his own tapes in that pizzeria, but those of Caz and his posse. 'Later, I asked him, "Whatsup?", and he said, "Sylvia already has two rappers and she wants one more. And she asked me to do it." So I said, "Well, okay, I understand that." If it was me I would have done the same thing. And he said,"Well, I want to use some of your rhymes."I threw my rhyme book on the table and said, "Take what you want".'[135] Which is what Hank and the Sugar Hill Gang did, without giving any credit or even paying a royalty to Caz. In the hip-hop communities of the Bronx everyone knew that 'Rapper's Delight' was a fake, and that the Sugar Hill Gang was not a real rap gang. Caz: 'When the record came out, I was going to high school at Roosevelt and every car had it on the radio. Every box on the street had it on. Everybody knew those rhymes were mine and half were coming up to me, "Yo, I heard you on the radio!" the other half was saying, "You're not getting' no money for that!"'[136] Kool DJ Herc ('I didn't really appreciate that Hank knew me personally... I was mad when Sugar Hill came first and did their thing'[137]), Grandmaster Flash ('Who is this?'[138]) and Afrika Bambaataa[139] considered the first rap hit a swindle.

Nothing about 'Rapper's Delight' was the expression of original artistic work. The song was the synthesis of many original set pieces for a quickly produced record. Sylvia Robinson got exactly what she wanted: a rap song that had nothing to do with the real ghetto rappers. For Jeremy J. Beadle the apolitical song embodies only one element of hip-hop culture: '"Rapper's Delight" had a surplus of arrogant egos.'[140] The assessments of rap experts are harsh, and, in the face of an obvious swindle, understandable. But anyone who hears the record now has to acknowledge how well produced it is, and how 'catchy' the hook sounds. Russell Simmons, the most important rap manager today, explains in retrospect that at the time everyone was annoyed by the song, but that afterwards they had to admit how much the record did to help subsequent hip-hop acts. All of a sudden all the doors were open.[141] If 'Rapper's Delight' had been as bad as 'King Tim III', it might have been a long time before many non-Bronx-dwellers found their way to rap.

A con or a breakthrough for hip-hop culture? A moral line is hard to calculate where works of art are concerned. The moral of pop is: be young, strong, handsome, clever and above all successful. Just as important as the beaming face of pop are sales figures and the popularity that goes with them. Anyone who enters the pop world must be able to cope with success and remain incorruptible whatever temptations come his way. Wonder Mike of the Sugar Hill Gang admits that he didn't want to sound like the New York rappers: 'My rap is unlike anything that came before. It is clearer and softer. Many people say I had a white voice.'[142] A remarkable statement for a black MC, and one that makes it clear just how far the Sugar Hill Gang were from the birth of hip-hop.

It remains plain that this record bears the historical burden of standing at the beginning of the biggest musical and social revolution since rock'n'roll,[143] as Reginald C. Dennis remarked when he put 'Rapper's Delight' at number one in his list of the 25 most important old school records. 'Rapper's Delight' was a huge hit, and sold over two million. The marketing mills of the pop industry started grinding. Young people throughout the world seemed to have been waiting for this sound, and the market needed feeding. Hip-hop became part of pop culture. Its isolation from the rest of the world had been broken, the shield of marginality was lost and the future in the confusion of interests in the music industry was uncertain.

Hip-hop was in the world, and the world was interested. Soon other rap records were being thrown into the market. Spoonie Gee's 'Spoonin' Rap' followed immediately from 'Rapper's Delight'. Spoonie Gee was the nephew of the famous R&B producer Bobby Robinson (no relation of Sylvia), who had a small record company called 'Enjoy'. After the success of the Sugar Hill Gang, Robinson decided to put together a rap song pretty quickly: 'When I saw the success of The

141. Cf. GEORGE, Nelson: Buppies..., loc. cit., p. 39.

142. OSSI, Rapneck/ MOONDUST, Ziggie, loc. cit., p. 39.

143. Cf. DENNIS, Reginald C., loc. cit., p. 54.

Sugarhill Gang and how crazy people went over this record, I said, well, I can't wait to get into my regular line of things. I'm gonna jump on this rap thing.'[144] Actually Spoonie Gee was part of the rap band Treacherous Three, along with L.A. Sunshine and the future superstar Kool Moe Dee. But as in the earlier records, the authentic artistic texture was destroyed for the record production. Kool Moe Dee relates how that depressed the rest of the band: 'We asked Spoonie, "Why didn't you take us down to the studio with you?"He said, "I didn't think it was no big thing."'[145] MCs and DJs jostled for contracts with the record companies. The success had shown that money and fame could be had from the 'cool thang rap', a reward that was at first denied the inventors of hip-hop. Kool DJ Herc never returned to his former supremacy and fame after being stabbed at a party, and Bambaataa and Flash had to watch late-comers and imitators overtaking him and getting famous.

Grandmaster Flash himself had had the chance to be the first hip-hop artist on record. As early as 1977 a record company representative offered to press his breakbeat mixes together with the raps of the Furious Five on vinyl, but Flash refused. 'I would have to admit that I was blind. I didn't think that somebody else would want to hear a record re-recorded onto another record with talking on it. I didn't think it would reach the masses like that. I didn't see it.'[146] Two years later, after the success of the Sugar Hill Gang, Grandmaster could clearly see how wrong he had been. When Bobby Robinson came to him after a party where Flash had been deejaying, and asked if he wanted to make a record with him, he agreed. Flash and the Furious Five went into the studio and were well paid for it. But the DJ wasn't sure whether the move from making parties to making records was the right one.

I'd have to say, I wasn't ready. I was content with what I was doing. I think what happened was when Herc stopped playing eight hours a night, Flash stopped playing, Bam stopped playing, the street thing flipped. Like one DJ would play eight different clubs in one night and not really have an audience anymore. You lost your home champion because there was nobody

144. TOOP, David: Rap Attack, p. 83.

145. HAGER, Steven, loc. cit., p. 55.

146. GEORGE, Nelson: Hip-Hop's Founding Fathers..., p. 49.

there. I would have personally liked to stay away from records a little longer. Not to say that I wouldn't want to make records 'cause records was the next plateau for spreading the musical word.[147]

Bambaataa and Herc also felt the radical change in the hip-hop environment. The parties were no longer so well attended, and instead anyone could buy records featuring the music that had previously been only available live.

The endurance test 'that would separate the men from the boys as far as the DJ was concerned',[148] had always been playing records at block parties that could last up to twelve hours. All of a sudden DJs were making careers for themselves without knowing anything about this foundation of hip-hop and without cutting their teeth in the Bronx. The hardest hit was Kool DJ Herc, who became a drug addict in the 80s and earned his money on building-sites, while the rising generation earned millions with rap.[149] When rap was pressed on vinyl for the first time, Herc was simply too content with his work as a DJ to worry about record production. 'My thing was just playin' music and giving parties. I wasn't interested in making no records.'[150]

147. Ibid. p. 50.

148. Ibid.

149. Cf. OWEN, Frank, loc. cit.

150. GEORGE, Nelson: Hip-Hop's Founding Fathers..., loc. cit., p. 50.

HIP-HOP TURNS INTO POP (I): THE BLACK WILL TO POWER

Russell Simmons doesn't come from the ghetto. His father was a schools inspector who taught black history in his free time, his mother was a city employee. Simmons grew up in Hollis, a middle-class area in Queens. He went to a good school and in the mid-70s started studying sociology. But like many middle-class children, Simmons was excited by the hard, raw, rebel culture of the ghetto. Even during his student days he and his friend Curtis Walker organized parties in Harlem that gave the young people there their first access to hip-hop. Walker, like Simmons, studied at the City College of New York, and worked nights as a DJ

151. GEORGE, Nelson:
Buppies..., p. 58.

152. Cf. BECKMAN, Janette/
ADLER, B., loc. cit., p. 21.

Russell Simmons

and MC. At some point Kool DJ Kurt became Kurtis Blow and his friend Russell Simmons his first manager. In 1977 Simmons and Walker alias Kurtis Blow organized rap shows in the Hotel Diplomat in Manhattan's Midtown, making hip-hop accessible to people outside the ghetto. When Kurtis Blow appeared with Grandmaster Flash, 15,000 flyers were distributed, and more than two thousand B-Boys came to the show. After that Simmons and Blow had a name in the hip-hop community, and their parties were major events in the emerging hip-hop scene. Simmons' talent for organization and his abilities to deal with representatives of the subculture as well as outsiders made him the first manager of hip-hop. Like other managers he was interested in the money, but he also had, as his friend Nelson George wrote, 'a love of music, at least his particular brand of it, that is real'.[151] With the emergence of Black Teenage Music, as Simmons called rap, he was there from the start – at any rate before people really considered working with rap musicians.

The situation changed rapidly in 1979, with the first rap records. Rap shows were now attended by up to 4,000 teenagers. Simmons sensed that this new music needed a manager who was devoted to it, so he started to put together the tools that a beginner – or one with a black skin – needed to survive in the white-dominated music industry. Kurtis Blow became the 'King of Rap' and, in line with the market, the two friends put out a 'Christmas Rap' in December 1979. At the same time Kurtis Blow became the first rapper to have a contract with a major record company, Mercury.[152] Blow abandoned deejaying in favour of rapping and became one of the first superstars of rap. This success encouraged Simmons, who started to promote and manage other rap acts as well: including Whodini, Dr. Jeckyl and Mr. Hyde and Run DMC, featuring Simmon's younger brother Joseph as a rapper. He assumed responsibility for helping a young culture, and one still in need of assistance, out of the economic ghetto and into the culture industry, to bring them affluence and good conditions of production and protect them against conformity and exploitation. Simmons was in his early twenties and so keen on his work that he often slept in record studios.

This enthusiasm was the big difference from Sylvia Robinson of the Sugar Hill label and Bobby Robinson of the Enjoy label. Russell Simmons was part of the hip-hop culture, and became its marketer and developer not for strategic considerations, but because Simmons saw himself as part of the new music and wanted to do something for it. And that remains the case today.

In 1984 the *Wall Street Journal* hailed the 26-year-old as the 'mogul of rap'.[153] At this point Simmons had founded the legendary label Def Jam with Jewish philosophy student Rick Rubin. The Beastie Boys, LL Cool J, Public Enemy and Slick Rick were only some of the artists that turned Def Jam into one of the most important and progressive record labels of the 80s.

Def Jam produced soundtracks for films like *Less than Zero* and *Krush Groove*, and its two founders were co-producers of the rap film *Tougher than Leather*. Although Simmons and Rubin parted company in 1987, and Simmons went on running the label on his own, the early years of Def Jam were an important step in the sucess of hip-hop as rebellious teenage music: 'I want to make successful black heroes, like what I've tried to do with Run DMC and Kurtis, I didn't say "positive" because that's a trap. It's got to be real.'[154]

This understanding of hip-hop made Simmons one of the few valued and revered representatives of the record industry. Mike D of the Beastie Boys called him 'the type of guy who isn't afraid to do the ill shit',[155] and Ice T presented Simmons (and himself) as one of the positive role models for black youth, who made it clear that you can be successful as a black man even if you're non-conformist and powerless: 'Regardless of what you got to do, you can still be a homeboy. That's why I still look like them and run this company. Russell Simmons doesn't need to put on a suit and tie to run Def Jam. He's another brother who's out there setting an example for these kids.'[156]

Fab 5 Freddy, born Fred Brathwaite, was in there at the beginning like Russell Simmons. Having grown up in Brooklyn, he had been influenced in his youth by DJs like Frankie D., Master D., Pete Jones and Grandmaster Flowers. Fab 5 Freddy spent his summers

153. Quoted in: Ibid. p. 25.

154. GEORGE, Nelson: Buppies..., loc. cit., p. 56.

155. MIKE D.: Yo, Wuss Thup? – An Impromptu Car Phone Conversation With Russell Simmons, in: GRAND ROYAL, Autumn/Winter 1993, p. 4.

156. ICE T, loc. cit., p. 16.

in the parks near the turntables. 'I used to follow these guys... I got the bug and was real curious when I saw those turntable techniques go down. I used to be one of those kids at a jam who used to stand in front of the DJ all the time. I would party a little bit, but I was more like, Damn, what is going on with the DJ? You know, like what's that record that he's playing? Or why does it sound like that? Or how come I ain't hearing this record nowhere else in my life? I used to ask them, and they would say, "Yo, it's the Uptown sound!"'[157] Fab 5 Freddy was a graffiti artist and, like all the other sprayers, he had a big collection of tapes by Grandmaster Flash.

The DJs' techniques had a lasting influence on the sprayers. Watching the DJs, Fab 5 Freddy saw the extent to which good art could inspire the masses and spread euphoria. Graffiti had to be part of this new black ghetto culture. 'Although my paintings were influenced by the way the music felt, I wanted to introduce the works as part of a complete culture because, I felt, they would have a bigger influence on people that way.'[158]

Fab 5 Freddy, who, like all graffiti artists, started out by spraying walls and subway trains, soon slipped into the chic Manhattan art scene. Along with artists like Jean-Michel Basquiat, Keith Haring, Futura and Zephyr, he was discovered by the downtown galleries and presented to the art public. His paintings were shown in museums and galleries around the world. Apart from Jean-Michel Basquiat he was the only black who made the leap into the world of elegant bohemia. At only 18, Fab 5 Freddy had access to white hipster culture with Blondie, Talking Heads, the B-52s and the Sex Pistols.

Fab 5 Freddy stayed true to hip-hop, rapped on a few rather average records, as did other graffiti artists like Futura 2000. They both saw themselves as visual artists, but wanted to use their performances as MCs to live out their close involvement with hip-hop music. In 1980, at the Mudd Club, Futura 2000 organized an exhibition of graffiti works by Keith Haring, Basquiat and Kenny Scharf, for which Fab 5 Freddy was to put together the music programme. The idea of the exhibition was to show graffiti art at the point when it was preparing to emerge from the subway and dive into

157. NELSON, Havelock/ GONZALES, Michael A., loc. cit., p. vi.

158. Ibid.

the art world. The exhibition was designed to show the stylistic diversity and artistic heterogeneity of the graffiti phenomenon. To emphasize the authenticity of the works on display, there was a programme of B-Boy dancing at the exhibition. This was how it was that Afrika Bambaataa first came downtown and deejayed for the first time to a predominantly white audience. The blacks in the audience were all graffiti artists. It was like a convention: 'Any nigger you wanted to meet who was your hero, he was there,' Fab 5 Freddy relates. 'Everybody was chatting and tagging up each other's books. It was a big deal.'[159]

159. Ibid.

160. Ibid. p. xi.

161. BECKMAN, Janette/ ADLER, B., op. cit., p. 17.

Fab 5 Freddy became an institution, linking the representatives of hip-hop culture with downtown bohemia. He worked on the talk show of the editor of *Interview*, Glen O'Brien, who knew all the major writers, artists and pop musicians. The exchange was mutual: white intellectuals and artists in particular were very impressed by the 'new thing', rap, and sensed the power and energy behind this new 'art'. In 1980 Blondie recorded 'Rapture', the first pop song to reflect rap in both its music and its lyrics which paid special homage to Fab 5 Freddy. After this he worked as co-producer and co-writer on *Wild Style*, the first film about hip-hop. The director was the white film-maker Charlie Ahearn. In the same year Fab 5 Freddy recorded the single 'Change the Beat', which, according to the artist, was very influential: 'It was the first rap record that used a laid-back, kinda mellow groove, a simple beat like a heartbeat... It became the most scratched independent record second only to James Brown's, of course. It became a real cult thing, and through it, everybody started knowing me.'[160]

Fab 5 Freddy in Wild Style

In the rap to 'Change the Beat', Fab 5 Freddy spoke of the great emotion that an artist feels when he steps on to the stage as an MC:

The hip-hop world is a fantasy
Groovin' to the rhythms of reality
Just a grabbin' the mike and takin' control
Being the monumental master, playin' the role
Pullin' the curtains back and lettin' you know
That when I'm on the mike, I'm rockin' the show.[161]

And yet Fab 5 Freddy had never seen himself as a rapper. He was rapping at this point because he saw it as a good way of paying his rent. Because despite his considerable success, he still wasn't bringing in much money as an artist.

In the mid-80s Fab 5 Freddy stopped painting and turned away disillusioned from the art world because blacks could barely make their way in it. He concentrated on producing hip-hop videos and shot clips for Queen Latifah, KRS One, EPMD, Shabba Ranks, Master Ace, Gang Starr and other rap acts. In 1988, MTV asked him to moderate a rap show they had just come up with. At this point in time it was a real sensation, because until then MTV had strictly refused to play radical, heavy, black rap music. On condition that he was able to have a say in the programme's design, and to pay attention to the quality (no fakes!) of the music, Fab 5 Freddy agreed. He wanted to present the show not in the studio but on the street – among the homeboys; in the settings where hip-hop had grown up. The first Saturday broadcasts achieved the highest viewing figures that MTV ever had.[162] Since then 'Yo! MTV Raps' has become the most important medium for the spreading of hip-hop culture. Thanks to Fab 5 Freddy's direct contacts with the hip-hop scene, this link to mainstream culture became a guarantee of the dissemination of hip-hop music and the hip-hop aesthetic, while remaining largely true to the originals.

Like Russell Simmons, Fab 5 Freddy had been a fan of hip-hop culture since its earliest days. As blacks, they were both vitally important in helping to bring the 'black thang' of hip-hop out of the ghetto and into the rest of the word without undermining or watering down its aesthetic. If Nelson George's fears that the death of hip-hop would follow closely on the death of R&B have proved unfounded, this is to a large extent down to these two highly influential media acrobats. As understandable as the position of a black nationalist like Nelson George may be, it is also senseless. The crossover of hip-hop into the mainstream had to take place because at the beginning of the 80s hip-hop proved to be one of the most interesting phenomena among all forms of artistic production. Dogmatists like

162. Cf. GEORGE, Nelson: Buppies..., p. 33.

Fab 5 Freddy as an MTV icon

George helped to criticize and comment upon intellectual errors within the black community, and within (not exclusively black) hip-hop culture. But black pragmatists and Machiavellis like Russell Simmons and Fab 5 Freddy have, with their activities in almost every area of the media, helped turn hip-hop into black pop music which, in the view of pop historian Reebee Garofalo, was distinctly more Afrocentric and nationalistic than the cultural mainstream had previously found acceptable.[163]

HIP-HOP BECOMES POP (II) – THE WHITE ACCOMPLICES

No whites were present at the birth of hip-hop. As so often in the history of pop music, they are the late-comers, the parasites. 'Being a parasite means: feeding on someone,' wrote Michel Serres. 'Exchange doesn't take place and will never take place.'[164] White artists and musicians started their hip-hop careers as parasites, but depending on the depth and seriousness of their engagement with it they soon outgrew this role and their position within the relationship of communication.

Hip-hop culture has a positive understanding of what it means to be a parasite. The DJ lives, like a parasite, on old records, in order to become an artist creating new products from old material. 'He chooses the path of genius – and becomes a producer. With that which he picks up from the floor, which has attracted no one's attention.'[165] For Michel Serres, the work of the post-parasite is 'a matter of life and death. He becomes a producer and puts his whole life into these raw materials. I have called him an archangel for two reasons: because he is the bearer of information, of new things, of novelty, and because he is clearly at the top of the line in reference to the parasitic chain... His novelty lies in his having put his life into the produced object instead of getting it from the object in question.'[166]

In this passionate reversal of the parasitic relationship, DJs and MCs turn dead records into living music. Only

163. GAROFALO, Reebee: Black Popular Music: Crossing Over or Going Under? in: BENNETT, Tony et al (Ed.): Rock and Popular Music, p. 245.

164. SERRES, Michel: The Parasite, p. 5.

165. Ibid. p. 211.

166. Ibid.

a very few of the records reawakened into new life were by white artists. Hip-hop built principally on the roots of black music. The separatist, confident slogan 'It's a black thing. You can't understand' would have seemed to be amply borne out by hip-hop, had there been a few white bands grafting an extra branch on to the black family tree of hip-hop. Among them was the supposedly whitest and most German band of all time: Kraftwerk. Otherwise, however, the raw material for hip-hop was reggae, funk, soul, predominantly black music. Nevertheless, the journey from the ghetto passed not only via black mediators like Simmons and Fab 5 Freddy, but also via white pop musicians and intellectuals who locked on to the ghetto's aesthetic practice with their own works, beginning a cultural exchange that was to rob DJ culture of all its hermetic orthodoxy.

ALWAYS CURIOUS: BLONDIE COMMITS RAPTURE

In 1980 Deborah Harry, the singer with the band Blondie, was a heroine of pop music, a punk veteran, a brilliant beautiful figure of the New Wave and the darling of downtown bohemia. She acted in films, had her portrait painted by Andy Warhol and was revered as an idol by the wild young post-punks. The first time she met Fab 5 Freddy she was very curious. She had heard of the new rap music, and the young graffiti artist now gave her direct access to ghetto culture. She heard Fab 5 Freddy rapping and Bambaataa spinning records, she heard 'Rapper's Delight' and Kurtis Blow, Grandmaster Flash and Spoonie Gee, and, because Debbie Harry was a clever woman and a far-sighted artist, she was immediately enthusiastic. When she saw the potency and power in this music, she decided to involve rap in her work. This produced the pop song 'Rapture', which The Source placed at number four in the 25 most important old school records, because for the first time a mainstream artist was acknowledging the existence of hip-hop culture and also paying homage to it. The New Wave artist's fascination went so far as to perform a kind of rap intermezzo, thus honouring the activities of Fab 5 Freddy as well as the scratching and mixing arts of Grandmaster Flash.[167]

These passages in 'Rapture' were as follows: 'Fab Five Freddy told me everybody's fly/ D.J. spinnin', I said, "my, my"/ Flash is fast/ Flash is cool.'[168] The hip-hop DJ, the DJ as an artist, had thus entered the corpus of pop history. In 1980 millions of young people learned that there were 'spinnin' DJs' who could be 'fast' and 'cool', and that their most famous representative was Flash. The video showed B-Boys dancing the Electric Boogie, and graffiti legend Lee, a friend of Fab 5 Freddy, was shown spraying. The informal relationships between Fab 5 Freddy and the downtown scene flowered into a serious collaboration first characterized by the white adaptation of black hip-hop culture. Blondie's 'Rapture' was one of the first products of this culture clash. It was a sign at once of hope and of new departure. The relationship between white downtown bohemia and the hip-hop underground was reinforced by 'Rapture' and the reciprocal exchange was strengthened. Debbie Harry became an icon of hip-hop culture and graffiti art. Her merit lay in musically reflecting rap before it had penetrated mainstream consciousness and been stereotyped. But not all representatives of hip-hop culture respected that. In Nelson George's *Chronicle of Post-Soul Black Culture*, 'Rapture' doesn't even appear.

167. Cf. DENNIS, Reginald C., loc. cit., p. 54.

168. BLONDIE: Rapture, in: STANLEY, Lawrence A., op. cit., p. 34.

ALL ART HISTORY: MALCOLM MCLAREN – A WHITE INTELLECTUAL DISCOVERS HIP-HOP

After Blondie, Malcolm McLaren, a white pop cynic, prophet and producer, was the next to take an interest in hip-hop. As early as 1981 McLaren was rushing around New York promoting his New Wave band Bow

Wow Wow after his massive success with the Sex Pistols. On his expeditions through the multicultural bustle of New York he quickly came across the first proud representatives of hip-hop and, as he once had with The New York Dolls, the first punks, he grasped the potency of the youthful subculture.

The New Yorkers were warned. McLaren's keen nose for new trends and intact subcultures had, since the early 70s, sent him roaming through pop culture. In 1968 McLaren was involved in the student revolts, and made contact with the Situationists. Along with his later punk comrade-in-arms, Jamie Reid, he translated their writings and published them in England. The Situationist strategy of *détournement*, of aesthetic subversion, was to be just as important for McLaren as his love of pop. McLaren's plan was to be a disciple of Guy Debord and Andy Warhol at the same time. 'Cash from Chaos'[169] was one of McLaren's slogans, and so, with his partner, the fashion designer Vivienne Westwood, he started selling fetish clothing in a boutique on London's Kings Road: from the style of the Teds to the perversions of the sex underground. But the project wasn't very successful, so in 1974 McLaren became the manager of the proto-punk band The New York Dolls. This group, designed for scandal, had style, attitude and an enormous media resonance. The singing of the Dolls was as confused and desperate as their lives. Bill Murcia, the drummer in the original line-up, died in unexplained circumstances; Arthur Kane was an alcoholic. Johnny Thunders came onstage in a swastika armband, and, in Bergen-Belsen on a tour of Germany, wanted to play a benefit concert for the Nazis hanged in South America. For McLaren, who was, as a Jew, not insensitive to flirtation with fascist symbols, this chaotic American band was a perfect dry run for pop music's semiotic guerrilla war.

In 1975 McLaren turned the swastika-wearers into the Maoist Red Guard of pop music. He had them perform in New York wearing brilliant red uniforms, with hammer and sickle banners in the background and slogans from the Chinese Cultural Revolution. The desired scandal occurred, and McLaren had demonstrated how to attract attention in an affluent culture that was dying of boredom.

169. TAYLOR, Paul: The Impresario of Do-It-Yourself, in: Impresario: Malcolm McLaren and the British New Wave, p. 12.

Malcolm McLaren

In 1976 McLaren formed the Sex Pistols and used all his knowledge of pop, provocation and the money to be made from it to hatch the 'Great Rock'n'Roll Swindle'. In Julian Temple's film of the same name, McLaren was to present punk as the brilliant and cynical trick of a clever manager and his wild young puppets. And most pop thinkers – headed by Greil Marcus, Simon Frith and Howard Horne – were happy to buy his view of things. McLaren's strategy for moulding four British dropouts into one of the most important pop bands of the century, and at the same time shaping the most striking youth culture of the 70s, is celebrated as an intelligent, *détournant* campaign by a manager as conceptual artist. Only Jon Savage, in his book *England's Dreaming*, concluded from McLaren's biography that rebellion and rejection had always been an emotional and existential matter for him. But after Duchamp, Warhol and pop rebellion, subversion had to be at least as clever as it was passionate, as intelligent as it was intense.

And here too McLaren used the history of the artistic avant-gardes as an example. Art history was McLaren's blueprint for almost all his actions in the pop world, as he revealed in a television interview: 'I learned all my politics and understanding of the world through the history of art.'[170] As an intellectual, he was too knowledgeable to give himself unironically to pop culture. While Sid Vicious sacrificed his own and his girlfriend's life for and with punk, McLaren saw it as merely a profitable variation on well-known avant-garde rebellions throughout the 20th century. McLaren's cynicism, offensive and, as with every great romantic, turned outwards like a shield, went hand in hand with his conceptual and strategic sense of subversion. But by 1978 it was probably the result of his outstanding success, and of watching his act of rebellion sadly degenerate into designer revolt. In 1977 a business magazine nominated McLaren along with the Sex Pistols as one of its 'businessmen of the year';[171] how could one not be cynical? But McLaren's curiosity about authentic, non-cynical subcultures was unbroken.

McLaren saw himself as a parasite in the positive sense, an artist in a new category. An artist who made artists,

170. Quoted in: Ibid. p. 13.

171. Cf. BEADLE, Jeremy J., op. cit., p. 55.

172. Cf. FRITH, Simon/ HORNE, Howard: Art into Pop, p. 130.

173. TAYLOR, Paul, op. cit., p. 13.

174. BROMBERT, Craig: The Wicked Ways of Malcolm McLaren, p. 255.

175. Anon: Definitions, in: DIABOLIS, Clara et al (Ed.): Situationistische Internationale 1958–1969, Vol.1, p. 19.

who were then – within the framework of his design – able to design themselves. The Sex Pistols were McLaren's most perfect artwork, constructed with the help of Jamie Reid and Vivienne Westwood.[172] The impresario as artist – it was in this sense the New Museum of Contemporary Art in New York devoted an exhibition to him in 1988. In a catalogue essay Paul Taylor, the curator, writes that McLaren embodies a new type of artist: 'A "producer" in more than one sense of the word, he has literally orchestrated new musical events and created provocative "cultural texts" within the mass-media. He has also shown that art in the post-avant-garde era is a question of synthesis, combining elements from radically different sources.'[173] McLaren sets out positions, and within these positions he places artists who can reasonably represent and shape them. 'Instead of using the canvas, I have chosen human beings,'[174] explained McLaren, who could neither read, write nor play music.

The idea of assembling artistic productions in new and higher aesthetic units also appears in the work of the Situationists, who propagated this as the 'alteration of the purpose of prepared aesthetic elements'. Current or old artistic productions were to be inserted into the 'higher construction of the environment'. 'In this sense,' as the central organ of the Situationist International had it in 1958, 'there can be neither a Situationist painting nor a Situationist music, but there can be a Situationist use of artistic means. In an original sense, *détournement* within the old areas of culture is a propaganda method displaying their exhaustion and loss of meaning.'[175] McLaren employs *détournement* in the context of pop culture, not in order to exhaust meanings, but to allow new meanings to grow through misuse.

After the massive success of punk and the complete sellout of all forms of punk innovation, McLaren turned his attention to the new romantics and the new wave. In 1981 he came to New York to promote Bow Wow Wow. Like all progressive spirits in the pop world he had become aware of 'Rapper's Delight', and listened around in New York for other products of rap music. Michael Holman, ace hip-hop expert and party-goer, described how he met McLaren in 1981 and introduced him to the world of DJs and MCs. 'I figured Malcolm's interest in new pop culture was important and influential enough to warrant taking him to the Bronx to see what this hip-hop thing was all about. There he saw for the first time quick cutting and scratching by DJ Jimmy Jazz and I could tell he was quite turned on by it all. I was hoping for a big breakthrough with this contact and it came.'[176] McLaren booked DJs Afrika Bambaataa and Jazzy Jay as support act for Bow Wow Wow, as well as the breakdancers of the Rock Steady Crew, and the first B-Boy video that Holman had produced, was shown at the concert. McLaren recognized the enthusiasm of the white pop audience for hip-hop culture. A little later, along with producer Trevor Horn he produced a new record, which used not only hip-hop but also other forms of rhythm-centred dance music from Africa and South America. On the LP *Duck Rock* he not only anticipated hip-hop hype, but also the trend of world music that became popular in the mid- to late 80s among listeners with a taste for the exotic.

The hip-hop influences were doubtless most important, however. The single 'Buffalo Gals' contained the sound of DJs scratching and MCs rapping. *The Source* puts this white appropriation of hip-hop in its top 25 old school list, because in the magazine's opinion, the 'urban street culture' of the Bronx was enriched with elements of new wave music and the related white pop rebellion.[177] And although the constructedness of the mix is apparent in every second of the song, it represents – much more than Blondie's 'Rapture', which only took note of the trend – a profound engagement with hip-hop. It was a good pop song, and at the same time a better-than-average hip-hop track. If you mix it, for example at an old school hip-hop evening in a club, with Bambaataa's 'Planet Rock' or Grandmaster Flash's 'The Message', it becomes clear how easily 'Buffalo Gals' fits in with its time. The collaboration with DJs and MCs of the reference culture had paid off.

McLaren had grown up as the scion of an upper middle class Jewish family in England, and was socialized in the art world. At first he didn't even try to fake his involvement with hip-hop, but instead – in the spirit of

176. HOLMAN, Michael, op. cit., p. 68.

177. Cf. DENNIS, Reginald C., op. cit., p. 55.

Cover of the album Duck Rock

his sense of himself as an impresario – put together the right team: The World's Famous Supreme Team, with himself at the top. 'Buffalo Gals' was released in a scratch mix and a trad square mix. The latter version sounded like traditional square-dance music, traditionally white folk music, and for everyone who listened to this obscure and incongruous track on a hip-hop record, McLaren had included only a small reference that makes it clear how ironically he intended the mix. After the end of the four-minute song you can hear McLaren briefly (but too distinctly to be ignored) laughing.

In the scratch version everything was meant seriously. The square dance instructions ('Three Buffalo Gals go around the outside...') were well integrated within the hip-hop song, and gave it an unusual charm which in turn had an effect on hip-hop culture. The decontextualisation of black pop music by whites was recontextualised by blacks. McLaren's mixture of white and black folk music – which is how McLaren saw hip-hop – was hailed by DJs like Afrika Bambaataa as both an aesthetic and a structural extension of the concept of hip-hop music. In 1983, on the basis of his understanding of this symbiosis, Bambaataa collaborated with the former Sex Pistols singer, John Lydon. The resulting record, 'Time Zone', puts Bambaataa at the beginning of all subsequent collaborations between hip-hop and rock musicians.[178]

Everything was possible. On the cover of 'Buffalo Gals', McLaren gave instructions for do-it-yourself hip-hop: 'Two manual decks and a rhythm box are all you need. Get a bunch of good rhythm records, choose your favourite parts and groove along with the rhythm machine. Use your hands, scratch the record by repeating the grooves you dig so much. Fade one record into another and keep that rhythm box going. Now start talking and singing over the record with the microphone. Now you're making your music out of other people's records. That's what scratching is.'[179] In *Duck Rock*, the subsequent LP, McLaren included a six-page pamphlet illustrated by Keith Haring, to explain the decontextualised music to the listeners. The music-collector thus became a music adviser, informing his audience about the collection. Thus, for example, in

178. Cf. SMALL, Michael, op. cit., p. 218.

179. Quoted in: TAYLOR, Paul, op. cit., p. 14.

'Buffalo Girls', among other things, DJ art is defined as 'using record players like instruments, replacing the power chord of the guitar by the needle of a gramophone, moving it manually backwards and forwards across the surface of a record. We call it "scratching".'[180]

These two short texts are the first theoretical definitions of the new DJ culture and the ancestors of this book. McLaren, trained in art history, discerned in DJ culture the huge possibilities that could arise from the repeated juxtaposition of old music with fresh elements. As a devotee of the aesthetic avant-gardes and thus of a Hegelian sense of history, all of a sudden he saw many of the postulates of the Dadaists, Futurists, Situationists and other deconstructivist approaches to art realized as part of pop music – not as an intellectual, high-minded product, but as a chartbuster that you could dance to. 'It's using the debris of old music... Finding little beats inside other people's records and mixing them together... doesn't follow the old-fashioned format of verse-chorus... it goes off at tangents. That's what makes it one of the most inventive, the newest and the most interesting types of music being made today. Scratching is probably the newest urban folk music,'[181] he explained in *The Face* of December 1982.

The video to 'Buffalo Gals' showed graffiti artists spraying and the Rock Steady Crew breakdancing, and the record cover of *Duck Rock* bore drawings by Keith Haring. McLaren had absorbed the whole context of hip-hop culture into his work and adapted it to his interpretation. He made appropriation seem quite natural. The idea of appropriation was as old as modern art itself. Marcel Duchamp's ready-mades shifted the emphasis in composition from self-creation to the act of selection and definition as an artwork. McLaren saw himself as working in that tradition, even if his act of selection (which also describes a great deal of the DJ's work) was followed by the act of synthesis, in which the selected pieces were connected. He introduced the 'DJ as Duchamp' into the pop world, and, like all other conceptual artists before him, scornfully rejected the blunt accusation of plagiarism. 'All I can say is that accusations of plagiarism don't

180. MALCOLM McLAREN: Duck Rock, LP, 1983.

181. Quoted in: TAYLOR, Paul, op. cit., p. 15f.

bother me. As far as I'm concerned it's all I'm useful for, but if people don't want me to plagiarize I'll have to stop work... I can't sit down and write a tune. I'm not interested. I can't write a tune as good as Puccini, so why bother? I can't write a soulful rendition with a big African rhythm like the Zulu, so why bother? Why not go and join them and bring it back because people here are so blinkered?'[182]

182. Quoted from: Ibid. p. 16.

Marcel Duchamp turned bicycle-parts and urinals into ready-mades, Andy Warhol multiplied soup can logos and washing-powder boxes, and McLaren stole various musical styles and introduced them as appropriations into pop music. For DJs in the Bronx, the use of old pieces of music was merely a technique for producing the sound effects they wanted, for McLaren the same activity is an aesthetic design, a grand project in the context of modern art. Not forgetting: everything he had learned about the world and politics he had learned from art history. The trend towards self-reflexiveness in 20th century art now functioned as pop with a lightness

B-BU-BUFFALO GALS
ITALU

PUNK IT

Buffalo Gals, recorded with the World's Famous Supreme Team in New York, 1982
The performance by the Supreme Team may require some explaining but suffice to say, they are d.j.'s from New York City, who have developed a technique using record players like instruments, replacing the power chord of the guitar by the needle of a gramophone, moving it manually backwards and forwards across the surface of a record. We call it 'scratching'.

In Kwazululand, man
King Shaka, who was
used to defeat the En
military training to th
their bare feet on the
kicking their feet in t
upon, they would fall
they pissed blood. N
to the beat. Boys and
We recorded this dan
I had to tell the Zulus
that of the Sex Pistol
the story at least a 1
Oh Yeah) was the res
jointly in Zulu and En

BREAKING

Spinning on your head. Back flipping, Demonstrating their prowess.
New Yorkers practise constantly on the sidewalks these amazing feats of the body giving themselves names like Crazy Legs.

ELECTRIC BOOGALOO

Give yourself An Electric Shock from your left fingertips thru your body to your right fingertips. Muscle poppin! Electric boogalooing then glide floating on air across the floor.

A Sex Pisto
A Sex Pisto
That's what
Irresponsibl
Mummy yea
I know you
I'm Horrible
Believe me
Never did II
No! Never Y

BUFFALO GALS (SCRATCH)

Girl it's a pity that you're so dirty
She's only dancing just to be friendly
So pretty she drive me loco
You're so silly you make me blush so–o–o–o Yeah
Ha, You're my Buffalo Gal Yeah

Zulu Chant
Bup Bup Bup Bup Bup Bup Bup
B– B– B– B– B– B– B– B– B– B– B– B–
All that scratching's making me itch
B– B–B–B– B– B–duck duck duck B– duck duck duck
B – duck duck duck B–b–b–duck duck duck
b–b–b–duck duck duck b–b–b– duck duck duck

It's a pity that you're so dirty
You're only dancing just to be friendly
So pretty she drive me loco
So pretty you make me blush so–o–o
Looking like a H–O–B–O) – Back up vox
Promenade–promenade–promenade – prom prom prom

Kiss Kiss Ba
Kiss Kiss Ba
It's all he ki
Heh Sex Pis

First Buffalo Gal go around the outside
Round the outside Round the outside

You know it

Two Buffalo Gals go around the outside
Round the outside Round the outside
Three Buffalo Gals go around the outside) Backing vocals 'Ah'

First Buffalo Boy go around the outside
Round the outside Round the outside ← AHA
Two Buffalo Boys go around the outside
Round the outside Round the outside –AHA
Three Buffalo Boys go around the outside – YOU KNOW IT
Four Buffalo Boys go around the outside

Kiss Kiss Ba
Kiss Kiss Ba
It's all he ki
Heh Sex Pis

Cover of the album Duck Rock

which, with no apparent effort, left all the contorted manifestos and demands of the avant-garde movements far behind.

In 1990 McLaren transferred his cultural tourism to house music, and, on an LP, asked 'Wherefore Art Thou?',[183] although without, of course, supplying an answer. Art had become irrelevant, pop culture and fashion had taken its place.

WILD STYLE: HIP-HOP IN/AS FILM

Charlie Ahearn was, like Malcolm McLaren, a punk in 1977, and shot a number of small super-8 films which, in their attitude and aesthetic, derived entirely from the rough-hewn pleasures of punk rock. In summer 1980 Fab 5 Freddy brought Charlie Ahearn into contact with hip-hop music. Freddy had brought him rap cassettes, and the ex-punk had listened to them with fascination. Even before, Ahearn had made a film with the title *The Deadly Art of Survival* on the Lower East Side of Manhattan, and many of the young people who acted in the film were graffiti artists. Amongst other things, the film-maker shot Lee Quinones, who had sprayed walls 30 metres long. The encounter with the sprayers and contact with Bronx hip-hop culture had so moved Ahearn that he decided to make a film about it.

To make himself acquainted with the places where these things happened, Ahearn had to go to the South Bronx, after being warned to stay away as a white man. Finally the rapper Busy Bee took him along to a concert and introduced him to other hip-hop artists. At first they reacted very sceptically to the white invader. But Ahearn stuck to his decision to make a film about hip-hop and tried to involve large numbers of original actors in the film project, whose authentic behaviour and language was to guarantee a successful mixture of fiction and documentary.

Fab 5 Freddy said that he and Patti Astor were just about the only actors. The rest of the cast list had been assembled from 'real people'.[184] The main role was

183. MALCOLM McLAREN presents The World Famous Supreme Team Show, LP 1990.

184. Cf. NELSON, Havelock/ GONZALES, Michael A., op. cit., p. x. This love of the original even went so far that Ahearn had armed gang members and criminals appear in the film with their original weapons. (Cf. OSSI, Rapneck/ MOONDUST, Ziggie, op. cit., p. 35.)

Back cover of the 12" single 'd'ya like scratchin"

played by 21-year-old graffiti legend Lee Quinones, who is called 'Zorro' in the film. The framing plot, kept deliberately simple, tells a fictional love story between Zorro and Sandra 'Pink' Fabara, who was one of the few female graffiti artists. Apart from many other sprayers, famous rap acts like Busy Bee, the Cold Crush Brothers, Double Trouble and the Fantastic Freaks gave long performances. The B-Boys of the Rock Steady Crew and the Electric Force Dancers breakdanced, and the DJs Grandmixer D.ST., Grandmaster Flash and DJ Theodore were seen on film for the first time. Scratching, which for many people was only a sound effect, could now be documented on film for the first time.

Rappers, DJs and graffiti artists form an aesthetic and single discursive unit. Even in the opening credits the direct relationship between graffiti and breakbeats is made plausible. The graffiti drawings dance to the rhythm of the music. The cinematic unity of the two art forms is a kind of kinetic cubism: 'It relates to a certain kind of style of cubism – cutting up and rearranging – like the way the records are heard in the background. Often you heard the same fifteen seconds – sometimes even five seconds – sometimes two seconds of record being repeated and remanipulated. Sometimes the needle would only go that far on the record for the entire night.'[185] The dancing letters visualize the work the MCs do on the English language, as well as the rhythmical output of the DJs, where the raps undertake the semantic shifts on the corpus of language. Signifying is made serious in graffiti art. The work of the sprayers is particularly important for a subculture whose influences are not textual but 'oral'.

Breakdancers are also, in Ahearn's opinion, part of the community of the sign manipulators. Their shifts within the semantics of body language obey the same paradigms. Ahearn sees his task as bringing these various aspects together, because unlike the whites in the film, he doesn't want to be a curious, arrogant observer. This synthesis legitimates the documentation of the white intellectual Ahearn.

"Wild Style" refers to pieces that are disjointed and then reput together and added with a great deal of style.

185. JACOBSON, Harlan: Wild Style, in: FILM COMMENT, June 1983, p. 66.

When the breakdancer comes off a dance he ends up like this, like that. If you look at the (graffiti) letters, they're doing the exact same thing – it's like a pose – I always hear graffiti artists going "He makes those letters dance". That's what it's like – he gives them animation, life. The letters have a kind of life. Graffiti puts kind of a muscular, acrobatic power into the style of the letters, and I think that's a big part of it.[186]

The rhythm of *Wild Style*'s cutting obeys the rules of the breakbeat. In symmetric montages of breakdance, graffiti spraying and DJ mixing art, hip-hop culture is explained. Most compellingly in a montage in which Grandmaster Flash scratches as a guest star and Lee – edited in – works on a large piece. In these scenes the camera comes very close to the artists. The focus is on the creative individual. 'The whole thing about rapping is about yourself but with style and narration added to it to describe something that you've been through. But you always come back to doing a rhyme about your name... it's the same process of trying to get your name out there like the graffiti artist.'[187] On this level, too, film works as a document. The film seems almost to burst with the desire for expression, which confidently pushes beyond the boundaries of the ghetto to realization. *Wild Style* shows not only the faces and gestures of the co-founders of hip-hop culture, their clothes, their weapons and their apartments, their jams and tools, but overall the picture of a subculture that is about to conquer the world.[188]

186. Ibid.

187. Ibid.

188. Even the former ghetto-dweller and advocate of black separatism, Nelson George, concedes that white director Charlie Ahearn's film is the first realistic representation of the up-and-coming B-Boy culture. (Cf. GEORGE, Nelson: Buppies..., op. cit., p. 22.)

ALWAYS NEW: HIP-HOP INNOVATIONS

Between 1979 and 1983 hip-hop grew up. Breakbeats and raps were remixed time and again, and each new successful mixture extended the spectrum of the music. DJs and MCs realized the enormity of the musical field that they had just begun to till. There was no scrap of recorded sound, no kind of music, no extra-musical sound that couldn't be used or put between breakbeats.

Scenes from Wild Style

Kittler has identified the maximization of all electro-acoustic possibilities as one of the fundamental practices of rock music[189] and refers to the wild, psychedelic phase of rock'n'roll, as in the Rolling Stones and Jimi Hendrix as well as the conceptual art-oriented new wave of Laurie Anderson. 'Writing can write no more about it,'[190] Kittler observed of the cymbal-crashes, jet engine noise and pistol-shots. Hip-hop now took this delight in pure sound to new levels. The DJ was the master of all sounds, his record-player and his needle, his mixing desk and the hands that controlled everything conjured food for the eternal groove out of everything available. Hip-hop was the music from which nothing was safe: not television theme tunes and classical music, not jazz and country. Nothing. Every year brought a new package of novelties and innovations for hip-hop music.

Source journalist Reginald C. Dennis' list of the 25 old school milestones include on the one hand 'Super Rappin' by Grandmaster Flash & The Furious Five – the first record by an authentic and respected hip-hop crew from the Bronx – and on the other, in 1979, the first female Rap debut of 'Funk You Up'. Kurtis Blow's 'The Breaks', in 1980, was the first record by a solo rapper to appear on a major label. 'Rapper Reprise' by the Sugar Hill Gang and Sequence is the first collaboration by two groups on one record, a predecessor of all the 'posse cuts'[191] of today. Milestones in 1981 included the revered 'Grandmaster Flash on the Wheels of Steel', the first Spanish rap on 'Disco Dream' by The Mean Machine, and on 'Showdown', Grandmaster Flash & The Furious Five appearing against the Sugar Hill Gang to document the first hip-hop battle on record.

His list revealed the speed with which the possibilities and varieties of hip-hop, once discovered, were being explored by the record industry, and by the artists themselves. Many of these innovations soon evaporated as pointless gimmicks launched by the record industry. Not so the works of Grandmaster Flash & The Furious Five. Their second single 'The Message' was the first inventory of everyday life in the ghetto with all its suffering and hopelessness. Hip-hop, as part of black realism, became part of an aesthetic practice which, all poetic extravagances aside, had been a constant within

189. Cf. KITTLER, Friedrich A.: Grammophon..., p. 169.

190. Ibid. p. 172.

191. DENNIS, Reginald, loc. cit., p. 54.

Afro-American culture since the early 20s. With 'The Message', rap as a ghetto CNN went on air and reported on drugs, unemployment, violence and police tyranny. Grandmaster Melle Mel of the Furious Five was surprised that listeners picked up on this realism: 'We didn't think anyone would listen to these really heavy lyrics. But when the record came out we noticed that people really wanted to know what's up and not what the news or the papers say. And they want to hear it from someone who's been through a lot like they have, not the President sitting behind his desk and saying: everything's fine, blah blah blah.'[192] For Melle Mel the purpose of these rap texts was both pedagogical and political. Both the individual and the system were responsible for conditions in the ghetto. There were no possible solutions such as those familiar from agitprop, but it remained certain that in hip-hop music the ghetto had acquired a powerful voice. The same year saw the release of Afrika Bambaataa's sensational single 'Planet Rock', which, by its creator's own account, introduced the synthesizer and the Roland Drum Computer 808 'as the primary rap instruments'.[193] Bambaataa's love of bands like Kraftwerk was clearly apparent in 'Planet Rock'. Hip-hop was now high-tech music, and the turntables could no longer be seen as the only sound sources for DJs. The drum computer made the beatbox look like a relic from ancient times, although it had made its debut with Grandmaster Flash only a year before. The ultra-deep bass-lines gave an idea of the possibilities provided by the latest electronic instruments. In 1982 'Planet Rock' sounded so weird that David Toop couldn't imagine anyone buying it.[194] The song was produced by Arthur Baker, who had already given disco music his cold, seductive electronic sound, and who now also started infecting hip-hop with his perfectionism as a producer. A soundtrack for the future of pop music. 'You gotta rock it, pop it, 'cause it's the century/ There is such a place that creates such a melody/ Our world is but a land of a master jam, get up and dance,'[195] rapped the Soul Sonic Force. The awareness of putting oneself in the most advanced position in music history was there, along with the knowledge that the advancing world-spirit was present in the Bronx at that moment. The

192. OSSI, Rapneck/ MOONDUST, Ziggie, op. cit., p. 80f.

193. SMALL, Michael, op. cit., p. 218.

194. TOOP, David: Rap Attack, p. 131.

195. AFRIKA BAMBAATAA & THE SOUL SONIC FORCE: Planet Rock, in: STANLEY, Lawrence A., loc. cit., p. 8.

rappers around Bambaataa had understood that their music was state-of-the-art. 'The DJ plays your favorite blasts/ Takes you back to the past, music's magic (poof)/ Bump bump bump get bump with some flash, people/ Rock rock to the planet Rock, don't stop.'[196]

Bambaataa didn't just want to make music for blacks and hispanics, but also for white, gays and heterosexuals, for Chinese and French people.[197] Music was taken seriously once again as a universal world language, and Bambaataa tried to incorporate as much of the world as possible into his Planet Rock. With 'Drop the Bomb', Trouble Funk had fused the driving go-go sound of Washington with hip-hop. Jazz alone was still somewhat alien to this planet when Herbie Hancock introduced a collaboration between hip-hop and jazz musicians with 'Rockit' in 1983. Together with the DJ Grandmixer D.ST., who scratched on 'Rockit', 43-year-old Hancock, a former pianist with the Miles Davis Quintet, tried out his own interpretation of hip-hop music. Hancock, who had already undertaken journeys to unknown galaxies of electronic music on his 1974 album *Head Hunters*, saw in hip-hop the possibility of using all the innovations of the synthesizer, the drum computer and the vocoder in the context of contemporary dance music, without having to abandon jazz's claim to produce intelligent music. His almost architectural, rigid understanding of the structures of hip-hop turned it into a kind of robotic music without soul or depth. Herbie Hancock wasn't a DJ but a jazz musician, and his understanding of hip-hop remained that of an outsider.

While Bambaataa's technical adventures were still connected to the original culture through his origins as a DJ and B-Boy, Hancock was thoroughly taken by the abstract structures of hip-hop. Since the techno beats harmonized well with D.ST.'s scratch sounds, there is a touch of authenticity – but the overall impression remains that of an 'art product'. The real fusion between jazz and hip-hop was not to take place until years later.

196. Ibid. p. 7.

197. Cf. NOBLE, Peter L., op. cit., p. 41.

DIGRESSION: WELCOME TO THE TECHNODOME

1. KITTLER, Friedrich A.: Grammophon..., p. 24.

KRAFTWERK, SAMPLES AND TURNTABLES

AURA OR RECORD BOX

The DJ carries his records into the clubs in metal boxes and square record-bags. They give him callused hands and a bent back. The DJ always carries his records himself, he never lets them out of his sight, and when someone gets too close to them the DJ gets nervous. The DJ loves his records and can't live without them. They are both his passion and the basis of his work.

The records are warehouses of information and history, and in this way they keep the melodies and notes of the past alive. 'The realm of the dead is as big as a culture's capacity for storage and communication,'[1] Kittler writes, referring to the immortality of culture through its recording media. The human sound archive stretches from Edison's 'Hullo' to the latest LP by New Order.

Since July 1877, sounds – properly preserved – can be preserved for eternity. That date is the beginning of history for the DJ and his little electronic homunculus. The rolling of horse-drawn coaches on the Medieval market-place is lost for ever, as are the echoing revolutionary cries of drunken republicans in May 1848. Since 1877 sounds have been able to survive, and since that point the sound archive has grown exponentially. The world of sounds has entered the age of its technical reproduction.

Until that point music had only been susceptible to reproduction in the sense that it could be played from manuscript. With the direct recording of sounds after Edison, the original sound could be preserved and replayed an infinite number of times. And while Benjamin regretted the loss of the aura as the disappearance of the work of art's here and now,[2] with increasingly advanced recording techniques, the reproduction of music seems almost capable of reproducing the aura. Benjamin's concentration on the visual makes the devaluation of the here and now seem quite reasonable as a core problem, since the development of printing technology, of photography and film relativizes the art's representational tasks. Realism in the sense of the most accurate possible depiction of reality had become obsolete, and art paid more attention to the possibilities of its medium. The self-reflexiveness brought about by modern recording media became one of the central criteria for modern art in the 20th century.

Music was different: it isn't realistic, and to that extent it has been spared the upheavals of the new media. Additionally, the possibility of recording notes rendered material something that had hitherto existed in absolutely ephemeral form – of all the arts music was the most abstract and immaterial. This has tended to remain so: notes can't be seen, they can be felt and measured but never touched. Nonetheless, notes and sounds can be captured, coded and stored as sound waves and then, by the same process, decoded and sent out again as sound waves. The better the technical storage, the closer the reproduction to the original. The loss of the aura is reduced to a hiss.

For Benjamin, this presents a new problem: what is the

2 . BENJAMIN, Walter: The Work of Art in the Age of Mechanical Reproduction, in: Illuminations, p. 221f.

relationship between the reproduction and the original? What effect does the existence of a reproduction have on the existence of the original? For Benjamin, reproductive technology freed that which was reproduced from the sphere of tradition: 'By making many reproductions it substitutes a plurality of copies for a unique existence. And in permitting the reproduction to meet the beholder or listener in his own particular situation, it reactivates the object represented.'[3] Despite his fear of the loss of the historical, Benjamin saw an element of catharsis in the upheaval of tradition, such that the reactionary old values could be overcome. The historical ballast of the original could be jettisoned, without the work of art losing its capacity for expression. So prying the object from its shell, destroying its aura, has a good side. What survived tended to be pure content. The sensual element was reduced. And this prying-away as a relativization of sensuality occurs only partially in the reproduction of music. Sound is so abstract and immaterial that nothing more can be stripped from it, and modern technologies of recording and reproduction have matured to the point that reproduction occurs practically without any loss of the original.

3. Ibid., p. 223.

For this reason the DJ has little sense of an aura. The original to which Benjamin refers would be live music, the authentic voice, the unmediated sound. For the DJ, the aura is limited at best to the scratching and crackling of the needle in the grooves of the vinyl record. The DJ works in a realm of reproductions. Originals aren't interesting, because they can't be used. And with the reproduction of the DJ's arts on vinyl the (reproduced) records have slipped into the role of originals, without being able or even wanting to be originals. So the DJ is completely at ease with the loss of the here and now, and frowns in surprise (amusement?) when told Benjamin's theory of pop culture.

Records as sound archive: motif from anonymous flyer

Reproducibility is the basis of democratic, progressive art, art for the masses, pop. With reference to the constant improvements in digital recording techniques and the minimization of the differences between studio-recorded sound and the sound reproduced in the consumer's CD player, Andrew Goodwin speaks of a mass production of aura.[4] The DJ has stuffed his record box full of almost-originals, his box is heavy, it's full of aura. Aura that no longer means anything. Aura is the dust on the record box.

BEATBOX, DRUM MACHINE, DRUM COMPUTER

The beatbox was the first instrument used by the DJ, apart from the record-players and the mixer. Grandmaster Flash had bought one of the first drum machines from a percussionist friend, who wanted to use the even rhythm of the beats to improve his drumming technique. The first drum machines, also known as rhythm boxes, came on to the market in about 1969 (Rock-Mate, Rhythm-Ace), and they were primitive devices that could store at most two dozen pre-programmed rhythms. The sound of the rhythm box was synthetic, clattering and metallic. It was a simple combination of a hardware sequencer controlling rhythmical sequences, and a mini-synthesizer limited to a few sounds of a drum kit. The sounds of the rhythm box were produced in analogue fashion using oscillators and filter switches, and for this reason rhythm boxes or drum machines were called 'analogue drums'.[5] The first musicians to use analogue drums included J.J. Cale and Leon Russell, the members of Kraftwerk, and even on the 1973 soul number 'Rock Your Baby' by George McCrae you can hear the beat of a rhythm box.[6]

In 1975 the first programmable rhythm box came on the market, but the possibilities of the Paia 'programmable drum set' were still extremely modest. The programmability of this pioneering instrument was so limited that most musicians remained loyal to their old beatbox. In 1978, with the CR-78, Roland presented the first drum machine with a microprocessor that made it possible for the user to record his own percussion patterns as well as the stored rhythm structures. The volume of the individual elements could be regulated, as well as the length of the

4. Cf. GOODWIN, Andrew: Sample and Hold, in: FRITH, Simon/ GOODWIN, Andrew, p. 259.

5. Cf. HALBSCHEFFEL, Bernward/ KNEIF, Tibor, op. cit., p. 319.

6. Cf. KUCKUCK, Thomas: Digital Delay, Mischpult, Vocoder – Die Wichtigsten Begriffe der Studiotechnik, in: FREDERKING, Klaus (Ed.), op. cit., p. 194f.

rhythm units, and the rhythm pattern could be faded in and out.[7]

The devices made by the companies Linn-Drum and Oberheim also permitted the complete storage of the rhythm sequences of a song with breaks, changes in tempo and varied drum sounds. The new instruments stored the acoustic signals digitally. The drum sounds could now – if the musician preferred – sound more like real drums. But ears accustomed to the dynamic and the different tone-colours of drums still found the sound of the digital drum sterile and boring. Others thought its flair was perfect. The right sound for disco producers who took their rhythm patterns from funk, but preferred to do without its 'soul' aspect. Giorgio Moroder and Arthur Baker wanted exactly that: heavy, fat bass-lines, combined with the glittering elegance of absolute artificiality. Electronic seduction.

In the studio, drum machines proved to have enormous advantages. Without having to set up every element of a drum set, from the bass drum and the snare drum to the hi-hat, and equip each with a microphone, the drum machine could be directly linked up to the mixing desk. Apart from making things easy for record producers, the drum machine also had the advantage that the drummer didn't have to be paid, and there was no need to worry about his flagging strength and deafness after a gruelling number of takes.[8]

Herbie Hancock and Afrika Bambaataa used the new rhythm instruments in the early 80s. Hancock was thus able to fake the rhythmical structure of hip-hop songs digitally, while Afrika Bambaataa's use of the Roland 808 drum machine was still closer to the DJ's breakbeat mix. The Roland 808 is probably the most famous rhythm box of them all: English rave band 808 State took its name from it, and it's listed as part of the line-up on the record cover of the hardcore band Big Black.[9] Its devotees extended from punk bands to disco productions to hip-hop crews.

The Roland TR-808 was already outmoded when it was introduced in 1980, because it produced its sounds in an analogue way and wasn't MIDI normed – which is to say that it wasn't compatible with the latest production technology. Despite, or perhaps because of

7. Cf. VAIL, Mark: Roland CR-78 TR-808

8. Cf. NEWQUIST, H.P.: Music and Technology, p. 91.

9. Cf. BIG BLACK: Go Atomizer Go, Touch-And-Go-Records, Chicago 1986.

its rather raw sound, the 808 had a legendary following among musicians, which meant that many of its sounds were pressed on sound archive CDs, and could thus be sampled. The programme's scope was not that much greater than that of the CR-78,[10] and yet the 808 seemed to fulfil all the needs of a computerized rhythm box because it was so easily programmed. In 1983, finally, the MIDI-normed model of the 808 was put on the market. The TR-909 was a hybrid between digital and analogue technology. Three of the eleven percussive sounds were generated digitally, and the other eight were analogue.[11]

Bambaataa saw the rhythm box as a digital servant of the DJ, who integrated its mix constructions in a solid rhythmical structure, thus freeing up the second record-player, which was mostly used for a continuous rhythmic line. Both record-players and the mixing desk could now be used to enrich and embellish the strict rhythmical structure with elements from the record box. Bambaataa used the Roland within the framework of the existing DJ poetic. More technology meant more possibilities as a DJ; it didn't mean that the DJ was superfluous, or even that he lost control. Bambaataa was always a DJ as well as a sound engineer: the man with the record box and the two turntables.

THE FIRST GERMAN B-BOYS: KRAFTWERK

Kraftwerk was one of Afrika Bambaataa's favourite bands. The four German electronic avant-gardists had, since the mid-70s, worked exclusively with electronic instruments, some of which they had made themselves. In 1974, they had a huge American success with their fourth LP, *Autobahn*, a hymn to the technological life in a technological world ('We're driving and driving and driving on the Autobahn'). What was particularly unusual was the symphonic length of the title track which, at twenty-two minutes, ignored the traditions of song duration, and even went far beyond the capacities of the Maxi-single, invented two years later. The

10. Cf. VAIL, Mark, op. cit., p. 84f.

11. Ibid.

German constructivists, who, in photographs, had a mask-like, mechanical appearance, had completely changed the pop world with their mixture of ice-cold electronic sounds, sweet melodies and seductive rhythms. Coming from Germany, the no-man's-land of pop, the two Kraftwerk musicians Ralf Hütter and Florian Schneider didn't even try to copy Anglo-American sounds. Since studying music in the late 60s they had experimented with synthesizers, which were still relatively unfamiliar in pop music. Their enthusiasm for new technology, and their interest in danceable rhythms made Kraftwerk one of the most influential pop bands of the mid-70s, whose music even today still sounds as modern and contemporary as ever. There were two other German bands who composed music in a similarly experimental and technological way: Tangerine Dream and Can, but it was Kraftwerk who enjoyed the greatest reverence and respect, particularly from black funk and hip-hop musicians.

1975 saw the release of *Radioaktivität*, a paean to nuclear energy, whose message was revised by Kraftwerk (the name means 'Power Station') in 1991 on their mix album, and turned into *Stoppt Radioaktivität* [Stop Radioactivity]. The LP cover shows an old radio loudspeaker; and apart from that only the name of the band and the title. Kraftwerk were thoroughly immersed in the world of machines. *Trans Europe Express* continued this trend in 1977. After motorways and radioactivity they turned their attention to the railways. In 1978, when ecological criticism of the idea of progress and technological positivism was starting to spread, Kraftwerk released what is probably their most famous LP with the programmatic title *Die Mensch-Maschine* [Man Machine]. The cover shows the four members of Kraftwerk in red shirts with black ties and grey trousers standing on a flight of stairs. Their hair is combed tightly back and their lips are painted red. The cover design and lettering recalls the graphics of the Bauhaus and the Russian Constructivists. The band look like a gang of German engineers who have escaped from Fritz Lang's *Metropolis* (the third track on the first shares its title with the film). The other titles on the LP are all famous, and became classics in both their German and

12. Cf. MALEVICH, Casimir: Introduction to the Theory of the Additional Element in Painting: in: CHIPP, Herschel B.: Theories of Modern Art, p. 339f.

13. One fact that is often forgotten is that in 1968 Kraftwerk was founded under the project name 'Organization', and saw itself as part of the movement of 1968. Hütter and Schneider's sympathy with socialism was taken as read. (Cf. POSCHARDT, Ulf: 1968er Aufstand, Popkultur und Technik, in: EICHHOLZBRIEF 3/94, pp. 81–88.)

14. CONSTANT: Über unsere Mittel und unsere Perspektiven, in: DIABOLIS, Clara et al, op. cit., p. 63.

Inner sleeve of Kreftwerk album Computerwelt

English versions: first the retro-futurist hit 'Die Roboter/ The Robots', with its manifesto-like slogan 'Wir sind die Roboter/ We are the Robots', which in its aggressive, Warhol-influenced affirmation of dehumanization, frightened even the most fanatical technocrats. Along with the title track 'Die Mensch-Maschine/ The Man Machine', the old 20th century dream of a fusion of man and machine was sung in the sweetest of melodies. The videos showed the members of Kraftwerk, their faces immobile, programming their music-machines behind enormous computers.

The futurist should never paint a portrait of the machine, but should always construct new abstract forms, Casimir Malevich recommended in the Bauhaus book *Die gegenstandslose Welt/The Non-Objective World*. Because, in the opinion of Malevich, and probably of Kraftwerk as well, the machine only produces new formal structures when injected with the creative energy of the futurist artist.[12] Malevich, as a socialist, had a completely different and more positive understanding of machines than the Italian futurists, who were especially keen on the violent, warlike and powerful aspects of technology. In their use of technology, Kraftwerk recalled the Soviet Constructivist aesthetic:[13] the *Man Machine* LP has Russian lettering on the cover, and Russian is sung in the song 'The Robots'.

Kraftwerk's charming yet highly modern music was the expression of high-tech's ability to produce absolute beauty. The Situationists declared the machine to be an indispensable tool for everyone – even artists – and industry the only means 'of taking care of the needs – even aesthetic needs – of mankind on the contemporary global level'.[14] This unshakeable belief in modern technology led Kraftwerk to write lines like: 'Radioaktivität/ für dich und mich im All entsteht' [Radioactivity comes into being for you and me in the universe]. The aggressive naiveté of these sentiments relativizes the confidence in technological progress and allows a glimmer of fear about possible technological disasters. The line between irony and affirmation is an extremely thin one.

In 1977 Kraftwerk travelled to America on tour, and played a sell out concert at the Ritz in New York to a largely black audience. They had to give four encores, and the enthusiastic audience still didn't want to let them leave the stage. Afrika Bambaataa remembers: 'That's an amazing group to see – just to see what computers and all that can do. They took like calculators and add something to it – people pressing it and start playing it like music. It was funky.'[15] After the Kraftwerk concert Bambaataa even took an interest in touch-tone telephones as musical instruments – 'I'm the operator with my pocket calculator', as Kraftwerk put it in their song 'Pocket Calculator'. Anything could be used for the purposes of composition. 'Positivity', the basis for the eclecticism and constructivism of hip-hop, had gained an extra dimension. Not only could all kinds and styles of music in the world be used positively, in hip-hop even the new electronic music technologies were an opportunity to extend the boundaries of music. For Grandmaster Flash the thirteen-minute version of 'Trans Europe Express' was the only record he wouldn't break or scratch. 'It was cutting itself. That shit was jumping off,'[16] he explained. Even today, Kraftwerk's records are part of the basic equipment of all hip-hop DJs, and their sounds and melodies are constantly being sampled. Rap historian Toop considered Kraftwerk's music the first attempt to produce the rhythmic finesse of black dance music electronically using advanced computer technology.[17]

Bambaataa's first hit 'Planet Rock' made direct and powerful use of Kraftwerk's 'Trans Europe Express', and documented the strong influence of the German band on the black hip-hop DJ. His interest in technological innovations also dated from the experience of the Kraftwerk concert in New York. In 'Renegades of Funk', Afrika Bambaataa & The Soul Sonic Force see themselves in the tradition of all progressive free spirits, from antiquity to the present day. 'We futureshocked the funk and added M.C. popping/ We blessed it with the force and the sound of electronics/... We're the Renegades of this time and age.'[18] Free spirits in the 80s – it seemed clear to Bambaataa – were people with technological knowledge and the intelligence to use that knowledge creatively.

15. TOOP, David: Rap Attack, p. 130.

16. Ibid.

17. Ibid.

18. Quoted in OSSI, Rapneck/ MOONDUST, Ziggie, loc. cit., p. 77.

THE DIGITAL RECORD BOX

The DJs' record box is full of history, stored on vinyl. The music is pressed in grooves that are scanned by a diamond stylus. The record is – in Adorno's words – 'as an artistic product of decline, the first mode of representation of music that can be possessed as a thing.'[19] He is referring to the fact, still remarkable to Adorno in 1934, that the most immaterial of all arts can be stored on a black disc. And like Benjamin, Adorno is also troubled by the damage done to the sense of history and time by the new recording medium: 'With records, time wins itself a new way to music... It is time as the past, lasting on in mute music. If the "modern age" of all mechanical instruments makes music seem ancient, in the fixity of all its repetitions, as though it had been there for ever, and subjects it to the merciless eternity of clockwork – then the past and memory... has been made manageable and obvious by gramophone records.'[20] The record makes music literally 'storable', and distances it from live production (Adorno speaks explicitly of living music) and the 'demand for the practice of art': the record absorbs 'freezing, this life into itself, that otherwise would flee'.[21] So for Adorno the record is the sign of the past and memory, and is at the same time frozen life. Dead art rescues fleeting and transient art 'as the only living' art, as dead writing captures living language. Writing and music find their way back to one another: music approaches its 'true character as writing' (!) through the grooves of the record. The record thus becomes a drawing of the music. Adorno's fascinated look at the form of the record is that of a textual man, influenced by words and language and their related media. Small wonder, then, that he sees the record primarily as a medium of storage that makes reproduced music visible and readable, in analogy to language.

About ten years before Adorno dreamed of a new visual form of music apart from manuscripts, the artist and photographer Moholy-Nagy sought to use gramophone records to design a 'groove-script ABC' that 'would render all previous instruments superfluous'. The graphic signs on the record would

19. ADORNO, Theodor W.: Die Form der Schallplatte, in: idem: Musikalische Schriften VI, p. 531.

20. Ibid. p. 532.

21. Ibid.

make it possible to draw up 'a new graphic-mechanical scale'.[22] While Adorno examines the similarities between the record and language, for Moholy-Nagy it is an analogue to drawing paper, on which great worlds can come into being on the blank page. The record is no longer a medium of storage or reproduction, but the basis of production which – in the artist's dream – would mean 'independence from major orchestral enterprises', and a 'vast dissemination of the creative originals'.[23] The freedom to improvise that was emerging in jazz at this time was made possible by freely scratching around on wax records, 'the acoustic results of which cannot be predicted theoretically'.[24] This materialistic consideration of the record as a dispenser of sound was rescued from its abstract existence as an idea and introduced into the reality of pop music by the scratching of the hip-hop DJs. With the major difference that what emerged was not Moholy-Nagy's 'graphic-mechanical scale', but the old, familiar scale used in a new form.

Artists' and philosophers' dreams of the possibilities presented by the new recording media were often distorted by their ignorance of the new technology. Adorno confesses these gaps in his knowledge and openly admits that true understanding of the record assumed a familiarity with the technology which allowed the transition from barrel-organ to gramophone. Until this has been understood, any approach towards the record remains philosophical and abstract: 'If we should later read the state of the spirit from the sundial of human technology rather than pursuing "intellectual history", then the prehistory of the gramophone may attain an importance that will consign that of some famous composers to oblivion.'[25]

Which would take us back to Afrika Bambaataa and his record boxes, crammed full of memory and frozen life. The sundial of human history stands shortly after the invention of the sampler, and if one is to understand a 'composer' like DJ Afrika Bambaataa, many aspects of his work require a technological explanation as well. The sampler brings memory back into the present and awakens frozen life into cheerful existence. The title of the first hip-hop track making use of a sampler is called

22. MOHOLY-NAGY, Laszlo: Neue Gestaltung in der Musik, in: BLOCK, Ursula/ GLASMEIER, Michael, op. cit., p. 53.

23. Ibid.

24. Ibid. p. 54.

25. ADORNO, Theodor W.: Die Form der Schallplatte, p. 532.

'Gramophone Record' by Laszlo Moholy-Nagy

'Looking for the Perfect Beat', and could hardly have been more programmatic. In the search for the perfect beat, Afrika Bambaataa had stumbled on the sampler and the emulator synthesizer.

The sampler is a digital record box; it digitizes sounds and makes the storage of sounds and notes a simple matter: a sound is recorded, and can then be repeatedly re-used and modified. The sampler consists of an analogue/digital converter, a memory and a digital/analogue converter, which makes the digitized form of the sounds audible again. By transforming sound events into digital form, they can be manipulated and reworked.

Sampled sounds are nothing but numerical codes. The original sound is recorded as an analogue signal with a microphone, and measured by an electronic switch 44,100 times a second. 44,100 times because the American mathematician de Shanon established, in his 'scanning theorem', that a sound can be transposed into digital values precisely enough if it is screened at least twice as often per unit of time as would be required for its frequency. If one is to record the whole range of audible frequencies (from 20 Hz to 20 kHz), a scanning frequency (also called a sampling rate) of more than 40 kHz must be used. Almost all manufacturers of samplers have agreed on a frequency of 44.1 kHz, which allows an adequate upward reserve and ensures that all sounds audible to the human ear can be converted. These momentary values are quantized, that is, they are turned into a 16-bit binary numerical value. 16 bits per digital number (byte) is standard. This makes it easy to calculate the capacity of digital storage: between the smallest number (16 zeros) and the largest number (16 ones) there are 2 to the power of 16, or 65,536 intermediate values. The dynamic that can thus be achieved, the relation between the largest and the smallest representable signal is about 96 dB. Compared with analogue sound storage this figure is extraordinary, but compared with the capacities of the human ear, which can achieve a dynamic of about 120 dB, digital technology is still in its infancy.

The first sampling instruments only had a very modest memory, limiting the sampling time to a few seconds.

With rapid advances in computer technology and the consequently rapid growth of memory capacity, sampling time has also extended to several minutes. The bit values per second are considerable, however. If we multiply the sample value per second (44,100) by the number of bits per sample value (16), and multiply the whole by two for the purpose of stereo technology, we arrive at a figure of 1,411,200 bits per second to be stored. The binary series of numbers are then reconverted, by a digital/analogue converter, after manipulation and compositional reworking, back into an audible sound.

26 . FAB 5 FREDDY: Fresh Fly Flavor, p. 54.

In Fab 5 Freddy's dictionary of the hip-hop generation the sampler had one of the longest entries, and the picture of an Akai S-1100 sampler was shown on one whole page – more space than was devoted to the photographs of Ice Cube, Slick Rick or Big Daddy Kane. The caption to the product photograph read: 'The Akai Digital Sampler, used to make the dopest beats around.'[26] By the time Fab 5 Freddy included sampling in his dictionary in 1992, the technology had already gained popularity in hip-hop.

Akai S-1100

When Bambaataa used sampling for the first time, he took the DJ away from the turntables for the first time. Until then, scratching and mixing had been the only way of transforming pieces of other songs into a new context. With sampling, reaching into the record box was digitized, the DJ busied himself with rows of numbers rather than vinyl. Instead of pushing the cross-fader to the other side on the mixing desk and playing the fragment of sound on the second turntable – or on the third, as Grandmaster Flash and some other DJs after him did – all he had to do was press the play button on the sampler.

The memory capacities of the first samplers were a long way from being a real substitute for the record box. When deejaying in the club, there was no way of doing without vinyl discs, but in the studio, when the DJ became the producer and musician, the further development of sampling technology transferred the storage of sound from the turntables to the sampler.

Even today many hip-hop groups use digital sound memories in the orthodox spirit of the DJ. That is, they use modern technology as a practical substitute for an action that would otherwise have to be performed by the turntables, but without undermining the fundamental structure of hip-hop music, which will always consist of the concept of the DJ plus MC. The traditionalism that keeps the old school poetic alive seeks to modernize the DJ–MC community by means of sampling, freeing up the DJ for other turntable experiments.

In addition, many of the effects that DJs can achieve manually, with cross-fader, pitcher, stylus and vinyl, cannot yet be produced with the sampler. Thus, for example, the mastermind of the high-tech projects Colourbox and M/A/R/R/S, Martin Young, explained in an interview in 1987 that scratching was more creative than sampling, and that sampling was generally limited to a staccato effect, while good DJs could do some really wicked things with their scratch technique,[27] producing new worlds out of chaos.

In addition, scratching is cheaper. Samples have become a matter for the lawyers. Biz Markie had to rename his 1991 LP for legal reasons because he had sampled a chorus from Gilbert O'Sullivan's song 'Alone Again (Naturally)' without clearing the copyright. He called his next LP, in 1993, *All Samples Cleared*. Sampling can get expensive, as the famous producer Prince Paul explains: 'I wanted to use "Family Affair" for one song. But Michael Jackson owns the Sly and the Family Stone catalogue, and he wanted 100 percent of the publishing. So I just scratched the record and changed it to something else. He already has enough money.'[28]

From the beginning sampling and scratching were thought of as going hand in hand. That the two were discovered and developed at about the same is pure coincidence, if there is such a thing as coincidence in history. But the five to eight year lead that the manual skill had over the high-tech version of creative musical reproduction gave scratching the aesthetic edge. The treatment of recorded music was defined by the first hip-hop DJs (and their forerunners in the discos), and modified only very slowly by new stylistic approaches. As with the drum machine, the new technology is used entirely in the spirit of the 'old' music.[29] It was only after 1986–7 that the second generation hip-hop bands overhauled this traditionalism, albeit in a very measured way.

27 . Cf. SINKER, Mark: Bytes and Pieces, in: NEW MUSICAL EXPRESS (NME), 14 November 1987.

28 . SMALL, Michael, loc. cit., p. 136.

29 . At this point the concept of hip-hop music is a whole seven to eight years old.

In hip-hop all kinds of sampling were used. Apart from the basic sampler, there would be a sampling drum machine, generally E-µ SP 1200, and a mixing desk that could record at least one sample. But for many hip-hop DJs who were just starting out, samplers were too expensive, so they put together their loops with a tape recorder. Loops are loops of sound that usually form the basic rhythmical unit (beat, groove) of a piece. With the sampler, the basic unit of an old funk piece with bass-line and percussion could be recorded and repeated endlessly using a sequencer. Eric Sermon, of the rap band EPMD, who experimented with samplers very early on, saw the selection of the basic units as a crucial element of composition. 'It became a technique of knowing what to sample to make a record sell – maybe a different kind of loop, a snare sound, whatever. What I'd do is, if I was trying to get a sample and there was something on top of it, vocals or whatever then I'd sample it and then filter off all the top.'[30] Even in sections of song that had a great diversity of sounds, the sound could be picked down to the rhythm section.

The new school of rap to which Sermon belongs has, despite intense use of sampling technology, seen the introduction of a certain amount of conservatism that keeps experimentation within regulated bounds. To keep his sound raw, Sermon uses the antediluvian-sounding 1995 Roland W-30 sampler – despite the fact that he has two E-µ Emax, several Akai samplers and drum machines in his studio. Because of its limited memory capacity, he can only lay eight sample sounds on one another or side by side. 'That's all the Roland W-30 lets you do. I love the way it sounds. It's dirty, and the bass is heavy.'[31] In the work of Sermon, who produces great rap acts like Run DMC and Heavy D., style is chiefly the result of the technology used. He doesn't think much of the idea of making the sampled passages strange. 'That's not being true. I have to get that (original) effect on my record. I have to get that funk.'[32] And at this very point it becomes clear how (self-)limited the use of sampling is in hip-hop. The particles of musical history should not be completely robbed of their significance. Sermon's records are supposed to sound like old funk.

30. RULE, Greg: The Good, the Bad and the Noisy, in: KEYBOARDS, 5/1994, p. 32.

31. Ibid. p. 33.

32. Ibid.

The young rap star Del Tha Funky Homosapien uses an E-µ 1200 sampler rhythm machine, although the Ensoniq EPS sampler, which he also uses, has much greater scope. 'You got cleaner samples, you get more sampling time, you can take out all the bass, you can take out all the treble, you can really fuck with the sample. With the SP, there's less things you can do, but since it's a drum machine, it sounds a lot rougher. I just like the sound of it.'[33]

33. Ibid. p. 36.

34. Ibid.

But despite the use of outmoded technology, the question of the innovative deployment of the instrument remains crucial in the use of the sampler. Homosapien resists the temptation to sample whole loops, instead breaking the rhythmic units down into their components. 'I don't start the loop from the one. Instead, I might start from the three, making that the one, and it won't even sound like the same song. And not even sampling four bars; I might only sample two and repeat it, or sample two bars and then make the third and fourth bars slower.'[34] It is at this point, where the artist and technician must form a creative unit, that the quality of a hip-hop artist is decided. Anyone can do beats, but the technique of re-inserting pieces and linking them up with ideas marks out the artist, particularly when he himself limits his possibilities by not using the most modern sampling technology. The style and character of hip-hop music arise out of a deliberate renunciation of the most modern technology. Only DJs who no longer felt connected with hip-hop traditionalism would exhaust the whole of sampling technology, as the next two parts of the history of DJ culture will reveal.

DON'T SWEAT THE TECHNICS – A RECORD-PLAYER WRITES MUSIC HISTORY

In 1980 Technics brought out the first record-player that met all the needs of a DJ. The Technics 1200 MK2 replaced the DJs' beloved 1100 A which Grandmaster

Flash – one of few – considers the best turntable of all time.[35] As early as the late 70s – when disco had conquered the world – Technics started to develop a turntable entirely adapted to the working needs of a DJ: with a big start and stop button, extendable record-lighting for working in the dark, with a thumb-wide pitch-regulator which, thanks to an extremely precise face-plate potentiometer, allowed fine pitch regulation of ± eight per cent. It also had a quartz regulated stroboscopic light that showed the norm rpms of $33\frac{1}{3}$ and 45 on the markings of the record deck, and, when the pitcher was regulated, showed a deviation of plus 3.3, plus 6 or minus 3.3 per cent if the position of the pitcher couldn't be seen in the darkness of the club. DJ culture had found its instrument of reference. A magic weapon that allowed DJs to do whatever they wanted. Technics had unwittingly launched a record-player which, as an instrument, was to shape the musical history of the 80s.

35 . Cf. GEORGE, Nelson: Hip-Hop's Founding Fathers..., p. 47.

36 . FAB 5 FREDDY, op. cit., p. 61.

37 . ROBERTS, Todd C.: Don't Sweat The Technics, in: URB, August 1992.

Today DJs think it quite natural to wear T-shirts printed with a picture of their turntable, they wear baseball caps bearing the 1200 trademark, or Technics stickers on their record box. For 14 years there have been no changes in the ways in which the Technics SL 1200 MK2 (in silver) and the Technics SL 1210 MK2 (in black) have been built, and since that time they have enjoyed a cult reputation among DJs. DJs call them 'technics', 'wheels of steel' (all turntables) or 'Twelve Hundreds'. The 1200 is so important in hip-hop culture (as in all other DJ cultures) that Fab 5 Freddy gives it its own entry in his dictionary: 'Technics 1200 turntables. The most preferred by hip-hop DJs worldwide for their ability to allow cutting and scratching at its highest.'[36] Almost all dancefloor magazines and fanzines have devoted articles to it – the Los Angeles *URB* magazine ran the headline 'Don't Sweat The Technics', also the title of a song by Eric B. & Rakim. The subheading was: 'The classic 1200 embodies the past, present, and future of the dj'.[37]

Technics SL 1200 MK2

In his history of turntables and DJs, Todd Roberts explains that it was disco that first brought record-player technology to its most secure place – the clubs. And if disco made the turntables necessary, it was the hip-hop DJs that brought them 'alive'. Roberts recalls that the first turntables in the Bronx at the block parties were self-made, converted versions of ones borrowed from the family home. In those days many DJs could only afford one turntable, and they had to mix their records with pieces on tape.

Today Technics 1200s are the 'standard tools of the trade'.[38]

Unlike many of its belt-driven fellows, the 1200 works with an almost friction-free direct drive. Twelve spools arranged in a circle brush against the diecast aluminium underside of the turntable platter as power passes through the circular permanent magnets surrounding them. The turntable speed thus achieved is controlled and corrected by a high-precision quartz-locked pitch control. The precision of this control permits minimal speed variations of only 0.01 per cent and thus, with the pitcher, permits the precise mixing of records even over lengthy periods of time, a technique that is of crucial importance, particularly in house music. Another advantage of the direct drive motor is the extremely short start-up and braking time. Within only 0.7 seconds the 1200 reaches a turntable speed of 33.3 rpm. And the direct drive motor is so robustly constructed that it withstands the resistance that is present in scratching despite slipmats,[39] for hours at a time. Raves sometimes last for over 30 hours, and the Technics works flat out for that whole time, without collapsing even when constantly pulled back and forth, and used for scratching and 'up-and-down pitching'. Technics 1200 are famous and popular not least because they are considered absolutely indestructible. Touring sound systems pack their 1200s in specially made aluminium boxes lined with foam rubber.

Even without the aluminium box, the chassis of the 1200 gives excellent protection against vibration near the loudspeakers or underneath the DJ monitor. This is achieved by the compact floor of cast aluminium and the turntable fitted with anti-vibration rubber on both sides. And the massive aluminium headshell moulded from a single piece of metal also absorbs the vibrations. The 1200's tonearm is kept in a friction-free gimbal suspension. One of its special features is height adjustment via a rotating ring on the tonearm plinth

38. Ibid.

39. Slipmats are felt plates placed on the turntable to absorb the resistance of the scratch movements on the platter. The slipmat slips over the turntable and thus weakens the braking effect of the DJ's movements against the spin direction.

which turns a precision gearwheel. This means that the height of the stylus can be regulated at will to an extremely high level of accuracy. With a variable anti-skating regulator and a possible modification of stylus weight from zero to 2.5 grams, any DJ can tune their 'instrument' to their own specifications.[40]

THE MIXING DESK

40. Cf. Technics spec sheet 1997–8.

The mixing desk is the true instrument of synthesis. It connects up the two turntables, and also connected are microphones, DAT machines or the third turntables. The cross-fader usually connects the two channels to which the turntables are connected. According to the quality of the cross-fader, the sound signals of the two channels can be gently faded in to each other. The slide controls for the individual channels can vary their output in volume. Particularly important are the rocker switches with which individual channels can be switched on and off in fractions of a second. For scratching and cutting, the rapid fadeout of a channel is extremely important, because the pull-back should generally be inaudible. And the exact cutting of a track in the rhythm of the mix-groove allows for dramatic syncopation. By precision cuts, a good DJ-craftsman can mix only the bass drum of a new piece into a running track.

The rapid development of mixing desks turned large, awkward boxes from the same family as sound studio mixing desks into small, handy units, generally narrower than a turntable. This gave them a user-friendliness that DJs soon used for more and more precise mixes. The growing market of DJ equipment inspired more and more companies to design machines which – like the 1200 – satisfied the needs of the DJs. In their hands, the cross-faders, controls and rocker switches became magic tools of synthesis with which more and more refined and intricate transitions could be hammered out. When the first mixing desks with equalizers were delivered, the DJ could not only vary volumes, but also separate out highs and lows within the sound landscape. Scope became particularly great when the equalizers, positioned over the slide controls, freed up the channels for deconstruction.

By now the mixing desk had been turned once and for all into a live remixing post. If there was a heavy bass-line, a good vocal sound or an exciting high-pitched Moog landscape on the right-hand turntable, the annoying highs, lows or middle frequencies could simply be faded out. Particularly for house and techno DJs, the equalizers became an indispensable tool for a 'beat flow' that allowed all kinds of filigree tampering. For dramatic purposes, high and middle frequencies were switched off to send only the dull roar of the bass into the club, or, the sound-corollary, the bass was completely removed so as just to hint at the groove with hi-hats or scraps of melody – until the powerful bass was once more unleashed on the bodies of the dancers. The DJs were now able to dissect every track and break it down into its component parts, combine the various parts wildly or harmonically and send new and changing versions pumping through the speaker system.

C. HOUSE

DISCO GOES BACK UNDERGROUND

In 1978 disco was the plague. As with every hype that ends in a sellout, the hysteria surrounding disco was such that creative artists with any integrity abandoned their projects, happy to renounce money and fame if only they could have the old fun back. Disco had to get back to the underground to guarantee self-discovery without alienation. And while the press announced the death of disco in 1979 after the last super-hit by Chic, 'Good Times', the true disco sound had plunged back into the fountain of youth. DJs like Larry Levan in New York's Paradise Garage worked in the old spirit, from which the beginnings of a new music soon developed. Levan played funk, soul and disco, but also New Wave by the Clash or Talking Heads. What linked all the pieces was their heavy rhythms and the power to make people dance and sweat till daybreak.

The 'fat' basses, combined with a love of soul-filled and gospel-type vocals were seen in the early 80s as typical characteristics of the so-called Garage sound. Garage was the continuation of disco by other means. The lines between disco and house are very hard to draw; it's a fluid transition.

The reciprocal influence was achieved by geographical proximity. The original sound of the Paradise Garage could be consumed by all house DJs and producers until the closure of the club on 27 September 1987, while Levan was sent all the latest house productions from New York, Chicago and Detroit, and was able to incorporate them into his mix for the garage sound. Until 1987, disco, garage and house existed at the same time. For DJs like Tony Humphries, who had been playing the new disco sound since the early 80s, the differences are irrelevant. For him there is actually no such thing as house music, or disco music, as he said in a radio interview, just R&B tracks with an upbeat tempo. Humphries, who is now, without a doubt, one of the best house DJs, still plays a very vocal-heavy house sound, the current version of garage. The constancy within the music's development is balanced by the extent of innovation. In the Sound Factory Bar in New York, one of the most important house clubs, this traditionalism was borne in mind. While in the club, DJ Little Louis Vega plays his heavy house sound, the DJs down in the lounge play the old disco sound, often mixed with more recent house pieces. An evening in the Lounge tells you more about the history of house music than any historiography can ever do. The separation between disco and house is just as arbitrary as it is important. The many varieties of house music prevent a rigidification of the concept and keep it deliberately open.

Before we can begin the actual history of house music we will have to take a brief look at Hi-NRG sound, which historically represented a transitional form between disco and house and is produced even today as a musical direction in its own right.

HI-NRG

Hi-NRG is the techno-sounding phonetic version of 'High Energy', and its very name stresses the intensity and rapidity of music. As club music without any gentleness or quiet breaks, Hi-NRG came into being at the precise moment when disco was going back into the underground. Gloria Gaynor's 'Never Can Say Goodbye' is considered to be the first record which, while still being disco, marks the beginning of Hi-NRG music with its tempo and pace. Producers like Patrick Cowley in San Francisco and Bobby O. in New York worked on a faster, more hypnotically driving version of disco that could soon be heard in gay clubs worldwide. The major influence of Hi-NRG was the Euro disco sound of Cerrone or Giorgio Moroder, which was characterized by a high degree artificiality and monotony and which was supposed to convey as little soul as possible, but a considerable amount of eroticism. The sensual totality of the rhythm was to be celebrated in the most uncomplicated way possible in its repetition. The Hi-NRG producers sought the effect of a decadent high-tech primitivism. The trashy robotic, mechanical music was produced solely so that it would work in the clubs. With the help of the drum machine and sequencer the small, stamping rhythmic units that shaped Hi-NRG were repeated throughout the whole piece, generally without breaks. The simpler the structures, the more seductive they seemed to be for the dancers; and the more simply the music welded together the unity of the dancers, the more useful it was in the clubs.

Hi-NRG was basically minimal music that you could dance to. Thus, by the end of the 80s, Hi-NRG would define the fundamental needs of gay dance music in its absolute simplicity. With the arrival of house, first in Chicago and New York, and its strengthening in the mid-80s, the dominance of Hi-NRG music in the clubs disappeared. Interestingly, Hi-NRG also managed to slip into the corpus of mainstream pop, and go on living there undisturbed when its underground existence came to an end. The American transvestite Divine, who became famous as an actor in John Waters' films, was still the only Hi-NRG star to make it in the charts. It was artists like Neil Tennant and Chris Lowe of the Pet Shop Boys who, as Hi-NRG fans, made the pilgrimage to producers like Bobby O. to have their songs mixed. The most successful team of British producers ever, Stock, Aitken & Waterman, who dictated the top end in the charts in the mid-80s, gave all their interchangeable puppet singers and artists an underlying rhythmical construction that made a modified form of Hi-NRG primitivism the most important pop music of the 80s.[1] Since then Hi-NRG has become an accepted part of mainstream pop, and is still played in its original version in some clubs in England and the USA.

THE BIRTH OF HOUSE IN CHICAGO

The birth of house music, like that of disco, began in the dark. But while disco was the object of a comparatively satisfactory historiography and reflection, house music has remained more or less undiscovered as far as academia is concerned. Articles and interviews from fanzines and DJ magazines have to serve as the basis for any carefully outlined history of house music. Only the American-Canadian DJ journal *Streetsound* took the trouble in 1992 to publish its first 'explorer's guide to house', in August 1993 its second, reworked version and in July 1994, the third, corrected version. The reactions of the artists and producers to the first historical outline, set out in the form of a circuit diagram, was so intense that *Streetsound* and its staff had to keep correcting dates and facts. As in the case of the history of hip-hop, with the summit meeting of the three most important old school DJs in *The Source*, *Streetsound* also attained a 'truth' about the beginnings of house that was acceptable to everyone. Since house music can be seen as a technology-friendly kind of music, it can hardly come as a surprise that the body of history can, as a modifiable databank, be corrected via email and the internet by the house subculture.

House arose out of the legacy of disco, and was a reaction to the dead end in which disco found itself after its sellout. The possibilities of the traditional disco track seemed to be exhausted, and the escape of the Hi-NRG producers into monotony struck the soul and technology-infatuated DJs in Chicago and New York as a mistake. They wanted an uptempo disco with about 120 beats per minute (bpm), with or without vocals.

1. In 1987 alone, Stock, Aitken & Waterman had thirty-one number one hits and sold a total of 35 million records world-wide. Between July and September of that year 9.82 per cent of all singles sold in England were Stock, Aitken & Waterman productions. (Cf. BRADLEY, Lloyd: The Rock Yearbook 1989, p. 46 and p. 122.)

While the Chicago sound was marked primarily by technical innovations over simple bass-lines and a 'four on the floor' rhythm, in New York it was vocal passages influenced by gospel and soul.

One of the fathers of house music is Frankie Knuckles. Like Larry Levan, Knuckles is the embodiment of the disco DJ who never played chart hits in the chic mainstream clubs of New York, but who operated strictly within the underground during the disco hype. He had made a name for himself there as early as the mid-70s. In 1977 the people who ran the Warehouse Club in Chicago invited him to spin records on their opening night. After a number of guest appearances in Chicago Knuckles was so pleased with the audience that he decided to move to Chicago. And he noticed that the 'kids' – as the gay Afro-Americans called each other – in Chicago wanted a considerably harder and faster sound than they did in New York.[2] In the Warehouse there was also a great love of avant-garde Electro-Pop from Europe. Kraftwerk were more important in Chicago than Barry White.

In 1981 Farley Keith founded the DJ collective Hot Mix 5. Keith, who later became famous as Farley Jackmaster Funk, gathered together his colleagues Mickey Oliver, Ralphie Rosario, Mario 'Smokin'' Diaz and Scott Key, first to make their own mix of dancefloor sounds popular with the help of the radio, and then to take it to the clubs and recording studios. Like disco and hip-hop, house was a DJ style before it was pressed on record. The Hot Mix 5 mixed a house-like sound out of the Afro-American dance music of the 70s, with opulently produced tracks like Loletta Hollaway's 'Hit and Run', Martin Circus's 'Disco Circus' or Evelyn King's 'Shame'. These classics of 'old disco' are still a major influence on the way 'we mix and produce records,'[3] Frankie Knuckles repeatedly stresses in interviews. Particularly popular were the productions of the New York Salsoul label that constituted the core of gay disco culture. There were also the influences of European disco and pop productions from Kraftwerk to New Wave. Stuart Cosgrove, the first European journalist to visit house's birthplace in Chicago, reported that Chicago had

2 . Cf. THOMAS, Anthony: The House the Kids Built, in: OUTLOOK 5, Summer 1989, p. 28ff.

3 . Cf. COSGROVE, Stuart: The DJs They Couldn't Hang, in: NEW MUSICAL EXPRESS from 9 August 1986.

astonishingly well-stocked import record-shops, in which even the most obscure productions of European electronic music were available.[4] Ricky Jones, the president of the Chicago house label DJ International, explains that house music derives from three sources: funk, imported European dance music and a 'technology factor'.[5] For Marshall Jefferson, one of the most famous house artists, house is simply old music like that of Harold Melvin or the O'Jays.[6] Everyone who engages with house music – as DJ, producer or historian – finds his own history of house music, whose roots are redefined according to the interpretation and definition of house. For the technology-infatuated house producers in Chicago, Kraftwerk are certainly more important than they are for Tony Humphries, who takes his inspiration from the hundred-year-old tradition of black gospel music.

Along with the DJs of the Hot Mix 5, Frankie Knuckles represented the core of the Chicago house scene. Even before the record labels, the DJs were often conduits for everyone who had recorded their own tracks at home using primitive technology. 'Tracks' was the house term for what had previously been called songs.[7] The term 'track' was supposed to indicate that the piece, apart from its relative autonomy as a song, had received its final aesthetic definition primarily as part of a DJ mix. Any DJs and producers who wanted to know if their track was working gave it to Knuckles, and he would then play the piece in the Warehouse or in the other famous Chicago club, Powerplant. Tracks that Knuckles wouldn't play had no future, and the ones that got people dancing appeared on vinyl six months later at the latest.

The transition from DJ style to an art form in its own right was a fluid one. The question of which black dancefloor record from Chicago or New York was the first real house single is still open. In the *Streetsound* story the productions of Jesse Saunders from Chicago are identified as the first house records. In 1986 Stuart Cosgrove described house music as the essence of ten years of club music – whether it be soul, disco, funk or Hi-NRG. 'House music is far from original, it's a celebration of ten years of club music, strung out and

4. Cf. Ibid.

5. Ibid.

6. Ibid.

7. One of the most famous house labels is called Chicago Trax.

Frankie Knuckles

re-mixed.'[8] For Knuckles, who worked as a DJ throughout that ten year period, in 1987 the novelty of house lay in the hypnotic groove, the 'very sexual feel', improved production values and the density of the music.[9] Knuckles is specifically referring to 'Deep House', as the classic house music from Chicago and New York was called after Knuckles' 1987 LP of the same name. 'Deep house' and 'garage house', as the New York sound was called, are often used as synonyms, but within the house scene, 'garage house' is used to describe a more vocal, gospel-like sound.

Aside from all the fact-based documents of the origins of house, there is also a mythical creation story telling of the beginnings of house music in almost biblical terms. The Minister of House, alias Fingers Inc., alias Larry Heard, identifies the lord of the universal groove as the ancestor of house music. 'In the beginning there was Jack and Jack had a groove. And from this groove came the grooves of all grooves. And one day while viciously throwing down his box, Jack bawled and declared: "Let there be house."And house music was born. I am, you see, I am the creator and this is my house. And in my house there is only house music. But I am not so selfish, because once you enter my house it then becomes our house and our house music. House music is the uncontrollable desire to jack your body.'[10]

Jack might be the term for the groove which has been the typical rhythm of 'gay black America' since disco. In his 1987 history of house music, Anthony Thomas described this groove as significantly 'more energetic and polyrhythmic' than that of heterosexual African-Americans, and simply more African than that of white homosexuals.[11]

After 1987, house groove had won world-wide acceptance. The 'desire to jack your body' had by now escaped all ethnic or sexual determinants.

'To jack' is a slang term meaning 'to trick somebody'. In the context of house music, 'jack' is only ever used in connection with the 'body'. Jack has a groove that is the ancestor of all grooves, and which, out of creative arrogance, creates house to make it first his house and

8. Ibid.

9. Cf. WITTER, Simon: Back To Jack, in: NEW MUSICAL EXPRESS, 15 August 1987.

10. BLACKMORE, Richie: House, in: MIXMAG, March 1993.

11. THOMAS, Anthony, op. cit., p. 25.

Tony Humphries

then everyone else's house, and then it takes possession of people's bodies. Beat and desire had already appeared as twins in disco.[12] In similar ways, the sexual instinct and the urge to dance to the rhythm of the music appear fundamental, basic and existential.

The imposition of conformity on individuals after the elimination of (almost) all their distinguishing features constitutes the community of slaves to the rhythm. In the house that Jack built, everything that distances people from one another is left at the door. The human being, in all his physicality, experiences himself in complete self-confirmation. The DJ sends Jack, via monumental loudspeakers, to the control centres of the dancers, and controls their actions. The DJ is Jack's most important ally: they both know of their power to conquer people. New York house DJ David Morales speaks of his audience like a dominatrix: 'You gotta peak'em, let'em relax, and then peak again. I gotta drive those kids hard. They wanna be driven.'[13]

The mood in the Warehouse was ecstatic in a similar way to the Paradise Garage in New York, and the dancers' desire for self-abandon was similarly passionate. Knuckles played eight to ten hours a night – until the sun came up and the dancers crept home exhausted. The audience had been worked over. 'Work It' shrieked one of the most frequently heard vocal samples of house music, standing up for the dancing public, and challenging Jack and the DJ really to work the dancers. The ambiguity of the expression and its S&M connotation once again demonstrate the identification of the language expressing the desire for sex with the language expressing the desire for house music. In a place without social repressions, being dominated and seduced becomes an act of safety and security. The beat, its ancestor Jack, and the lord of beats, the DJ, pull on a string to guarantee this euphoric self-abandonment, as the lyrics of a 1985 song by JM (Jack Master) Silk testify:

The beat won't stop with HM Jock
If he jacks the box and the party rocks.
The clock tick tocks and the place gets hot,
And believe it or not all your troubles forgot.

12. HUGHES, Walter, op. cit., p. 10.

13. WALTERS, Barry: Last Night a DJ Saved My Life, in: VILLAGE VOICE, 7 June 1988.

So ease your mind and set yourself free
To that mystifying music they call the key.[14]

Once the mood had reached its peak, Knuckles would switch off all the lights in the Warehouse and, at deafening volume, would play the soundtrack of a speeding express train. The windows in the Warehouse were painted black, and the club fell into absolute darkness. The audience, mostly under the influence of drugs, was so excited by the volume of the noise and the weirdness of the darkness that everyone would start screaming like mad. 'It was like fear and entertainment,'[15] said Knuckles about that particular stunt.

Staged events like that made the Warehouse and Powerplant DJs celebrities just a little later than the DJs who had made hip-hop popular in New York. The club audience was soon full of experts about what made a good DJ, a good mix and a successful evening. Chicago is a DJ city, Farley Jackmaster Funk put it in an interview: 'If the DJ can't mix, they'll boo him in a minute because half of them probably know how to do it themselves.'[16]

14. Quoted in: COSGROVE, Stuart: The DJs..., loc. cit.

15. Ibid.

16. THOMAS, Anthony, op. cit., p. 29.

17. REYNOLDS, Simon: Blissed Out, p. 174.

THE HOME OF HOUSE MUSIC

The most current misunderstanding of house music is the misrepresentation of its soullessness and placelessness. For the British pop writer Simon Reynolds, house is the sound of machines talking to each other. A dry, superficial music that exerts its fascination more through the question of sounds than of truths. In 1990, 27-year-old intellectual Reynolds could discover no depth, no human truth, no social truth, not even an atmosphere of any kind in house music; rather he saw it as 'an illegible, arbitrary alteration of torques, vectors, gradients, whose opacity is endlessly resistant to the attempts of white rock critics to read anything into it'.[17]

Reynolds' emphasizes this 'opacity' in the word's dual senses of 'lack of transparency' and 'incomprehensibility'. The failure of the white rock critic to engage with highly modern pop music is apparent, in Reynolds' case, in his ambivalent despair at the euphoric celebration of the synthetic in house music. While house musicians long ago understood that modern technology and the alienation of the 'natural expression' of human truth and profundity can be used positively and aestheticized, Reynolds, a lover of British guitar bands, laments the withering of non-superficial, non-dry rock music. For him and for many pop writers and thinkers, guitar plus singer-songwriter is still the format in which pop music should produce truths. The apparently natural expression of profundity and commitment should be carried over into the age of synthesizers and samplers.

House music is music that is no longer able to believe in this innocent expression. DJs in Chicago, New York and Detroit were not interested in the composition of an autarkic work that lived completely on its author's will to expression and creative possibilities. Like hip-hop and, to some extent, disco, house music is DJ music, because its signifiers are only rediscovered in the music and then – by implication – in non-artistic, non-signifying reality.

Possibly, house producers are not so much authors as engineers and architects whose music is not an expression of the soul but a product of expert skill. For house musicians this at first sounds like praise. At each point in cultural developments, theorists have established their norm for a 'healthy, correct form of expression'. In pop music technological developments over the past eight to ten years have made them do this more and more.

Reynolds is not alone. Postmodernism made many intellectuals insecure, because the previously unassailable truths of the great narratives that shaped the west had fallen apart, and few people wished to embrace this new insecurity. Only in the pop world did everything seem to have remained whole, because it had a consistency of development that didn't need to be called into question. Rebellious rock'n'roll, existential soul and every kind of intellectual avant-garde pop music, from Pink Floyd to Einstürzende Neubauten, promised a foothold for insecure intellectuals and gave them confidence that an unbroken, quasi-naïve authorship can still function even at the end of the 20th century – even if the author was long ago called into question in visual art, literature and film.

Strangely, it is disco and dance music – maligned as 'dull' and 'stupid' – that is expelling pop from this stage of innocence. Pop critics like Reynolds react sensitively to this expulsion: just as Hegel scorned all art after classical antiquity as a culture of decline, and Adorno identified jazz and pop music as absolutely inferior, they have their problems with house music.

The verdicts of normative aesthetics are fundamentally crude. While Beethoven 'represents the undiminished experience of external life, returning internally', for Adorno pop music was merely a 'somatic stimulus' and therefore, in terms of aesthetic autonomy, 'regressive'.[18] This regressiveness is not least a product of the technical progressiveness of pop music, which the lover of Beethoven saw as a potential attempt to curry favour with the culture industry. 'To recommend the acceptance of jazz and rock-and-roll over Beethoven does nothing to dismantle the affirmative lie of culture. All it does is give the culture industry an excuse for more profit-taking and barbarity. The allegedly vigorous and uncorrupted essence of such products is in reality synthetically put together by the very powers that are the target of this supposed Great Refusal.'[19]

House is ruined, Reynolds would agree with Adorno. And rather than taking Beethoven as one's standard, the pop thinker speaks of the old, organic language of pop music, from which house has broken away. For Reynolds as an outsider, the music appears like a non-decodable computer programme. 'It's difficult to imagine a genre more placeless or hostile to an infusion of ethnicity. Although it comes from a place (Chicago) it does not draw anything from its environment.'[20] For someone who can't find any soul or warmth in house music, the music remains hostile and incomprehensible. The communication of the music to the listener breaks off at the point when one side denies the soul of the other. Even the most technophile house producers would see their music as being misunderstood if this occurred. The soul is the heart of communication. Without soul there is no exchange.

For conservatives, the accusation of soullessness is

18. ADORNO, Theodor W.: Aesthetic Theory, p. 170.

19. Ibid. p. 441.

20. REYNOLDS, Simon, loc. cit.

related to the accusation of placelessness and homelessness as a circumlocution for insecurity, a lack of reference, and finally a lack of sense. For Heidegger, the purest form of distracted inconstancy is 'Aufenthaltslosigkeit', or 'abodelessness', in which being (Dasein) is everywhere and nowhere.[21] Indifference finds its most menacing but also its clearest image in the combination of homelessness, referencelessness and meaninglessness. The culture industry turns the individual into 'a complete identification with the generality'.[22] But indifference is strength. 'I never fall apart because I never fall together,'[23] as Andy Warhol put it.

If we can now come to talk about home, identity should be understood as the added value of liberating indifference. The ambivalence of spatial determination is deliberate. Information as enactment requires victims.

House music isn't just an urban music, from a city environment, but – more precisely – it comes from all the cities of the American East Coast with a tradition of black pop music. New York has been home to every kind of black pop music, from gospel, jazz and R&B to hip-hop. In Detroit there was the Motown label that had a Detroit sound of its own. In Chicago too they had their own styles of blues and R&B, not to mention Chicago jazz.

But more important than geographical sources are musical origins, which we have already examined. One of the many places, one of the many 'homes' to which house bears witness is the DJs' record collection, which brings together fairly precisely all the roots of the house sounds, and provides a pretty thorough documentation of the prehistory of house. At this point we might recommend once again the Wednesday evenings in the lounge of the Sound Factory bar, where this genealogy of the house sound is retold by various DJs over and over again. As in hip-hop, the history of the music is told in its samples. DJ culture turns chains of signifiers into roots of its own historicity.

One other home must be the technology with which house is produced. The mixing of old soul vocals that can be found on many records with heavy, deep bass-

21 . HEIDEGGER, Martin: Being and Time, p. 347.

22 . HORKHEIMER, Max/ ADORNO, Theodor W.: Dialectic..., p. 154.

23 . WARHOL, Andy: From A to B and Back Again, p. 81.

lines and bright, jangling synthesizer sounds was not least an expression of the technical equipment at the disposal of the DJs. House, like underground disco and hip-hop, speaks eloquently about the means of production behind its existence, while mainstream pop remains silent on the subject. For Diederichsen, one characteristic of underground music is that the audience is always fully aware that it is using new technology, and what kind of new technology it is using, 'while the regressive side still keeps its media under wraps. In the mainstream and stadium rock of our own times, excessive use is made of the technology of sampling',[24] but always in such a way that the listener thinks he's listening to authentic playing. Underground musicians work quite differently. They are 'traditionally proud of the properties of their equipment'.[25] At first it was above all the rawness of the tracks recorded on 8-track recorders and the limitations of the instruments used. With improvements in technology the sound improved as well, telling of the technical innovation that often preceded musical innovation. In many cases it was the house DJs and producers whose unorthodox use of technology, the *détournement* of the user's manual, determined technical innovation. Reynolds looked for the roots, fertilizations and mutual influences that underlay house, and neglected to look in the circuit diagrams and studio equipment. Music has always been the expression of its means of production, but in disco, hip-hop and now house, this basis was more important than it had been in any previous pop music. One of the many variations of house music, acid house, owes its existence entirely to a single instrument, the Roland TBR-303, a bass-line computer which, with six modifiable resonance filter regulators, allowed undreamed-of opportunities for sound manipulation (see next chapter, pp. 254–7).

The home of house music was not only the place where it came into being, but the place for which it was produced: the club. House music was so-called because it was first played in a Chicago club called the Warehouse. Like disco, house was by definition a kind of music to get people dancing. If the clubbers danced to it it was house, if they stood there and smoked a

24 . DIEDERICHSEN, Diedrich: Vom Ende der Wahrheit, loc. cit.

25 . Ibid.

cigarette, it wasn't. 'You Can Dance to It, But Is It Worth a Listen?' asked the *New York Times* in 1990, in the headline to an article on house,[26] referring to the old problem that the bourgeois understanding of culture has with any art that seems to be exhausted in its functionality. The supposed contradiction between functionality and the liberal arts is, like every contradiction, an ideological problem of the recipients of art. Someone who can't listen to house music because he's just dancing to it is never going to understand house music.

The club as a home requires knowledge of what's happening on the dancefloor. House music is DJ music because only DJs know the needs and requirements of night-life, and they alone are familiar with the means of drama and seduction that make club music a medium of absolute abandon and consequently of devotion to music and dance. The rules of the music, and also the rules of a successful evening, are stored in every good piece of house music because house (like all other kinds of club music) has relinquished the unity of the song and its inviolability. Of course the creator of a house song thinks at first in terms of his single track, but he also thinks of it in the context of a club evening, into which his track can be inserted at a particular point.

The home of house music is, not least, also the subculture in which it comes into being. Like disco music, house comes from the background of a black and/or gay club scene, whose needs for fun and abandon provided the basis for life in the subculture. In the disco chapter we examined the extent to which club culture might be seen as the product of a gay aesthetic. In house, in direct descent from disco music, the music's origins in a gay club context are equally important. And where disco, which tends to be composed in major keys, sounded cheerful and always had an uplifting effect, house music has become a melancholy dance music, at once tender and heavy. In combination with the calculated sadness of industrial and electronic sounds, house became both euphoric and melancholy.

Subordination to the dominance of the beat became even more rigid in house music, since Roland computer bass-lines are a great deal heavier, cruder and more precise than the 'hand-made' or beatbox-generated bass

26 . Cf. FREEDBERG, Michael: You Can Dance to It, But Is It Worth a Listen?, in: New York Times, 29 April 1990.

-lines of the disco era. House is to disco as punk is to rock'n'roll: all the important elements of the aesthetic are preserved, but the stance becomes more relentless and aggressive. House music is disco after punk. Even if the influence of punk on house DJs might be described as peripheral at best, the aesthetic shock of punk rippled into the little bedroom studios of the house producers. Anthony Thomas attempts another comparison, describing house as retro-disco in the sense that hip-hop is retro-funk.[27] But in the end it's a similar analogy because hip-hop is also funk after punk. The radicalization of origins as a form of self-creation functions similarly in both.

House music isn't the product just of many different homes, but also of its age. Between the peak of disco (1976–7) and the first high of house music (1986) there are just ten years, in which a lot happened. The difference between disco and house is not least a testimony to the general changes of that period: in pop culture (after punk), in dance music (after hip-hop), in technology (after sampling) and in the gay subculture (after AIDS), to mention just a few factors.

The accusation that house music was hostile to the infusion of ethnicity is a nonsensical one, since house music, as an open construction system, does not close itself off to new infusions but, if they work in the context of the song, gives it a warm welcome; and also because ethnicity, in an electronic culture, can have no point of reference in the origin or the home of the piece. The nicest twist to the idea of home was provided by Andy Warhol. His love of America, which he repeatedly and passionately declared, is based on an image of America in which the blessings of flourishing capitalism and populist democracy are militantly eulogized. The indifference of the Americans thus retrospectively contradicts any idea of home as a form of definition. The laconic view emerges triumphant: 'What's great about this country is that America started the tradition where the richest consumers buy essentially the same things as the poorest. You can be watching TV and see Coca-Cola, and you can know that the President drinks Coke, Liz Taylor drinks Coke, and just think, you can drink Coke, too.'[28]

27 . THOMAS, Anthony, op. cit., p. 33.

28 . WARHOL, Andy, op. cit., p. 100.

Home thus becomes a meaningless definition through everyday consumption. America is the supermarket in which Americans like Warhol grow up. Homelessness as placelessness doesn't exist. The global network via media and consumer goods has not only changed the forms in which identity is registered. House music reveals far more significant definitions than any form of everyday culture. Within these definitions one can also discern the soul of house music, which is not the same as saying that pure placelessness and insecurity cannot have a soul.

29 . TOPE, Frank: Holding On, in: DJ 2/1994, p. 26.

THE IDEA OF SALVATION AND RELEASE IN HOUSE MUSIC

House music is club music in that it can be considered in terms of song units than of abstract structures such as tension and release. Gospel music has found shelter in house music via the secularized pop variants of R&B, soul and disco. American house vocalist Michael Watford grew up with gospel music and transferred its spirituality and power into his garage songs.

Because I write about love, a lot of people seem to think I'm just writing about girls, but it's much deeper than that. The phrase 'Holding On' comes from Church. It means, before you give up on anything, especially when you know it's right, you should just Hold On, because then you're guaranteeing yourself the chance that something might come of it. I based that song on my career, my relationships and my music: I was just holding on, because I knew what I was doing was right.[29]

Gospel quotations are secularized without relinquishing their spirituality. The distance from the religious context and the transfer to the intimate sphere of private life is not an act of blasphemy, but is supposed to bring the spirituality of the singing even closer to the (hearts of the) listeners than gospel tried to do. The 'Hold On' that people are dancing to always tends to speak to the souls of the dancefloor underground, who see themselves as a close community and a family.

Michael Watford isn't an exception; many of the garage house vocalists were connected to the ethical essentialism of gospel both in their singing technique and in the content of their lyrics. House music is the document of a lost innocence that can be restored by soul-based vocals. House is the church for people who have sinned (and who go on sinning),[30] explains Professor Funk. House music speaks, in its spirituality, of an ineradicable longing for a pure life full of love and righteousness. That house is never kitsch, but always the document of a struggle, is apparent in its definition as dancefloor music. The beat and the melodies speak of seduction, while the samples represent the rest of the world. House music doesn't escape the world for a reconstructed church (although disco started out in a former Baptist church in New York), but seeks to rescue the power and purity of emotions for the community. The autonomy of the underground produces a new form of innocence: a longing for purity along with an awareness of the evil of the world. Longing is the driving emotion behind almost all soul-based tracks. This longing is constantly catching up with vocalists like Michael Watford in the production of their music: 'Once I get to a certain level inside a song, my emotions just take over. My character is spiritual and I can't help that. I can't sing any other way.'[31]

The hope of salvation creates detachment from worldly life. The 'other side' of salvation remains vague – a state between tension and release. The word salvation is closely linked to religion, as the antithesis of despair. But just as house music has brought gospel out of the church and into the club, house transforms the metaphysical quality of salvation. No one in the club has to be saved from guilt; salvation, like the build-up of tension, is the product of house. Over long, monotonous rhythmical passages dotted with sparse samples, repeatedly interrupted by sugar-sweet dissonances in the minor key, a tension is built up that generates a diffuse excitement. DJs have ample opportunities to build up tension. The German house

30. Cf. COSGROVE, Stuart: The Djs..., loc. cit.

31. Ibid.

DJ Westbam defines his form of tension as a wave: his strength lies in 'building waves and not just letting a thing go on till it fades away, but rather building the music up and down in a sine curve'.[32] Other DJs use dark sounds (industrial samples or horror film noises) or an extremely heavy bass-line to produce a threatening, frightening or alienating atmosphere which is then released with a liberating vocal or a piano riff. The DJs' work with tensions and dissonance emphasizes the extent to which house, for all its freedoms, obeys the old concept of harmony and order.

In its earliest days house music was almost exclusively the music of a gay subculture, and the concept of release must also be understood in a sexual sense. 'Release me!' and 'Set me free' always has the secondary meaning of the release in orgasm. Many 12-inch singles, depending on the remix (with or without groaning), offer various different readings of 'release'.

The highly sexualised nature of semantics in the context of house music is also shown by the shifts in body language in vogueing, which transcend all sexual boundaries. Vogueing is the posing of African-American or Hispanic homosexuals as seen in fashion magazines like *Vogue*. 'I learned everything by watching,'[33] explains Willi Ninja, one of the most famous voguers.

The appropriation of a stylized, highly aestheticized form of white female behaviour is characterized by exaggerations that turn imitation into self-dramatization. Organized in 'houses' that worked like families, particularly at the dances of the late 80s, the dancers battled for the predominance of their house over the others. As in breakdancing, the hegemonic forms of body language were deconstructed, and then reassembled according to the dancers' own ideas. What was especially striking was the mixture of female and male body language, which was extraordinarily important for the dual minority of non-white homosexuals.

What was being celebrated was the release from the patriarchal gestures that are such a torment to homosexuals. How charged this version of femininity was apparent in Jennie Livingston's film *Paris is Burning*.

32. BÜCKERT, Heike: Bam! Bam! Bam!, in: FRONTPAGE, 10/1991, p. 7.

33. NINJA, Willi: Not a Mutant Turtle, in: ROSS, Andrew/ ROSE, Tricia (Eds.): Microphone Fiends, p. 162.

For non-vogueing homosexuals, too, house music as a whole acted as an instrument of release. The possibility of feeling part of a house community was as liberating in its effects as the knowledge that one could completely be oneself within the subculture. Within this permission to be oneself, the music could also become a sublimation for sex. The orgiastic release occurred on the dancefloor itself and no longer in the toilet. 'Jack your body' – to the music.

THE FAMILY TREE

In the period between 1981 and 1985 a DJ style played in clubs and on the radio emerged as the new musical form, house. In clubs in New York and Chicago, and on those cities' radio stations, DJs worked eclectically on their own sound. Apart from Hot Mix 5, Frankie Knuckles and Ron Hardy, one of them was Tony Humphries, who, from 1983, had a mixing show on New York radio station Kiss FM. In 1985 the first house labels were founded: Trax Records and DJ International in Chicago and, in New York, Easy Street Records. The first tracks by Marshall Jefferson, Larry Heard, Frankie Knuckles, Rocky Jones, Joe Smooth and Fingers Inc. appeared.

In the same year, acid house was invented in Chicago, and techno in Detroit, both of them clearly characterized less by soul, more by high tech. In 1986 a fusion of hip-hop and house occurred; the result was, predictably enough, called hip-house, and was based on a simple pattern: rapping rather than singing over classic house beats. In Europe, particularly in England, they developed their own house scene in 1987, interpreting and modifying trends from Chicago and New York. 'House Arrest' by Krush even made it into the British Top 20 in 1988. In Italy in the late 80s an indigenous variant of house music emerged, called Italo house and characterized by seductively sweet melodies, catchy piano riffs and a speeded-up tempo. Italo house is considered the definitive good-mood music, designed for straight enjoyment and to get people dancing. *Streetsound* magazine adds other variants of house music – pop house, rave, hardcore, new beat and ambient house, all of which – along with acid house and techno – will be dealt with in the next part of the history of the DJ.

HARMONY OR RHYTHM?
HARMONY AND RHYTHM!

34. ROSE, Tricia, op. cit., p. 66.

35. SCHÖNBERG, Arnold: Komposition mit zwölf Tönen, in: Stil und Gedanke, p. 151.

Black cultural historian Tricia Rose identifies rhythm as a central element of the construction of black cultural production. 'Rhythm and polyrhythmic layering is to African and African-derived musics what harmony and the harmonic triad is to Western classical music,'[34] she writes in her book on rap. In rap music, complexity is generated principally by the rhythmic and percussive elements of music, while in western music it is achieved by expansive melodies and complex harmonic structures. Rose sees the distinction between harmony and rhythm as one of the most important characteristics in the explanation both of western classical music and all kinds of music with their origins in Africa. The clear and rational harmonic theory of classical music is clearly opposed to the intuitively and emotionally generated sense of rhythm in black music. Western culture, informed as it is by writing, books and theories, has introduced a logical order, operating according to distinct laws, even to such an immaterial, essentially free thing as music. Even a rebel against the old orders of music thinks in its categories. Schönberg, the founder of twelve-tone music, asserts that his new sounds 'obey the laws of nature and the laws of our way of thinking'. The 'conviction that order, logic, tangibility and form cannot be present without obedience to these laws' sends the composer on voyages of discovery. 'He must find, if not laws and rules, at least ways to justify the dissonant character of those harmonies and their sequence.'[35] The obligation to support musical orders tends to make theorists of all classical composers.

Classical music is intellectual music. Even more than that, like the whole of western art it is logocentric, and its theoretical abstraction derives from the fact that the notes are written down and it is thus designed (via a mediating authority) in a detached way. This act of abstraction through written notes has no tradition in Afro-American music, even if jazz musicians like Duke Ellington and Billy Strayhorn put compositions and arrangements down on paper. There were originally no written symbols in Afro-American music. Thinking about music occurred – as a part of oral history – primarily via mythical descriptions. There were no theoretical texts or poetics by Afro-American musicians, or indeed by pop musicians.

36 . ADORNO, Theodor W.: Aesthetic Theory, p. 407.

The classical ideas of harmony were based not only on the perceived unity of dissimilarities, but also on a mathematical, logical relationship adapted to the manuscript system. The god of reason was always immediately subordinate to the god of hearing. Even the praise of disharmony was only secondary to the dominance of harmony. Nevertheless, Adorno, who sees harmony as an inescapable aesthetic category, warns against mathematizing aesthetic phenomena: 'The notion of two things being equal is not the same in music as in mathematics.'[36]

The very intellectualism of western harmonic theories and the related restriction of the complexity of its rhythms have favoured the openness of contemporary composers for the clear and simple structures of ethnic music.

Dance music is primitivist, to the extent that it is not interested in any harmonic theories or melodic developments, but only in the groove. In this sense, house embodies dance music in a pure cultural state. Steve Hurley and Keith Nunnally, who produce music together under the project name JM Silk, see one problem as lying in the integration of more instrumentation and more melodies within the open concept of house.

On the dancefloor it's the drums that make you move, so the closer you are to that, the better. That's where House originated, but you've got to do a bit more to achieve national success. We write all our songs from four tracks, so there's a lot of drive in the drums, bass and vocals. You can strip all our songs back to that. On the dancefloor, it seems that the more meaning, the more lyrics and the more music you give them, the less they appreciate it.[37]

That was in 1987. Today the statement would have to be retracted, because the dancefloor has come so far that no melodic complexity, no instrumentation, no sound, not even difficult lyrics are strange to it. On many levels, a wide-ranging experimental journey into the realm of unlimited sound possibilities begins in 1987. 'This is a journey into sound' – these are the first words of 'Pump Up The Volume' by British project M/A/R/R/S, which was to bring DJ music and DJ culture to a new level. Not rhythm rather than harmony, but rhythm *and* harmony give the dancefloor a quality which, in the late 80s, turns this music into an interesting field of cultural production.

That DJ culture as a culture of the sublimely disharmonic and dissonant – even for Adorno – not only rescues Modernism but even sends it dancing, the synthesis of harmony and rhythm becomes a pleasurable matter. And rhythm is always, in the end, the 'sensually agreeable' (Adorno) that brings the composition to a close, torn though it may have been by dissonance.

37. WITTER, Simon: Moving House, in: NEW MUSICAL EXPRESS, 20 June 1987.

D. THE DANCEFLOOR PLANET – 1987–1995

THE JOURNEY FROM POP TO M/A/R/R/S

The DJ's domination of the world started around 1987. With disco, hip-hop and house all the important forms of dancefloor music had come into being. New developments occurred at cyclical intervals, extending the original concept of the style in question and making it more sophisticated. Added to this, pop music was integrating more and more patterns and stylistic elements from the dancefloor into its own productions, and slowly beginning to breach the boundary between dance and pop.

1987 was the year of the release of 'Pump Up The Volume' by M/A/R/R/S. This record, cobbled together from a crazy selection of samples, fundamentally changed the pop world. As if from nowhere, the avant-garde sound collage, unusual for the musical taste of the time, made it to the top of the charts and became the year's highest-selling 12-inch single in Britain. The piece emerged from a collaboration of the three DJs Martin 'Colourbox' Young, C.J. Mackintosh and Dave Dorell and the experimental British rock duo A.R. Kane. The only organic sounds came from the guitars of the two rock musicians, who saw themselves more as sound-scientists, preferring to see their music being treated in the context of classical music or experimental jazz.[1] Rudi Tambala, one part of the duo, had studied as a biochemist, and compared A.R. Kane's abstract psychedelic sound collages with catastrophe theory: music would reach a point of maximum energy level and then collapse.[2] In collaboration with the DJs, A.R. Kane recorded their deconstructivist rock'n'roll ruins for a dancefloor piece, and, modern though their understanding of rock music was, only laid the groundwork towards a piece conceived by three DJs. Almost parasitically, the DJs took what they wanted from A.R. Kane: the organically warm sound of the guitars at maximum energy level. Where A.R. Kane's music collapsed again, the DJs had another sample ready.

The roles of the DJs in the production were clearly distributed. Martin Young was primarily responsible for the technical development during the composition in the studio, while Dave Dorell, with his knowledge of musical history and his extensive record collection, ensured that there was sufficient material to be plundered. Over hours of experimenting they tried out all manner of samples and scratches.[3] Through trial and error the three DJs achieved a multi-layered rough version of the piece, whose individual parts then had to be tuned against one another. Finally, the technically brilliant DJ C.J. Mackintosh scratched live elements like the title line 'Pump Up The Volume' of rapper Eric B. on the grooves. Many of the supposed samples are perfect scratches by C.J. Mackintosh, Martin Young explained in an interview.[4]

After several lengthy sessions in the studio, Martin Young's fiddling, Dorell's record archive and the

1. SNOW, Mat: Sampling Secrets of Sound Scientists, in: THE GUARDIAN, 8 July 1988.

2. Cf. Ibid.

3. Cf. O'HAGAN, Sean: Life on M/A/R/R/S, in: NEW MUSICAL EXPRESS, 14 November 1987.

4. Cf. Ibid.

technical finesse of C.J. Mackintosh produced 'Pump Up The Volume'. The first version of the piece was put on the market as a white label for DJs. Although there was nothing written on the label, and no advertising was done for the piece, it made its way astonishingly quickly from the clubs on to the radio station playlists, and finally into the front racks of the record-shops. By 1987, the time was apparently ripe for this kind of new music.

'Pump Up The Volume' by M/A/R/R/S meant the beginning of a synthesis of all forms of dancefloor music into a new whole. The British team of DJs used house, hip-hop and even disco to enter the world of music in a programmatically artificial form – montage – as a pure 'art product'. An 'art product' because nothing in this music was related to an extra-musical reality. Nothing was designed to recall the ghettos of the Bronx or the gay clubs in Chicago and New York; it was the music of young DJs who liked house and disco and hip-hop, but were infinitely far removed from the culture of reference.

Just as Godard and Truffaut turned from film-lovers to film-makers, at first imitating their loves (neo-realism, B-movies, film noir), DJs tried to incorporate their favourite records and styles in a song. Despite their infinite remoteness from the original scenes and conditions of production of this music, the DJs' passions brought them very close to the music. So why not bring disco, house and hip-hop together and link them into something new?

M/A/R/R/S

M/A/R/R/S embodied the dialectic of the turntables in a pure form: two turntables and the mixer as a technological magic spell for the synthesis of the two. Being a DJ means connecting everything and letting it communicate; and if something audible emerges from the process, you can start work on the professional synthesis.

'Pump Up The Volume' was the product of a scattered love of music. The samples extended from 'classical' material such as old soul and funk to wild techno sounds or sermons by Ayatollah Khomeini.

In *New Musical Express*, Stuart Cosgrove identified the most important samples, starting with the chatter of DJ legend Wolfman Jack. After this come sound quotations from Pressure Drop's 'Rock the House', Trouble Funk's 'Pump Me Up', Montana Sextet's 'Who Needs Enemies' and sampled trumpet sounds from Tom Browne's 'Funkin' for Jamaica'. Also, the intro to the song 'Put the Needle to the Record' by Criminal Element Orchestra and the intro from James Brown's piece 'The Grunt' were used, along with songs by people like Jimmy Castor and The Last Poets, and the Jazzy Fives' 'Jazzy Sensation'. The title 'Pump Up The Volume' is taken from 'I Know You Got Soul' by Eric B. & Rakim.[5] 'Play it loud!' was a challenge from the DJs to all the listeners to discover the DJ in themselves and turn up the volume control. The song's self-reflexiveness is almost obsessive: this is a piece of music is a piece of music is a piece of music.

'Pump Up The Volume' was danceable *détournement*. According to the vision of the Situationists Debord and Wolman, every sign and every word, and of course every musical quotation was potentially always also another one, and even had the potential to be transformed into its opposite. M/A/R/R/S united the constructive elements of the montage with the destructive conception of *détournement* and left half the changeability of a sign unused, in order to use the part of the quotation that was left intact as an element of authenticity and power. On the other hand, the wildness of the montage and the juxtaposition of black American soul and Islamic fundamentalism perverted the musical signs to a degree, placing them in contradictory contexts. But while *détournement* was based on intellectual control, and its strategy on semiotic considerations, the DJs' construction work was based entirely on musical principles. *Détournement* was only the side-effect of a sampled music that had, above all, to sound good. What the various levels of meaning of the quotations then did amongst themselves was beyond the responsibility of the DJ producers.

In 1959, the Situationists exhorted people either to reinvest all elements of the cultural past or to allow them to disappear. Situationist *détournement* was supposed to be the negation of the old and the model of the new. 'The two fundamental laws of *détournement* are the loss of importance – which can go as far as the

5. COSGROVE, Stuart: Pump It Up, Homeboy, in: NEW MUSICAL EXPRESS, 12 September 1987.

loss of original meaning – and at the same time the organization of a new and meaningful whole which gives each individual element its new meaning'[6] as the central organ of the Situationist Internationale put it. Where Malcolm McLaren still deliberately staged *détournements* in the Situationist tradition, they occurred unconsciously in the work of M/A/R/R/S.

How helpless the DJs were in the face of an abstract and theoretical understanding of their production is shown by a quotation from Dorell, who says he discovered the collage in 1987 as a new and effective art form.[7] The DJs knew nothing of the history of classical Modernism and all the artistic avant-gardes, they were children of pop culture – they had grown up with radios, cassette recorders and stereos. Their knowledge was concentrated on music, particularly pop music.

DJs, and not only the ones in M/A/R/R/S, were avant-gardists thanks to their origins in pop and youth culture, and their knowledge of pop history: like the visual artist, who must constantly relate to art history in an infinite self-reflexive loop, the DJ refers in his work to the history of pop music. But he does this without theoretical or historical reflection; he has heard the old tunes and knows how to use them. An intellectual understanding of this self-reflexiveness is superfluous.

And why should DJs devote any thought to their aesthetic practice if it works so well? Their studio foolery links all their abilities together in the best possible way, and once the piece has been mixed no further explanation is necessary: it sounds good, and you can dance to it. Debord and Huelsenbeck probably didn't know this feeling of security. Their intellectual doubt called for manifestos and essays; the artists of M/A/R/R/S saw hundreds of people dancing to their work, and then thousands of people buying their records, and then could be pretty sure that in 1987 they had (at least in youth and pop culture) got to the heart of the world-spirit.

The fusion of the disparate parts of 'Pump Up The Volume' was successful thanks to the driving house rhythm, and only for that reason did such a wild piece

6. Internationale Situationiste, No. 3., in: DIABOLIS, Clara, et al (Ed.), op. cit., p. 85.

7. Cf. O'HAGAN, Sean: Life on M/A/R/R/S, op. cit.

8 . WEIBEL, Peter: Von der visuellen Musik zum Musikvideo, in: BODY, Veruschka/ WEIBEL, Peter: Clip, Klapp, Bum, p. 126.

9 . O'HAGAN, Sean: Life on M/A/R/R/S, loc. cit.

of unheard-of musical deconstructivism become a club hit. But if people were able to dance to it, they could understand it as well. If the synthesis had been unsuccessful, the dancefloors would have stayed deserted, and 'Pump Up The Volume' would just have been a little display piece for cultural critics and art theorists. But M/A/R/R/S even made it into the pop charts. Everyone could understand the synthesis. By 1987 the deconstructivism of hip-hop and video clips, computer games and ever-more weird advertisements had so altered the perception of the inhabitants of industrialised nations that they could hear the melodic cut-up, scratching and constantly changing sound-sources as a unit. It is certainly no coincidence that Dave Dorell and Martin Young worked on the production of video clips at MTV. Music videos, in their deconstructivism, were a fairly accurate audio-visual equivalent to what the DJs were trying to do in sound.

For Peter Weibel the postmodern mixture of high and low forms of pop art is best expressed in music videos. 'What is celebrated in high culture as "appropriation", music videos have been doing for ages. Music videos are to the modernism of the avant-garde film and video art as postmodern art is to its modernist past. Music videos are a postmodern text, a postmodern use of the historical discourse of the avant-garde of the moving image and rock music itself, because in them the distinction between popular realism and subversive avant-garde strategies, between underground and electronic culture, between commerce and art, between today and yesterday, no longer applies.'[8] But while most video artists have been through art school or design colleges, and therefore have an academic background, DJs are pure autodidacts – educated, you might say, by the heart that taught them to love the music. This 'purity of the heart' makes it difficult to talk of DJ music in terms of postmodern aesthetics. In pop music the sense of history was still intact: progress had not yet been called into question. On the contrary: DJ culture suddenly presented a whole world to be discovered.

According to *i-D* magazine, 'Pump Up The Volume' made the world sit up and listen.[9] Pop theorist Jeremy

J. Beadle saw the song as a turning-point in pop music, from which there was no turning back: 'It wasn't merely a showcase for the possibilities of all the technology... it showed that all that sophisticated machinery could put together something which could shift units.'[10] The traditional construction of the consumer commodity known as a 'pop song' was revolutionized. Even more than in disco, hip-hop and house music, which, in all its disunity, was at least still the intact product of an intact subculture, 'Pump Up The Volume' came into the world as the result of an experiment in the DJ laboratory. The laboratory was in England, and that was surely no coincidence. The synthesis of house, hip-hop and disco had occurred a long way away from its origins, but it had happened in the centre of a new dancefloor culture that was forming in England at that time.

In the previous chapters we have tried to show how the prior history of dancefloor music had its roots in the subcultures of oppressed minorities, particularly those of the gays and blacks. In the mid-80s, the pale-faced middle-class child entered the arena of dancefloor music with his record collection and mixing desk. The question of soul and existential expression that had been manifest particularly in house and hip-hop, and to some extent in disco as well, disappeared in favour of the question of fun and innovation. The children of affluence longed for excitement and a style of their own, their own music, their own life. The DJs made music for their contemporaries and coevals, who had similar experiences of life and culture.

The emulation of the black American lifestyle was now a matter of interest to only a few white B-Boys; most other young people were longing for something that was closer and more familiar to them. In this respect, 'Pump Up The Volume' was something familiar because it brought together channel crossing, the favourite passages from one's record collection and a diffuse, 'postmodern' sense of life.

10. BEADLE, Jeremy J., op. cit., p. 141.

Beastie Boys (1994)

11. Cf. MAJOR, Clarence, op. cit., p. 26f.

Picture disc (1987)

AFTER OLD SCHOOL – THE NEW HIP-HOP

Between 1983 and 1986 little changed in hip-hop. It was a time of relaxation, in which young bands like Run DMC went on developing and old stars like Kurtis Blow and Grandmaster Flash went slowly out of shape. Around 1986 there was a new impetus in hip-hop music, bringing fame to artists who didn't necessarily come from ghetto culture, but who were prime among their admirers and emulators. The Beastie Boys were three young Jewish boys who had grown up as members of the New York middle class. They started out as punk rockers, and, under the influence of hip-hop, became a rap band. In African-American slang, the word Beast means 'white', and in the 60s it was generally used by black nationalists. In the 80s the word enjoyed a revival with the renaissance of black nationalism.[11] So even in their choice of name, the Beastie Boys were making a self-ironic statement, anticipating criticism by presenting their invasion of Afro-American youth culture as something ambivalent. Like M/A/R/R/S, the Beastie Boys were unconscious descendants of the great decontextualist Malcolm McLaren. In their work, decontextualization was not an intellectual matter, but an everyday feeling that saw no contradiction between the love of black ghetto music and life in white affluent society. Decontextualization was something completely normal and undramatic. And the actual quality of the work lay in this relaxed attitude towards any form of authenticity. In their raps the Beastie Boys didn't talk about poverty and criminality in the ghettos (how could they?), but challenged their contemporaries to fight for the right to party. 'Fight for your Right to Party' must have sounded like naked mockery to black rappers and DJs. And yet this unbridled desire for more fun was just as important a work of realism as 'The Message' by Grandmaster Flash & The Furious Five. It was the reality of white middle class teenagers, who had found their chroniclers in the Beastie Boys.

You wake up late for school, man you don't wanna go
You ask your mom, 'Please?' but she still says, 'No!'
You missed two classes and no homework
But your teacher preaches class like you're some kind
of jerk[12]

For Nelson George a band like the Beastie Boys is historically inevitable, since in his opinion every successful kind of black pop music is sooner or later copied by whites. It is typical of America that these copies should often be more successful than the original, he said of the Beastie Boys.[13] Just as it took white rock'n'rollers to bring R&B to a wide public, in 1987 the Beastie Boys were the first rap band to go platinum four times over with their LP *Licensed to Ill*. This white hip-hop, heavily mixed with rock samples, made the crossover into the mainstream. In 1993 black rapper Ice T said in an interview: 'You've got to cross over. If you're speaking to a purely black audience you'll barely move over 650,000 units if you're very successful. To get to 1.5 million you need white buyers.'[14] Black buyers are – according to Ice T – poorer, and would just sell the tape, while the white fans bought the CD, the T-shirt and the tour jacket.

The music of the Beastie Boys was not the result of commercial calculation but the expression of an enthusiasm for hip-hop music. As we mentioned before, the Beasties, as their fans called them, started their musical careers as punk rockers with crude productions that stylized their own dilettantism, their own roughness. It was the raging noise of real 'white negroes', who saw the fact that they were growing up in an affluent white area as some kind of oversight. In the mid-80s the Beasties decided to produce rap music without denying their past as punk rockers. Their samples from records by AC/DC and Led Zeppelin – produced by Rick Rubin and Russell Simmons for Def Jam – became an important bonding element between white rock and black rap culture. The synthesis also prompted enthusiasm among black rap fans, as the two rap authors Nelson and Gonzales put it: 'I think it's one of the best hip-hop albums every produced... This shit is fly!'[15] The energy of hip-hop was fused with that of punk rock and heavy metal. The Beastie Boys' LP was

12 . BEASTIE BOYS: Fight for Your Right (to Party), in: STANLEY, Lawrence A., op. cit., p. 12.

13 . Cf. GEORGE, Nelson: The Death..., p. 194.

14 . DIEDERICHSEN, Diedrich: Präsident Bush's Most Wanted – Unterwegs mit Ice T, in: Freiheit macht arm, p. 204.

15 . NELSON, Havelock/ GONZALES, Michael A., op. cit., p. 12.

a monument to the euphoria of rock and rap, and evidence that the two could be so effortlessly combined. Their music is like a bouillabaisse, explained Mike D of the Beastie Boys: 'In making the bouillabaisse you might have fishermen from all around the village bringing in different fish. You might have a coupla farmers bringing in some tomatoes to just thicken the stew.'[16] Postmodern eclecticism had become a simple recipe for the New York rap hipsters. And while the colour supplements and philosophical conferences were racking their brains over a heterogeneous cultural practice, among the Beasties and many other dancefloor projects at this time they had been the simplest reality for a very long time. As with M/A/R/R/S, it was outsiders to the reference culture who made this bouillabaisse and thus reformed the original concept of hip-hop culture. The traditional 'racial colour bar', according to which hip-hop was only made and designed for young male blacks, was untenable. Where Blondie and Malcolm McLaren had flirted and experimented with rap, the Beasties took hip-hop seriously and saw themselves as part of the hip-hop community. In 1986 they went on tour with Run DMC and LL Cool J.

With the Beastie Boys, the white B-Boy had entered pop history. As in all decontextualisations, the white hipster used the art forms and arenas that had been fought for so that they could more freely assert their own identities. In London *i-D* magazine saw the Beastie Boys as 'a trio of spoilt white brats who namechecked brands of beer and hamburgers in their raps, wrecked hotel rooms, humiliated female go-go dancers on stage, did everything in the worst possible taste'.[17] If furious self-assertion and self-adulation sounded rebellious and heroic among members of oppressed minorities, among white middle-class children the self-praise typical of rap became an act of hysterical narcissism. James Brown's 'I'm black and proud' was a courageous political feat, while the announcements of pride by the white Beasties were nothing but the expression of social conditions – the children of affluent parents demonstrating the self-confidence of the offspring of the ruling class, not forgetting to denounce that very establishment. Although the Beasties saw themselves as hipsters,

16. TOOP, David: Rap Attack, p. 173.

17. COLLIN, Matthew: The Beastie Boys, in: GODFREY, John, op. cit., p. 29.

Beastie Boys (1994)

society's outsiders, the arrogance of the privileged was also at work in their music. In their programmatic hymn 'Rhymin' and Stealin'' they provide eloquent testimony of their excessive confidence: 'Most illin-est boy, I got that feelin'/ 'cause I am most ill and I'm rhymin' and stealin''".[18]

The rhyming and stealing quickly brought the Beasties fame and success, and a few years of the over-indulgence and bad behaviour typical of stars. A good five years later the Beastie Boys were to apologize to their fans – particularly the women – for their incorrect and cynical behaviour. If 'Fight for Your Right to Party' was the central message of the old Beasties, the title of their third LP *Check Your Head* gave a clue to a new, more mature and self-critical ease.

18 . BEASTIE BOYS: Rhymin' and Stealin', in: STANLEY, Lawrence A., op. cit., p. 13.

The Beastie Boys, M/A/R/R/S, the British house hit 'Rok Da House' by the Beatmasters and the rap hit 'Paid in Full' by Eric B. & Rakim in 1987 marked the beginning of a new era in DJ culture. Almost every month there were new feedback loops, new interpretations, new approaches. In the record-shops and on the radio stations of the world's great cities revolutions occurred every few weeks. DJs in America and England – encouraged by their success – brought their experiments into the public eye. The DJs were slowly coming to understand that they held the fate of pop history in their hands. Their consciousness grew with their responsibility. DJs started to ask other DJs for remixes. Black hip-hop duo Eric B. & Rakim brought out a remix of their hit single 'Paid in Full'. As with their M/A/R/R/S remix, Coldcut used the vocals from Ofra Haza's 'Im Nin Alu' and contrasted Rakim's ultra-deep bass voice with her provocatively feminine voice. To this were added techno sounds and a house-inspired remix of a rhythm section that loosened the heavy, sliding beat of the rap piece, making it sound lighter and brighter. Without any lack of respect, the British remixers had cut the masterpiece of authentic hip-hop for listeners who had put experimental sounds like those of M/A/R/R/S at number one in the British charts. The woman's voice and the many 'disco' elements in particular made Eric B. & Rakim hate the Coldcult remix, and describe it as an inappropriate emasculation and feminization.[19] But the Coldcut DJs who, because of their work in clubs and on pirate radio, had a better understanding of the taste of the British public, managed to take what had originally been an extremely raw piece of hip-hop into the British Top 20. This remix made it very clear that ghetto authenticity was a hindrance to a wide reception of rap music. The popped-up version of the rap piece was authentic in a new way: as the expression of the listening habits and preferences of young white Europeans, who wanted to hear a renovated hip-hop sound.

The Coldcut remix was one more monument to the white European dancefloor underground which had access to a poor level of technology and little money. The first copies were only pressed for DJs as white labels, and had been produced with two turntables, a mixer and a tape-deck: 'Pause button assembly'.[20] The crudity of the original had its match in the crudity of the remix, and yet in the remix – both respectful and and cocky – Eric B. & Rakim's original was turned completely upside down. Using unusual samples was like bombarding the original with enemy signs. These new details overwhelmed the rest of the piece. Coldcut had swallowed Eric B. & Rakim's track and spat it out in a different form. The British fans had become authors, and the hip-hop authors had, for the first time, become victims of their own DJ poetic: DJ culture stops for nobody.

19. Cf. BEADLE, Jeremy J., op. cit., p. 143.

20. NIEMCZYK, Ralf: Coldcut/ Justified Ancients of Mumu und die anderen, in: SPEX 5/1988, p. 37.

'BEAT DIS' AND FRIENDS

In 1988, 'Beat Dis' by Bomb The Bass meant the end of experimentation and the beginning of a new phase, in which mainstream pop absorbed and accepted all new innovations as a matter of course. Bomb The Bass was a project of 20-year-old London DJ Tim Simenon. Where montage was still apparent as such in the songs by M/A/R/R/S and Coldcut, Simenon achieved a cold and technically perfect synthesis of sound out of samples, synthesizers and what was at the time an incredibly fast beat. Simenon was one of the many 'bedroom programmers', as the British dancefloor magazine *mixmag* called the new DJ producers; he had recorded the original version of the track in a ministudio, and it had to be re-recorded in a recording studio. By the late 80s the technology had become so cheap that it was possible for a part-time DJ who also worked as a waiter to compose and pre-produce a number one hit in his own bedroom. A good two years previously, Coldcut still had to assemble their tracks with the pause button, while by 1988 Simenon was able to use samplers and computers.

Like the DJs of M/A/R/R/S and Coldcut, Simenon used his own record collection as the raw material of the piece. Even the name was a quotation, referring to Afrika Bambaataa's 'Looking for the Perfect Beat'. The samples were assembled from radio frequency noises, speeded-up morse codes sounding like a Braun alarm clock, a Thunderbirds countdown, the refrain from the song 'Everybody in the Street' by Funky Four Plus One and the official command to a pirate station, 'Keep the Frequency Clear'. Like 'Pump Up The Jam', the song had no non-musical content or themes. 'Beat Dis' was pure music-music, DJ music. 'Beat Dis' essentially consisted of clippings from his personal top ten of 1987, Simenon explained: 'We found a common denominator between the songs we wanted to use, and settled on a speed of 114 beats per minute. The tracks of the individual songs were adapted to this beat either by speeding them up or slowing them down. I recorded the bass-line on the keyboard, and what sounds like a guitar isn't one, just a single note from a wah-wah guitar, sampled and reconstructed on the keyboard.'[21]

The Bomb The Bass album *Into the Dragon*, which the record company Rhythm King advertised on posters and in newspaper advertisements as 'The First Great DJ Album', contained love songs, but even these sounded like genre studies of the classic soul love song. The songs were performed by young vocalists Maureen, Lorraine and Aurra, all of whom were members of the London club scene.

Apart from 17-year-old rapper Merlin, a number of other musicians worked on the Bomb the Bass project. Simenon, as a DJ, wasn't interested in a band, but wanted to use Bomb the Bass as a kind of forum for young talent from the club scene, under his musical

21. MANSCH, Jenny: Bomb The Bass – Leader of the Pack, in: ZITTY, 19.5.1988.

Bomb the Bass: Into the Dragon *album*

direction and produced by him. Despite his many collaborators, Simenon insisted on sole authorship and declared in a number of interviews that all the ideas were his own. But the openness of the Bomb the Bass project made Simenon's originality and his exclusive authorship look extremely questionable.

Jeremy J. Beadle considered it a myth that Simenon had recorded 'Beat Dis' all alone in his bedroom. But the myth grew until Simenon started believing it himself. The rise of a 20-year-old from waiter to pop star determined the general reception of the work. The DJ as individual artist was easier to explain than the abstract projects of M/A/R/R/S and Coldcut, who were celebrated by the music magazines but could never be reduced to personalities. The mainstream press in particular was delighted that the DJ and sampling had found a nice, young, hip face in Simenon. And in the figure of Simenon the active, spontaneous and creative individual could once again be celebrated.[22]

Much the same thing happened to DJ Mark Moore, who had a hit with the project name S-Xpress, with 'Theme From S-Xpress'. Moore, predestined to be a pop star with his platform shoes and colourful 70s suits, played a crazy mixture of glam pop, disco, house and hip-hop as a DJ in London's Mud Club. His first single reflected precisely this cheerful insouciance in his treatment of various stylistic elements. 'Theme From S-Xpress' was the perfect fusion of house and disco, and didn't fit perfectly under either heading. The subsequent LP *Original Soundtrack* examined further possibilities in the blurring of musical categories.

An analysis of the British charts between mid-September 1987 and mid-June 1988[23] reveals that the success of M/A/R/R/S was the start of something big. On 19 September, 'Pump Up The Volume' rose to number two in the Top 20 and stayed there for seven weeks. A fortnight later, the Coldcut remix of 'Paid In Full' entered the Top 20 for two weeks. Early in 1988 the house anthem 'House Arrest' by Krush rose to number three; at the same time 'Rok Da House' by the Beatmasters & Cookie Crew and Jack'n'Chill with 'The Jack that House Built' were also climbing the charts, so that in January and February there were three real house

22 . Cf. BEADLE, Jeremy J., op. cit., p. 162ff.

23 . The 1989 Rock Yearbook contains the British Top 20s from August 1987 to July 1988. (BRADLEY, Lloyd, op. cit., pp. 169 – 95.)

tracks in the Top 20. On 20 February 'Beat Dis' by Bomb the Bass reached fifth place and stayed in the Top 20 for four weeks. Coldcut's 'Doctorin' the House' followed. Finally, in mid-April, 'Theme From S-Xpress' entered the charts, reached number one twice and stayed in the Top 20 for seven weeks. Then came the sample-heavy songs 'Check this Out' by L.A. Mix and 'Doctrin' the Tardis' by pop Situationists The Timelords, who were to unsettle the pop world with prankster mayhem a year later under the name KLF. KLF stood for Kopyright Liberation Front. The two art students Jimmy Cauty and Bill Drummond had realized that sampling opened the doors to new subversive aesthetic practices.

Within nine months the face of pop music in Europe had completely changed.

24. SINKER, Mark: Bytes and Pieces, in: NEW MUSICAL EXPRESS 14 November 1987.

25. MI.: Beutezug der Klang-Klauer, in: MUSIK EXPRESS 7/1989.

SAMPLING IN THE AGE OF ITS ABSOLUTE USABILITY

M/A/R/R/S, Coldcut, Bomb The Bass and S-Xpress were the first to make full use of sampling. While in hip-hop and house sampling still took second place to composition technique as a method of construction, the young European DJs were no longer interested in pre-established construction plans. Their cross-fertilizations and syntheses were characterized by the unorthodoxy and wildness of their montages. The work's remoteness from tradition and authenticity encouraged all kinds of experimentation. Everything could, would and should be tried out. 'The whole history of recorded sound is waiting there for us to murder,'[24] Coldcut said cheerfully.

But it was a question less of murder than of bringing old recorded sounds back to life. The 'murder' of sounds is a clue to the lack of respect for the original life of the sampled and scratched elements. 'It's the best game since the invention of Scrabble... The harder it is to hear the original in this chaos, the more interesting the piece is to me,'[25] said Matt Black from Coldcut. An uninhibited celebration of the chain of signifiers. And yet this freedom is still bound up with the traditional understanding of pop music. Matt Black: 'We see ourselves as cut creators, scratching, sampling and mixing is basically the same thing for us as guitar-playing for Johnny Winter or Jeff Healey.'[26] And as with guitar players there are the amateurs and the experts. 'It's exactly the same with the sampler. Either you use it as a toy or you become a virtuoso.'[27]

The Beastie Boys say sampling is an emotional thing. Sampling that isn't musically inspired remains dull formalism. MCA of the Beasties stresses that it isn't a matter of plundering, but about the feeling in the sound particles. Beastie Boy Mike D sums it up: 'We just go to where the feel is on the tape.'[28] Sampling, seen this way, preserves not only sounds and noises but also the emotions bound up with them. Even more: it is almost as though the original goes on living in a new context thanks to its immaculate reproduction.

Andrew Goodwin, in his article about pop music in the age of digital reproduction, distinguishes between three different forms and levels of sampling based on different conceptions of realism.[29]

The simplest form of sampling is the copying of sounds and noises with a view to replacing the original instruments with the sampler. This use is based primarily on economical rather than aesthetic considerations. Musicians are expensive, and their instruments are often unwieldy, while a sampler is comparatively handy and inexpensive. In this case realism is restricted to an attempt at simulating the most realistic possible representation of the original sound. The progressive perfection of sampling has meant that the differences between the original and the reproduction can no longer be heard. The question is whether we can even speak in terms of realism, since realism is always characterized by the appearance of reality and its representation in the art work. Goodwin ignores this problem and turns this simple use of the sampler into the basic form of realism in sound.

The second form of sampling is more complex, and refers to the use of the sampler by producers and remixers. Sampling opened up whole new areas of possibility for the producer. Where he had previously been restricted chiefly to the mixing of songs, he could now add whole string sections to the composition without bringing any

26 . Ibid.

27 . NIEMCZYK, Ralf, op. cit., p. 38.

28 . JARRETT, Michael: Beastie Boys, in: PULSE 7/1994, p. 52.

29 . Cf. GOODWIN, Andrew: Sample And Hold, in: FRITH, Simon/idem.: On Record, p. 271ff.

extra musicians into the studio. Jeremy J. Beadle says that producers have always been thwarted musicians, and have only been able to realize their desires with sampling technology.

There were 'artist-producers' in classical music as well, like Wagner experts John Culshaw and Walter Legge; Beadle demonstrates how they interpreted 'their' Wagner in the context of their production.

Phil Spector was probably the first master-producer with the vision of a whole sound-world. The essence of a song was its sound, the melody and lyrics were secondary.[30] At the age of eighteen, Spector wrote the song 'To Know Him Is to Love Him' after a line on his father's grave. The song, recorded by the Teddy Bears, was a million-seller. At nineteen Spector was producing songs for Atlantic Records in Philadelphia; shortly after that he went independent, founded the Phillies label and was a millionaire at twenty-one.

For Cohn the Phil Spector sound was the apocalypse: 'Through multi-tracking, he made his rhythm sections sound like armies, turned the beat into a murderous massed cannonade. No question; his records were the loudest, fiercest, most magnificent explosions that rock had yet produced, or dreamed of.'[31] Spector loved exaggeration and total drama. Pop music has always been dramatic, exaggerated and over-stylized, and with Spector these tendencies became fully apparent. Spector seems to have brought hosts of violins and brass, of choirs and drummers into the studio to make the sound as bombastic as possible. What emerged was 'heroic combustions... soundtracks for a one-shot, one-man millennium'.[32]

Spector produced hits for bands as diverse as the Ronettes, the Crystals and the Righteous Brothers, but all of his productions were influenced more by the typical Spector sound than by the musical personalities involved. Each of these pop symphonies burst with power and passion, testimony to the desire to forget the rest of the world. Spector's Walls of Sound threatened the traditional understanding of pop music less through rebellion and aggression than through seduction and intensity. For Cohn, the actual characteristic of Spector's works was their charming dissonance between romance and rawness:

30. Cf. BEADLE, Jeremy J., op. cit., p. 32.

31. COHN, Nik: Phil Spector, in: MILLER, Jim (Ed.), op. cit., p. 153.

32. Ibid.

In his original songs, by utilizing the massed writers of the Brill Building, he nurtured the purest, the most aching and idyllic of all teen ballads. Into this sound, meanwhile, he poured out his rage and vengeance. Three pianos, half a dozen drummers, rattlers and assorted thumpers, whole battalions of brass and strings, all crashing and smashing away, in deafening, murderous release. So his songs might be pure romance, but his sound was pure slaughter. Together, they meshed as absolute energy.[33]

The massive sound of Spector's productions derived from the fact that almost all the tracks were given equal value, and the vocals were mixed in as one instrument among many. The result sounded as dense and massive as a wall. Speaking of the new psychedelic music of Pink Floyd in 1965, Kittler calls the mixing desk a 'fifth instrument';[34] rather earlier, in Spector's work the mixing becomes the super-instrument that organizes walls of sound rather than notes and melodies.

Completely egocentric, Spector organized not only his productions, bands and artists, but also his label, distribution, manufacture, contracts, advertising, everything. Spector was the first artist who was no longer satisfied simply to be an artist and creator, but wanted to use his creative power and stylistic awareness in a broader context within the entertainment industry.

In Beadle's view, Spector's production aesthetic captured something like the spirit of the age, 'something combining youth, naivety and the exuberance that can go with both, to produce a unique document.'[35] Spector changed not only the charts for a few years, but the whole face of the record industry. Although things got very quiet for him in the late 60s, he had provided the blueprint for many artist-producers after him, who turned engineering work into composing work. As further examples, Beadle adduces Brian Wilson of the Beach Boys and Beatles producer George Martin, who saw himself more as a musician than an engineer.[36] While Wilson's and Martin's 'sound' was conveyed by a band, the band assuming the upper hand in the process, Spector found fulfilment in the form of other artists and bands. Phil Spector

33. Ibid. p. 155.

34. KITTLER, Friedrich A.: Der Gott der Ohren, in: idem.: Draculas Vermächtnis, p. 132.

35. BEADLE, Jeremy J., op. cit., p. 34.

36. Cf. MR. BONZAI: George Martin & John Burgess, in: STONE, Terri: Music Producers, p. 75.

compilations make the Ronettes and even Ike and Tina Turner into parts of Spector's great work. The autonomy of the pop artist – a hypocritical construction on the part of the record industry – had developed cracks thanks to Spector.

Before sampling and high tech, the producer wasn't much more than a recording director, who made sure everything went according to plan in the studio. Producers like Spector and Martin, like Felix Pappalardi, who produced Cream, the Youngbloods and Mountain, or Mickie Most, who mixed, among others, the Animals and Donovan, were exceptions. But they did make it clear that the organization of musicians and studio equipment was just as important for the final sound of the record as choosing the songs to be pressed and their sequence on the record. Producers reorganize artistic products on a second level, charging the creative energies of the artists with their ideas of how a song and an LP should sound. The choice of producer by the artists – an aggressive business since the days of Spector – makes it clear that artists desire and demand this interpretation of their music by the producer. They see criticism and alteration of their compositions as an enrichment.

Rick Rubin compares the role of the music producer with that of the film director (rather than the film producer): the sound engineers are the cameramen, the songs the play that is being staged. Rubin's stagings often come close to the boundaries of what the authors of the 'play' find acceptable. The Beastie Boys rebelled when Rick Rubin asked a guitarist from speed metal band Slayer to record solos to be used as loops for the Beastie Boys' rap record. Rubin won the battle. Rubin's staging of the first alliance of rap and rock music became famous in the cover version of Aerosmith's 'Walk this Way' by the rappers of Run DMC. Former DJ Rubin mixed rock and rap together, not on the record deck but in the recording studio. The white rockers and the black rappers recorded the piece together; after that rock and rap were less strange to one another than before. With the Beastie Boys' rap album *Licensed to Ill*, which was run through with heavy metal riffs, this crossover was extended to LP length. For music-lover Rubin, the differences between the various styles are unimportant, what matters for him is intensity.[37] For 'real teenage music is always angry, loud and aggressive'.[38]

For Goodwin, artist-producers are the most interesting users of the new technologies, because their 'aesthetic radicalism' is played out in the mainstream. The best example of this is Arthur Baker's remix of Fleetwood Mac's 'Big Love', which turns the respectable rockers into modernist avant-gardists. In his reworking of the songs Baker refused to obey the rules of the typical pop song and created something completely new of his own. Goodwin stresses that this has nothing to do with postmodern game-playing: 'This aesthetic isn't postmodern at all – it is modernist, with a dance beat. It is Theodor Adorno mistreating Fleetwood Mac, not Walter Benjamin celebrating them.'[39] The critique of the culture industry as dance material.

Goodwin sees the third and last form of sampling as the uninhibited use of digital sound recording as a central element of composition. Sampling thus becomes an aesthetic programme. Theft from other records is part of the meaning of the new 'text'.[40] Goodwin wrote his article on sampling in 1988, when M/A/R/R/S, Bomb The Bass and Coldcut had just demonstrated what sampling could do in the hands of free spirits and anarchists. For the British music theorist, these DJ projects saw theft not only as an aesthetic, but as politics as well. Especially bands whose history goes back to punk, like Cabaret Voltaire, Big Audio Dynamite and KLF, saw the do-it-yourself ideology of dancefloor music as a rebirth of the spirit of punk and its politics: anyone can do anything, he only has to want to. Technique (craft-based skill) can safely be forgotten, in its place there was now simply technology (samplers and sequencers). In the meantime sampling has become so normal that only a few people talk of stealing and plundering, most of them speaking instead of a form of musical quotation that lawyers and professors of jurisprudence might argue about, but without which pop music is unimaginable. Simon Reynolds, whose conservative reservations about house music we have already looked at, also has a problem

37. Cf. BLAIR, Ian: Rick Rubin, in: STONE, Terri, op. cit., p. 98f.

38. SCHNEIDINGER, Dirk: Der Hexer, in: SPEX 10/1990, p. 17.

39. GOODWIN, Andrew, op. cit., p. 271.

40. Cf. Ibid.

with sampling; in 1990 he published an article about it under the headline 'The End of Music'. While Goodwin is calmly aware that sampling certainly doesn't mean the end of traditional ideas of authorship and creativity, but at best a confusing way of calling them into question, Reynolds paints a darker picture. In his anti-technological view, sampling is linked with disorientation, destruction, futurism and the end of the song.[41] And while for Goodwin the 'Age of Plunder' is less an age that has forgotten history, and more the age of the deliberate acceptance and reworking of one's own past, Reynolds sees an unstoppable decon-structivism at work, one which isn't particularly interested in historicity.

Reynolds' position is not an exception, it stands for a faction even within younger pop intellectuals, which votes for a moderated traditionalism within pop music, and only receives new technologies and their aesthetic products sceptically and hesitantly. Because Reynolds is the clearest, most polemic and original thinker among these 'conservatives', it is worth looking more closely at his arguments.

Sampling makes it possible, as in the days of punk, to make music quickly and cheaply as a do-it-yourself process. But this easy access to the means of production does not, in Reynolds' view, promote the democratiza-tion of artistic brilliance. This is a myth, he says. People with talent always rise to the top – in the case of the DJ artists they are the ones with more sense of rhythm and architecture and less sense of music and melodies. The independence from the industry celebrated by both punks and sampling pirates was unrealistic, sampling technology has to be bought from companies directly linked to the record industry. The political dimension of sampling is, for Reynolds, pure whitewash.

Although Reynolds concedes that sampling can be kept exciting by constant aesthetic innovations, he also sees the popularization of the progressive cut-up and bricolage technique as a destabilization of the listener, his values and his perception: 'Blip culture means the death of sequential, linear thought, an erosion of people's ability to plan and manage their lives. There is only a NOW that is either blissed-out, or dreadful.'[42] Sampling is thus seen as a consciousness-manipulating

41. Cf. REYNOLDS, Simon: Sampling, in: idem., op. cit., p. 171.

42. Ibid. p. 169.

technology of confusion. What Reynolds doesn't see is that both house and hip-hop have used sampling for the construction rather than the deconstruction of consciousness. Even the mid-80s European synthesizer-based projects, for all the pleasure they take in disunity and heterogeneity, are driven by the desire to create an internally consistent pop song, and worked as such.

One other danger in Reynolds' eyes is the reworking of old soul classics, torn from their soul context and swallowed up by the unemotional coldness of the machine, to be called up at the push of a button: 'With one push of the button, black heart becomes white noise, detached from its original context, a piercing bleep in your cranium, an abstraction.'[43] A heartless, futurist world opens up for the British lover of guitar bands: soul becomes technique, passion becomes volume. By the time soul has died, artistic passion is an irrelevance, and a 'new sonic architecture'[44] is born.

Andrew Goodwin is much more relaxed in his view of the consequences of sampling, establishing that the death of the author is further off than ever and the old discourses about the creator have not been interrupted but continue in a modern form: 'Pop might be eating itself, but the old ideologies and aesthetics are still on the menu.'[45] The new sonic architecture merely requires a more complex and free idea of the author, which not only comes closer to the general truth of the creative act than all forms of post-idealist aesthetics and frees the artist from the duty of being a genius, but also the hitherto undervalued conditions of production such as the technology employed, material resources and the fact of being rooted in a subculture. That pop musicians must turn themselves inside out in the course of a song is not only 'bourgeois nonsense', but no longer corresponds to the state of productive forces, Diederichsen declared in 1987.[46] And yet people who cannot imagine culture without authors should not despair: 'If a piece by LL Cool J consists of one quarter Chuck Berry intro, one quarter Bill Haley lyrics, one quarter Isaac Hayes' "Shaft" and only one quarter LL Cool J's rap, the artistic achievement... is still one hundred percent his.'[47]

The human need to see everything in existence as being

43. Ibid. p. 171.

44. Ibid.

45. GOODWIN, Andrew, op. cit., p. 272.

46. DIEDERICHSEN, Diedrich: Copy Right, in: KONKRET 12/1987.

47. Ibid.

somehow the product of human labour is a fundamental one. Postmodern theory and a considerable array of zeitgeist-monitors and columnists, in the information age in a post-industrial society, speak of the death of the subject, of the bourgeois individual, the monad of the ego. There are many reasons for the death of the subject. Some thinkers draw historical comparisons and establish that the subject is being increasingly broken down by new technological, media and bureaucratic structures. Connections within society have become so complex that a self-centred individual can work only in a fragmentary way linked up to the apparatus. Marxist theorists turn this death of the bourgeois individual into a phenomenon of late capitalism. Absolute alienation means the disappearance of the subject.

Philosophers such as Foucault have unmasked the subject as a human construction of the humanities. The idea of the creative subject, responsible for himself, is just that – an idea – and as such susceptible to transformation within the history of the mind. For thinkers within this tradition there is no death of the subject, because the subject has always been a fixed construction of the humanities. The attempt is made to imagine the individual and the author in a decentred way, without generals and without bosses, as Deleuze and Guattari have demanded. The two French thinkers counter the old centred systems with 'non-centred systems, networks of final automata, in which the communication occurs between one neighbour and another, in which stems and channels are not pre-existent, in which individuals are all interchangeable, defining themselves solely by one *state* at one particular moment, so that local operations are coordinated, and the final overall result is synchronized independently of a central authority.'[48]

In this context the image of man and the artist becomes a highly political question, about centres, hierarchies and power. Deleuze and Guattari's rhizomatic model sympathizes with an absolute absence of hierarchy, and knows that such a state can only be achieved when the old subject dies as an idea: if the old artists and the old subject fall, at some point the state apparatus will fall as well. If this is to be our goal, we can put Warhol,

48. DELEUZE, Gilles/ GUATTARI, Félix: Rhizome, p. 50.

Godard and M/A/R/R/S in the front line, along with the artistic productions promoting decentralization and the breakdown of hierarchies. But the old problems remain here too: however much quoting, sampling and stealing is done – in the end it is the old subjects that undertake their own modernization. Even an examination of technology and the conditions of production does not rescue aesthetics from finally having to believe in the author. He just looks different.

ENGLAND – THE START OF THE EUROPEAN DANCEFLOOR SCENE

M/A/R/R/S and Coldcut, Bomb the Bass and S-Xpress were all products of a dancefloor scene that developed from the mid-80s in England, and not only in London. Apart from the country where all dance music originated, the USA, England was the only country with a lively and wide-ranging club scene. The Young Soul Rebels fused punk and soul in 1977, and after that it was the '81 pop of ABC, Heaven 17 and Duran Duran that kept interest in dancefloor productions alive. At Northern Soul parties and Soul Weekenders, American soul was played alongside funk and disco. After disco disappeared from the mainstream again, there was a small underground disco scene dancing first to Hi-NRG and then to house music. But from quite early on, this disco scene influenced pop musicians from well-known bands like New Order, Bananarama and the newly founded Pet Shop Boys. As if on a conveyor belt, the most successful team of British producers, Stock, Aitken & Waterman produced a series of number one hits with stars like Samantha Fox, Mel & Kim, Bananarama, Kylie Minogue and Jason Donovan. Underlying all their productions was a watered-down combination of disco and Hi-NRG components.

ACID HOUSE

Acid house was the first dancefloor movement in Europe to enjoy mass success. In 1987, a group of Londoners who had spent the summer in Ibiza throughout the mid-80s, gave Ibiza reunion parties, first in the Project Club in London, and then, from November, in Shoom and in Heaven. The DJ at Shoom was Danny Rampling, in Heaven it was Paul Oakenfold. Both clubs played a mixture of Chicago acid house, indie guitar music and hip-hop. More stylistically distinct than the music was the fashion – summer clothes only, particularly white T-shirts – and a great deal of strobe-lit dry ice that transformed the clubs into unreal landscapes. Within a very short time acid house nights had become a sensation in London's night-life.

Acid house as a musical style was invented in Chicago as a variant of the city's house sound. The music was based around the sounds that could be produced with a Roland TBR-303. This bass-line generator was put on the market in 1981 by the Japanese electronics firm Roland to complement its TR-606 rhythm machine. The little silver box with an octave keyboard and six knobs sold so badly that production was packed in after two years. With the introduction of the first MIDI model TR-909, the old Rhythm Composers became obsolete.[49] But not among Chicago's house musicians, who only really discovered the 303 in 1985. When DJ Pierre and his friend Spanky bought the Roland bass computer, they originally wanted to use it – as the instruction manual suggested – to programme bass-lines. But then they discovered that the six knobs and the resonance filters they controlled could distort, stretch and twist the beats of the bass-line. DJ Pierre was enthusiastic: 'We were trying to figure out what knobs do what. The machine already had acid in it. At first I thought it was some kind of shit we gotta erase out of it before we program it. Spanky had a fifteen minute beat track he'd programmed a couple of days earlier, it was just the beat that happened to be playing and I kept turning the knobs to see what kind of effect they had on the bassline.'[50] The result was one of the

49. MIDI stands for 'Musical Instruments Digital Interface' and was invented in 1981 by the American company Sequential Circuits. With the help of MIDI, the compatability of electronic instruments was normalized, and digitalized exchange of information between the instruments regulated. MIDI-connected instruments can be served by a central control unit. (Cf. NEWQUIST, H.P., op. cit., p. 37–58.) MIDI technology was integrated into almost all studios at the end of the 80s.

50. MARCUS, Tony: Acid's Back, in: i-D 7/1992.

DJ Pierre

first acid house tracks, which was recorded on tape and then given to Ron Hardy, who played the tape four or five times in the Warehouse. Via bootleg tapes recorded in the club on Walkmans, the tracks by DJ Pierre and Spanky were quickly passed around, and people asked desperately for these exotic-sounding tracks in record-shops. The name 'acid tracks' was derived from acid rock, and not because LSD was the drug of choice in the Warehouse, as DJ Pierre explains. 'We thought of acid rock. I was very naïve, I didn't think of drugs, I don't do drugs, I never have. There were rumours going round about acid tabs in the water of the Warehouse.'[51] But at first acid house was not drug music, just – like the Detroit techno sound – a variant of house music.

At the same time as DJ Pierre and Spanky, Phuture, in 'Phuture Trax', uses the Roland TBR-303. Then came the DJs Sleazy D, Adonis and BamBam with their attempts to test out the scope of the six resonance filters. The European acid imitators, who discovered the music two years later, didn't use the Roland 303 but the next model, the 909. But in 1992 many DJs and producers were still raving about the individual sound of the old 303, which was actually designed only to complement the bass-line. For Mike Banks of Detroit's Underground Resistance label, the 303 is an unachieved classic. 'I guess the basic reason I like using the 303 is because the sound variation is almost endless thanks to those damn knobs. It's one of the most basic synthesizers you can have and I assimilate it to the wheel. A wheel is the type of invention that trendy people might say is old, but every time that fucking aeroplane lands, your ass is riding on wheels. Like the wheel, the 303 is a perfect invention.'[52]

For Diederichsen acid house is 'the first completely anonymous and largely atonal mass music in history'.[53] Acid house doesn't only seek the right notes or melodies, but sounds whose consumption, in combination with the consumption of drugs, can lead to an Overdose (the name of one of the bands). The names of the bands and projects, most of which are masks for DJs, were often artistic products with a notable preference for machine-like titles such as MD 11, Chip E and Modell 500. Anonymity can thus be interpreted as a transfer of authorship to music-

51. Ibid.

52. Ibid.

53. DIEDERICHSEN, Diedrich: Vom Ende der Wahrheit, loc. cit.

generating technology. In Manchester at this time a band took the name 808 State to prove its reverence for the Roland drum machine. Acid is 303 State.

And the expanding 303 State made lifestyle history: the Ibiza-inspired fashion of T-shirts, shorts, bandannas, shades and trainers relativized the fashionable hipsterdom that had previously been the rule in the clubs. Dressing down was tolerated by the doormen, and within a very short time the white T-shirts, most of them printed with yellow smiley faces, went on sale in stores and supermarkets. The former symbol of love and happiness in the drug-filled hippie underground became part of the 'pimp' style of soul stars like Isaac Hayes in the 70s, and was rediscovered by the clubbers of 1987.[54] Smileys represented sun, good times and fun. The Smiley outgrew the London underground within only a year, and became a mass icon that was seen on the streets of Budapest by 1988. Europe had experienced its first mass-based dancefloor subculture.

54. Cf. GODFREY, John/ COLLIN, Matthew: Smiley, in: GODFREY, John (Ed.), op. cit., p. 200.

55. Cf. SHAW, Arnold: Dictionary..., p. 372.

SUMMER OF LOVE

In England the summer after acid house, 1988, was baptised the 'Summer of Love'. In deliberate reference to the first 'Summer of Love' celebrated in San Francisco in 1967, the big parties and club evenings sought to revive as much as possible of the euphoric values of the hippie age. The children of the hippie generation were expressing their hope that the world and society could be changed with 'flower power' and 'love'. And although none of the DJs, record producers and i-D journalists had been at the Monterey Festival in 1967, where policemen wore flowers in their helmets,[55] many people hoped for just such a peacefully idyllic atmosphere in their warehouse parties.

Warehouse parties were events which, as the name suggests, were generally held in empty hangars and storehouses. Mostly organized at very short notice, the venues were equipped only with the barest necessities. Most important were the DJ and speaker systems, which were often set up on a lorry so that they could quickly be taken to safety if the police threatened to clear the place. The parties were promoted via flyers and/or chains of phone-calls. Anyone switched in to the subculture's information channels always knew where and when the next warehouse party was taking place. The police sought out the parties because alcohol was served there without a license, and they suspected the dancefloor culture of being a hotbed of all kinds of drug consumption.

Most of the young people who attended these parties in their hundreds and sometimes in their thousands were not members of disadvantaged minorities, but were looking for the excitement of the underground. After punk, the dancefloor scene was the next major teenage revolt in Europe. But where punk lived off hatred, fury and shock, the acid house movement and its successors tried to achieve a fundamentally aggression-free, peace-loving attitude. It was about fun, sex and drugs. It was pure hedonism, according to *i-D* magazine, which, as the central organ of the club scene, had joined in hailing the Summer of Love. Unlike the political consciousness and radical moralism of the first summer of love in 1967, the activity in the clubs and warehouses was one of ecstatic self-gratification: 'Undoubtedly fuelled by Ecstasy, thousands of perspiring bodies danced under one roof screaming their heads off. Paisley patterns, face-painting, peace symbols were worn with benign smiles, no more than the trappings of a past era.'[56] The children of the generation of '68 had learned from the mistakes of their parents and punk. They no longer wanted to protest for some vague utopia, but rather to realize their idea of a happy life in the immediate present.

The DJs were the great heroes of the warehouse movement. Hunted by the police, badly paid and still resolutely good-natured, they embodied the pure and good spirit of the dancefloor underground. Without light effects and without a license (drinks were generally brought by the dancers themselves or sold in cans) the warehouse parties were the purest and rawest form of 'clubbing'. This purism necessarily put the work of the DJs at the centre. Many of the famous English DJs who also enjoyed success as producers in the late 80s, began their careers at warehouse parties.

56. GODFREY, John: Summer of Love, in: idem, op. cit., p. 207.

RAVE

Rave was the continuation of the dance euphoria of acid house and the Summer of Love. Rave represented a new music, a new youth culture and a new kind of party and club night.

The text of a 1992 flyer for New York rave club Nasa attempted a definition of rave, or rather intelligently avoided doing so: 'Do not try to interpret or explain the word Rave to someone who has not experienced the pure extasy [sic] of being in total harmony with his or her surroundings, i.e. the feeling of safety dancing within a crowd of smiling faces, of the rush of a DJ taking you on a mind trip down into deep dark caverns of trance and then up to the highest peeks of spiritual utopia. Do not try to explain. Just tell them to open their minds.'

The word rave first makes its appearance in the dancefloor context in Jamaica, where dancehall evenings were called 'ravings'. In England the term 'raver' was used for primarily black clubbers who listened to rap and house music and who chiefly visited underground jams and warehouse parties. Their taste for soul was to provide decisive encouragement for this music in England from 1986–8 (see next chapter, pp. 292ff).[57] Around 1988, under the influence of acid house and the Summer of Love, Manchester developed its own club scene, in which music by guitar bands was played alongside house and disco. In the Hacienda, one of the most important clubs of the 80s, musicians of all hues met up and, however different their musical origins, quickly agreed about the new dance beats. The product of this euphoria was a new kind of music that put house beats underneath well-known British guitar sounds. In 1990 the new rave music, as it was called, had conquered the world. German music magazine *Spex* had the headline 'Rave-O-lution' on the cover of its October 1990 issue, and could hardly contain its enthusiasm:

There hasn't been so much so good music from England for years! Primal Scream, Happy Mondays, Stone Roses, The Farm – in 1990 they're groovier, higher and more mental than ever. And they all have a

57. Cf. COLLIN, Matthew: Ravers, in: GODFREY, John (Ed.), op. cit., p. 176.

star DJ like Andy Weatherall or Paul Oakenfold, who remix their pop songs into dancefloor killers. England's at a massive endless rave. The whole world's talking about Manchester. We're talking about the whole world: rave mania has started to overflow on to the continent.[58]

Once again it was the DJs who allowed a new pop music style to arise out of the fusion of guitar bands with dance beats. Before the guitar band concerts, house DJs span records, and the audience, which until then would at best have wiggled their heads or tapped their feet, danced throughout the gigs as well, as though at a club. Bands like The Shamen mixed club night, concert and multi-media shows into so-called 'Synergy' evenings held every two weeks in London. These nights, according to the band members of The Shamen, were no longer about an individual band or characters, 'but about the clubs and the streets'.[59] That tried-and-tested fossil of pop, the 'band', was on the point of dissolution, yet at the same time was showing new signs of life. But as with the putative disappearance of the author, the creator or the artist, the type of organization known as a band was only being rethought in a more open and complex way. DJs could belong to a band project in the short term without forfeiting any of their autonomy. As in M/A/R/R/S and Bomb The Bass, the artists saw themselves as project-oriented.

Andrew Weatherall saw a new form of freedom being realized for the DJs, both in the playing of records and the remixing of music. The final barriers between dancefloor music and the styles of pop music that were not club-oriented seemed to disappear. A philosophy of 'open-mindedness',[60] as Weatherall called it, brought together pop scenes that would previously have had absolutely nothing to do with each other. But for Weatherall the new possibilities of remixing had their darker side. 'The slogan "If it moves – remix it!" produced a lot of crap... I've been offered songs by the Clash or the Cure, but why destroy things that stand on their own with a remix?'[61] Weatherall mixed, and continues to mix, only songs that interest him, songs that he likes. Because of his penchant for pure sound he

58. ZABEL, Sebastian: Children Of The Rave-O-lution, in: SPEX 10/1990, p. 6.

59. KLINKMANN/ SCHNEIDER: Peace, Love, so was in der Art, in: SPEX 10/1990, p. 11.

60. ZABEL, Sebastian: loc. cit., p. 8.

61. Ibid.

often does without vocals, giving the song a powerful bass-line instead. But he won't be pinned down to a particular style or a preference for particular kinds of instrumentation. When he was accused of liking brass too much, he composed an extremely bass-heavy song that he called 'The Death of the Timbale'. The repertoire of Weatherall remixes ran from old industrial veterans like Throbbing Gristle to Swiss neo-pop artists Yello. Since 1992 he has run his own label, on which he releases both his own productions and remixes and the works of younger DJs.[62]

DJs like Weatherall, Paul Oakenfold and Terry Farley shaped the sound of rave music, and rave music in turn made them famous. In the music papers and the colour supplements, DJs suddenly enjoyed the same status as musicians. The conquest of pop music by dancefloor had turned the DJs into stars, not only for producing records, but for playing them. Other DJs like Adamski moved from playing records to the live playing of keyboards and drum computers, thus blurring the distinctions between concert and DJ set. His LPs are studio recordings based on live performances with the greatest possible opportunities for improvisation.

Raves became mass events, and rave culture was one of the chief pillars of youth culture in the early 90s. In 1990 Colin Angus of The Shamen predicted the great future of rave.

Rave is the entertainment form of the future! Sooner or later it'll happen in Europe as well, and blow away the boring old rock concerts! It's our feeling, since we discovered the acid scene. Rock music's a goner, no doubt about it. Raves are so much more fun, and musically better than anything that came out of disco. The difference from disco is… that people come for other reasons. You just went to the disco to pull women. Now it's about feeling communality, a shared social experience, a feeling of life. From that point of view our roots are still in the sixties. The rave is about the combination of drugs, light and music. Of course there's the escapist, hedonistic moment. But what's crucial about the event is the communality thing. Peace, Love, Unity, something like that.[63]

62 . NEEDS, Kris: Andrew Weatherall, in: MIXMAG 3/1993.

63 . KLINKMANN/ SCHNEIDER, op. cit., p. 11.

Andrew Weatherall

RARE GROOVES, ACID JAZZ, MODERN SOUL

64. COLLIN, Matthew: Rare Groove, in: GODFREY, John, op. cit., p. 176.

65. Gilles Peterson explained in an interview that the name acid jazz was created as a joke in 1988. 'A friend of mine had just come back from Spain and had brought some acid house records with him, which he announced were the latest thing. But the dancefloor stayed empty. Then it was my turn and I put on a few jazz pieces. The dancefloor was full. To take the piss out of him I called my music acid jazz.' (GORRIS, Lothar: Der Acid-Bluff, in: TEMPO 5/1989.)

66. Cf. KÜNZLER, Hans-Peter: Acid-Jazz, in: WIENER 5/1989.

While acid house and rave were turning thousands of young people in England into clubbers, a whole variety of other dancefloor subcultures was making their way from the underground to the public. In a club in Southall between 1983 and 1984 DJ Norman Jay played old soul and funk records. The sound got its name from a radio show that Norman Jay had on the then pirate station Kiss FM in London: *The Original Rare Groove Show*. 'Rare groove' because it played songs which, when they were made (in the 60s and 70s), no one (or no white people) had bought. Clubs in other towns in England organized rare groove evenings.[64]

Even in the 1960s the mods in England had danced to black American soul from Chicago, Detroit and Philadelphia. In England since that time, particularly in the industrial cities of the North, there had been clubs that were open every night. The tradition of Northern Soul was, apart from the rare groove scene, a major influence on the new form of soul that was produced in England from the mid-80s.

In 1988, London DJ Gilles Peterson brought a new sound to the club-going public. Peterson mixed old jazz with hip-hop and funk, and produced a sound which – for want of anything better – was called acid jazz.[65] For Peterson the music is the expression of an attitude as close to Coltrane as Big Daddy Kane.[66] He sees himself as the typical representative of this new generation of jazz-lovers and clubbers. At the age of 18 he started playing records in a jazz club, where he tried to bring more life and more young people to the dancefloor. During the Summer of Love, Peterson produced a compilation of new acid jazz productions from young British musicians who were distilling a new kind of music out of a revival cult. He also got involved with two record labels and produced samplers of old, danceable jazz material. Since then Peterson has played records in the new acid jazz clubs everywhere in Europe.

STRICTLY TURNTABLIZED: FROM SOUL II SOUL AND MASSIVE ATTACK TO TRICKY AND MO'WAX

Jazzie B. from Soul II Soul

In the mid-80s Soul II Soul was founded in London by two black DJs, Jazzie B. and Daddy Harvey. They worked together on a sound system playing soul, hip-hop and funk and their parties attracted so many people that they opened a shop in Camden Town selling their own designs and accessories. The style was a mixture of ethnic African and sporty club outfits (T-shirts, hooded pullovers, bomber jackets). Underlying all their enterprises, however, was the sound system – 'the knowledge of business came from that foundation, of running and organizing the sound',[67] explained Jazzie B.

Eventually Jazzie B. decided to bring out his own records. In 1989 Soul II Soul had massive hits with 'Keep On Moving' and 'Back To Life', and with their debut album *Club Classics Volume 1*. Over the next few years Soul II Soul was built up into an entertainment business that produced videos, had its own club evenings, designed fashion and opened record and fashion shops. It was so successful that in 1989 the National Association for the Advancement of Colored People (NAACP) in the United States gave Jazzie B. an award for being 'an outstanding black role model'.[68]

Soul II Soul's motto was 'A happy face a thumping bass for a loving race', and they sought to overcome barriers between black and white, rich and poor in favour of an all-encompassing club culture. Soul II Soul's music tried to provide something like a common denominator of the British club scene in the late 80s. The *Club Classics* combined heavy hip-hop beats and sweet soul vocals with the sensual grind of reggae rhythms and the erotic vibe of house.

Soul II Soul is a product of DJ culture. Its beginnings as a sound system bear this out, as do the biographies of Jazzie B. and his partner Nellee Hooper. They both

67. BAKER, Lindsay: Funki Like a Dred, in: THE FACE 4/1989, p. 62.

68. Cf. HAMACHER, Adriana: Soul II Soul and Sound Systems, in: MIXMAG 3/1993.

began their careers as DJs, with Jazzie B. standing behind the turntables at the age of eleven. 'We were both DJs,' explains Jazzie B. 'We've spent most of our lives listening to other people's music. Now we're fillin' the stuff that gets us high and putting it back.'[69] Both are trained musicians, but they know how to programme drum computers and arrange samples. While Jazzie B. prefers reggae and soft house, Hooper clearly prefers (heavy) hip-hop. They share a love of soul music and the desire to take the production of dancefloor music in new directions.

The stubborn four-four rhythm of many American productions is, in the view of the two members of Soul II Soul, a sign of poverty. Soul II Soul doesn't want to fit into the well-worn schemata of dancefloor productions. 'Our music captures a lot of elements people know but have been left out recently, like R&B, jazz fusion, real instruments. The way our production works, you can turn it down and use it as background music or have it as loud as you like... Nobody is alienated by Soul II Soul.'[70]

Like other DJ projects before it, Soul II Soul was more an idea and a concept than a fixed band, and disunity has often been the basis of their compositions. The creative battle between different ideas and notions is fought out in the studio, 'until we end up with something completely different. And what we achieve together always seems to work better than any of the ideas we come up with on our own.'[71] DJ culture.

At around the same time as Soul II Soul started working on a musical style of their own, four Bristol DJs got together to produce hip-hop records on their own label. Pop stars like Boy George, Lisa Stansfield and Neneh Cherry commissioned remixes from the Wild Bunch, as the production team called itself. Nellee Hooper, who was originally part of the Wild Bunch, switched to Jazzie B.'s Soul II Soul sound system in 1988, and strengthened its hip-hop influence. The three remaining members of Wild Bunch, who called themselves Massive Attack, produced their debut LP *Blue Lines* in 1990 with singer Shara Nelson: three streams of consciousness (male) with the good fortune to find a voice (female).

Massive Attack had no line-up and no fixed structure in which individual members could be assigned a

69. SANDALL, Robert: Soul II Soul, in: ROLLING STONE, 12 July 1990, p. 105.

70. Ibid.

71. Ibid.

Massive Attack

72. Ibid.

particular function. The musicians saw their community – as did Soul II Soul – as a 'loosely-based idea', in which unity isn't produced by pulling on a single strand, it's already present in the work's diversity. 'The difference between now and The Wild Bunch is that we're not fighting for supremacy all the time, we agree to differ. We all know we hate each other and that's the way it is.'[72] Withstanding and thinking through differences, and allowing them to become part of the creative process is a fundamental idea in the DJ aesthetic, in which difference is always reflected in the separateness of the two turntables. In the first non-band-based DJ projects, this difference is built into the idea underlying the project. The heterogeneity of the music makes it easier to understand and experience heterogeneity within the group. With *Blue Lines* unity as diversity attains a new level of perfection. The synthesis of components that had battled against each other and seemed impossible to bring together exploded the traditional order of old musical categories and stylistic divisions. And while in all earlier DJ projects collage and fragmentation appeared as part of the aesthetic – in whatever form – *Blue Lines* seemed like the first work of a new whole, on which further work could now commence. This kind of music had no name, it was something completely new. *Blue Lines* is without a doubt one of the masterpieces of DJ culture. This record was to be the epitome of the refined and brilliant achievement that DJ culture was capable of. Dirk Scheuring, one of the first German journalists to draw attention to Massive Attack, described the sound as a transcendence of dancefloor according to its own laws. The musicians of Massive Attack 'take a music that is pretty strictly functional, strip it down to a skeleton of rhythms and bass sounds and redefine it according to its rules... The music of Massive Attack is – given the effect-charged breathlessness of most contemporary dancefloor productions – organized in unusually long and peaceful stretches; melodies, song, whispering and strange noises float whirring in and out of the arrangements, producing a hypnotic atmosphere; and the lyrics follow associations that can lead thematically within five lines from Kleenex tissues via Maggie Thatcher to a list of old records that have influenced the band.'[73]

As DJs, the members of Massive Attack wanted to make music that went beyond DJ territory and could not just be defined with reference to its danceability. 'We don't want to make music that's just aimed at the feet, for the club environment with the strobes and the drugs and the whole vibe. Ours is more of a... mood thing which you can play anywhere, any time. We'd rather do something which we feel is going to last.'[74] Like Soul II Soul, Massive Attack wanted to transcend the dancefloor and create a music that does more than make people move. As an intellectual construct with diverse layers and forms of discourse, *Blue Lines* is an adventure in perception that taxes the average pop listener just as much as it does the average clubber. Massive Attack followed their streams of conscious-

73. SCHEURING, Dirk: Die LP des Jahres, in: VOGUE 5/1991, p. 112.

74. DALTON, Stephen: Herb Crawlers, in: NEW MUSICAL EXPRESS, 15 January 1992.

ness, which drew not only on fragments of text but above all on music. In the song 'Daydreaming', rapper 3D speaks of being lost in the world of sounds: 'living in my headphones' isolates the musicians from all events going on outside the record-player. The headphones feed the main strands of perception, so that words, images and smells are made secondary to the music.

For 3D the danger of dancefloor culture is that the consciousness of the listeners risks wasting away. Lines like 'rock your body' are nothing but stupid imperatives that objectivize the dancer – which is exactly what disco and house want – and make reflection impossible – another thing that disco and house want. The music of Massive Attack is aimed at the 'roof of your head'. 'We just write as we think,' explains 3D, 'which is fragments of ideas and the idea they conjure up. You end up with raps that are almost stream of consciousness, cut up and put back together like something in William Burroughs, it doesn't have to have a point, so long as there's information in there which people can retrieve if they want to.'[75]

75. THOMPSON, Ben: All Shipshape and Bristol fashion, in: INDEPENDENT REVIEW, 26 May 1991, p. 18.

In 1994 their second LP appeared with the title *Protection*, which, in its rhizomatic flourishing, was easily a match for the sensational debut. Particularly in the song 'Sly', the carpet of sound reached symphonic levels. Rich string sections and the ethereal voice of Nicolette established something like a new genre of Black Romanticism within hip-hop-related DJ culture.

Just a year after the appearance of *Protection*, Massive Attack brought out a dub version of the record under the title *No Protection*, in which the tracks were remixed by reggae producer Mad Professor. The treatment of sounds and rhythm structures appears even freer and more associative, and only occasionally do the vocals attain any kind of order. It is a sound that can simply be described as 'free music', a sound that has turned its back on the demands of the dancefloor. The functionality imposed by the requirements of night-life is only fragmentarily present in the ideas underlying the music. Just as Pink Floyd moved beyond the old ideas of pop music with their concept albums and concerts, the hip-hop avant-garde is transcending all previously accepted understandings of DJ music and culture.

76. Cf. VERRICO, Lisa: Welcome to Portishead. Please Read Carefully, in: DAZED & CONFUSED 9/1994, p. 95.

Dummy *cover by Portishead*

Dummy by Portishead was the sensation of 1994. Beth Gibbons' fraillly beautiful voice moaned lines like 'Give me a reason to love you/ Give me a reason to be a woman' over dark sounds that could only be held together with difficulty by the provocatively slow breakbeats. *Dummy* was to be just as groundbreaking an album as *Club Classics Vol. 1* and *Blue Lines*, demonstrating new possibilities within DJ culture and documenting a sense of life that had previously been somewhat rare in dancefloor: despair as beauty, interrupted with wonderful, sensitive melodies and samples from James Bond and Western soundtracks. Before Portishead Geoff Barrows, the mastermind behind the band, had only composed one song for Neneh Cherry's LP *Homebrew*, and yet his arrangements for *Dummy* sounded wise and mature. To make the whole spectrum of his sound ideas accessible, Geoff released countless Portishead remixes, whose delicacy and refinement came close to the boundaries of ambient kitsch.

Geoff's models were hip-hop bands like Black Sheep, Leaders of the New School and A Tribe Called Quest. Despite these roots in hip-hop, which give the record its fundamental character, the musician wanted Portishead's music to rise above all the categories of dancefloor music. Like Massive Attack and Soul II Soul, Portishead aims to be music for life, not just night-life. The perfect Portishead concert would be a club evening with a DJ playing 'mellow music', where the audience can sit and drink tea while the band plays on stage.[76]

Tricky also comes from Bristol, from the same part of the city as Massive Attack. After a number of twelve-inch singles, early in 1995 he released his first LP entitled *Maxinquaye*. Even darker and more melancholy than Massive and Portishead, *Maxinquaye* documents an almost Kafkaesque hopelessness. When he was younger, Tricky says, people were always telling him to 'get a life', and he wondered what that could possibly mean. After he saw all the lost creatures in the clubs who didn't even know they were lost, Tricky sensed what the phrase meant. He knew he was lost, and in writing his song lyrics he tried to rediscover himself. In the end it was all an attempt to 'get a life'.[77]

Like feverish dreams, Tricky's songs revolve around misery and violence. The dragging breakbeats draw the listener hypnotically inside the music and on into the head of the musician, where there is also room for punk and new wave songs, or for a new form that might be called hip-hop blues. The insistence of the depressive mood gives the music its inevitability and it is the fate of the artist to give voice to it. 'The terrible world I have in my head. But how to free myself without tearing. And a thousand times better to tear than restrain it or bury it in me. That is what I am here for, that is quite clear to me,'[78] writes Kafka in his diaries. Calmly, confidently and stoically, the musicians of Massive Attack, Portishead and Tricky set about their task of making the world between their ears available for everyone to hear.

Less self-destructive and isolated than a writer like Kafka, these musicians experience the liberation of their cerebral worlds as something that brings peace and salvation. The anti-hermetic and anti-autistic aspects of the DJ culture removes the self-tormenting aspects of their journeys within. In *Maxinquaye*, Tricky stresses musical kinships. He radicalizes Public Enemy's 'Black Steel' into a 'white' piece of punk rock, while he gives another track a soul feel by looping a Tom Jones song. The title of his ironic self-reproach: 'Brand New You're Retro'. Tricky demonstrates the new as the old, the retrospective as the basis of all innovation in countless references. His participation in Massive Attack's Karmacoma is apparent in lyrical quotations scattered throughout his own album. The network of references becomes particularly dense in the song 'Hell Is Round the Corner', which is based on the same Isaac Hayes loop as 'Glory Box' by Portishead – most of the lyrics are familiar from the Massive album *Protection*. The Bristol community, whose music between 1994 and 1995 represents the highest state of DJ culture, is thus loosely yet distinctly connected. *Maxinquaye* documents working structures of communication.

Within this freeform exchange, Tricky concentrates on the typical Bristolian, dub-heavy, dragging sound. The references to Massive Attack and Portishead outline the idea of a communal project. The rest of the world is

77. Cf. O'HAGAN, Sean: The Wilde Bunch, in: THE FACE 2/1995, p. 46.

78. KAFKA, Franz: Diaries 1910–1923.

Tricky (right) with singer Martina

carefully excluded. 'You have to live with yourself, beware of our appetite, I can't breathe and I can't see, M.T.V. moves too fast, I refuse to understand,' say Tricky's lyrics. There are limits to openness: that's how it finds its way to form.

Another project closely connected with new hip-hop-derived adventures in sound is London's Mo'Wax label. 'Abstract Musicology' is the phrase that James Lavelle uses to describe the label he founded in 1992. Lavelle was 18 years old at the time, and had borrowed the money from friends and acquaintances who, like himself, believed in the future of a new music beyond jazz and hip-hop. Encouraged by the success of Massive Attack and the Talking Loud label, Lavelle started pressing records which soon enjoyed cult status.

In 1987, when M/A/R/R/S were first unsettling people's listening habits, James Lavelle was eleven years old. He grew up with hip-hop and acid jazz, as well as the Beastie Boys and techno raves. In this sense he represents a newer generation that is making the next leap after M/A/R/R/S and Bomb The Bass, and producing DJ music in even freer forms. If James Lavelle is honest, he isn't interested in giving his label a clear profile. There are no contradictions between techno, house and trip-hop. Lavelle likens his own label to the eclectic techno label Warp rather than an acid jazz label.[79] Both Warp and Mo'Wax produce 'soundtracks of experimentation'. Within the realm of techno and house there have also been musicians (see the techno section, pp. 313ff.) who have emancipated them-selves from club life and tend to liken their compositional work more to Stockhausen than to Giorgio Moroder.

Listening habits fragment as fast as new sounds hit the record decks. Every form of deconstruction and information is eagerly and intelligently received. It almost seems as though the 'soundtracks of experimentation' cannot be too outlandish to be successful. Pop music as the 'sole and positive feedback between sound and the listener's ears'[80] works better than ever. 'Hear Between the Silence' is one of the pieces by Monday Michiru on Mo'Wax. And almost all Mo'Wax records constantly demand just this

79 . Cf. CRYSELL, Andy: Mo Wax Than Most, in: DAZED & CONFUSED 9/1994, p. 53.

80 . KITTLER, Friedrich A.: Der Gott der Ohren, in: idem: Draculas Vermächtnis, p. 144.

James Lavelle

way of listening.

As Stockhausen used to like pointing out, you don't invent new music, you find it. The new is not created but made possible. Innovative artists are therefore working prospectively: for them 'the experiment is not something temporary, but a permanent condition'.[81] The openness of the hip-hop innovators is constantly making things happen, despite the fact that the focus of the work is always based on concrete construction.

In England, filigree dancefloor music is called ambient hip-hop or – because it sounds so like a drug soundtrack – trip-hop. Melodies only emerge as ruins from sound landscapes that seem to follow a new tonality. The notes are strangely familiar, as if from past dreams, and when a voice breaks through the fog of abstract sounds and 'concrete' breakbeats, it sounds like the voice of a shadow. There is a DJ Shadow track which poses the question, 'What Does Your Soul Look Like?' and as with all good questions there are no simple answers. Mo'Wax twelve inches sound like insoluble riddles and eternal secrets. DJ Shadow, a former old school DJ from California, gives the breakbeats a poetic aura that answers the question of the design of the soul, at least for him. The soul lies somewhere between the headphones, and in it there are thousands of records from Rachmaninov to Gillespie, from Pink Floyd to Public Enemy. The soul is made of vinyl. 'What Mo'Wax wants is mostly to experiment with the music we produce,' explains Lavelle. 'There's no plan, no rules. We just do it and try to make a few heads spin.'[82] His fellow combatants come from all parts of the world.

Particularly exciting is the jazz hip-hop scene from Japan, with cult band Major Force (also a record label) and the two DJs Krush and Takemura. In the Japanese variant of hip-hop it is clear just how far the style has developed. No culture, no society and no generation is excluded. Dancefloor has become the universal language of pop music.

The credits on the *Headz* sampler run from Sun Ra via Josh Davis to Detroit techno, ambient house and artificial intelligence. The graphics on the cover feature an orange matchstick-man whose head is shown against the background of a turntable. The tonearm is

81. STOCKHAUSEN, Karlheinz: Elektronische Musik und Automatik, in: idem: Texte zur Musik 1963–1970, p. 234.

82. POSCHARDT, Ulf: Klang eines Schattens, in: VOGUE 1/1995, p. 84.

Cover of Headz *sampler*

resting in his head. There is no better illustration of a DJ's stream of consciousness. The records of Mo'Wax try directly to capture the melodies and rhythms whirling around our heads.

This approach is pursued programmatically. 'A JIGSAW PUZZLE FOR THE INTELLECT – TECHNOLOGICAL SIMULATION OF CONSCIOUSNESS – A MENTAL MYSTERY MOVIE – ELECTRONIC IMAGERY' reads the cover of a Major Force twelve inch. The extent to which consciousness can be simulated technologically seems only to be a question of equipment as far as Major Force are concerned. The same cover features greetings to the EMS sampler, the Moog synthesizer and the old VCS 3 that even Pink Floyd used to use, showing the various oscillator knobs and filter frequency buttons on the old synthesizer. The journey into undiscovered galaxies of 'possible music' is made with old equipment, because historicism in the digital age mainly occurs via the use of *historic* instruments. The electrically generated sounds announce the birth of the switching circuits.

If we take the idea of directly recording consciousness a little further, its technological stringency becomes apparent. Life in the headphones as sung by Massive Attack feeds consciousness with the whole of musical history, which then fuses into new sounds as if by itself. By this point, the DJ principle of two turntables and a mixing desk has become a metaphor for the DJ's consciousness, even if the instrumentation of this new music long ago ceased to be limited to just these machines. *Strictly Turntablized* is the name of the record by DJ Krush, which, with its strictly modernist hip-hop essentialism, follows on directly from the masterpieces of DJ music by Grandmaster Flash and DJ Premier of Gang Starr.

DJ Krush

DANCEFLOOR STYLE

In line with the evermore filigree aesthetic of the music, a sense of style also grew within club culture. The truly innovative redefinitions of fashion and design remained the elitist concern of a few people, most of whom worked directly in the subcultural environment of the clubs. But club culture was such that the hipsterdom of the experts and fashion professionals made its way, with breaks and trivializations on the way, into the tastes of the dancing masses.

Disco had only changed fashion, people's behaviour when they went out, and musical taste, but hip-hop as a phenomenon had its own artform, graffiti, its own dance style – breakdancing – its own fashion and its own lifestyle. The dancefloor movement in England and Europe extended the sphere of its influence to every imaginable area of design: magazines came into being, fashion was designed with the club in mind, graphic design, furniture and skateboards were inspired by night-life. As in the wake of punk, the youth culture and subculture 'revolution' was followed by an avalanche of by-products outside the clubs and the recording studios. More than anything else, the 80s were the decade of night-life, according to the 1990 i-D guide. Clubs, fashion and music were based on a youth culture that saw the chance once more to create a world on the basis of its own ideas.

In a 1991 collection of photographs reflecting the diversity of dancefloor style, Cynthia Rose tried to take stock:

During the latter half of the 1980s, London witnessed the making of remarkable social history. From illicit radio stations through improvised nightclubs, young Londoners helped to construct a completely alternative leisure landscape. Its aim was celebration, its glue was music and the changes it engineered and explored now affect the music industry, the advertising business and many related areas of design. Socially, this world united Britons of many ages who differed widely in background, race and taste. And the inspiration they took from each other was broadcast across the globe.[83]

The narrower spectrum of dancefloor style, which also influenced the mainstream of fashion and graphic design in the late 80s, ranged from club fliers via television advertisements to music videos. What had hitherto been the characteristic feature of a subculture now became the universal actualization of the media.

83. ROSE, Cynthia: Design After Dark, p. 7. Other documents rich in material, particularly about European dancefloor culture, are contained in the excellent i-D Lexicon of the 80s, *A Decade of i-Deas* and in Liz McQuiston's *Graphic Agitation*.

As in the last days of punk, the sellout into content-free formalism happened pretty quickly, and innovations in graphic design and semiotics were robbed of their faults and fissures and trivialized. This led to such media manifestations as a television advertisement for a bank featuring breakbeats, computer graphics and/or a teenager with a baseball cap and sideburns.

Growing levels of trivialization promoted levels of sophistication within the semiotic system of club fashion. In elite circles in London, New York, Tokyo and perhaps even Berlin, the guidelines for the prominent sign-shifts within the subculture were constantly being redefined. Companies like Goodenough, Acupuncture, Hysteric Glamour and X-Large, run by the Beastie Boys, keep their product circulation deliberately low to bring the number of customers down to a hard core and prevent mass commercialization. Even if these protective mechanisms are gradually becoming less effective, the authentic can still be distinguished from the plethora of fakes. As in all areas of cultural production, intelligence, stringency, a wealth of ideas and charm decide the quality of creations in fashion and design.

Fashion is particularly important for DJ culture. Nightlife lives on appearance, and the appearance must be really clever, radiantly beautiful or skilfully malicious to radiate around the DJ's desk. Viennese fashion designer and orthodox modernist Helmut Lang, who has two Technics and a mixing desk in his studio, answers the question of why the word 'Backstage' is printed in grey on a black Helmut Lang T-shirt: 'Here we have a word that has become a sign. Signs speak differently from words. If you want to understand it you have to know the code. Backstage – literally: behind the stage. Where it happens. Where not everyone is allowed. Where the language is English and work is a battle of nerves, alcohol is served in paper cups and the most beautiful beauties are suddenly standing there in their underwear. The code also says something that might sound a bit presumptuous: This is serious – this is our life. Real life. Not the show.'[84] And if real life is like a show, the show is superfluous. It is at precisely this point that club fashion also works in the rest of life. What looks to non-experts like either

84 . USLAR, Moritz, from: 'Ich bin nur zufällig hier. Meine Kleidung ist mitgekommen, ohne mich zu fragen.' In: SZ-MAGAZIN, 3 March 95, p. 39.

show or sloppiness is a celebration of real life. As Helmut Lang stresses, it's serious. The opposite of indifference and amusement. Fun.

RAINALD GOETZ – LITERATURE UNDER THE DJ'S DESK

In Germany in the early 80s, stimulated by the shocks of punk, the 'Neue Deutsche Welle' came into being, trying to develop an autonomous pop music in the Federal Republic. The Neue Deutsche Welle consisted on the one hand of mainstream-oriented musicians like Nena, Markus and Extrabreit, and on the other of avant-garde bands like DAF (Deutsch-Amerikanische Freundschaft), Palais Schaumburg and Der Plan. The same period saw the development of the new figurative, neo-Expressionist painting of the 'Junge Wilde', all of whose artists have been influenced by punk music. And finally, after some delay, there came a literary scene of journalists and writers, who didn't want to 'cancel out every feeling, every *idea* with the critical hole-punch',[85] as people tended to do in the 70s. The resistance of the generation of '68, which the system had tolerated as a critical supplement to itself, was, as the 'Junge Wilde' Peter Glaser put it, 'an intellectual dead duck'.[86] In 1977 punk changed the world: punk's song-writers were 'the first writers at the end of the languishing literary 70s who finally had enough: [in Germany they called themselves] "Rawums".'[87] But it was quite a long time before a really autonomous literature came into being. For Glaser, the best book of 1981 was a record: the album *Monarchie und Alltag* by the German band Fehlfarben. 'Adrenalin-rush, disturbing and unrestrained. Snappy, edgy, witty. Appropriate…'[88] – these are the terms in which he describes the new writing. 'Strategies between ruthless rejection and offensive affirmation are being tested out.'[89] The new narrator freed himself from all his ideological models and antiquated notions of the purpose of literature.

With each step he writes the ground beneath his feet,

85. GLASER, Peter: 'Zur Lage der Detonation – Ein Explosé', in: idem: (Ed.): Rawums, p. 12.

86. Ibid. p. 13.

87. Ibid. p. 14.

88. Ibid. p. 15.

89. Ibid. p. 16.

and other people's feet. And he finds magnificent pieces in the cellar: excitement, comprehensibility, entertainment value, wit, thrills; 'Rawums'. The narrator is attentive, thorough, *straight* and precise, a global spy in no-one's employ, and yet out there for many people (not everyone). He's in tune with the times, he writes about them and he knows that awakening longing and giving an image of liberation still works.[90]

The Rawums writers included, alongside artists Georg Dokoupil, Gottfried Distl and Martin Kippenberger, story-tellers like Peter Glaser, Joachim Lottmann and Rainald Goetz. But only Rainald Goetz kept the impetus from the pop disturbances of the early 80s going, with plenty of interruptions, through to the present day in his writing.

Goetz' first novel *Irre* [Insane], published in 1983, told of the slide of the hero, a psychiatrist, into 'night-life life' and the pop music scene. The importance of painting and music for the author Goetz is apparent in many passages in the novel. '...I could play you a load a load of music or paint you pictures on the theme of *space*. I'd love to. But I've got to write words, poor sod, and from my word-gaol I greet the comrades of Freiwillige Selbstkontrolle[91] and the dear old expertfuckingpainters way up, far from here, in Hamburg. Greetings! I cry through my gaol window and wave longingly... I have to go on writing the words, but I have to put on a different beat.'[92] The beat of the music and the violence of the images become a standard for the speed that literature should try and reach.

In the text 'Subito', which Goetz delivered along with his famous 'blood performance' at the Klagenfurt Literary Festival in the same year, the author stresses that painting and music are the forerunners of the new literature: 'The painters are the best, the painters and pop musicians are the best, and the rest, particularly the writers, they don't even exist because their heads are full of craaaaap sensibility and imagination or they're self-ironists, and most of them are the craaaaappest, that is committed. And for that they'll be shot, bam bam bam.'[93] At the end of his text Goetz puts a manifesto, in the style of the early 80s, picking up much of the programme of the first pop generation in the 60s:

90. Ibid. p. 20.

91. FSK is a Munich pop band.

92. GOETZ, Rainald: Irre, p. 302.

93. GOETZ, Rainald: Subito, in: GLASER, Peter (Ed.), op. cit., p. 158f.

'We don't need a defence of culture. Just go for it bold totalitarian raw belligerent and funny, that's how you've got to write, the way the violent-thinking person lives. I don't need peace because I have war within me. Least of all I need nature. I live in the city where it's much prettier. Go and watch tv instead. We need even more stimuli, even more advertising beat cars fashion hedonism pop and more pop.'[94]

A lot of young intellectuals apart from Goetz had found their main field of activity in pop. Writers like Diedrich Diederichsen, Michael O.R. Kröher and Olaf Dante Marx wrote music reviews in the music magazine *Sounds*, which, apart from the usual orgies of adjectives, brought ideas, structures, stories and history into pop music. In *Sexbeat*, published in 1985, Diederichsen tells the story of the first subculture that had to get by without progress: 'The elements of clothes, image, interview statements, the so-called externals, were emancipated into independent expressive devices. Pop music had become a complicated but funny and efficient art.'[95] For intellectuals who see themselves as leftists, pop has always been a place of truth. Either the brilliance and glamour of pop are the lie that tells the truth, or the realism and simplicity of pop are the more perfidious lie that may express harder truths. In any case, good pop always has access to 'very un-kitsch, intellectually digestible descriptions of that world. However you stack it, its descriptions of the world satisfy all the needs of a historian.'[96]

But fundamental to the intellectual engagement with pop was complete devotion to pop music, its trivial solutions and its multi-layered ways of looking at problems. Living with and in music was, for the hip dissidents, a space of survival with plenty of freedoms and the possibility of great happiness.

Rainald Goetz, who studied as a doctor and a historian, and who is a successful literary critic, tried to describe happiness through music as it presents itself to someone shaped by words and writing. 'Pop's good fortune is that pop has no problem. So you can't think pop, you can't criticize pop, you can't write about it analytically. Pop is living pop, looking with fascination at pop, studying it obsessively, telling it with as much material

94. Ibid. p. 165.

95. DIEDERICHSEN, Diedrich: Sexbeat, p. 42.

96. Ibid. p. 173.

as possible, celebrating it. There is no other sensible way of talking about pop than, thrilled, pointing out what's thrilling about it, hey, brilliant.'[97]

For Goetz, even in *Irre*, this 'hey, brilliant' was the crucial discourse about pop, but it's impossible to avoid having further thoughts about something you love so much. Because with blank affirmation 'pop throws up problems for the thinking person, but problems of thinking, not problems of pop. Simple as the distinction is, it's hard to realize in writing about pop.'[98] And yet, 'in the two most relevant branches of science and pop'[99] there arises the new 'holy scripture of the everyday, rejigged in German, comprehensible to everyone'.[100]

By 'pop', Goetz means not only the music, the bands, songs, lyrics and records – art, in short – but above all the social practice to which pop music is connected: concerts, clubs and parties. The hero in *Irre* is constantly cruising through night-life in search of authentic and beautiful people and the music that brings together these true and beautiful people and serves as the basis of their attitudes and actions. In his works Goetz thus becomes the chronicler of night-life. His fascination with the bright, fast, loud world of the clubs and discothèques leads him, after his years of apprenticeship in Munich, to Hamburg, Berlin, New York, London and Ibiza. Goetz, who took a particular interest in dancefloor music in the late 80s, also turns his attention to the DJ at the beginning of the acid house movement. For Goetz, in 1988, acid house is the right kind of music: 'In the heartbeat measure of beats per minute, the IQ was redefined for everything (fft fft fft fft ssptssptsspt fft fft fft fft fft fft sspt sspt fft fft fft fft), can you feel it, the arms turn into nervous dendrites that reconnected the human body, the world brain cell, with the surrounding dancing electrified other brains into a collective fun body. Release your body. Vinegar. Angiiie. Pusher party. Everything.'[101]

'Can you feel it' and 'release your body', the classic house samples, find a sensitive sounding board in Goetz, stretched out in the minefield between body and mind. For an intellectual, the spaces within (and not outside!) rationality, where the life-threatening arsenal of words can take a break, are important. For the dancer, shaking his body to the house beats, the only relevant thoughts

97. GOETZ, Rainald; Krieg, p. 188.

98. Ibid.

99. GOETZ, Rainald: Kronos, p. 295.

100. Ibid.

101. Ibid. p. 258.

the music allows are: Free your body! Can you feel it? The experience of the coincidence of all the senses, emotions and the otherwise dissident body becomes fundamentally existential. Goetz is made particularly happy, as in his adventures with punk and heavy metal, by the sense of community with other devotees of the subculture. The hammering beat and the dance movements unite the various individuals into a collective body of fun. 'Can you feel it?' means not least the euphoric feeling of that community and the transcendence of one's own ego into a dancing unity. Existential isolation breaks down, as it usually only does with sex (and then only if it works), when the isolated individual opens himself to the other person. Goetz describes this experience as infinitely romantic. He takes a tab of ecstasy, sees other people, greets them, and knows 'that he is connected via the fundamental force of anti-gravity with the moving pointing finger of a dancer on the other side of the dancefloor by my fingertips'.[102]

Goetz, the highly academic intellectual and logocentric man of letters, was so deeply shaken by these experiences that he questioned his own capacity for perception. Goetz felt 'neither screwy in any way, nor was the self-observation of my thoughts dulled, but on the contrary, everything was more, more natural, more wonderful, more clear'.[103]

Goetz' enthusiasm for acid house was originally prompted by Lothar Gorris' article 'Der Acid-Wahn' [Acid Madness] in the August issue of the magazine *Tempo*, about the parties, the makers, the fans and the music in England. For Goetz, that was it: it 'was immediately clear. I immediately drove via Paris to London, but then I didn't dare go in anywhere. But just seeing the fashion for real made me believe, all of a sudden, what all the magazines between *i-D*, *NME*, the *Face* and the others told in pictures and stories.'[104]

At the first acid house party in Munich, with fog, fights and police, Goetz was 'soo happy'.[105] And it's clear to whom Goetz owes that happiness: 'D.J.: mix master G. HELL. I'll never forget it. Incipit vita nova.'[106]

That night in October was the beginning of a beautiful time for Goetz: '... my most partying autumn for many years... The nicest people were suddenly around anywhere with Acid written on it.'[107] For Goetz, night-

102. Ibid. p. 270f.

103. Ibid. p. 271.

104. Ibid. p. 265.

105. Ibid.

106. Ibid.

107. Ibid. p. 268.

life was reborn. 'New kings, new princes, a real revolution in the life of the night, and the old game of shame renewed, who's the first, the more authentic, more knowing, more original acid man and so on. Tormenting and embarrassing it all was again, but really only in the record shop, really only in my head.'[108] But not only in the record shop: in the club too Goetz is alone with his thoughts. His thoughts separate him from the rest of the night-life people. He breaks out of the community of the dancers and sees himself isolated in the middle of the noise and the fog. 'Where the stroboscope white came from, in the high-energy pulsating round ice-light source up in the ceiling I saw myself, out of the heat of the dancing bodies, suddenly seen by the familiar appearance of the death's-head shadow in the ice-white light.'[109] The desire to be one with the dancing mass doesn't rescue the artist from his latent autism. The battle between sociability and reclusion is particularly apparent in the work of Goetz, who is repeatedly shaken by existential crises and finally finds his way, through discipline and intelligence, out of self-preoccupation and out into an unlimited openness to the world. The story of the artist as an autistic genius who cuts himself off from the world, is, for Goetz, a tale of misery. Art must communicate, and where art is hermetic and inaccessible it loses its own definition. For Goetz, this struggle for communicability is one of the main elements in his work. The spectrum runs from partially cryptic essays on art like 'Kadaver' to clearly and simply written portraits of DJs for the magazine *Tempo*.

For Goetz, DJs are perfect examples of universal communicability, even of the most difficult and abstract art works. The claim to be able to address as many people as possible is not essentially populist, but more of an attempt to try to speak to everyone. It is clear that this will lead to real but necessary reductions of the mass base. 'But it's in the nature of the thing,' DJ Westbam explains, 'that some records are so weird that only four hundred people will ever hear them, while others have the potential to appeal to 100,000 people.'[110] The only important thing is that neither populist nor elitist preferences should distort the essence of communication about art.

DJ Westbam from Berlin, who has been one of the

108. Ibid.

109. Ibid.

110. BÜCKERT, Heike, op. cit., p. 6.

leading figures in the German dancefloor scene since 1987, is, for Goetz, 'the master of the art of doing people, clearly a brain'.[111] Goetz even goes so far as to see him as a kind of brother with whom he can discuss all kinds of issues involving work, life and the world. Goetz often stands beside Westbam's DJ booth and watches him at work. 'After the last number I went up and asked what it was. "That was one of mine," he said, "my new piece: CELEBRATION." – "Totally gorgeous," I said, and laughed and was pleased.'[112]

Goetz has a different kind of close relationship with the Munich DJs Hell, Olaf and Woody. They are friends of the author, and at the same time his heroes. In the article 'Ästhetisches System' [Aesthetic System], he mostly discusses Olaf, who is called Alfi in the article, and Woody.

Olaf 'deals in records but also, like most good record retailers, in information, knowledge and, above all, in moods… He has a precise feeling for the right balance of power, manipulation and service. Or maybe it's a bit too good?… He hates everyone who's weak, he despises all the people who like him. He's a malicious game-player in groups and in the social act an extremely perceptive artist in cruelty. He's a destroyer… an amoral exploiter of situations.'[113]

Goetz is also making the DJ as a social figure the focus of his reflections. Olaf above all embodies all the qualities that make the DJ not just an exciting artist figure but a leading figure within the subculture. He decides who's part of it and who isn't, what gets worn and what doesn't, which sound is right and which isn't. The DJ influences not just most of the party-goers and clubbers, but also the illustrious milieu of the nerve centre of 'night-life': the fashion designers, party-designers, gastronomes, journalists, musicians, producers, designers and artists.

The DJ thus becomes a leading figure who holds all the strings of the night-life world. Sven Väth, one of the most successful techno DJs, is described by Goetz as 'DIONYSUS': a shaman with a little rucksack, a medicine man, Napoleon, Lucifer with a white mask and a husky voice – a lonely sage.[114] Thus the DJ becomes not only an artist and a figure of social crystallization, but a myth and a legend with meta-

111. GOETZ, Rainald: Kronos, p. 291.

112. Ibid. p. 377.

113. Ibid. p. 397ff.

114. Cf. Ibid. p. 396.

Rainald Goetz carrying Sven Väth's record box

physical qualities: the shaman, who brings the masses under his power and heals them as a medicine man. A power-conscious hero and at the same time a brooding sage, to whom Goetz devotes a ten-page article in the September 1994 issue of the magazine *Tempo*. The article, co-written with Michi Kern, describes – in emphatically simple language – a visit that Väth made to Tokyo, and contains lengthy interviews about music, drugs and a DJ's life as an artist. In conversations lasting several hours, Goetz tries to investigate the essence of the DJ and his work, and at the same time to make the character and biography of the shaman comprehensible. The article clearly demonstrates the familiarity that has grown up between Goetz and Väth. What remains is admiration for Väth and the hint of myth that gives him his fascinating aura.[115]

Woody is a completely different kind of DJ. He isn't powerful, he isn't a shaman or a Napoleon, he isn't an amoral exploiter of situations. Woody has devoted himself completely to the music, for him it's the only thing that counts. He is one of the DJs 'who by being even more lost in the music somehow has a different weight, a kind of moral strategy or goodness, which secretly, when you've stopped counting the hours after a few days, when you sit there uninterruptedly listening to music, entering spaces between the beats and sounds, and are more unnoticeable in the midst of these people than right in their heads'.[116]

For Goetz, the 'greatest, most fantastic thing, fulfilment itself'[117] is when you can abandon yourself completely to the music and lose yourself in it. On the other hand, the thoughtful enjoyment of the DJ's art can be exciting as well. The adventure then is 'sitting on the receiver side of one of these mood dealers and being sold record by record a new idea and a constantly shifting, changing structure, and thus getting an insight into the inner form of another, unknown human mind and character. You sit there you listen and you practically SEE someone else THINKING, what he's about and what's going on inside him.'[118]

Goetz's writings are testimony to the greatest feeling of happiness in night-life – literature 'near the speakers and music machines',[119] 'under the DJ's desk'.[120] In 1994, this proximity to the rave and techno subculture

115. GOETZ, Rainald/ KERN, Michi: Sven Väth – Maniac Love. The Tokio Tapes, in: TEMPO 9/1994, pp. 70–80.

116. GOETZ, Rainald: Kronos, p. 398.

117. Ibid.

118. Ibid.

119. Ibid. p. 377.

120. Ibid.

led Goetz to produce a triple CD for Frankfurt's Eye-Q label, on which texts read from *Kronos* were laid over techno tracks. Like his fellow-writer William S. Burroughs, who recorded with The Disposable Heroes of the Hip-hoprisy, Goetz dared make the step from music fan to music producer, and introduced his literary work into the context of DJ music. The fascination and love of music provides – in the DJ tradition – the step to production, without suppressing or even forgetting the artist's own activity. Burroughs and Goetz act as literati in the context of dancefloor, but with different poetics. While Burroughs, as a cut-up writer, has an artistic affinity with the montage works of the hip-hop MCs, Goetz sets his texts contrapuntally against the music. The lyrics, a disturbance of the music and an antithesis to its lightness, only reluctantly fit in with the logic of the dominant music.

Techno is defined, amongst other things, by the fact that language – however reduced and mutilated – is often omitted. This is a big enticement to Rainald Goetz, so he reintroduces language into the space that has been cleared of words. Language's lost state in the face of the dominance of the beats and sounds gives it its charm. The writer who throws himself into the arms of the verbal enemy brings his two passions together and documents their reciprocal destructions. But, as ever in DJ culture, every form of confrontation, if it is properly and authentically felt and thought, is rewarded with a wonderful synthesis. Difficult lyrics and fragments suddenly assume what Goetz calls a 'melancholic plausibility'.[121] The CD works in both contexts, and also constitutes a new whole. After Burroughs' hip-hop record, the DJ aesthetic once again reaches directly into the aesthetics of literature. The words are controlled by the mixing desk.

121. LAARMANN, Jürgen: Words don't come easy, in: FRONTPAGE 2/95, p. 59.

TECHNO – THE NEW HEAVY

Techno, short for technology. Since 1985 the word has been used for a variation of house music that became one of the most successful kinds of dancefloor, and which was incarnated in dozens of versions in the early

90s: from dreamy ambient via hip-hop-related breakbeats to the relentlessly hard and fast sound of Gabba. 'Techno is music made by humans; in its most definitive forms it sounds like it could have been made by machines,'[122] wrote John McCready in his 'A–Z of Techno'.

Techno is music on its way to pure sound. In an interview, Kittler points out that music, if its melodies are not grasped as a formation of three sounds, 'but as a distribution of probability, as the improbability of leaps, in the sense of a mark-off chain',[123] is actually hiss. In the abstract sense 'that everything that isn't regulated by laws and periodicity, is hiss'.[124] The only period in techno is the beat. As a development of house and acid, techno is to its predecessors as free jazz is to ragtime. The idea of the breakdown of solid structures and experimentation with the music as sound material are foregrounded in techno. 'This is a journey into sound', promises the often-used vocal sample.

Kittler points out that hiss has only become a theme in music since the media for recording it became available. 'Previously, hiss was always there, but it was what was removed from all recording and broadcasting, and thus from its cultural practice. And music is, of course, a cultural practice. So if the music is hiss, then it hisses in the name of everything that goes on hissing in science and technology.'[125] Techno makes hiss into a norm. Any form of non-music can be swallowed up by this music. Techno shifts the boundary between noise and music into the infinite void of that which can no longer be perceived. No screeching, shouting, bleeping and beeping is horrible enough not to be salvaged by techno and integrated as a sample into the minimalist order of a four-four house beat. Kittler describes the history of jazz from Parker to Coltrane as a process of acclimatization to the fear that this music gives you the first time you hear it. Hearing Charlie Parker for the first time was, for him, an indescribable shock: '...so it was really cutting, truly cutting, this music, cutting! And you stuck it out with your teeth clenched, listening, or with little shivers down your spine.'[126]

The story of house and hip-hop contains many similar shocks. The development of synthesizers, samplers and beatboxes enabled house music to generate new terrors

122. McCREADY, John: A–Z of Techno, in: THE FACE 12/1991, p. 56.

123. LÜCKNER, Michael: Tenorsaxophon Lysergsäure Bleep, in: SPEX 12/1991, p. 81.

124. Ibid.

125. Ibid.

126. Ibid.

in its experiment. While hip-hop is more moderate in its treatment of pure sounds, and begins only slowly, with the second generation of musicians (the new school) to discover the infinite range of possible sound signals, house music is immediately a more open field. DJ Westbam sees the classic house sound as typified 'by sparse studio equipment and the unconventional dilettantism of the DJs, none of them sound engineers or musicians'.[127] Without the sneaking desire for perfection of disco or pop, tracks were mixed on 8-track machines, bass-heavy and, in the high notes, so hysterically exaggerated that – according to Westbam – 'it would have made any sound engineer throw up.' The free use of technology gave rise to new sounds. Richard James, alias Aphex Twin, went so far as to build his own sampler because he didn't feel that existing samplers could be adequately manipulated. Underground music is defined not least by the fact that the technology employed is used against the grain of its original purpose. As hip-hop DJs discovered a new sonic dimension to the turntable with the scratching of records, techno entices all possible and impossible sounds from computers, synthesizers and samplers. 'Much more important than any kind of music already in existence' are, for techno musician Markus Schopp, 'the means of production, which is to say the instruments. They are the true roots of our music.'[129] For Diederichsen this also means making the journey to a new tonality. 'The tracks of these pieces that aren't rhythmically functionalised, the ones that live where melody is, are neither tonal nor atonal. A huge number of "fractal" tones are retrieved from "between" the notes, not to disappear into an infinite chaos of possible combinations, but to establish new rules from one case to the next, rapidly revealing to the listener how they elude musicological classification.'[130] Absolute freedom without structure or law – the perfect space for creation. Goetz puts it this way: 'An uninterrupted process of experimentation; of testing, rejecting, deciding and deciding again: like that, exactly like that. An absolutely intellectual act.'[131]

Techno was a wildly flourishing cousin of acid house, with the difference that the sound of techno was able to incorporate any kind of malicious and irritating noise, not just the drug-addled bleeping and beeping of acid house.

127 . BÖHM, Thomas: Was ist house Music?, in: MUSIK EXPRESS 5/1988.

128 . Ibid.

129 . AMARETTO, Joel: Neue Europäische Elektroschule, in: FRONTPAGE 2/95, p. 42.

130 . DIEDERICHSEN, Diedrich: Vom Ende der Wahrheit, loc. cit.

131 . GOETZ, Rainald/ KERN, Michi: Sven Väth, op. cit., p. 80.

Foucault tells a story of madness in the age of reason, Bataille tells a story of the eye and – for Kittler – in Pink Floyd's 'Brain Damage', there is a short story of the ear and madness in the media age.[132] In the face of three-minute techno blitzkriegs at speeds of up to 200 beats per minute, the track sounds like idyllic relaxation music. The 'story of the ear in the age of its technical explodability'[133] had clearly advanced since Pink Floyd's day, and in the late 80s, after M/A/R/R/S and acid, young people's listening habits had become so radical that notes that scraped past your ear, practically amounting to torture, nestled in the midst of pleasant dance music. 'The explosion of the sound media becomes an implosion that falls right into the centre of perception itself. The head, not just as a metaphorical seat of so-called thinking, but as the actual nerve switchboard, becomes one with the information that comes in and which is not just so-called objectivity, but sound.'[134]

Techno is the music of absolute immediacy and the sound of pure physics. While disco and house still tried to produce immediacy via seduction, glamour, charm, eroticism or elegance, techno, with brachial violence, directly entered the nerve centre and sent signals from there to the body. Subsonic bass-lines and squeaks that had previously been beyond the pain threshold, landed on the dancefloor with techno.

'It's all a matter of hearing and listening,' says Rainald Goetz, pointing out that techno demands a new form of listening, 'of immersion listening again and again to the depths of the tracks: to distinguish individual voices in their sound, alone, in friction with one of the others or with all of them; to recognize rhythms, precise and distinct, in the pecking, thundering, clattering and furiously complex mechanics of their motor activity; to sense the range of simple melodies, as against the elephant-skin penetration and banality, to understand the truth of simple great themes consisting of five or seven notes.'[135]

TECHNO – THE FAMILY TREE

After Kraftwerk, it was above all the house sound of

132. Cf. KITTLER, Friedrich A.: Der Gott der Ohren, in: idem: Draculas Vermächtnis, p. 133.

133. Ibid. p. 139.

134. Ibid.

135. GOETZ, Rainald/ KERN, Michi: Sven Väth, op. cit., p. 80.

Chicago and Detroit that paved the way for acid and then turned into techno. The first DJ artist to produce techno, in 1985, was Juan Atkins. Atkins says that the most important influence of his youth, apart from the P-funk of Parliament and Funkadelic, was a DJ called Electrifying Mojo, who played Kraftwerk as well as hard funk and thus influenced not only Atkins but certain other rising musicians and DJs in Detroit. In 1981 Atkins, along with the Vietnam veteran Richard Davis, who called himself 3070, formed the band Cybotron. Davis was a solitary tinkerer who had a Roland MSK 100, one of the first Roland sequencers, at home, and knew how to use it. Playing with his Roland he soon came very close to the house sound that Atkins and 3070 were after: 'I wanted to make electronic music but thought you had to be a computer programmer to do it: I found out it wasn't as complicated as I thought.'[136] Cybotron's first single sold 15,000 copies almost immediately – mostly in and around Detroit.

'Unlike Los Angeles and New York, Detroit has no ghetto glamour, no community. Detroit is grey and monotonous, the killing is more absurd, people do it as a leisure activity,'[137] explained Detroit DJ artist Jeff Mills in 1991, making it clear that techno has the same function in Detroit as hard hip-hop in LA or New York. The motor-town of Detroit, hard hit by the recession in the USA, was considered one of the heaviest cities in America in the 80s. A situation reflected in the melancholy hardness and violence of the techno sound, despite Atkins' assurances that techno wasn't originally to be equated with hardness and violence, but amounted to a form of escapism. 'With Detroit being such a desolate place, it's depressing and there's a lot of crime and decay, you really want something to take you away. I always saw techno like as dreaming.'[138]

In their music, like Kraftwerk and Warhol (in his art), Cybotron yearned for the end of purely human feelings and hybrid existence between man and machine. Atkins: 'We had always been into futurism. We had a whole load of concepts for Cybotron: a whole techno-speak dictionary, an overall idea which we call the Grid. It was like a video game, which you entered on different levels.'[139]

In 1985 Cybotron released the single 'Techno City',

136. SAVAGE, Jon: Machine Soul, in: ROCK'N'ROLL QUARTERLY, Summer 1993, p. 20.

137. NIESWANDT, Hans: Vive la résistance, in: SPEX 12/1991, p. 27.

138. WILSON, Tony: Juan Atkins, in: i-D 8/1993, p. 51.

139. SAVAGE, Jon; Machine Soul, p. 20.

Juan Atkins

140. Ibid. p. 19.

141. The ideological centre of underground resistance is Mad Mike Banks. This black musician and label manager refuses to speak to whites. Dialogue could only be resumed if the whites were to stop using black innovative work and perverting it for their own ends. For him, underground resistance means resuming the struggle where militant Black Panthers in the 60s had to give it up: with a radically aggressive position and with no desire for compromise. Mad Mike Banks lives in exile in the USA, and doesn't see himself as part of the culture that exists there – he's invisible as far as it is concerned. The work that he does in internal exile is understood and valued above all in Europe. Nonetheless, he puts no value on dialogue. The old-fashioned concept of the subversive refusal of communication still strikes him as the most effective way of avoiding exploitation by the white culture industry. Although Banks rarely appears in public, he remains the invisible centre of the Detroit techno movement: revered as a hero, even by those who value the effectiveness and power of dialogue.

giving the new music its name. In the same year 3070 failed in his dream to become a man-machine. He died, and Juan Atkins continued as Model 500. His musical companions were now Derrick May and Kevin Saunderson. They shared a love of Kraftwerk, electronic music and the latest musical technology. 'Techno is technological. It's an attitude to making music that sounds futuristic: something that hasn't been done before.'[140]

Together with Blake Baxter and Eddie 'Flashin' Fowlkes, in 1987 the techno pioneers made it to Europe for the first time, encountering the emerging dancefloor culture in England. British techno fans like Adamski and Baby Ford became producers, distilling a European version of hi-tech music in a mixture of techno and acid. After the death of acid as a mass fashion, many DJ artists and labels, and also many club DJs and clubs stayed connected up to highly technologized house music. The techno virus was spreading, but, a few exceptions apart, it remained in the underground for the time being.

One of the exceptions was Technotronic, which familiarized the pop world with the merciless 'Abfahrt' in 1989 and 1990 with its magnificently produced album *Pump Up The Jam*. 'Abfahrt' in German techno slang means immediate abandon, the inescapable command of the music, the brutal violence of the musical dramatization. 'Abfahrt' was the condition for each 'Brett' – in English, 'killer', or 'floor killer' – as German DJs called particularly brutal techno tracks. The bulky-sounding arrangements of Technotronic made 'Abfahrt' into something quite natural, and anyone willing to listen more closely was rewarded with the finer details of the music. Delicately floating, barely audible melodies, perfectly proportioned breaks and rhythmical constructions created a sense of musical masterpieces. The brutality of the trivial: nowhere in the mainstream did basses sound fatter, louder. Technotronic were first in an ancestral line of pop bands that drove every form of DJ music into the charts with a view to making it as popular as possible. Certain representatives of the underground saw these bands – Technotronic and Dune – as dangerous trivializations.[141] The unboundedness of superpop (Cohn) was only accepted by the subculture when it expressed solidarity with that subculture by means of unambiguous dual coding, or pursued its own strategies directly.

Technotronic were making sugar-sweet techno pop at a time when the best techno DJs were putting on uncompromisingly heavy music in dark ruined cellars and concrete halls, and for that they were punished with contempt.

Techno was hardcore, and for all their differences DJs in Belgium, England, Germany and the USA all agreed on that.

BELGIUM – THE LEAP FROM INDUSTRIAL TO EBM AND TECHNO

In Belgium the R&S label put out techno twelve inches that resumed the Belgian tradition of Electric Body Music (EBM) and the New Beat, the slower variation of EBM. Both EBM and New Beat had emerged as hybrids between the experimental sounds of Industrial Music and the poppy synthetic sounds of the new wave in the mid-70s. The iconography of records and the ideology of the bands were violent and despairing. Musicians in bands like Front 242 and à; Grumh resembled warriors from science fiction films or hysterical hooligans. The war that was being waged was diffuse, as diffuse as the violence which, in the opinion of the musicians, could be found everywhere in society.

Industrial music, from its beginnings, presented the discourse of violence. Bands like SPK (which, according to legend, was founded in Australia in a psychiatric clinic) and Throbbing Gristle made high-tech music about fear, hate and despair. Singles by Throbbing Gristle were called things like 'United/Zyklon B Zombie', and an LP with a concentration camp on the cover was entitled *Music From the Death Factory*. The musicians – who had all trained as artists – wore camouflage battle gear, and for their vocal tracks they used tapes of psychiatrists interviewing murderers, or old cut-up texts by Burroughs. In the dissonant, noise-related music, a world of terror and violence was presented. For Genesis P. Orridge, who later became the founder of a sect and then a house musician, this violent aesthetic reflected the horror that was documented daily in the media.

I don't see why music or painting or writing should be excluded from this set of problems. I don't know why a group that makes music should be forbidden to mention things that are current everywhere else in the media. Why isn't it ok for someone with a guitar to mention or discuss Zyklon B or violence, or simply refer to it or remind people about it? And as it turns out it's good if it still has a certain surprise effect – because people aren't used to music telling them something about reality, because normally they just know music as an escape from reality. Like opium, music's now the opium for the people, instead of booze or tv.[142]

142. HARTMANN, Walter: TG: Show me the bunker darling..., in: idem./POTT, Gregor: Rock Session 6.

Industrial music wasn't interested in prettying up the everyday, and tried, with the aggressive representation of its own terror at the world, to come close to Adorno's injunction that lyric poetry was no longer possible after Auschwitz. Like a lot of great 20th century art, from Picasso's *Guernica* via Beckett's hopeless plays to Cindy Sherman's images of war, industrial music had not yet got used to death, suffering, violence, hatred and terror, and spoke in tormenting collages of sound of the continuous shock that these deplorable aspects of life made on the individual musicians. On the verge of fainting, German journalist Reinhold Brunner describes a performance by Throbbing Gristle in 1980 in the Städel in Frankfurt, where two films of the band were shown. The first was called *After Cease To Exist*, and was shown over menacing synthesizer sounds:

Wide shot pans to the surface, to the playing group members of TG, silhouetted in the environment of their instruments. The back of one member comes into the picture. On his dark pullover the words Death Factory are printed in white. Dark. A small, bare inner space. A door opens, Cosey and a younger man walk into the room, both uninvolved; maybe the man has a sense of resignation. They both know what to do: without the slightest resistance the man allows himself to be tied to a table, the woman gags him. She takes a pair of scissors, and cuts open his trouser legs, revealing his private parts. She pushes the big member upwards, and seems to massage it... The man's gagged face starts twitching and jerking, his head tosses helplessly back and forth – the woman cuts the man's scrotum open, pushes out his testicles, with no hurry, pleasure or hatred, no emotion, and severs the cords... The screams of the man, suppressed by the gag, are engulfed by the merciless music. It makes them all the more loud and urgent. Terrible. It all seems to happen in slow motion. Time nearly stands still, the music goes on sawing painfully away to this unspeakable horror. Slow, endless pan around the bloodbath of the private parts; the man lies still.[143]

143 . BRUNNER, Reinhold: Lähmende Begegnung mit der Gewalt: Throbbing Gristle am 10.11.80 im Frankfurter Städel, in: HARTMANN, Walter/POTT, Gregor, op. cit., p. 176.

Throbbing Gristle, whose actions and art certainly derive from the context of art history, are obsessed by evil and wickedness in the world. Torture and executions are the only motifs that seem appropriate for artistic reproduction.

At concerts by the Belgian EBM band à; Grumh the singer spits breadcrumbs into the audience. Monitors show videos of rapes or film-clips of s'n'm doctors operating on the pulsating hearts of young boys. The back cover of the 'Underground' twelve inch shows two malformed stillborn babies. According to the musicians, the representation of horror is supposed to move the audience to make statements and communicate with the musicians.

The aesthetic of horror also determined the sampling practice of the EBM bands. Samples of war films, horror films and porn films turn up alongside snapshots of everyday life in a post-industrial information society. Front 242, who are considered the inventors of EBM, begin their productions by sampling everything that interests and impresses them. 'Other musicians, take a guitar band for example, are just as influenced by their surroundings and their environment as we are. We take it a step further and work directly with that environment, without the detour via instruments and tunes.' These scraps of sound, recorded at random, are first selected and then lined up and overlaid to the greatest possible density. The pieces are run through with uprooted and decontextualized information from the samples in such a way that the rhythmical structures of the piece have to be intensified to bear the weight of the sampled material. 'There's so much information in music that you're quickly sated by it, it gives the music a certain dynamic, you can listen to it ten times,'[144] explain the musicians of Front 242. Being overwhelmed like this by deliberately diffuse information and sounds forces the audience simply to leap over the incomprehensible diversity by dancing. What is presented is not so much a reworking but a working-through of the mountain of information. Front 242 don't think on behalf of their listeners, they collect and present – and deliver their own lost state to the world. In contrast to disco, dancing assumes a sad and hopeless quality. The musicians of Front 242 aren't DJs.

For young Belgian musicians, the Detroit techno sound provided the possibility to integrate the hardness and relentlessness of EBM within the comparatively cheerful context of house. Techno was more playful and experimental, and above all it didn't want to make existential statements about human life and the nature of the world. Or at least not as centrally as EBM and Industrial Music did. The 'Dominator' of Human Resource might have shouted, 'I'm bigger and bolder and rougher and tougher/ In other words, sucker, there is no other/ I wanna kiss myself', but his exaggerations could be unmasked as such. Many tracks on the Belgian R&S label were able to combine hardness with playfulness.

ENGLAND – SUBSONIC BASSES AND A WUNDERKIND

With the successes of Coldcut, M/A/R/R/S and Bomb The Bass, the British charts had proved that the English mainstream audience could understand futuristic-sounding, techno music. Acid house and outsider projects like KLF formed a tradition that techno was able to build upon.

One of the first techno labels was Warp from Sheffield.

144. GROTELÜSCHEN, Frank: Kartoffeln-Sound, in: SPEX 11/1988, p. 44.

It was founded by Rob Mitchell, who had a record-shop in which house music from Chicago and Detroit was sold alongside indie music. The record-shop became the first stopping-point for all the DJs who bought house tunes and had started producing their own pieces. They would play house and techno productions to Mitchell on cassette or as test pressings, and after a while Mitchell met the two DJs of Nightmares on Wax, who had pressed a thousand white labels of their piece 'Dexterous'. Mitchell didn't understand why the huge number of white labels were ignored by the record companies, and why no one would license them.

This led to the foundation of the Warp label. 'All that was needed was for all the exciting things that were being done in Sheffield and Leeds to have a more effective outlet. I had already heard "Dexterous" in a few clubs and thought it was incredible. But I didn't know Nightmares on Wax, and you couldn't get hold of the recordings.'[145] The first edition of 3,000 sold out in three days, and the next 3,000 sold almost as quickly.

Warp's first great success was LFO. Mitchell discovered them in a club when a DJ played their newest piece as a tape. 'It was the craziest thing I'd ever heard... slowed down samples, weird drum patterns and the heaviest, deepest bass you can imagine. I really froze when the bass-line started in. Maybe people are familiar with stuff like that from reggae sound systems, but not from clubs, from a house context.'[146] LFO was the result of a collaboration between two Leeds lads, who had gone in search of new boundaries in sound with their keyboards and their sampler. What had emerged was the subsonic bass, in frequencies that marked precisely the transition between what could be heard and what could only be felt. When Mark Bell and Jez Varley recorded the piece, the amplifier in the recording studio burned out three times.[147]

Techno meant using technologies contrary to the purpose for which they had been designed, and extending this *détournement* to the instruction manual of a sampler or a synthesizer. Techno, like industrial music, house and acid, came from cities and areas with a tradition of electronic music. The young people who

145. ZABEL, Sebastian: Warp – Subsonic Business, in: SPEX 6/1991, p. 30.

146. Ibid.

147. Cf. Ibid.

Nightmares on Wax

had grown up with videos and computers had no respect for the new machines, and they weren't afraid of them either. They approached the keyboard and sampler just as they approached the Gameboy, to find out what possibilities lay in the sound generators. The European techno sound is primarily the work of the first generation that was no longer afraid of new technologies but wanted to use them in a sense of fun. When 'LFO' by LFO sold 130,000 copies, the two lads from Leeds were amazed, and refused to appear on *Top of the Pops*. One other success on Warp was Tricky Disco. This duo produced its repertoire of sounds on an old synthesizer that Stockhausen had used, and which represents a symbolic link between the electronic avant-garde of the 50s and 60s and the techno musicians of the present.

The Wunderkind of Techno music, Richard James, invented new sounds to make the sounds in his head audible. Since his childhood he had controlled his dreams, to rework them into new pieces shortly afterwards in his parents' garage. 'I've been able to control my own dreams since I was about eight... Then I started making tracks when I'm asleep, either in my studio or in an imaginary studio. I can fall asleep for twenty minutes and write five songs.'[148] To bring the sounds in his head into the real world, the boy from a little village in Cornwall needed more than a piano or the keyboard he had played since the age of eight. So he opened up the cover of the keyboard and started rearranging the circuits. Soon afterwards, he started looking for bits of instruments on scrapyards and building sites, and cobbled together his own equipment out of electronic waste. For Richard James, electronic music has always been the most personal of all kinds of music. 'It's a much more direct link of getting expression into a song, even more so than your voice. You can't change the sound of your voice.'[149] Because James built all his instruments himself, the synthetic sounds weren't cold and artificial, but just as much products of artistic expression as the melodies and rhythms that they emitted. Asked whether he saw himself as an artist or a technician, he answered: 'Both... I'm a technician most of the time because a

148. MYERS, Caren: Dead Ringer, in: DETAILS 5/1994, p. 152.

149. Ibid. p. 153.

LFO

technician repairs things, he doesn't make things. That's a wicked definition. At the moment I'm repairing things. I'm a musician as well.'[150]

First of all James used his tape machine to 'sample' sounds; at college he built his own sampler, to satisfy his own needs. For James, traditional samplers are unsatisfactory because of the limited possibilities for the treatment of the sounds. Industrial samplers are too similar to DAT machines. What he really wanted was absolutely variable sampling rates, with several resonance filters and many more control units providing space for sound experiments.[151] During his youthful experimental phase, Richard recorded material for a number of double LPs which are now gradually being released, after his initial successes, under the name of Aphex Twin.[152] Aphex Twin is seen as one of the most important and intelligent techno projects. Ambient techno, in particular, which James helped to define as an architectural music reminiscent of Pink Floyd and Brian Eno, opened up new possibilities and freedoms for DJ culture. The 'tyranny of the beat', which still shaped disco, house and hip-hop, was abandoned in favour of an almost classical space in which everything was possible.

Asked what his goal was in 1991, DJ Westbam answered: 'The most absolutely abstract, weird dance music that has ever existed in the history of mankind.'[153] The music that Westbam has in mind no longer adheres to any rules, and the DJ has complete freedom in which to research.

Techno music, according to Rainald Goetz,

belongs entirely to the brain. That's the greatest advance of Techno over the old music made with skilful hands. It's the great thing about this new music, and it's also its danger. As everywhere else in the sphere of complete abstraction, ideas, concepts, rigidity of mind, ideology lie in wait. But this purely intellectual music is only made for the body: the body of the dancer, the raver, and not an individual; for the body in the collective, for the party of everyone all together.

If you get all that right, techno music is tragic: the voice of the life of people in the world.'[154]

150. PHILLIPS, Dom/ MARCUS, Tony: Aphex Twin, in: MIXMAG 3/1993.

151. Cf. RULE, Greg: 'They're Making Samplers Wrong', in: KEYBOARD 5/1994, p. 49.

152. James uses other pseudonyms like Polygon Window, Dice Man, Caustic Window and AFX.

153. BÜCKERT, Heike, op. cit., p. 7.

154. GOETZ, Rainald/ KERN, Michi: Sven Väth, p. 80.

Richard James

GERMANY – WESTBAM AND THE REST

Maximilian Lenz, alias DJ Westbam, described his use of records in the mid-80s as Record Art. At the age of 20, in 1985, he arranged 'Seventeen/ This Is Not A Boris Becker Song' out of computer rhythms and samples.

155. ENGELHARDT, Ingo: Herr der Rille, in: Tip, 2 August 1990.

Westbam 1989

The name Record Art actually refers to the claim that this is an emancipated, free-floating musical concept. A compositional art form in its own right, and not just a DJ standing there and trying to make a few nice transitions. It was important to establish that and distinguish it from musical presentation, and no one had done that in those days. People only speak of DJ music after "Pump Up The Volume", and that's about two years old. To that extent I'm a good two years ahead.[155]

Westbam's first models were hip-hop DJs like Afrika Bambaataa. At that time there was no dancefloor culture in Germany and Westbam himself had to create the environment in which he could produce and mix.

Along with his brother Fabian Lenz and three friends, Westbam founded the record label Low Spirit in Berlin, and in 1986 he organized the first house party in Germany. As the first prominent DJ he toured German clubs to arouse interest in the new dance music from the USA.

The former bassist in a punk band, Lenz opted in favour of turntables as his instruments, and practised until he could use them to his own satisfaction. Aside from his permanent work as a DJ, Westbam went on working on his Record Art in the studio. But he was unfamiliar with the technology, and so it was down to his schoolfriend Klaus Jankuhn, a former student of computer science, to realize what Westbam had in his head with the help of computers.

Westbam is also a confirmed advocate of sampling technique. For him, questions of authenticity and authorship are obsolete. 'If I suddenly discover a new record in the shop where someone's nicked something from us I'm proud of it. Some musicians should be really grateful to be sampled,'[156] explains Westbam, seeing the fight for copyright as being above all an argument about money, which completely ignores the fact that it was samples that brought artists like James Brown back into the public eye, a piece of PR that money couldn't buy. You can't talk about theft, says Westbam, 'because what already exists is left completely untouched. It isn't like you take James Brown's "Huh"and then there's a gap at that point in the composition, everything's still where it was. So nobody's taking anything away from anyone, they're just making something new.'[157] For Westbam, musical quotation isn't just legitimate and artistically valuable, it's indispensable for the work of composition. If you've run out of your own ideas, your record collection is a horde of material. 'I leave everything to chance. There are moments where I really reach into the pile of records because I think something's missing, and then I put the needle down on it somewhere and it fits precisely.'[158]

For Westbam the DJ is a kind of scriptwriter (we might recall Rick Rubin's comparison of the record producer with the film director), who's concerned with content and less with its incarnations. So Westbam also refuses all forms of live presentation, and says the party is the only possible 'concert' form for techno music. The live principle is realized in the DJ, who keeps replaying the tracks. 'The function and the background of this music is that I press it on record, that the DJ can play at and that people can party. It comes into being in the studio, with records being played, and its function is that it starts living again in a DJ mix.'[159] At the party in the club, it doesn't matter who produced the piece. Westbam isn't interested in the old notion of fame of which pop used to be so protective.

The same is not true of Sven Väth, the second German DJ superstar, who was not only honoured with the opening piece in *Der Spiegel*'s culture section in 1993,[160] but also got paid up to 15,000 Deutschmarks (£5,000) for two hours' work as a DJ. The massive success of his debut LP *Accident In Paradise* brought Väth global

156. Ibid.

157. Ibid.

158. BUG, Christian: Tanz den Hitler!, in: Tip, 18 August 1988.

159. BÜCKERT, Heike, op. cit., p. 6.

160. HÜETLIN, Thomas: Der Gott aus der Maschine, in: DER SPIEGEL, 8 November 1993.

fame, and *Musik Express* named him 'Germany's only pop star'.[161] Apart from the records he produces and the three labels that he runs, Väth is particularly interesting as a cult figure who has turned the DJ, as 'record-spinner' and 'party-maker', into a pop star. What distinguishes Väth is his charisma and his ability to get people into his thrall. His appearance also contributes to this, as do his dramatic performances at parties and raves. Like a prophet, he stretches his arms out wide and throws back his head. His eyes seem to be constantly sparkling, and anyone who has seen him dancing in his DJ box with tight leather trousers and a bare torso knows that Väth has found a style not unlike the live appearances of Elvis or the Beatles, while other DJs, mostly immersed in the music, are chiefly concerned with making good transitions and building up structures of tension and release. Väth turns the DJ's desk into a stage, and attracts the dancers' eyes to his show. Sven Väth is the greatest pop star among German DJs because he has precisely studied the history of pop music and is a passionate exhibitionist, for whom an ecstatic stage show seems entirely natural. 'Techno is body-music... There are always people who think I'm producing myself there, it's all show, but that's me, that's what I feel.'[162]

161. REINBOTH, Michael: It's All in the Mix, in: MUSIK EXPRESS 1/1994, p. 30.

162. Ibid.

Sven Väth

Apart from the two DJ superstars, every city in Germany now has at least one techno label and a dozen good techno and house DJs who have their own evenings or clubs. Records by German house labels are sold in DJ record shops in New York, Tokyo, London and Milan. For the first time Germany has made its own contribution to dancefloor culture. The most gripping phenomenon on the German house scene is the Love Parade, a mixture of demonstration, party and festival that has been celebrated in Berlin at the beginning of July every year since 1989.

LOVE PARADE

'Freedom, unity, equality, respect, fun and love. These ideas also underlie all possible theories about the improvement of the world, with one difference: in the House Nation they work,'[163] wrote the Techno fanzine *Frontpage* in 1992 on the occasion of the forthcoming Love Parade in Berlin. In 1987 two hundred people moved to house music through the centre of Berlin, a year later it was 2,000, in 1991 5,000, in 1992 15,000 and in 1993 the crowd of ravers was estimated at about 25,000. The demonstration on Berlin's Kurfürstendamm is the largest event of this kind in the world: by 1997 one million ravers assembled in Berlin for a demonstration 'for our house culture' (*Frontpage*) which is about 'celebrating the people who feel connected to house and have understood the spirit of coming together and partying'.[164]

'House culture is a counterculture against normal, dull, fun-free everyday life, but it's also a counterculture against traditional discothèque and leisure culture. House sets the energy of its grooves against all that. Everyone who was present at the last Love Parade felt that spirit. Not without reason, there haven't been any fights or any other kind of aggression at any major house event, and all the parties have been peaceful and happy. House music makes you and me happier, and makes us all get on better and party.'[165]

The Love Parade is a massive monument to DJ culture. The great utopias of peaceful and fulfilled co-existence seem realistically possible during those three days in early July. The Love Parade probably has a similar effect on the people who attend it as Woodstock had on the hippies who went there in the late 60s.

The Love Parade shows the ravers who come from around the world that they belong together, and how natural and simple that co-existence can be if everybody shares the same love of music. The identity that comes from the meeting of fans of techno and house isn't just formed by the music, which is played by the various Love-mobiles with their huge stacks of speakers, but from the shared feeling of power and strength. The mass of demonstrators, the line of 'mobiles' from all the major rave cities in Germany occupy the Kudamm in something almost like a military action. But rather than prompting fear and terror, the laughing dancers do little more than divert the passers-by on their long Saturday.

163. O.A.: Love Parade 1992, in: FRONTPAGE 6/1992, p. 8.

164. Ibid.

165. Ibid.

Fraternity – Love Parade

Demonstrations are generally taken to be manifestations against measures by the government or political opponents. The Love Parade drops the demanding, critical character of the demonstration and simply demonstrates itself. What you see is what we want. The Love Parade is an almost entirely non-verbal demonstration, the banners all show red hearts or shaking hands. When passers-by ask the demonstrators what on earth they are demonstrating for, they just answer with a broad grin and move on.

Equality – Love Parade

This book began with an attempt to show the extent to which DJ culture is also a relevant underground culture. With the Love Parade the underground has assumed a political quality. The Love Parade doesn't promise anything – unusual in political discourse – but it demonstrates in the true sense of the word: it presents, it shows. No blank cheques for the future. The way of the house and techno underground leads not from theory to practice, but from practice to practice, or to a theory derived from it. The happiness of the 'good world' is presented to the rest of the world, with such glamour and euphoria that even the sceptical police who close off the streets for the demonstrators are sometimes seen to dance. It is the seduction of the here and now, not the seductive power of an idea, that makes the Love Parade such a major act of conversion to the 'good world'.

Given the thousands of people demonstrating unity without the enticement of any kind of transcendence, without any plan for a utopia, faith is permitted at least for the three days of the Love Parade.

Liberty – Love Parade

DJ CULTURE – ATTEMPT AT A THEORY

BRIEF REMARK ON THE POP RESEARCHER AS PARASITE

The parasite rubs his eyes. He's seen a lot over the last two years. He'd come in with a stack of philosophical works, his head full of the great aesthetic theories of the 20th century. The doormen know him by now, and let him into the club without reservation. But the suspicious expression remains. The parasite has learned a lot during this time.

The big ideas have been gradually forgotten, and instead – ever the collector of stories and myths – he has looked for real material. In the club he felt the need less for the big designs than knowledge of music, style and technique. The parasite became a collector of pop history. His fellow-parasites have become even more suspicious than the doormen. The parasite with the tight Comme des Garçons T-shirt, the old Adidas trainers, the short (sometimes even blond) hair and the goatee has brought in the laws of high-falutin ideas and extravagant interpretations. The homeboy parasite and part-time DJ became a conservative archivist and collector during this work, and the more old stories and old knowledge he dragged back to his cave, the more he had the feeling of being on the trail of big ideas. The ideas, as always, stood behind the facts waiting to be discovered.

THE BIG IDEAS

Sooner or later almost every thinking person opts in favour of an idea. He sees the world in this way or that, and, following the fundamental idea, tries to subordinate everything as sensibly as possible to this first of all premises. He thinks hierarchically: down from the big ideas to the smallest things of life. The freedom to be able to opt for one of the big ideas is a human privilege granted particularly to those people who can afford to organize their life according to an idea, and don't have to fight to survive.

But in the end ideas are always helpless, as Marx and Engels observed in *The Holy Family*: 'Ideas can never lead beyond an old world system but only beyond the ideas of the old world system. Ideas cannot carry anything out at all. In order to carry out ideas men are needed who dispose of a certain practical force.'[1] For intellectuals and artists the idea is a practical force, because these people work within a non-material, intellectual reality. Material force must be toppled by material force, wrote the young Marx, referring to the fact that the theory becomes a material force 'once it seizes the masses'.[2] Ideas can become practical force if they settle in the human consciousness and develop the potential for action there.

Without an idea, the writer cannot write and the thinker cannot think. This work first presented itself as an idea, has a lot of ideas within it, and has tried to pursue every idea arising during thinking about the facts. But since the parasite who was in love with metaphysics became a historian, ideas have been made subordinate to the phenomenon. Of course that doesn't mean that facts can be written down without an idea. Ideas have, of course, always been there, governing things from the background. But the parasite's attempt to allow facts to arise as such was at least worth the try. Ideas, always identified as such, made reciprocal influence possible via comparison with the facts, and at least the revelation of the secret metaphysical weapons.

1. MARX, Karl/ ENGELS, Friedrich: The Holy Family, p. 160.

2. MARX, Karl: Critique of Hegel's 'Philosophy of Right', p. 137.

HISTORY AND PROGRESS

'(The world spirit) goes ever on and on, because spirit is progress alone.'[3] For Hegel, history and progress were inseparably linked, even if he avoided the term progress and generally spoke of a 'process' and a 'development'. In the course of this process the world-spirit is realized as the motor of historical progress in the world, and makes the world reasonable. For Hegel, the history of the world was the interpretation of the spirit in time, as the idea is interpreted as nature in space, but only in the spirit was each change progress. Becoming, as history 'presents a slow-moving succession of Spirits, a gallery of images, each of which, endowed with all the riches of Spirit, moves thus slowly just because the Self has to penetrate and digest this entire wealth of its substance'.[4] At the end of this process of digestion, which leads matter into the purity of the absolute concept, is the rule of the absolute spirit. Hegel's dialectic of history, with the omniscient world spirit sat in its central headquarters, was turned upside down and materialistically brought down to earth. Engels:

Just as Darwin discovered the law of the evolution of organic nature, so Marx discovered the law of the evolution of human history: the simple fact, previously covered over by ideological overgrowths, that people must first eat, drink, dwell and be clothed before they can practise politics, science, art, religion and so on, that the production of immediate material food and thus the economic level of development of a nation or an era forms the basis from which the organs of state, jurisprudence, art and even the religious ideas of those people in question have developed and from which they must also be explained – and not, as has happened hitherto, the other way around.[5]

The idea of progress is one of the great constructs of western metaphysics and has, particularly since the beginnings of the philosophy of history in the 18th century, played a major part in the context of rationalist enlightenment thinking. Hegel saw history in

3 . HEGEL, G.W.F.: History of Philosophy, Vol. III, p. 546.

4 . HEGEL, G.W.F.: Phenomenology of Spirit, p. 492.

5 . ENGELS, Friedrich: Das Begräbnis von Karl Marx, quoted in: MARX, Karl/ idem: Über Kunst und Literatur, p. 15.

the world as 'progress of the consciousness of Freedom'[6] whose necessity had to be acknowledged. Marx added a political dimension to the optimistic image of world and time, and constructed a social utopia that went far beyond what Hegel and his world spirit could imagine in a bourgeois state. The radicalized demands of the French Revolution for liberty, equality and fraternity were to end in a socialist ideal community in which all people would be happy and peace would be stable, and the world spirit, constantly pushing forward, would finally be able to rest. For Marx, this world spirit was only a fellow-traveller of material history and not, as for Hegel, its guide. The world spirit was pure superstructure.

The experiences of two world wars and the holocaust have destroyed the euphoric idea of progress among the 20th century thinkers. Given the millions of victims of war and the mountains of corpses in concentration camps, the notion that we might be able to see something like progress in history was unthinkable. Could the horrors of National Socialism still be understood in terms of the old dialectic of history, or did they hint at new dangers for humanity which could no longer be understood in the categories of class antagonisms?

'The concept of progress is one of our dearest and most important,'[7] insisted Ernst Bloch. To rescue progress as a 'radiant concept',[8] in Bloch's view 'differentiations in the concept of progress' must be undertaken. Progress does not occur clearly and in a straight line, but is an inconstant process, which can look different from the base and the superstructure. To avoid allowing progress to end up in a loss of culture, the multiverse of cultures – as a fundamentally humanist safeguard of the process – must be found. Although the idea of progress has been relativized, its fundamental seductive power remains that of a utopia that must be held on to in the face of all setbacks. 'What we must think of as progress at this moment in time we know vaguely but precisely: for that reason the term cannot be used coarsely enough,' Adorno postulated in 1962, referring to the dangers of a clear definition of the term: 'Pedantry in its use deceives us merely of what it promises, an answer to doubt and the hope that things will finally get better.'[9]

6 . HEGEL, G.W.F.: The Philosophy of History, p. 19.

7 . BLOCH, Ernst: Differenzierungen im Begriff Fortschritt, in: idem: Tübinger Einleitung in die Philosophie, p. 146.

8 . Cf. Ibid. p. 118.

9 . ADORNO, Theodor W.: Fortschritt, in: KUHN, Helmut/ WIEDEMANN, Franz: Die Philosophie und die Frage nach dem Fortschritt, p. 30.

Progress thus ceases to be a catchword or a substitute religion in which one can simply believe, but becomes instead a call to arms. The eschatological positivism that could be formed in the 19th century in a rush of technological, medical and to some extent political progress has avoided a desperate effort to hold on, in the face of all dangers and resistances, to the idea of progress. A demand that goes hard to the edge of Adorno's paradox when he defined progress as 'resistance to this on every level'.[10]

There can be no alternative to the idea of progress for humanity. In a new, reformed and thoughtful version the concept can survive. Often the concept of 'progress' is then reduced to an open conceptual negation of reaction: one is progressive if one is not reactionary. In the state of paralysis in which the concept of progress has ended up after its ill-starred misuse, it may still be worthwhile to devote a little more attention to progress as concept and idea. Similarly, in this work historiography is carried out in the knowledge that writing history is always also a terrorist act in which discourse is established, in the face of all relativizations and misgivings that that implies: not as a salvation-bringing totality, but as a furious insistence on the remnants of the enlightenment and emancipatory understanding of politics. The goal must be defined by the minorities in question. To see the new intellectual as 'the destroyer of evidence and universals', as Foucault would like to, constantly changing his place and never sure for certain 'where he will be tomorrow or what he will think'. He may ask 'whether revolution is worth the trouble, although it is obvious that the only people who can answer this question are those who are prepared to put their life on the line'.[11] The boundaries of doubt in the idea of progress run along the lines at which they face the political practice of those that break on the dominant relations. The critique of ideology comes to an end where political actions prove to be necessary. In the case of DJ culture, this means wherever the ghetto sets about becoming the world, erecting autonomous zones in the sphere of influence of power, or directly approaching power's mechanisms of suppression. The intellectual as Foucault saw him must then – after the most precise examination – always stand on the side of

10. Ibid. p. 48.

11. FOUCAULT, Michel: Nein zum König Sex, in: idem: Dispositive der Macht, p. 198.

the weak and the oppressed. With almost Leninist partisanship, Foucault offers, in the context of these real engagements to make a tool-box out of his intellectual instruments and use all the philosopher's intellectual achievements as a means of resistance.[12]

In this sense, in this book 'progress' as an idea and concept that has feet of clay. The ideological critique forbids the handicapped concept all growth within a multiplicity of discourses, and yet offers it a possibility of peaceful co-existence in the context of dancefloor history. The underground in disco, house and hip-hop has done its work instigating aesthetic and subcultural revolutions, and now the parasite creeps along in the rear to explain their achievements to the revolutionaries. The DJ sees progress captured for eternity on vinyl in a record box, and at every brand new live mix in the club one becomes more aware of standing at the spearhead of a new pop revolution. With this idea, the old terror version of the concept 'progress' has served its time – time for a remix. What follows are suggestions, not promises. At every line the author is aware that the discourse of progress is always also a violence that he is doing to things. Nonetheless (nonetheless, time and again) the attempt must be made if one doesn't want to reduce the achievements of DJ culture to that of another bright and entertaining phenomenon of the postmodern entertainment industry, but to subject it to a strict and, in an unorthodox sense, disciplined struggle.

12. Cf. FOUCAULT, Michel: Von den Matern zu den Zellen, in: idem: Mikrophysik der Macht, p. 45.

CULTURAL PROGRESS AS POLITICAL PROGRESS?

After the end of communism in world history in the late 80s, some conservative intellectuals rediscovered the Hegelian idea of the end of history in free, bourgeois society. The time of revolutions and revolts has come to an end, they argue, and the superiority of the bourgeois, capitalist state has been proven with the disappearance of the Eastern Block as a communist alternative to capitalism.

But in many places in the world people are in revolt and revolution against this new, apparently homogeneous world order. Many of these combatants have not abandoned faith in more liberty, equality and fraternity, and are trying, as reformers or revolutionaries, to realize their ideas. This front of resistance extends from Christian trade unionists in German industry to the members of the Marxist Guerrillas in El Salvador. Part of the resistance does not fight through the medium of politics, but has organized itself in the sphere of culture. For many people fighting solely with the medium of political engagement, the resistance of the cultural activists is peripheral, paltry and pointless. But again and again, these sceptics must be shown the extent to which politics has changed, and the extent to which politics articulates cultural practices. Images of the world and humanity have become media constructs, like the multiplicity of political arguments. Pop culture has become part of political culture, and cultural resistance has increased its significance.

For Marx and Engels, art and culture were merely notable side-shows of history, whose independent qualities were quickly and painlessly eliminated. Thus Marx, the lover of the arts, was struck by the nature in the development of material and artistic production, which led to the situation whereby, in the face of modern art, one could no longer – according to Marx – use the term 'progress' in its traditional 'abstraction'. He had recognized that the arts at their greatest do not always 'correspond to the general development of society; nor do they therefore to the material substructure'.[13] Given his enthusiasm for the works of Greek art, Marx was forced to ask whether progressive linearity could still be rescued within history. 'The difficulty is that they still give us aesthetic pleasure and are in certain respects regarded as a standard and unattainable ideal.'[14]

The dilemma of a freely wandering superstructure can no longer be solved so simply, plainly or disinterestedly. The limitation of aesthetic thought as it appears in Marx and Engels must be understood against the background of the political and social arguments of the 19th century. Art and culture were leisure activities,

13. MARX, Karl: A Contribution to the Critique of Political Economy, p. 215.

14. Ibid. p. 217.

and had practically no importance in political argument. Marx and Engels only toyed superficially with the question of the extent to which the superstructure can distance itself from the base without completely contradicting it, because there was no need for any further reflection. In a post-industrial information society, the dialectic between base and superstructure has to a great extent become unrecognizable, because in many places the two have merged into a whole. Large areas of the culture industry produce the ideology of the ruling system on a quasi-industrial basis; the variety of the bourgeois entertainment routine, which considers itself the bearer and ultimate guarantee of a democratic capitalist world order, extends from musicals via pop-songs and television series, from operas and paintings to dance theatre. Cut off from it, the underground sees itself as an order of dissidence.

The dancefloor subcultures described above are only parts of an underground culture that fights for freedoms from the ruling society, and by entering the mainstream changes its values and its worldview (sound included). Underground culture is above all culture, and is thus also a double agent, because it occupies a side-room off from the political argument and transfers much of the power of resistance to subsidiary problems such as lifestyle and everyday life and attitudes towards them. The line between resistance to the system and affirmation of it is a fluid one. It is, not least, a question of interpretation.

'Pop music speaks of social movement and mobility, and thus in principle it knows only one direction,' wrote Diederichsen. And that leads from 'the absolute exclusion of the individual (whether he be excluded politically, racially, economically) to the utopian inclusion of all (liberation, revolution, unity, communication).'[15] The extent to which pop music, and more particularly minority cultures in the context of DJ music, have broken down that exclusivity, can be seen in disco and house where the homosexual and ethnic minorities are concerned, and especially in hip-hop. Even before dancefloor music, DJs like Alan Freed and the activists of underground radio opted in favour of resistance at the end of the 60s. Freed turned black

15. DIEDERICHSEN, Diedrich: Wer fürchtet sich vor dem Cop Killer, in: SPIEGEL SPEZIAL 'Pop und Politik', p. 23.

R&B into a kind of music whose ground note of rebellion addressed all young people, and broke down any reservations young whites might have had about black pop culture. With his dances and concerts, he brought blacks and whites together, and as his reward received piles of letters describing him as a 'nigger-lover'.[16] But Freed, who, as a Jew, belonged to a minority that was still the victim of discrimination in the US, would not be dissuaded from playing black R&B music, which was cut off from the mainstream of American popular culture, and so, if not actually abolishing cultural segregation, he was at least knocking holes in it – and influencing the development of pop history. By 1952 the US charts demonstrated that the racial lines separating popular music and R&B were blurring. Songs like Johnnie Ray's 'Cry' – promoted by DJ Bill Randle – were successful in both hit parades.[17] With the beginning of pop culture, black music became integrated – often to its disadvantage – into the white-dominated mainstream. Black separatists like Nelson George have spelt out the dangers that this integration implied for Afro-American culture. The mainstream often conquered and subjected the cultural terrain of the blacks.

The mainstream lives on the power of minorities and exploits it for its own ends. Where pop lacks direction from exclusion to utopian inclusion, it is 'dead', proclaims Diederichsen. 'Even in the most dilapidated forms of the mainstream there still remain trace elements of the countercultures and minority cultures and their challenges, from which even the dreariest hit derives its form.'[18] This formative power of counter-cultures and minority cultures is nowhere more obviously apparent than in all the varieties of DJ music and the multiplicity of its mainstream hybrids.

After the failure of the student rebellion in 1968, political progress in the affluent First World has vanished into the distance. Many young people have turned their backs on politics, and completely forgotten that the decisions of politicians have a great influence on their everyday lives. And those who find little joy in the world as they see it do their fighting in the world of night-life. The extent to which the potential rebels of yesterday are today's artists, musicians or DJs is hard to

16. Cf. JACKSON, John A., op. cit., p. 34.

17. Cf. Ibid. p. 44f.

18. DIEDERICHSEN, Diedrich: : Wer fürchtet sich vor dem Cop Killer, loc. cit., p. 23.

establish. But it is certain that the alternative of joining up with a party or a protest movement rules many people out from the start. For young people who don't want to conform, the wide field of youth, minority and countercultures provides a space in which they can try out a partially unalienated life. The rejection of the ruling life practice and the dominant aesthetic is the starting point of all DJ cultures formed in the underground. It was sexual, ethnic or religious emancipation that encouraged disco, house and hip-hop. The socially marginalized have always played a crucial part in the establishment of any new subculture. Aesthetic innovations have not merely been powerful documents of proud independence, but also the hard-fought booty of the self-assertion – which arose within the cultural space – of otherwise oppressed minorities. Although innovations can be seen as documents of dissatisfaction with that which already exists, disco, like house and hip-hop, emerged not from the negation of that which already existed, but from the desire to create, from a threatened and precarious position, a kind of music that corresponded precisely to the needs of the subculture and its notions of beauty. The negation of existing music was not only superfluous, but was annulled by the curatorial tendency of the DJ's work (as an archivist with a record box). But at the same time the work of the underground DJ is always involved in disassociating himself from the dominant aesthetic, whether in the application of technology, the use of music or the planning of a club evening. The possibilities of self-realization were almost infinite in the subculture, while in everyday life they were, for blacks, gays and Latinos, extremely limited. Apart from the activism of the gay movement as a reaction to the Aids crisis in the 80s, the political actions of the culturally active minorities were relatively modest.

Their emancipation occurred primarily in the cultural underground. The DJ has always been at the centre of a subculture in which music played the most important part, with artistic, literary or fashionable forms of expression following on from it. This was particularly apparent in hip-hop, which at first, as DJ music, provided only danceable breakbeats, and then got people rapping and reciting poetry, dancing and breakdancing, painting and spraying. There were traditions of rapping, wild dancing and graffiti in ghetto culture, but only the DJ with his two turntables and his arts of composition defined the cultural field so broadly that B-Boys, sprayers and MCs could see themselves as part of a subculture. In absolute isolation, the politically marginalized ghetto secured itself a culture that was to conquer the rest of the world in the 80s and become more famous than the speeches of Malcolm X and Martin Luther King – indeed, which sampled the speeches of Malcolm X and Martin Luther King out of oblivion and into the consciousness of the present. A radical black resistance unseen in the USA since the 60s was strengthened by the propaganda of hip-hop musicians in their music and in the interviews they gave as political artists. The revival of black nationalism and the Nation of Islam was primarily down to hip-hop music. Public Enemy's 'Fight the Power' and other aggressive pop lyrics threw up the question of the point at which this resistance referred to a socio-political practice which, just as radically, preached resistance to the bourgeois capitalist world order. In previous revolts and revolutions the artists were either sympathizers or followers, never leaders or influential thinkers. That role belonged to the intellectuals, philosophers and politicians. Here something seems to have changed. Has the advancing world spirit been forced out of history into aesthetics, or is history bound to aesthetics more closely than ever in the media age?

Rodney King video

The case of the Rodney King video, the amateur shots that showed four white policemen beating a black car-driver, proved that the presence of the media and their recording capacities not only form political conscious-ness but can also lead to political activism.

Astute experts at media manipulation, hip-hop musicians filled all their anti-racist songs with the Rodney King incident, either in their lyrics or, as visual quotations, in their videos. When the images first appeared on television and then as visual samples in a number of rap videos, the abstract notion that blacks were mistreated by the white police was given a definition and concreteness that drove people into the streets. At the end of April 1992 the police in question were acquitted, and parts of Los Angeles went up in flames as the ghetto rebelled. A video camera had taken a single case that represents thousands of similar incidents, and turned it into a document that shook the internal stability of the USA, albeit for a short time.

This video tape rescued realism as an aesthetic strategy for political art – the direct and immediate representation of an injustice provoked a bloody revolt. The justified fear of many left-wing aestheticians, that the *realistic* documentation of exploitation and suppression was necessarily inadequate proved to be false. All one needed was the right example that turned abstract accusations into concrete political arguments, and could even force the American President to investigate a scandalous ruling. Realist art had a future after the Rodney King video. Even the straightforward idea of 'reflection' became negotiable again thanks to the shaky video recording and the reaction to it in rap videos.

From the heart
It's a start, a work of art
To revolutionize, make a change, nothin' strange
People people, we are the same
No we're not the same
'cause we don't know the game
What we need is awareness, we can't get careless,[19]

Public Enemy rapped in 1989.

The contradictions and injustices of the bourgeois world order are denounced in the pop charts, yet political systems remain stable. The revolutionary aesthetic of Public Enemy sells well, white record companies earn millions of dollars with it. In this confused situation, the consciousness of an artist like Chuck D., Public Enemy's spokesman, may be clear, but the political dimension of artistic creation becomes questionable. For Chuck D., hip-hop is the last black cry for help. Hip-hop 'is the only authentic, loud voice that black culture has produced. Today the oppressed of the whole world can identify with rap.'[20] The extent to which this identification with a kind of music that considers itself revolutionary leads to political activism or at least to a political attitude remains an open question.

The history of modern art is full of artists, writers and

19 . PUBLIC ENEMY: Fight the Power, in: STANLEY, Lawrence A., op. cit., p. 259.

20 . CHUCK D.: Arbeiten wie James Bond, in: SPIEGEL SPEZIAL 'Pop und Politik', p. 57.

directors that put – or want to put – their work at the service of revolution, and have had to watch their aesthetic projects fail in the reality of political arguments, or degenerate into complete nonsense. Chuck D. knows about the limitations of his work, and still believes that a society can only be changed if one owns its symbols. 'You can move people and make them think with symbols. And I and other rappers have managed that. Whites don't first learn what's up with blacks from whites: how they dress and think, how they dance and feel. Rap is something like an introduction. If my people really want to become politically active it isn't enough for them to listen to my records. They have to start reading books.'[21]

Hip-hop deserves to be considered principally in the context of a politically progressive art history. But even the separatist and isolationist projects of revolt of disco and house are forms of clashes with power. While hip-hop represents a clash with the system, disco and house tried to secure niches and freedoms in the context of the system and then – with as little alienation as possible – to organize them according to the needs of the minorities who are to bear them.

21. Ibid. p. 57f.

22. Cf. KOSSELECK, Reinhart/ MEIER, Christian: Fortschritt, in: BRUNNER, Otto et al (Ed.): Geschichtliche Grundbegriffe, Vol. 2, p. 392.

NONETHELESS: THE PROGRESS PROJECT

Anyone who principally measures progress in historiography in terms of political development is following an outdated notion. Technology, aesthetics and the organizational form of the subculture feed the hope of more and bring the project of modernity into the 21st century.

TECHNICAL PROGRESS

Since the Renaissance, scientific progress, inventions and discoveries have encouraged people in their belief that their own time is superior to previous eras.[22] Since then philosophers and apologists have adduced science and technology as evidence for the validity of the principle of progress. Paul Feyerabend describes the technology-dependent concept of progress as 'quantitative' or 'additive'.[23]

It's even easier to establish progress that can be measured in decibels, bits and watts. Its history can be read in tables, charts and circuit diagrams. An aesthetic that is closely linked with its technical means of production can be shown to be progressive, in the sense that it improves from the technical point of view, simply by using slide-rules and electrical gauges. More important than quantitatively measurable improvements are the qualitative leaps which, thanks to the achievements of engineers, grant musicians a new form of production. In 1991 the techno pioneers of Kraftwerk were delighted that technical development had gone so far 'that recording possibilities keep pace with our ideas, that the idea and the product are to a large extent identical. Only now has software developed to the point that it can appropriately convert the software in our heads.'[24]

The great anti-idealist among German literary academics, Friedrich Kittler, has examined the extent to which the artists' software was dependent on the hardware of the history of technology. In his aesthetic theory the development of the arts is connected via the history of technology to the gear-wheel of the (material) world. His history of the modern era begins where Foucault left the archives and the libraries and concluded his 'order of things'. In the 19th, and particularly in the 20th century, the history of a homogeneous logocentric culture became an audio-visual avalanche of information, which was recorded in various electronic media. 'Mouths and scripts fell out of prehistory', because 'otherwise the events and their narratives (hi/story) could not have been joined together'.[25] And now mouths and scripts are coming back and, in many places, taking over historiography. In the literary history of the modern era, Kittler documents how writing stores 'the fact of its loss of power'.[26] Within a century, writing's storage monopoly has been transferred to an 'omnipotence of electrical

23. Cf. FEYERABEND, Paul: Wissenschaft als Kunst, p. 89.

24. GRAF, Andreas: Chipsy Kings, in: MUSIK EXPRESS 7/1991, p. 45.

25. KITTLER, Friedrich A.: op. cit., p. 12.

26. Ibid. p. 16.

circuits',[27] but Kittler refuses to speak in terms of progress, despite the multiplication of possibilities for information and storage. As a literary academic and a futuristic computer-fan, he only refers to the transition from writing's monopoly on storage to that of pictures and sounds.

The history of DJ music begins with the history of radio, and is thus immediately connected to the history of technology.

In 1906, when Reginald Fessenden played Handel's *Largo* on a gramophone, and merged the tinny sound of the recording with the hissing of the first radio broadcast, the range of frequencies was restricted to a 'pathetic'[28] 200–2000 Hertz. Music could be recognized but hardly understood. The coarseness of the sounds generated by gramophones, and the shortcomings of the broadcast left little room for musical niceties. In 1923 Laszlo Moholy-Nagy was moved to carve graphic structures into gramophone records, and thus turn the gramophone as an instrument of reproduction into a productive instrument. 'The graphic signs allow us to establish a new graphic-mechanical scale, which is to say a new mechanical harmony, by examining the individual graphic signs and bringing their relationships into a law.'[29] This primitive idea of the equivalence of graphic and musical creation could only come into being at a time when the crudity of the product corresponded to the crudity of the hardware, although Moholy-Nagy observes that the efficiency of the gramophone was 'considerably furthered by certain technical improvements'.[30] What he was referring to was the electrical powering of the gramophone and the new, refined membranes of gramophones. This 'modern' technology, linked to the avant-garde scratchers on records, was to bring an end to the old scales and the old melodic system.

At the same time DJs tried not to destroy the old scales, but to communicate their musical results. Transmitting installations became stronger and stronger, and almost every year new records were established for the wattage and range of the radio transmitters. The future of radio was a transmitter that everyone could hear at once, and

27. Ibid. p. 33.

28. Cf. KITTLER, Friedrich A.: Der Gott der Ohren, in: idem: Draculas Vermächtnis, p. 135.

29. MOHOLY-NAGY, Laszlo: Neue Gestaltung in der Musik, in: BLOCK, Ursula/ GLASMEIER, Michael, op. cit., p. 53.

30. Ibid.

which would unite humanity. Velimir Khlebnikov, who, like Moholy-Nagy, was fascinated by the possibilities of radio, saw it as a medium for the intellectualization of the people and the democratization of knowledge. Radio libraries, radio clubs, radio lectures, even radio diagnosis and therapy: Khlebnikov wanted to use radio to bring happiness to people.[31]

The first DJs had no time for an emancipatory, humanist understanding of their radio practice. Martin Block, the first DJ superstar, wanted and had to sell in order to keep his music programme's financial head above water. For him, the extended range meant above all the possibility to reach more potential customers with his commercial breaks, and attract more sponsors to his programme. Trained as a travelling salesman, thanks to radio he was able to spare himself the arduous trek from door to door, and at the same time he was able to speak to all potential customers at a time of day when the usual, non-media-based salesmen couldn't be received. Block also managed to flatter, not only with his rhetoric, but with the addition of pre-pop hit music.

For Bertolt Brecht, the invention of radio was an example of technical development in advance of social development. When radio was invented, it spent the first period of its existence as a substitute: a substitute for theatre, opera, concerts, for lectures, for local newspapers and other forms of art and media. Block's *Make-Believe Ballroom* was a typical example of what Brecht called the halcyon youth of radio.

As a utopian socialist, in 1932 Brecht dreamed of a radio that would not only spread knowledge, music and the arts, but make communication possible. The one-way character of radio, from the transmitter to the receiver, would be cancelled by direct feedback or other communication opportunities for the hitherto disparate and isolated audience. Radio should not try to mask loneliness with entertainment, but get rid of it altogether.[32]

The visions of radio as a democratic apparatus of communication remained daydreams. The only opportunity for listeners to shape the programmes was the listeners' requests which were first institutionalized in the hit parade in the 30s, and continued in the Top

31. Cf. KHLEBNIKOV, Velimir: The Radio of the Future, in: STRAUSS, Neil: Radiotext(e), pp. 23–5.

32. Cf. BRECHT, Bertolt: The Radio as an Apparatus of Communication, in: STRAUSS, Neil, op. cit., p. 15.

40 programmes. 'For innovation, against renovation!' was Brecht's rallying-cry, but the technical innovations never happened, and were simulated by modifications in programme design. The hit parade as a pathetic feedback loop revealed the opportunities for audience influence to be mere primitive populism. Worse than that: the extraordinary PR actions by DJs for particular songs proved how much in thrall the audience was to the 'tribal drum' (McLuhan) of radio. Block managed to use this thraldom in the service of capital in exemplary fashion. Block's work is the ancestor of all the successful commercial breaks to be found on radio or television or in the cinema.

33 . Cf. HEBDIGE, Dick: Subculture, p. 3.

Pop culture is a reaction to the bombardment by the media that reached a new peak after the Second World War. Radio, television, records, cinema define a new reality, a subsidiary media reality which, for those teenagers of the post-war era who could afford entertainment, soon became a glamorous super-structure of their everyday life. Pop culture rescued the audience from the passivity of pure reception. Alienation in the enjoyment of media productions was undermined if this media world was declared to be the real world, and started to exist entirely in the symbolic reality of music, film images and fashion. Youth cultures after the Second World War reacted to the undemocratic structure of the capitalist entertainment industry without having any of their fun taking away. Teenagers recoded rock'n'roll from Bill Haley to James Dean according to their own conditions, and adapted it to their own lifestyles. Hebdige describes the process in which objects are given meaning, and in which they enter new signifying contexts as style, as a constitutive element of youth culture.[33] This creative remake of an already existing object changes nothing about the power structure of the media communication process, but the receiver escapes the passive role by accepting what is broadcast in his alienation, exaggerating it and finally categorizing it as a part of pop reality.
Alan Freed is one of the first figures in pop culture. His decontextualization of R&B and his definition of rock'n'roll make him one of the leading culture makers in the young pop world. Subcultures organize their own

symbolic hierarchies and create their own realities. The first pop DJ, Freed became involved in the construction of this new reality, organizing concerts, composing songs, writing lyrics and acting in films. For him, media reality was an area of immediate self-realization. If the media were not organized and structured communicatively, the use of the various media had to be recognized as formal possibilities. But Freed, who ended up as a tragic figure, knew from the first how narrow those possibilities were, and that all further development of the media would sooner or later be swallowed up by the dominant discourse. But the public liquidation of his legend on the occasion of the payola trial could do nothing to prevent Freed being among the first to show that radio could influence and define a subculture, or the DJ masterfully shaping taste via the transmission installations.

In 1958 the stereo record was introduced, making pop music even more enticing. The development of Hi-Fi technology made sound experiments and fine tuning in the studio a possibility, changing the design of pop music. The mixing desk was first used by artist-producers like Phil Spector and George Martin, and a good five years later by the first DJ-musicians. Bands like Pink Floyd and later Kraftwerk investigated how far listening habits and the traditional understanding of music could be challenged.

Singles music became LP music, and the underground DJs on the FM band broadcast songs which, because of their length and also of their experimental character, were unsuitable for mainstream radio. The innovative application of technology separated the underground from the conservatives, and once again it was DJs who found the appropriate representation for the new sound on the radio. The student leader Abbie Hoffman challenged hippies and subversives to install 'Guerilla Radio': 'If you rigged a small tape recorder to the transmitter and tuned it to a popular AM band, the patrol car as it rode around could actually broadcast the guerilla message you pre-recorded.'[34] But this rather theoretical, one-dimensional understanding of radio remained the hobby of ivory-tower students. DJs like Tom Donahue made the ultra-short-wave FM

34. HOFFMAN, Abbie: Guerilla Radio, in: STRAUSS, Neil, op. cit., p. 301.

frequencies hugely popular as transmitters of underground music. The 'guerilla' news played on these wavelengths came from records and spoke of realities that had left the realm of words and pamphlets far behind.

But the technology of recording and reproduction had improved not only in the recording studio, but in the musical instruments as well. The American pop writer Robert Palmer describes how the traditional instrument, the guitar, was turned into a solo instrument by the introduction of the amplifier in the mid-30s, and in the 'electric music' of rock'n'roll became the instrument of pop music. 'Since the 1960s rock&roll fanatics have been, ipso facto, guitar fanatics.'[35] Although the artistic use of the electric guitar was totally different in the work of Eric Clapton, Jimi Hendrix, Duane Allman or Keith Richards, they were still all working with the same simple instrument, and trying to create a universe in sound out of six strings and the associated technology.

The infinite space of notes and sounds was promised by the invention of the synthesizer. As early as the beginning of the 1950s, musicians like Stockhausen were trying to use the sound possibilities of electronic systems. The difficulty and complexity of the beginnings of electronic music are documented in a description of Stockhausen, who, as a 23-year-old in Paris together with his colleague Pierre Schäffer, 'experienced and experimentally systematised everything... that was then current in Musique Concrète': with a sine generator in a basement studio 'I systematically produced the first sound spectrums by overlaying sine tones, an endlessly arduous task (there was no tape-recorder in the studio, and I had to copy each sine tone on record, and copy it on from record to record!!)'.[36] Fifteen years later synthesizers were introduced without much difficulty into pop music. The struggle with a reluctant technology had never really taken place in pop music, with the possible exception of some tracks by Kraftwerk.

A new era in pop music began with the mature generation of synthesizers which were first used in intellectually demanding projects by student bands like Pink Floyd and Kraftwerk. 'The present day is great,

35. PALMER, Robert: Church of the Sonic Guitar, in: DeCURTIS, Anthony: Present Tense, p. 14.

36. STOCKHAUSEN, Karlheinz: Elektronische Musik – Brief an Douglas M. Davis, in: idem, op. cit., p. 342.

particularly for musicians,' Ralf Hütter of Kraftwerk raved about the 'incredible' expressive possibilities of the new instruments. 'In the 19th century the job must have been an incredibly bleak one: all those people crouching on chairs and scratching around on their violins – what a terrible idea! Today, on the other hand, anyone well-versed in technology is a sorcerer in the universe of sound!'[37]

In contemporary electronic music, too, technology is crucial to composition. Boulez challenges scientists and musicians to form a close collaboration which will finally give rise to a new and innovative music: 'In the end, musical invention will have somehow to learn the language of technology, and even to appropriate it. The full arsenal of technology will elude the musician, admittedly; it exceeds, often by a big margin, his ability to specialize... in other words, musical invention must bring about the creation of the musical material it needs.'[38] Boulez was writing in 1977, when Kraftwerk was programming the LP *Menschmaschine*, and DJs were beginning to invent hip-hop.

After Kraftwerk, DJs were the next technological sorcerers in pop music. At first using primitive mixing desks and relatively orthodox access to the record-player, in the late 60s they begin mixing a new music out of soul, funk and R&B. Disco principally uses the new electronic instruments such as synthesizers and rhythm-boxes to produce a synthetic sound that is technologically contemporary. The first DJs who created a sound of their own with their mix of records reached their own work via the detour of record production, but not through the consistent development of their work as DJs.

The maxi or twelve-inch single was the first media product of DJ culture, and enabled remixing to gain acceptance, a process that DJs had conceived for DJs and were now able to produce.

Hip-hop DJs were the first to recognize that two record-players could not only provide their own mixture of existing music, but could also allow something completely new and autonomous to come into being. What sort of sounds can a record-player and

37. FUCHS-GAMBÖCK, Michael: Kraftwerk, in: WIENER 7/1991, p. 108.

38. BOULEZ, Pierre: Technology and the Composer, in: idem: Orientations, p. 491.

a record produce? A question raised by Moholy-Nagy in the early years of the century, out of dissatisfaction with the limited tonal systems, was posed once again by the DJs. The question was not governed by artistic or theoretical considerations, but amounted to the expression of a ghetto situation, in which two record-players and a mixing desk constituted precious objects. Precious objects which were first used to provide the sound for parties and which, in the course of party-making, were gradually discovered as musical instruments in their own right. Graffiti painting, breakdancing and rap established a new, revolutionary aesthetic order around the two turntables and the mixing desk. For black rap theorist Tricia Rose, hip-hop is a product of the cultural tradition of the blacks, of the post-industrial transformation of urban life and the state of technology. In this context Rose points out that many of the hip-hop musicians had trained as technicians, to repair and maintain the new technology for the privileged classes, but instead used this technology for an 'alternative cultural expression'.[39] So technicians and frustrated engineers formed the beginning of hip-hop music.

Grandmaster Flash put his own system together, modified his mixing desk and turned the beatbox into a fixed component of hip-hop music. Of the three original hip-hop DJs the trained electrician was the only one who forced through technical innovations and integrated them within the aesthetic concept of the music. Kittler challenged the unbelievers, who still appreciated the beauty of laser guns and samplers in terms of older art to open the covers of their technical instruments. Once the black boxes were unscrewed anyone could tell that art wasn't going on in there, 'but coming to an end in a piece of data processing that was taking its leave of humanity'.[40] Grandmaster Flash opened all the covers and put together a system entirely according to his own needs. One faction within the DJs was to follow this passion for engineering: a prime example is the techno wunderkind Richard James, who put together his own sampler as a teenager. But neither Grandmaster Flash nor his youngest descendant in the tribe of engineer DJs ever saw musical 'data processing' as taking its leave from humanity. Unlike Kittler, who

39. ROSE, Tricia, op. cit., p. 63.

40. KITTLER, Friedrich A.: Fiktion und Simulation, in: BARCK, Karlheinz et al (Ed.), op. cit., p. 196.

came from high literature and jazz to high-tech, Grandmaster Flash and James grew up in a sound-world that was technical through and through. For them the new technology was not a farewell to humanity but a new start for people who were able to use it to communicate through new music. Even more than this: the record changed from being merely a medium of recording to being one of communication, because the ghettos of New York and LA were able to communicate via rap songs pressed on vinyl. The gramophone was just 100 years old when the DJs in the Bronx discovered it had more uses than merely playing records. The playful rediscovery of the record-player resulted in some strange noises from the vinyl discs, and the transformation from a piece of reproductive equipment to an instrument took place. The unorthodox use, contrary to the instruction book, was rewarded with sounds that had previously never been heard. The scratching of the stylus to the rhythm of the breakbeat was originally an act of raw accentuation within the rhythmical structure. As with all innovations, whether technical or 'playful' in nature, primitivism rapidly became highly skilled.

Technology wasn't something – certainly not in the ghetto – to be afraid of. Heidegger saw the essence of modern technology as a metaphysics that estranges people from truth and revelation [*Entbergung*]. Heidegger speaks of the '*Gestell*' [frame, enframing] as 'that way of revealing that holds sway in the essence of technology, and that is itself nothing technological...'[41] but rather a form of western metaphysics of civilization based on modern science. This enframing 'blocks the shining-forth and holding sway of truth. The destining that sends into ordering is consequently the extreme danger. What is dangerous is not technology. Technology is not demonic; but its essence is mysterious. The essence of technology, as a destining of revealing, is the danger.'[42] In his desperation Heidegger takes refuge in a line from the poet Hölderlin: 'Where danger is, grows/the saving power also.' The greater the danger, the closer the possible rescue. 'But human reflection can ponder the fact that all saving power must be of a higher essence than what is endangered, though at the same time kindred to it... The closer we come to the

41. HEIDEGGER, Martin: 'The Question Concerning Technology, in: idem: Basic Writings, p. 302.

42. Ibid. p. 309.

danger, the more brightly do the ways into the saving power begin to shine and the more questioning we become. For questioning is the piety of thought.'[43] Heidegger, a conservative enemy of progress and a reactionary prophet of *Kehre*, or reversal, is concerned about people, because as a 20th-century philosopher he is in a position to see how quickly the world is developing – and with a technology that is entirely alien and incomprehensible to him. His distance from technology and his incomprehension provoke anxiety and insecurity. The fact that Heidegger is always fundamentally right in his warnings about the dangers of modern technology has been understood for some time, even before Hiroshima and Chernobyl. If we wish to criticize the rule of technology we can always fall back on Heidegger's fundamental critique, but to insist and rely upon it in the late 20th century would be both senseless and impotent.

Anxiety about the development of technology in the 20th century had also gripped non-reactionary thinkers like Marcuse and Horkheimer. In 1947, in his *Critique of Instrumental Reason*, Horkheimer expressed the fear that the advance of technology would be 'accompanied by a process of dehumanization', and that progress threatened to destroy the goal that it was to realize: 'the idea of man'.[44] Horkheimer and Adorno unite in lamenting that technical rationality is the 'rationality of dominance' itself, and thus the 'coercive nature of society alienated from itself'.[45] The danger of an all-levelling and standardizing culture industry is linked in the *Dialectic of Enlightenment* with the growing penetration of the production process by technology. The victim of this development is the work, whose logic is no longer distinguished from that of the social system. 'The ruthless unity of which in the culture industry is evidence of what will happen in politics.'[46] The alignment of the new technology with the culture industry and the political logic of the dominant class becomes the harbinger of a new barbarism.

In their work, DJs pervert both the logic of the new technologies and that of the culture industry. Their blasphemous treatment of the instruction manual and its deliberate distance from the premises of the culture industry (or a perverted affirmation of it) undermines

43. Ibid. p. 315f.

44. HORKHEIMER, Max: Kritik der Instrumentellen Vernunft, p. 13.

45. HORKHEIMER, Max/ADORNO, Theodor W.: Dialectic..., p. 121.

46. Ibid. p. 131.

the totalitarian unity feared by Horkheimer and Adorno, but remains unable to escape it. The capacities of the culture industry to absorb and to standardize grow with the resistance that it encounters.

The artists in DJ culture form the first artistic avant-garde in the context of pop music that recodes modern technology. Video and computer art have tried to do this, but the artists used the media as the manufacturers had intended. The techno rebels from the Bronx were neither familiar with the users' manuals nor with avant-garde manifestos about the conquest of technology by the arts that were churned out in the early years of the 20th century. The piety of their thinking began when they questioned: what is a record-player, and what can it do? And then they questioned what two record-players could do if linked up by a mixing desk. And then they questioned what a stylus connected to an amplifier could do on a vinyl record. And so the ghetto DJs questioned and questioned their way to a new musical aesthetic. And because the ghetto DJs were not philosophers who were content with questioning, but practitioners, DJs and trained electricians, they only wondered briefly, and then they tried it out. The piety of questioning coincided with the piety of action.

People generally react to technology as technicians expect the users of objects to do. A great deal of video and computer art appears, in its meaningless, pointless tricksiness, to be interesting only as a bit of PR for the manufacturers. The electronics and high-tech industry ornaments itself with an avant-garde, which stands out from it, which is infatuated with technology and forgets what it really wanted to do with that technology. The concentration on hardware and software relegates the art product to second place. The gesture of the hip-hop DJs in scratching their styli to pieces on the records, turning the records against the direction of the motor, or simply regulating the speed of the record with their fingers on the edge of the deck, was originally the violation of technology. Many record-players, pick-up systems, loudspeakers and amplifiers were sacrificed to sound out the possibilities of the technology. If something was broken, there was always somebody somewhere in the community who could repair the damage caused by experimentation. In an act of courageous and autonomous redefinition, the record-player became an instrument. 'Ceci n'est pas une pipe', Magritte painted beneath the picture of a pipe, thus referring to the unreal character of art. It isn't a piece of reproductive equipment, it's an instrument, a much-scorned, simple device that you can do so much with if you're creative enough, the DJs said. Thus they were referring to the real character of art and a pop culture that wasn't afraid of technology. Until then it had been engineers and DIY men who had invented synthesizers and electric guitars; with the DJ, the artist-inventor entered the arena of art history.

Grandmaster Flash painstakingly put together a cross-fader on the monitor junction of his headphone box so that he could hear the beats of the record that wasn't going out over the loudspeaker system, which were to be mixed into the song he had just been playing. By this time there was already a mixing desk with this capacity on the market, but fitting the existing machinery to one's own requirements in this way became a feature of the technologically innovative hip-hop culture. Record-players had been reinvented under the hands of the DJs, and a little later the electronics industry constructed record-players corresponding to those same needs. Violation was taken up and re-evaluated by the industry as a creative act. The unorthodox treatment of technology brought dividends.

Something similar happened with the transformation of the beatbox that Grandmaster Flash had bought from a drummer. Flash mounted the beatbox on his mixing desk, which had already been fitted with a pre-hear system. With the beatbox, the narrow, primitivist concept of DJ music was extended for the first time; it became the first instrument to be used by DJs. As one excursion into the history of rhythm machines has shown, in the late 70s, when Flash first used the beatbox, there were already much more highly developed instruments on the market, but once again it was the DJ-led appropriation of technology that turned this one into the standard instrument for old-school breakbeats. Throughout the development of DJ culture many of these anachronistic products, originally used

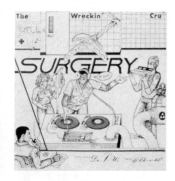

The celebration of the means of production: covers of hip-hop records

for want of new equipment, became the machines of reference for the original sound of DJ music. The best example of this, perhaps, is the Roland 303 drum machines, which made acid house possible, and are still used by artists today if they need sounds close to acid.

The lack of the latest technology gets people interested in the technology that already exists, particularly if there has been no opportunity to get close to the new, more expensive technology. Grandmaster Flash had to beg and plead from one of the first disco DJs before he was allowed to use his mixing desk. The DJs from the ghetto fought until they achieved their own technical progress. This struggle produced a familiar relationship with technology, which turned hip-hop, and later house and all other forms of DJ music into a kind of confessional hardware poetry. The hip-hop DJs hid their systems from their competitors; they gave their record-players pet names like 'Wheels of Steel' or 'Ones and Twos', and in DJ battles the DJs often shouted the wattages of their systems into the microphone. For a long time Kool DJ Herc was uncontested as number one among the DJs, simply because his speakers and amplifiers were louder than those of all his competitors. In the mid-70s the battles were still like car races, and what mattered above all was who had the more powerful engine. The refinements of the mixing were secondary. The dexterousness of the DJs only really became interesting when the most important DJs had equipped themselves with comparable systems.

The first raps rhymed to the breakbeats praised the DJ and his sound system. Before hip-hop ever spoke of violence and sex, about the ghetto and poverty, about love and despair, it raved about speakers, vinyl and turntables. And when DJs grew better and more virtuoso in their use of the turntables, the MCs had to distract the people from the arts of the DJs with rhythmical verbal art, and communicate a party mood. Nonetheless, many B-Boys and fly-girls stood as if rooted to the floor, to see how these unfamiliar sounds could be produced from a stack of old records and two ordinary record-players. While spray-can graffiti painting could immediately be understood *technically* as art, the actions of the DJs were initially a mystery.

That soon changed, as all the famous DJs started to train up the new generation, and these pupils in turn passed on their knowledge.

When the technical foundations of hip-hop music were in place in the form of the beatbox, the turntables and the mixing desk, and all the foundations of DJ technique were in place with scratching, mixing and back-spinning, the focus within the music shifted from the breakbeats to the rhymes. The MCs put the DJs in the shade. The poets and literati concealed the fact, with their loquacious signifying, that it was the DJ engineers and technicians who had allowed them to perform like this. The references and declarations of respect for the DJs went into a distinct decline, and the lyrics were generally filled with a heroic poetry glorifying the MCs' own verbal power and their (apparently) related potency in more general terms. The first successful rap record was produced by a thrown-together band of MCs, and not by a famous DJ. The Sugar Hill Gang didn't come from the Bronx, and had no respect for the innovators of hip-hop. Only a year later could Grandmaster Flash and Afrika Bambaataa hit back with their first hits.

But even they couldn't prevent the MCs being the focus of interest both of the record industry and that of the audience. The man clutching the microphone came significantly closer to the traditional idea of the pop star than the DJ crouched over two turntables, constantly rummaging around in his record boxes. The marketing of rather reticent technophiles who were entirely immersed in the music was much more difficult than that of the loud-mouthed party-givers and self-adulators, so the record industry put the record industry into the spotlight. Breakbeat music turned into rap.

Of course the input of the DJs remained crucial for the success of a song or the quality of a band project, but many of the old school pieces had little instrumentation, or only ran over a simple bass-line. Today these productions sound thin and monotonous.

The use of the sampler by Afrika Bambaataa in 1981 marked a second new impulse in DJ technology. The sampler was not the invention of a creative ghetto DJ but a product of digital high-tech that only became affordable when DJs were able to abandon their involuntary isolation in the ghetto. In the case of the sampler, the DJ could not indulge in the violation of the user's manual, since the recording and ordering possibilities of the samplers appeared to correspond precisely to what the DJs had previously constructed by hand at the mixing desk. With the help of samplers and sequencers, loops could be endlessly repeated, and breakbeats ceased to require concentration and back-breaking labour. But just as painting only seemed to become obsolete with the invention of photography, and then had to find tasks other than those of representation, the DJ was now able to concern himself more fully with the musical embellishment of the breakbeats. The development of rhythm equipment was an additional help, and within a very short time several high-tech devices had assumed the classical functions of the old school DJ without calling his activity into question, because DJs were the first to make purposeful use of these new technologies and experiment with them. Scratching and mixing remained a formal blueprint for the use of machines. Here too, then, there could be no alienation from production technology, because from the start it had been seen not as a problem but as a great support to the work of composition.

In the mid-80s the second great impulse in hip-hop music began, and many of the sceptics who had denounced rap as pop's original mayfly were forced to acknowledge the great musical power that lay within it. The fundamental revolution of hip-hop lay in the fact that the music had not been created by instruments, but by joining two pieces of reproductive machinery. Hip-hop as a product was the first pure music-music, while it was only in its DJ roots that disco existed as music-music, or music that consisted only of parts of other, old music. All technical equipment used by hip-hop first of all served to reproduce stored or recorded sounds, and only became instruments in their use and application, their combination and networking. The only exception is the rhythm box, although even this was originally less of an instrument than a beat counter. The self-referentiality of art as a chief characteristic of both modern and postmodern culture was technically inherent in hip-hop.

While self-reference in classical modernism had a philosophical focus, aimed at the discovery and definition of the art in question, self-reference in postmodernism is a vehicle of cheerful eruption into the playful irresponsibility of self-referential chains of signifiers. 'What is painting?' asked Casimir Malevich's white squares on a white background, 'What is art? asked Marcel Duchamp's ready-mades, while the historicism of an architect like James Stirling didn't so much ask questions as tell cheerful stories. Commonly, hip-hop and the other forms of DJ music fall under the heading of postmodern cultural practice because of their eclecticism. Certainly, nothing could leave a DJ more indifferent that the notion that his work was being assigned to some tradition or other by some philosopher at some conference somewhere. Nonetheless, it must be pointed out that the historicism and eclecticism of the DJs cannot be understood as such, but can be seen as a derivation of production technology. Record-players reproduced, while the drawing-boards of James Stirling were the same as those at which Mies van der Rohe sat before him: historicism/eclecticism was a purely intellectual construct and a matter of taste, and not something derived from production technology. And while the historicism of the postmodern architects left the fundamental aesthetic premises of house-building untouched, DJ eclecticism created a new musical genre (more about this in the next chapter).

Sampling represents the beginning not only of a new chapter in the history of hip-hop, but in DJ culture and pop music in general. In hip-hop, the recoding of turntables and mixers had been undertaken by a small community in the Bronx. When rap reached the rest of the world, musicians and DJs in Europe and the USA began first to copy the orthodox old school style, and gradually to modify it, eventually leading to the completely autonomous works of Soul II Soul and Massive Attack. Each of the innovative DJs read the user's manual of his systems and equipment in his own way. The individual appropriation of technology in each case was a crucial characteristic for the diversification of DJ music as it has occurred since 1987.

Band names like Digital Underground and 808 State tell us how much the technical bases of production shaped the aesthetic of the projects. Hip-hop bands like EPMD were photographed for the cover of their first LP *Strictly Business* in front of flashing studio equipment, making it clear that their system of reference is not so much the ghetto (as shown on many other hip-hop covers), but the place where bass-lines were looped and funky guitars sampled. The conquest of pop by the DJ was not least down to the fact that within a very short time the new technology – samplers, computers and mixers – became affordable. Where the first DJs had to cobble together their systems out of scrap, the DJs who weren't from the ghetto, but from terraced houses, were able to put together their own mini-studios at home, as teenagers. M/A/R/R/S, Bomb The Bass and Coldcut are early examples of these bedroom producers who appeared in their thousands in the late 80s and early 90s and sold their songs to small independent labels. In the rapidly growing dancefloor culture these DJ producers occupied the place held by guitar bands in rock culture. If most cool guys had previously dreamed of being the singer or guitarist in a rock'n'roll band, now they dreamed of being a DJ and putting on records at parties and clubs and making new tracks at the computer during the day.

The first great pop engineers after the producer kings like Martin and Spector were the musicians of Pink Floyd and Kraftwerk. It was no coincidence that three of the four original members of Pink Floyd had been students at Regent Street Polytechnic in London, where they had studied architecture, a subject that precisely marks the boundaries between the visual arts and engineering. Faced with the choice, Syd Barrett opted to study art. His brilliant madness gave early Pink Floyd their consciousness-expanding power and ecstasy, and catapulted him out of the band in 1968. But the journeys to the borders of acoustic perception were not just the hallucinations of extended LSD trips, but always electrically powered. Like no pop band before them, Pink Floyd used all the advances of sound distortion and sound treatment. They unscrewed their amplifiers, over-modulated their systems, violated their electric instruments and used the mixing desk as a 'fifth instrument'.[47] But again, it was the non-technologist and madman Barrett who gave the band a 'technical head-start' with his Azimuth Coordinator: 'As the name suggested, the Azimuth Coordinator was a sound system which meant that any events, tracks and layers within the mass of sound could be placed in any position, variable according to all three spatial dimensions, and brought to the listener's ear.'[48] By the mid-60s Pink Floyd had overtaken the rest of the world, technically, and as a result, aesthetically as well. On the cover of their masterpiece 'The Dark Side of the Moon', the list of band-members is followed by the abbreviation VCS3, an acknowledgment of the synthesizer which enabled the band to make their poetic trip to the dark side of the moon. For Kittler this isn't going far enough. He wanted to see the circuit diagrams of the music systems in place of the names of lyricists and composers. Only the DJs of acid house would supply this pleasure, when they explained the functions of the 303 Roland drum computer on T-shirts.

Kraftwerk replaced Pink Floyd at the head of the techno avant-garde, and in the wake of the drug-hazed British hippies, they embodied the sober German engineering spirit. But the two Kraftwerk masterminds Hütter and Schneider both began as music college students who could read music, and gradually lost themselves, in their debate with synthesizers and computers, in circuit diagrams that wanted to transform them into man-machines. Like Pink Floyd and their interpreter Kittler, Kraftwerk come from the western cultural tradition. As intellectuals and artists with an academic training they devoted themselves – fascinated by the creative capacities of new technology – entirely to this new world, without forgetting, however, that they had been socialized in a completely different way.

The DJs are the first musical engineers to have brought no cultural knowledge to their work. They are not trained musicians, they can't play instruments and only a few can read music, but they can repair televisions and assemble mixing desks. The DJs from 1987 onwards are also the first children to have grown up

47. KITTLER, Friedrich A.: Der Gott der Ohren, in: idem: Draculas Vermächtnis, p. 132.

48. Ibid. p. 137.

with televisions, stereos (which have only existed since the mid-60s), and then with computers. Today's DJs have additionally been socialized by video games, cd players, video recorders and laptops. For them, the tradition of western culture is irrelevant. They grew up with high-tech, and learned to use it quite naturally. Anyone who has seen the photographs of 14-year-old computer specialists who earn more money programming than their parents do will know that there is a rising generation of intellectuals and technocrats with little time for the old system of writing and manuscripts, not out of laziness but out of lack of time. There isn't much to get excited about in the field of the old recording media, while infinite possibilities lie in the digital world of wonders. Pink Floyd and Kraftwerk moved from classical culture to the sovereign territory of the engineers and sound technicians. The question of the future will be whether there will be any DJ producers willing to take the trouble to think their way back to classical culture without abandoning their progressive aesthetic practice.

In his half-academic, half-mythical book *The Third Wave*, Alvin Toffler draws a vision of the future. The third wave of civilization means the end of industrial society and the transition to a new era of humanity in which, in Toffler's view, everything from everyday life via culture to technology will be changed – forming a new, more pure and better society, as the book's cover has it. For this to succeed, the leaders and pioneers of this new civilization will have to win the fight against the representatives of the old, second wave. Toffler calls the advance guard of the new man the 'techno-rebels'. These rebels are environmentally conscious, humanistic and anti-nationalistic. Their leaders are generally trained as representatives of technical intelligence. 'The techno-rebels are, whether they recognize it or not, agents of the Third Wave. They will not vanish but multiply in the years ahead. For they are as much a part of the advance to a new stage of civilization as our missions to Venus, our amazing computers, our biological discoveries, or our explorations of the oceanic depths.'[49]

49. TOFFLER, Alvin: The Third Wave, p. 169.

Toffler wrote this in 1980, and became one of the cult authors of the techno (house) scene in the mid-80s. Twelve years later the first lexicon of the techno rebels was published by the magazine *Mondo 2000*. It was originally the fanzine of the new computer hippies, who started out, like the original hippies, in California, but it soon became the most important magazine for cyberpunks, hackers and techno-nomads, whose digital dreams longed for the end of the boring 20th century. The makers of *Mondo 2000* see themselves as the avant-garde of a cultural revolution, 'the hip youth stoked on technology!'[50] This technological development occurred so quickly that almost every form of alternative lifestyle was able to find a place in it. Apart from this, the rapid and compelling development of high-tech could not be left to the engineers and techno-positivists of the big companies and the military. Rebels could only intervene in the development of things if they were ready to work with the new technologies. A lexicon that the authors of *Mondo 2000* call a 'User's Guide To The New Edge' declares the engagement with computers and other high-tech equipment to be both a lifestyle and a world-view. The book refers to drugs and aphrodisiacs, virtual sex, cyberspace and computer graphics, but also to the cultural strategies for the techno future. Hip-hop and house each win the honour of their own chapter.

The aesthetic strategy of appropriation as the 'hallmark of postmodernism'[51] is only realized, after Duchamp and Warhol, with the sampler. Computer philosophers define postmodern art via the act of appropriation of ideas, material and data from the existing 'database' of information and experience, to make something of their own from it. The fact that appropriation has made it into the mainstream is down to this digital recording instrument. 'The media have emphasized virtual reality as the central technology of the New Edge, but I say that the central technology is the digital sampler,'[52] writes *Mondo* thinker-in-chief with the Dadaist name R.U. Sirius, making it clear the extent to which non-musical techno rebels refer to the aesthetic practice of the DJs. Hip-hop as cyberpunking: 'Sampling is the auditory of hacking through a data base. A certain functional anarchy is involved which one might argue

50. SIRIUS, R.U.: A User's Guide to Using This Guide, in: RUCKER, Rudy et al: MONDO 2000: A User's Guide To The New Edge, p. 14.

51. SIRIUS, R.U.: Appropriation, in: RUCKER, Rudi et al, op. cit., p. 26.

52. Ibid. p. 24.

Cover of Mondo 2000 guide

is good for the soul.'[53] This hacking through databases, linked with a functional energy, is explained in the lexicon with reference to the aesthetic practice of deconstruction: 'Deconstruction is the program of taking texts or cultural phenomena and trying to see what they are really saying in a social, political, and sexual context. In practice, deconstruction is performing art, a process of systematically breaking set and setting to violate people's expectation.'[54] And hip-hop does precisely this by shaking up verbal codes along with the traditional ways of sound perception.

But the techno rebels feel even closer to house music than to hip-hop music, seeing it in the context of the world-wide techno hippie movement. What they mean, of course, is not the traditional house sound from Chicago, New York or Detroit, but the new synthetic rave sound taken with large amounts of ecstasy. This new chemical drug marks the most notable difference between the old and the new hippies, otherwise it is the old 'love-ethic with a new high-tech implementation'.[55] The intoxicating practice of dancing to the point of ecstasy led to a new cult described as 'techno-shamanic'. The techno rebels note with fascination that the preferred bpm number of 120 corresponds precisely to the heartbeat of a baby in the womb. The whole of high-tech culture is thus brought back to a naïve form of humanism. And after all the fanatical excursions into the world of robots, cyborgs and computer viruses, one of the writers of *Mondo 2000* writes under the heading 'Me': 'The New Edge is not particularly personality oriented. You stick around about only as long as you remain interesting. They say the youth of the seventies and eighties were the "me generation"…The nineties may be the "it generation", as technology takes over. Personally, I like a bit of personality. The nerds feel that MONDO has TOO MUCH.'[56] In the intoxication between flickering screens and computer monitors, in the delirium of sampled scraps of melody and plundered databases, the techno rebels, as neo-hippies, yearn for humanity. And maybe the reference back to western intellectual history occurs here. The death of the subject is not something that even the self-declared prophets of the techno rebels have in mind. Rather, the rebellious romanticism of the cyberpunks and hackers

53. Ibid. p. 29.

54. O.A.: Deconstruction, in: RUCKER, Rudi et al, op. cit., p. 80.

55. ST. JUDE: House Music, in: RUCKER, Rudi et al, op. cit., p. 140.

56. Anon.: Me, in: RUCKER, Rudi et al, op. cit., p. 168.

indicates that they are using their technological know-how to carry their 'Me' as intact as possible through postmodern times into the world of the Third Wave. Fun and enjoyment reconstitute the ego even on excursions into cyberspace and in the act of virtual sex. The thoughtful, self-determining and natural treatment of the newest technology doesn't make them gravediggers of the subject. On the contrary it turns the techno rebels, many of them DJs, into prophets of self-liberation in a completely alienated environment. At the end of the techno chapter we might once again quote the first techno-rebels: Kraftwerk. 'We have always defined ourselves as man-machines. In society, the use of machines often appears like a battle between people and their own inventions: against this disastrous misinterpretation of the situation we set a counterpoint in our own work... with its fully electronic sound, Kraftwerk symbolically shows that machines are not evil, but that they can produce harmony. It's just a question of using them.'[57] And in an interview Hütter adds: 'Technology isn't strange, it's part of our world. There's a destructive power in this strange schismatic thinking – exploit something here, throw away something there. That can only stop if a unified thought process occurs.'[58] Kraftwerk have a 'friendly relationship' with their machines.

'People who mistrust their machines and people who glorify them show the same inability to use them,' explained the Situationists in 1958. 'Mechanical work and mass production offer unheard-of creative possibilities, and people who know how to put them at the service of a bold imagination are the creators of tomorrow.'[59] For Beastie Boy Mike D, the music of the future is the noise that 16-year-olds produce when they 'let the computer rock'.[60] 'That's the whole future of music, not just sampling, but like, say, the kids that are going to pick up technology that we've used. They are going to do something that we've never thought. It's inevitable. And that's going to be music.'[61]

57. FUCHS-GAMBÖCK, Michael, loc. cit.

58. O.A.: Wir sind die Roboter, in: SZ-MAGAZIN, 31 October 1991, p. 40.

59. CONSTANT: Über unsere Mittel und unsere Perspektiven, in: DIABOLIS, Clara et al (Ed.), p. 64.

60. HÜETLIN, Thomas: Drei Jungs im Müll, in: DER SPIEGEL 31/1994, p. 142.

61. JARRETT, Michael: Beastie Boys, p. 52.

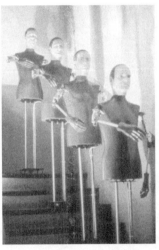

Kraftwerk as machine-men

AESTHETIC PROGRESS

Speaking of aesthetic progress is a risky business. Normative aesthetics and histories of art necessarily run the risk of being merely matters of taste. Hegel's love of antiquity made him see the remnants of art history as an interesting but decadent epilogue to classical Greek art, which, in the philosopher's opinion, produced the perfect ideal. The art of antiquity strives for the ideal, and art after antiquity goes beyond the ideal as 'the general Idea of artistic beauty'.[62] Hegel is the best example – grotesque to us today – of a normative establishment of the core of an aesthetic that is constructed as the history of art. How can we interpret progress in art history? Is there anything more beautiful than a painting by Botticelli? Is Beethoven better than Bach? Or Godard more than Eisenstein? Joyce than Cervantes? Such questions immediately make it apparent how senseless it is to fit art into the context of a story of progress. 'Works of art are remote from each other in their perfection',[63] as Benjamin put it.

At the end of the 16th century, in the closing days of the Renaissance, Giorgio Vasari formulated an idea of qualitative progress in art history, according to which art, from its lowly beginnings, gradually 'attained the summit of perfection, producing the more valuable and renowned modern works'.[64] From the painting of the Greeks to the works of Cimabue with which Vasari begins his history of art, via Giotto to Michelangelo, art historian and artist Vasari finds a continuous progress within the artist, along with their refinement and improvement. He repeatedly relativizes his judgments on earlier ages with his historicism. 'But although the artists of the second period made great additions to the arts…, yet they did not attain to the final stages of perfection, for they lacked a freedom…'[65] The criteria for progress in painting are its increasingly lifelike and natural representation, perfection in the reproduction of perspective and its general attempt to come close to reality. While Hegel, an early 19th-century idealist philosopher, made art part of and secondary to the realization of the absolute substance or spirit, Vasari, as a late 16th-century artist and critic, deals quite

62. HEGEL, G.W.F.: Lectures on Aesthetics, p. 105.

63. BENJAMIN, Walter: One-Way Street, p. 66.

64. VASARI, Giorgio: Lives of the Painters, Sculptors and Architects, p. 151.

65. Ibid. p. 153.

concretely with differences between the old and new kinds of art. His normative art history works with a 'qualitative' (Feyerabend) concept of progress about whose definition Vasari supplies precise information. Of course this historiography is difficult to sustain today, since art transcends the ideological treatment of its history, firstly because the categories documenting progress are always relative and secondarily because they cannot, as in the history of technology, be represented in bare figures. Only the 'qualities' and 'quantities' of an art produced with modern technologies – as in the previous chapter – can be counted and measured. 'All kinds of progress in cultural spheres are those of the command of material, of technology,' said Adorno, warning that progress in the command of material in art 'is by no means immediately as one'[66] with progress in art itself. In art, progress always operates – if at all – in quite a different way. Progressive art cannot run counter to a development that is necessary to its own logic: 'The complexity of progress only ever unfolds historically.'[67]

In the context of DJ culture, the idea of 'aesthetic progress' should be carefully reintroduced, in full awareness of its relative untenability, and explained as plausibly as possible. This is not to say that the author wants to evaporate the whole of art history on the idea of progress. Botticelli's *Mars and Venus*, painted in 1483, can still be considered the most beautiful painting of all time even if one acknowledges that Malevich's reflections on the ending of painting were clever and justified, and that all painting is transcended in his white square on a white background. Knowing about the history of painting before him, and with the potential knowledge of every picture painted before this one, Malevich was able to create this picture. In that sense the painting was progressive.

The concept of 'progress' (as an idea) can only be used if it is not used to defame and destroy the very art that runs against this idea, since a more highly developed historical stage in art cannot ensure any better result, as it can in the exact sciences, particularly in technology.[68] A higher degree of stylistic development does not – according to Hauser – imply a 'higher level of quality'.

66. ADORNO, Theodor W.: Fortschritt, in: idem: op. cit., p. 44.

67. Ibid.

68. Cf. HAUSER, Arnold: Kunst und Gesellschaft, p. 109.

This heterogeneity in values is unknown in science. Despite his faith in historical progress, which exerts its influence on art via various factors, Hauser speaks of the 'value-free nature of artistic development'.[69]

Both the genesis of art and its scientific reflection in art history follow the 'principles of succession', which, as Hauser observes, must be understood 'unlike the continual process of achievement-accumulating civilization, as shown by the history of the exact sciences and technology': as the example of an 'erratic, irregular, not necessarily progressive "cultural movement"'.[70] The construction of a history of art thus becomes an ideological matter. This is clearly apparent in the work of Arnold Schönberg, who derives the history of progress in music via Bach, Beethoven and Brahms to twelve-tone music, and declares his works, from the point of view of the avant-gardist, to be the spearhead of musical development. The writing composer thus becomes a historian and an establisher of norms for classical music. The ideological is nowhere more clearly apparent than when artists construct their own art history with their own work at the end of it. Or to put it more simply than that: artists who take history seriously must – if they understand their work as an absolute – put their work at the end of their normative historiography, or else it would be worthless. Thus they are falling into the same trap as art historians. Hauser soberly notes the distorting work that no art historian can escape: 'One values, overestimates or neglects artistic trends and artistic creations of the past according to the goals and standards of one's own time.'[71]

This work has also been unable to escape that risk. The ideological task of these reflections is manifestly and conclusively to rescue the idea of a progressive, cultural production with reference to the phenomenon of DJ culture.

DJ culture is thus to be connected with the practice of the innovative avant-gardes of classical modernism and the DJ avant-gardists be seen as the legitimate inheritors of Malevich, Duchamp or Warhol. At the same time it seeks to make clear that DJ culture as pop culture does not realize the achievements of the avant-

69. Cf. Ibid. p. 108ff.

70. Ibid. p. 151.

71. Ibid.

garde as if in a natural progression, but goes beyond them and shows new perspectives and possibilities of aesthetic practice at a time in which almost all of them can agree on a playful eclecticism or a non-committal 'anything goes'. The following aspects of DJ culture are thus to be emphasized. On the one hand the dissection of the idea of the author/artist, on the other the self-reflectiveness inherent in the work. Other starting-points are the growing complexity of the DJ's work, their capacities for absorption and integration as well as the almost effortless transformation of the 'most difficult' concerns of the 'high' art avant-gardes into the cultural mainstream, pop culture.

72 . REDON, Odilon: A Soi-Même, p. 9.

73 . HAUSER, Arnold, op. cit., p. 201.

74 . Ibid.

THE DEATH OF THE AUTHOR/ARTIST

'I made an art from my self'[72] is the first sentence of Odilon Redon in his journal to himself. Redon, who died in 1917, grew up in an age in which the artist saw himself as a confident, autonomous individual on his way into the modern age, one who was not understood by the majority of society, but who, from the margin of society, had absolute control over his work. The cult of the artist reached its peak with superstars like Picasso, Dalí and Warhol at a time when the idea of the self-determining artistic genius had long fallen into disrepute.

Until the Renaissance, the artist acted 'as an assistant, earning his livelihood and dealing with good and evil spirits, as a spokesman in religious services, as a prophet and seer, a eulogist and propagandist, educator and teacher, clown and master of ceremonies in life', and was thus wrapped up in the life of society, 'after he had formulated the ideal of knowledge, morals and beauty of the ruling class, churches and elites'.[73] At the time of the Renaissance the artist becomes fully aware of his subjectivity and never – according to Arnold Hauser – 'loses sight of it, whatever he undertakes'.[74] This awareness of subjectivity is not new, since it makes brief appearances throughout antiquity and is also apparent in the Middle Ages. What is new is the 'consistent pursuit' of subjectivity, 'the intensification of subjectivism as a sufficient meaning and value'.[75]

Michelangelo, Leonardo and Raphael are the first artists in the modern sense who see their work as the artistic expression of themselves, and not as drudgery or labour for clients from the church, the state or the new class of the bourgeoisie. Dependence on state or clerical powers continued to exist in the Renaissance, but the respect for the artist grew in a climate of intellectual refinement and taste. This reformation of the artist was apparent in the context of the rise of the first rich, bourgeois businessmen and the predominance of humanist ideas.[76] The intellectual, aesthetic hegemony of the feudal lords and the clerics was undermined by the money of the bourgeoisie. 'Money was the great political equalizing power of the bourgeoisie,' wrote Engels, 'Wherever a personal relationship was repressed by a financial relationship, a natural achievement was repressed by a financial achievement, a bourgeois relationship replaced a feudal one.'[77] Art was no exception, the bourgeoisie was able to afford art and with it a representation that only the aristocracy and the church had enjoyed hitherto. The Renaissance not only marked a new beginning in culture, but more importantly represented the beginning of the cultural hegemony of the bourgeoisie.

The artist is generally defined by the part he plays in society.[78] The concept of the author/artist is, for archaeologist-in-chief Michel Foucault, 'a privileged moment of individualization in the history of ideas, knowledge, and literature, or in the history of philosophy and science'.[79] The author functioned as a 'principle of the rarefaction of discourse'.[80] Discourses grouped around him. He was also seen as the origin of their meanings. The author was taken seriously according to the form of the discourse. Banal messages had no need of an author, any more than they needed contracts or technical instructions. Science in the Middle Ages not only needed authors, they became guarantees for the scientific value of a work, an 'index of truth'.

But with the victory of the sciences the function of the

75 . Ibid.

76 . Cf. WOLFF, Janet, op. cit., p. 27.

77 . ENGELS, Friedrich: Über den Verfall des Feudalismus und das Aufkommen der Bourgeoisie, quoted in: MARX, Karl/ idem: Über Kunst und Literatur, p. 341.

78 . Cf. HAUSER, Arnold, op. cit., p. 153.

79 . FOUCAULT, Michel: What Is An Author? in: idem: Language, Counter-memory, Practice, p. 115.

80 . FOUCAULT, Michel: L'Ordere du Discours, p. 28.

author in scientific discourse shrank, and its role consisted 'solely in giving a name to a theorem, an effect, an example, a syndrome'.[81] Numbers and empirically demonstrated facts seemed so objective that the scientist as an interpreter and discoverer – a subject – became entirely uninteresting. Quite unlike this was the role of the author/artist in the sphere of unlimited subjectivity, in the terrain of the arts. While in the Middle Ages all forms of literary fiction circulated more or less anonymously, with the beginning of the Renaissance the question of the author entered the consciousness of the public. 'The author is asked to be accountable for all of the texts placed under his name; they demand that he reveal, or at least bear within himself, the hidden meaning that runs through them; in his personal life, in his lived experience, in its real history; he is asked to articulate them, about his personal life and his lived experiences, about the real history that gave birth to them. The author is what gives the unsettling language of fiction its unities, its nexi of coherence, its integration within reality.'[82]

The author/artist as creator is a construction that gives the bourgeois individual the certainty of identity through the form of the self. 'It would certainly be absurd to deny the existence of the writing and inventing individual,' Foucault observes, pointing out at the same time that 'the individual who sets about writing a text that might become a work, assumes the function of the author.'[83] This function of the author regulates and shapes the artistic work. The function of 'author' is 'probably only one of the possible specifications of the function of material', because the function of 'author' must not remain constant 'in its form, in its complexity or even in its presence'. Foucault dreams of a culture in which a discourse 'would circulate without any need for an author'.[84]

DJ culture deconstructed the function of the author. As we have shown in the chapter on sampling, in high-tech art the author has on the one hand disappeared behind the circuit diagrams of the beatboxes and samplers, and on the other he has, with his wild use of other people's works, refused all respect to the function of the author. The literature of modernism, for which Foucault cites Flaubert, Proust and Kafka, required the relinquishment

81. Ibid. p. 29.

82. Ibid. p. 30.

83. Ibid.

84. FOUCAULT, Michel: What Is An Author?, loc. cit., p. 138.

of the author in favour of the immortality of the text.[85] As an idealistic abandonment of the author to the eternal substitute religion of art, the ego was relinquished, and not simply dissipated and ignored. The abandonment of the 'ego' is the product of an excessively strong 'ego'. The 'ego' of the DJ is dispersed. Depending on the situation of the record deck and the position of the slide control on the mixing desk, the creator's ego has a different consistency, fed by the works of other creator egos which the DJ brings into a new artistic unity. Violation and expropriation produce a new piece of art. The process of the expropriation of the original work that is the DJ's material, leads, through the mixing of the records, into a new work-unity that the author-ego or the original work (Foucault would be furious) transcends in a Hegelian sense, at once negating, preserving and elevating it. The 'death of the artist' is inadequate as a concept, being at once a deliverance and an extension.

Roland Barthes also spoke of the 'death of the author'. For him, the author/artist is above all a spectre of literary, art and music criticism which still like to interpret works as the expression of the character and personality of an author. Although the realm of the author is still a very powerful one, according to Barthes there are some writers who have tried to destroy it. Barthes is thinking of quite different authors from Foucault. Thus, for Mallarmé it is language that speaks, and not the author; writing then becomes an act in which language presents itself rather than the author.[86] A tradition that reappears in psychoanalytically banal form in the 'écriture automatique' of the Surrealists. The author cautiously retreats, although he does not quite disappear.

Barthes wants to see him replaced by a 'scriptor'. He is not absorbed in the unity of the work; he is not its past, whose suffering and happiness is represented in the work. Writing is no longer an act of representation, observation or copying, but is fully absorbed in the speech act that is being played out, like the king's 'I decree', or the troubadour's 'I sing'. The scriptor works without passions, without moods, feelings or impressions, he works with a vast dictionary that makes his writing incessant. Life, according to Barthes, merely

85. Cf. Ibid. p. 117.

86. Cf. BARTHES, Roland: The Death of the Author, in: idem: The Rustle of Language, p. 49ff.

imitates the book, and the book itself is nothing but a network of signs, an endless imitation.[87] The self-referentiality of the texts consequently transcends all reference to the author. The short circuit of the reception 'artist's life = work' is destroyed once and for all.

The text of the future is freed of the burden of old identities. It should no longer offer a unique, 'theological' meaning (the message of the author-God), but act as a multi-dimensional space in which a number of texts are married and disputed and none is original. As a conglomerate of quotations, the work feeds on thousands of sources.[88] The tradition of polyphonic literature, which Bakhtin began with Dostoevsky, gave a number of voices and bearers of consciousness an equal status, and thus broke down the monolithic one-dimensionality of the narrator's consciousness. This more open form of representation created the possibility of texts that contain and express meanings which – according to Janet Wolff – 'extend beyond those of the individuals who authored them'.[89] But Barthes' approach goes beyond this; he wants to transfer this openness of representation, whose unity we must still think of in terms of the person of the author, to an ambiguity of the text which not only allows various voices and consciousnesses to appear, but makes every form of quotation possible. The text/art work as a potentially endless store of signs which is then decoded by the reader, who, for Barthes, is the new sovereign after the death of the author.

Although William S. Burroughs is still seen as a traditional writer in line with the old function of the author, his 'cut-up method', taking the textual collages of Dada and Surrealism further, breaks with the persistence of the old authorial writing. 'When you're writing, the best results seem to have happened almost by chance, but before the cut-up method assumed clear contours – (all writing basically consists of extracts) – writers had no procedure for producing the chance of spontaneity. You can't force spontaneity. But you can introduce the unpredictable spontaneous factor with a pair of scissors.'[90] Take a page of extracts of poetry and a pair of scissors and you've got a poem. Or even: 'As many poems as you want.'[91] A literary art which, in Burroughs' opinion, anyone can do. 'Collages are there

87. Cf. Ibid. p. 51ff.

88. Cf. Ibid. p. 53.

89. WOLFF, Janet, op. cit., p. 129.

90. BURROUGHS, William S.: The Cut-Up Method, in: RIESE, Utz: Falsche Dokumente, p. 84.

91. Ibid. p. 85.

Disposable Heroes of Hiphoprisy with William Burroughs

for everybody... This is experimental in the sense there's something to be done with it. Write now, right here.'[92] No wonder, then, that as an old man Burroughs was keen on hip-hop, and in 1993 made a record with the Disposable Heroes of Hiphoprisy entitled *Spare Ass Annie and Other Tales*. Thanks to the breakbeats, his cut-up texts become fascinating rap monologues which give voice to disparate opinions either in hypnotic alternation or simultaneously, or simply 'sound' to the beats as verbal or sound material. Cut-up texts are then suddenly funky.

Dramatic texts are storehouses of polyphony. In his plays, Rainald Goetz uses the stage as a mixing desk and distributes the various textual samples around the various characters. Many of the speech acts are recognizable as quotations from the media, pop or advertising. Goetz, who quotes pop music in his novels and even on their back covers, has been a great fan of DJ music and its aesthetic at least since acid house. His 1993 media notes are nothing but skilfully assembled samples from endless television and radio recordings. Like Burroughs, Goetz has also collaborated with DJs and house producers. Goetz' readings, over house beats, were first produced for radio broadcast, and in 1994 they were tackled by the Frankfurt Eye-Q label as a record project. So the resurrection of the author by DJ culture is not just a theoretical suggestion but a cultural given.

Which takes us back to DJs. Right on the turntables, beside the mixing desk and above the record boxes. The death of the author coincides with the resurrection of the reader; transferred to music, the death of the composer would coincide with the resurrection of the listener.

The DJ is both: he is at once a composer and a listener, and has nothing to do with the death of anybody. The DJ listens to records as a consumer and uses this act of artistic consumption as the starting-point for his own creation. The Barthesian reader is not a person in the sense of having a history, a biography, a psychology. He is not only the *someone* who accumulates within himself all the voices and tracks that constitute the text. The DJ as a listener is only very distantly related to that

92 . Ibid.

'someone' because he has a particular history and biography that is generally explained with reference to the subcultural environment. And he usually has an extraordinary amount of musical knowledge. Nonetheless, the DJ is first of all always a listener, before he becomes a musician.

As soon as the music fan becomes a DJ, his way of listening to records changes. It becomes a process that directly precedes the act of mixing. Perception becomes more precise. The DJ does not wish the author dead, because he can use him better alive. The fear of the 'theological' definition of a work is superfluous because the piece of music no longer seeks to be understood in the sense intended by the author/composer (and in any case this is impossible), but is already one of the conditions of the DJ's work, whether it be in the initial stages as a raw material for mixing or later as material for remixing or sampling. Listening to music was, at the beginning of disco, house and hip-hop, the beginning of the DJ's own production. Only later was it joined by considerations about representing both music-music and the outside of music in the songs.

The Barthesian scriptor leaves the field of representation, while the DJ is primarily interested only in the mixability of the sound material used, and only after the use of the new music aesthetic goes towards using these to report on the social, subcultural, but also 'artistic' conditions of the artist's music and life. The transition in hip-hop music from the dominance of the DJ to the dominance of the MC marks precisely this point at which the representation, the 'depiction' of reality interrupts the strict autonomy without taking that quality away from it. The hip-hop DJs discovered that MCs put them in the position of telling stories, giving hints for a better life and also telling about their own work. DJ culture is less about the death of the author/artist than about the extension of its structure, in whose context music is produced.

The death demanded and prophesied by Foucault and Barthes appeared long ago in DJ culture – and was overcome. But while, in the old written culture, which knows only the lonely writer and his typewriter or computer, the act of 'creation' occurs in the head of the writer, and so his death is bound to be an apocalyptic idea; in DJ culture the notion of a creator-god doesn't even exist. The record box is full of creator-gods, and this fact relativizes every form of monotheism. The mixing itself is a further act of relativization, creating a new 'deus ex machina' out of the many creator-gods. Many of the pioneer dancefloor DJs were feted for the achievement of inventing this process of musical mixing. Because of the previous relativization, this reverence, which has also appeared in this history of DJ culture, possesses a new quality that is only interested in questions of authenticity and originality of creation in the 'transcended' sense, and no longer in the form of the creator genius.

The DJs, from the first moments of underground disco to the complex, abstract creations of Massive Attack, lay bare the bases of their work and their conditions of production, and thus do not mystify the production of music. The influence of production technologies described in the previous chapter, and its progressive use in the sense of the revelation of samples and quotations (rather than obscuring them) is another element that makes the process of creation[93] transparent. All forms of intellectual obscurantism become ineffective if aesthetic practices and their development are precisely derived from the development of the technology used, as one can see from the early days of creative DJs in the late 60s, with simple record-players and an archaic mixer, to the newest computer-generated productions. The death of the author/artist then coincides with the birth of the musician as producer and engineer. But here too the author/artist doesn't die, but becomes sovereign in an area that has been occupied by only a very few 20th century artists: that of high-tech. The Futurists depicted their pitiful glorifications of war and technology with the oldest media known to humanity: painting, speech and writing. Their enthusiasm for the new wonders of technology such as cars, planes and weapons coincided with their complete ignorance of technical processes. For this reason Duchamp called Futurism the 'impressionism of the mechanical world'.[94] The DJ as engineer can not only use the new technologies precisely for his own ends, but also works on the further development of these means of production. A

93 . Janet Wolff has put the word 'creation' on the index of reactionary art theory. Instead, she recommends the term 'production'. (Cf. WOLFF, Janet, op. cit., p. 138.) But Janet Wolff, in her examinations of the social conditions of the production of art, also bases her work primarily on the classic art forms of the visual arts and literature. As the DJ is clearly distanced from this old process of creation, the use of the term 'creation' with reference to the DJ seems unproblematic, and thus undergoes a process of modernization. The term 'creation', compared with the term 'production', still expresses a final moment of the cultural unconscious that does not quite disappear in the work of the DJ. For that reason the term 'creation' should remain usable – freed from all quasi-mystical idealizations of the author-genius.

94 . Cf. DUCHAMP, Marcel: 'Painting... at the Service of the Mind', in: CHIPP, Herschel B., op. cit., p. 393.

tradition that extends musically from the non-DJs Pink Floyd and Kraftwerk to the computer kids Richard James or Kid Paul. The Futurist mystification of technology is unthinkable for these young people, since they have grown up with it and cannot see it as anything strange, disturbing or even demonic and divine, but simply as a means of transferring their musical ideas to reality. Technology is no longer an element of alienation, but rather an element of unfettered self-realization.

One further element in the elaboration of the author/artist structure is the emphasis on the work of the producer/remixer. While in literature and classical art, creation is transferred directly from the consciousness via the hands to paper or canvas, the production of a piece of dancefloor music is only possible with the help of a great deal of technology, studios and producers. According to the DJ's systems, the original compositions in the piece undergo a clearly audible modification that is supposed to give them a better sound or make them more club-viable. Often remixes by other DJs are pressed on the twelve-inch single as possible interpretations of the original. This by now completely normal relativization of the idea of the 'original' changes the understanding of the idea of the author/artist. A growing lack of respect apparent not only in all the many samples and cover versions, but also in remixes that completely ignore the original, by famous DJs like MK, who observed at the New Music Seminar in New York in 1993: 'If I had to hear all the crap in the original I'm remixing I'd stop doing it. A vocal sample is enough for me to do a remix.' Rock bands like U2 and INXS profit from this lack of interest, which makes their names – in however distorted a form – famous in the dance charts and in clubland, with all its promise of fame and money.

The future of cultural production wished for by Foucault, Barthes, Deleuze, Guattari and others started long ago. The questions, '"Who is the real author?" "Have we proof of his authenticity and originality?" "What has he revealed of his most profound self in his language?"'[95] have – outside of the record companies' rights departments[96] – become relatively unimportant in DJ culture, which is concerned with quite different

95. FOUCAULT, Michel: What Is An Author?, in idem: Language, Counter-Memory, Practice, p. 138.

96. An excellent article on the legal problems thrown up by the new DJ-creators is David Sanjek's '"Don't have to DJ no more": Sampling and the "Autonomous Creator"', in: WOODMANSEE, Martha/ JASZI, Peter: The Construction of Authorship. See also: NEGATIVLAND: (Copyright) Fair Use & the Law, in: KEYBOARDS 6/1994, pp. 88–94 + 134–140.

things: "'What are the modes of existence of this discourse?' 'Where does it come from; how is it circulated; who controls it?' 'What placements are determined for possible subjects?'"[97]

These questions as Foucault imagines them are easily posed from the point of view of the engineer and the DJ, and are apparent in their work. The anti-author/artist question par excellence, 'What matters who is speaking?' is quite obvious in the club, the mix makes everybody equally important and insignificant at the same time. The greater unit of the 'club evening' replaces respect for individual works. The DJ speaks, but even that isn't so important if all you're doing is sweating to the beats flowing from the subwoofer.

The death of the author/artist is embedded within the theoretical renunciation of the classical idea of the subject. The unmasking of the subject as a 'young' construction of the arts, as envisaged by Foucault, was a spur to deconstructivism, which decoded concepts like 'subject' and 'ego' as the expression of ideologies. The psychological structure of the bourgeois individual was full of generals and bosses, as Deleuze and Guattari put it. Capitalism produces schizophrenics because they stop at its boundaries: they throw all the codes into confusion and bear the decoded streams of desire. 'Schizophrenia is desiring-production at the limit of social production.'[98] Capitalism as a syndrome makes psychiatrists and philosophers hope for a rhizomatic revolution or at least a reform. 'Be neither one nor multiple, be multiplicities!... Be the Pink Panther, and love one another as wasps and orchids, cats and baboons.'[99]

For artistic production, the consequence of this decentralization and de-hierarchization of the subject is a multiplicity of 'streams' in art works. Here too quotation assumes a central position. 'Most of the books we quote are books that we love,'[100] the philosopher and psychoanalyst confess, challenging the reader to sample at will. 'Find passages in books which you can use or which suit you... Combinations, permutations, uses are never inherent to the book, but depend on connections with something or other outside it. Yes, take what you want.'[101] The de-hierarchized

97. FOUCAULT, Michel: What Is An Author?, loc. cit.

98. DELEUZE, Gilles/ GUATTARI, Félix: Anti-Oedipus, p. 35.

99. DELEUZE, Gilles/ GUATTARI, Félix: Rhizome, p. 74.

100. Ibid. p. 70.

101. Ibid. p. 72f.

subject (or should that be 'subject-multiplicity'?), freed from a power centre, perceives with many different channels and processes the amounts of information with ideologically fixed priorities. In DJ music it is the bass-line and the groove that co-ordinate the multiplicity without destroying its heterogeneity.

The theories of artistic productivity are coupled to the idea of the productive human subject. The avant-gardes of the 20th century have alternately negated and intensified the disappearance of the individual. The Expressionists and the artists who saw themselves within that tradition were entirely devoted to the idea of creative monads; the Dadaists are the beginning of the line of development of that art which, from Duchamp via the Situationists, via Andy Warhol to the most recent conceptual artists, shows little interest in salvaging the individual. But all of these positions, which called authorship and original creativity into question, repeatedly found themselves in paradoxical situations that showed escape from Cartesian ideas to be almost impossible. Because however much Duchamp and Warhol scorned and denounced the artistically creating subject, they – creators – were always the ones who carried out this destruction and thus actively salvaged the author's honour. This inescapability of the self, the finally active and reflecting person, recalls the foundation of the modern understanding of the subject in Descartes. He found, in the metaphysical thought experiments in the course of which he placed doubts and questions upon everything, one solid and motionless point that is 'certain and indubitable'.[102] Even if God is constantly and ingeniously deceiving him, it is nonetheless true that 'I exist, since I am deceived; and let him deceive me as he may, he can never bring it about that I am nothing, so long as I shall be conscious that I am something. So that it must, in fine, be maintained... that this proposition I am, I exist, is necessarily true each time it is expressed by me, or conceived by my mind'.[103] The unavoidable fact that every idea hostile to the subject is, in the end, thought by a subject, renders the discussion of the death of the subject meaningless. Duchamp and Warhol, M/A/R/R/S and Godard recognized this, and speak of redefinitions in the context of old structures of thought, from whose

102. DESCARTES, René: Meditations, p. 79.

103. Ibid. p. 80.

simplest metaphysical basic definitions it is difficult to escape. The subject isn't dead, but simply clearly relativized, and freed from the weight of uniqueness. The subject is a free forum of all kinds of influence, whose mixture and consistency define something like a momentary state of the subject. The subject is not a rigid puppet, but a freely defined, fragile, heterogeneous project that is constantly changing. The individual is many people and many things – and so is the artist.

104. REINHARDT, Ad: The Philadelphia Forum: 'The Idea of the New', in idem: Schriften und Gespräche, p. 99.

105. SEDLMAYR, Hans: Die Revolution der modernen Kunst, p. 16.

106. REINHARDT, Ad: 'Art as Art' in: HARRISON, Charles and WOOD, Paul: Art in Theory, 1900–1990, p. 806.

SELF-REFERENTIALITY – THE GOAL OF MODERNISM, QUITE NATURAL FOR THE DJ

The idea of progress as reflected in the work of the avant-gardes was based on the idea that an avant-garde referred to what had gone before, and in the process produced something like art-immanent discourse. 'The new is the new awareness of the development of art, of what is',[104] as Ad Reinhardt put it. Of course, all art spoke first to the genres of its own form, but in Modernism self-referentiality became one of the central endeavours on the way to a pure, absolute art. Art, cleansed of all elements of the other arts and of all references to the reality lying outside of it, is then exposed as a pure, autonomous and autarkic product, which seeks the absolute as 'that which is unconditional and self-detached'.[105]

The definition of pure art comes close to tautology. This is documented particularly impressively in the writings of the abstract and absolute painter Ad Reinhardt. 'The one thing to say about art is that it is one thing. Art is art-as-art and everything else is everything else. Art-as-art is nothing but art. Art is not what is not art.'[106] For Reinhardt, the way to absolute art is one of continual exclusion, in which art is separated and defined 'more and more, making it purer and emptier, more absolute and more exclusive – non-objective, non-representational, non-figurative, non-imagist, non-expressionist, non-subjective. The only and one way to say what abstract art or art-as-art is, is to say what it is not.'[107]

In DJ culture, self-referentiality does not work by exclusion, but by inclusion and absorption. The removal of art, in this case music, from the rest of the world leads to the rediscovery of that same world, which is inscribed within the musical quotations used. The positive nature of DJ production lies in the fact that the basic compositional form of this music consists of two reproductive media and the mixing desk as a conjunction always connects the two elements with a 'plus'. Reinhardt's idea of modern, absolute art knows only the minus sign in the sense of a line of 'negative actions and reactions',[108] whose threshold constantly approaches the pure void. Reinhardt's thought and writing experiments mark a transition from abstract art to pure idea, as realized in the conceptual art of the 60s and 70s. In panel painting, idealistic purism reaches its boundaries, where the material consistency of art

107. Ibid.

108. Ibid. p. 808.

Modernist manifesto: Ad Reinhardt's 'Autocritique de Reinhardt' (1963)

prevents its absolute transcendence into the sphere of the mind. This very boundary is erased in conceptual art, in which art and philosophy are connected and cross-fertilized to the advantage of both. 'If philosophy (and religion) is finished, it is possible that art's viability may be connected to its ability to exist as a pure self-conscious endeavor. Art may exist in the future as a kind of philosophy by analogy,'[109] explains conceptual artist Joseph Kosuth.

Music only escapes this rigorist tendency in modern art by virtue of the fact that it can ignore immaterializing transcendence because of its own immateriality. In its search for absolute sound and absolute music, the music of DJ culture never gets stuck in minimalist cul-de-sacs. There is too much in DJ music that has either not yet been heard, or has not yet been tapped into, as Shaheed of the hip-hop band A Tribe Called Quest points out: 'I just want to continue to learn about music because there's so much to learn. I didn't realize how much we don't know. We know a few things, but we want to just be able to step into a room and tell people what the formula is for this. It's cool to know that stuff because you can take your music to other levels.'[110]

For artists to be sure they are not reinventing Impressionism, they must know their art history and have it in mind at all times. 'Because: Art is New Art',[111] as Schönberg has it. The history of innovations stakes out the framework of those actions which no longer need to be reinvented, and which can either be used quite naturally in the work or reflected as historicism. For the DJ, the knowledge of (pop) music history is constitutive of the work. The DJs' record boxes are themselves archives of sounds stored on vinyl, which the DJ uses not as dead knowledge but as the basis of his own production.

Self-reflexivity and self-referentiality have always been core definitions of DJ music. The first underground DJs had neither instruments nor refined technology at their disposal, just their record collections of old soul, funk and R&B records. Within this archive they looked for elements of a new sound that got people dancing in the clubs. In the mixture and sequence of the elements of their archives, the first forms of a new music were

109. KOSUTH, Joseph: Four Interviews (with Arthur R. Rose), in: idem: Interviews 1969–1989, p. 14.

110. STERN, Adam Keane: Quest For Fire, in: SECONDS 27, 7/1994.

111. SCHÖNBERG, Arnold: Neue Musik, veraltete Musik, Stil und Gedanke, in: idem, op. cit., p. 86.

A Tribe Called Quest: Midnight Marauders *LP*

discovered, and, over time, transformed into a style of their own. By reorganizing the archive, a new pop music and the beginnings of dancefloor or DJ music were laid down. All other kinds of DJ music like hip-hop, house and the various hybrids that came into being after 1987 had their origins in the reorganization of the existing sound archive. Anyone who integrated strange or unheard sound elements into his mix was considered a 'master of records' in the hip-hop community'.

Since most DJs didn't play a musical instrument, music history pressed on vinyl was their only expressive and structural possibility.

Thanks to sampling, music history no longer had to be arduously mixed from one deck to the other – it could be introduced directly and digitally at the desired point in the mix, remix or original composition. The other-worldly notion of 'living in my headphones', as Massive Attack put it in their song 'Daydreaming', clearly touches the idea of being lost in music. Repeatedly, it is the artists such as rappers or singers working with DJ music who refer to the world outside of the record collection.

Hip-hop, house and the many stylistic hybrids after 1987 have huge numbers of self-reflexive and self-referential lyrics, only speaking of 'beats' and 'bass-lines', of Coltrane and James Brown, of disco and clubs, and how one will lose oneself irrevocably in music. But being 'lost in music' does not mean the loss of the self, but its recovery in the realm of sounds.

The self-reflexivity of DJ music is not a matter of intellectual debate, but the result of the DJ's production method, as deejaying begins with the linking-up of two reproductive media. But the autonomist tendency within modern art remains alien to DJ music, because it is structurally much more open than the art and the literature of the 20th century and, because of its youth, doesn't have to speculate so doggedly on the possibilities remaining to it. Clement Greenberg, one of the most partisan modernists and art critics, defined the essence of modernism as the use of the methods unique to and characteristic of the art form, in order to criticize that art form. This should not occur in order to destroy it, but to strengthen it in its area of competence, which is to say art itself.

But the DJs' 'critique' is not negative and solipsistic, as it ended up in Minimal Art. Rather it is a critique by fans like that practised by the film-makers of the Nouvelle Vague, from film criticism to direction, a critique of unorthodoxy much like that which led in Deleuze and Guattari to the construction of the 'rhizome', and which DJs now introduced – sampled – into pop music.

COMPLEXITY OF THE SYSTEM AND PRODUCTION

Everything that is loved can be used by the DJ. The openness of compositional structures has led, in the course of its development, to a growing complexity of productions. The quest for new sound quotations and undiscovered or unused pieces from music history led to a broad-based conquest of 20th century music by the DJs. Once disco and hip-hop had discovered soul and funk, and house had grown out of those, the sound after 1987 opened up to all forms of cross-fertilization. No imaginable hybrid model was left out. The jazz archive was investigated particularly intensely; with the result that at the end of the 80s a new sub-species of hip-hop developed, which at first bore the name of acid jazz and gradually won its independence under that logo.

At around the same time some American dance labels attempted to bring jazz-house into the clubs. The collaboration of the rapper and producer Guru of Gang Starr with many veterans of jazz music in turn influenced both the jazz and hip-hop scenes, and led to a lively exchange of musicians and producers that is still going on today.

This and similar stylistic syntheses led broadly to a growing complexity in DJ productions. The idea of DJ music, namely synthesizing two different musical works with a mixer, was now transferred to the creation of a new style. In the early 90s there can hardly have been a single possible hybrid that was not tried out by one dancefloor project or another. Malcolm McLaren's Opera House or the rapid breakbeats of jungle demonstrated the wide spectrum under the roof of the house nation alone. One hybrid fertilized the other, and at the end of these syntheses were productions like that of Massive Attack, whose refinement and delicacy could almost make one forget that the (raw) ancestors of their music were barely fifteen years old. Technological progress encouraged the rapid development of DJ music, and created the possibility of the rapid realization of every DJ idea. Borne along by the success of the dancefloor subculture, the growing number of DJ producers absorbed and integrated more and more elements, more and more quickly, not only from musical history, but from the archive of perceptible sounds: from subsonic bass-lines of the Warp label to the beeping feedback of Acid House productions.

While in the history of modern art self-reflexivity as self-referentiality has closed in and paralysed artistic production, thanks to the openness of structures of communication, in the work of the DJ it has led to a diversity in pop music that had never been there before. As the death of the old idea of the author/artist brought with it a freer production practice, the restraining effect of old ideas of identity fell away. 'We're open to everything,' explains Shaheed of hip-hop group A Tribe Called Quest. 'To be a real musician, you gotta be open to anything. Once you close your mind off, you can't be a musician.'[112] The new author/artist no longer had any problem understanding his unity as diversity – and vice versa.

This is taken so far that bands like Tricky or Portishead appear live without DJs, and apply their compositions to band-based structures. Turntables then disappear as instruments, but remain inherent to the music as its ideal basis. The most progressive productions of DJ music have internalized the unity of turntable and mixer to such an extent that – paradoxical as it may sound – they manage to get by without it.

As DJ music grew in complexity, it also led to counter-movements which rejected refinement and sophistica-tion and either turned back to the simplicity of the old school works or cultivated a highly technological neo-

112 . STERN, Adam Keane: op. cit., p. 40.

primitivism of unheard-of rawness and brutality. Hip-hop and house and techno had, and continue to have, strands which produce dance music of an extremely high quality from the technical point of view, and whose simplicity recalls the ritual rhythms of uncivilized peoples and tribes. Genre names like Tribal House and Jungle Techno, which are used by musicians, producers and the public, make this proximity apparent. This too could be interpreted as a typically modernist trait within DJ culture which, at the peak of its refinement, comes close to the art of the primitives, as has often happened in the art history of the 20th century. Neo-tribalism tries to reconnect the dancers to the archaic roots of their actions – preserving the violence of the music rather than transfiguring it – and thus to close a circle which reveals that it is a fundamental definition of human life to move and dance to (certain) rhythms. German tribal DJs have organized evenings with African drummers and produced a cross-link to ethnic music. As an extension of DJ culture, this form of conceptually guaranteed primitivism is a characteristic of the complexity of DJ music. You can do everything. That which lies outside DJ music is non-sounds.

But the search for complexity cannot become an end in itself, if one doesn't wish to come close to a normative aesthetic. Then, if the simple becomes difficult, the solution of a musical problem leads via the reversal of complexity. The next stage of the music is then determined not by 'more', but by 'less', which is also a kind of more. The primitive which is familiar with decadence, which has understood it, is refined in simple structures. The work of the musician in the supposedly narrow range of minimal structures as heard in non-experimental hip-hop or house, requires, under the premise of the greatest possible freedom, the command of all rules of minimal structures. Thus reduced complexity does not become 'excluded complexity, but transcended complexity'.[113] In Luhmann's systematic philosophy, it is stressed that complexity means the compulsion to select, and the compulsion to select involves contingency, and contingency, in the end, means risk. Music is structured by the laws of rhythm

113. LUHMANN, Niklas: Soziale Systeme, p. 12.

and harmony, but their immaterial structure makes them an area of the greatest possible freedom. The compulsion to select is a stylistic device.

The minimalism of pop music is not thoughtful self-reference but the mission to serve the masses. What German techno jargon refers to as *Abfahrt* has made sophistication even more difficult. How can you be fine and refined, and at the same time universally comprehensible and trivial? Nik Cohn doesn't care. Superpop 'has to be both intelligent and simple, it has to carry its implications lightly and it has to be fast, funny, sexy, obsessive, a bit epic'.[114] In German that's now called *Abfahrt* (literally: takeoff, departure), and particularly in DJ music that departure is concentrated on the activation of the body on the dancefloor. So the complexity of DJ music must be able to disguise itself in the realm of the dancefloor if it's to be sure of providing fun. From this point of view, too, it was pioneering of Grandmaster Flash to employ an MC to distract from his virtuosity and complexity. Many musicians in DJ culture no longer wish to relativize their complexity and inaccessibility in the context of pop. They demand the freedom to understand *Abfahrt* as intellectual sublimation. Massive Attack stress 'Daydreaming', a particular kind of departure, lonely, introverted and relaxed in a way that makes its own complexity a stylistic device. Then that becomes relaxed, sexy, possessed and powerful. DJ culture has no problem with complexity. Both the reduction of complexity and its nonchalant promotion are made seductive via the mechanisms of pop aestheticization.

114. COHN, Nik: AwopBopaLooBop..., p. 239.

AVANT-GARDE GOES POP

Avant-gardes are serious matters. The avant-gardists fight for noble goals, aware of their meaning and viability. Since the 20th century at least art history can be read as a sequence of declarations of war on that which was present and dominant as an aesthetic. 'An avant-garde in art advances art-as-art, or it is no avant-garde,' declared Ad Reinhardt, battling with his texts for the victory of art-as-art. All debates within art are carried along by the will to power, to establish one's own state of knowledge as the state of things in the art world. Everything produced by avant-gardes occurred according to or at least under the influence of manifestos which explain and communicate the aesthetic, cultural or political concerns of the group. Art history as the history of the avant-garde has always implied the intentionality of that which came into being in the studios, at the typewriters or during filming. The penetration of modern art by theories peaked in the quasi-philosophical works of conceptual art, which entirely subordinated the material aspect of art to the intellectual aspect, and shifted art to the sphere of theories. What survived was ideas without traces. An ending.

Pop works completely differently. The intention of pop musicians is to sell records, get famous and write beautiful songs. The intention of underground music, which always turns into pop, is self-expression. Having fun and working and producing with as little alienation as possible. The idea of an avant-garde, a manifesto or even a wide-ranging cultural history of which one is a part seems infinitely remote. Pop works according to patterns of its own. 'Superpop is mass media,' Nik Cohn announced at the end of his history of pop, 'it is teen music always, it has to hit.'[115] To disguise his cleverness and complexity, he avoids intellectualism. The intentionality of the avant-gardes is integrated within his work via the direct, material connection with music history. More than any other form of pop music, DJ music refers directly to the earlier works of pop musicians. And the methods of construction, the authorial sense, of DJ music are so progressive that it can put itself at the end of the 20th-century avant-gardes. But all the difficult matters have now moved from the elite circle of galleries and universities, symposia and academic bookshelves and into the pop charts. The most complicated verbal experiments, the wildest experiments with montages and collages, the most difficult semiotic fractures and shifts have become common property. Where Greil Marcus construes punk as a renaissance of Dada and Situationism, the links via intellectuals like Malcolm McLaren and the many art students in punk bands are obvious. In hip-hop there

115. Ibid. p. 241.

are no links of any kind with the classical avant-gardes, apart from latecomer projects by McLaren and William S. Burroughs. DJ culture came into being in an isolated side-room of culture: in the ghetto, cut off from the rest of the world. However much store one might set by the idea of a *Zeitgeist*, the origin of DJ music is just as much a miracle, a miracle of human creativity and self-assertion. That this marginalized ghetto culture should have conquered the whole of popular culture within a decade is testimony to the great perception of pop and the correctness of its aesthetic. The ears and consciousness of youth around the world were ripe for the *summa summarum* of pop culture and the modern aesthetic of the 20th century.

116. Cf. JAMESON, Frederic: Postmodernism, p. ix.

HIGH MODERNISM – NOT POSTMODERNISM

Postmodernism is generally seen as the sphere of unlimited possibilities. Anti-dogmatic, free, liberal, hoping for every narrative fragment after the end of the great narratives and prepared to accept everything. Thus postmodernism detaches itself from the great designs of modernism, and tries to take its bearings, as a pragmatic attitude of mind, from the realistic conditions of the here and now. No utopias and no attempts to draw up a new concept of the world. Some postmodern thinkers, reworking Hegel, spoke in the anti-Hegelian sense of the end of history, of the age of the simulacrum, of the era of simulation. A few computer games, more electronic media than books and the failure of old left-wing projects left the way open for a mass of metaphysical post-left theories, which sought a liberating lack of seriousness in wild whirls of language.

Many thinkers and artists in late capitalism made their own hopelessness the underlying tenor of their apocalyptic excursions into a cynical world-view that spared itself any constructive element, and seemed to be afraid of history. The postmodern is above all an age that has forgotten how to think historically,[116]

117. Ibid. p. x.

118. BENHABIB, Seyla: Kritik des 'Postmodernen Wissens' – eine Auseinandersetzung mit Jean-François Lyotard, in: HUYSSEN, Andreas/ SCHERPE, Klaus R.: Postmoderne, p. 120.

119. Ibid. p. 121.

according to Frederic Jameson, who assessed this attitude of mind in the context of his Marxist design as an – extremely entertaining – superstructural phenomenon in late capitalism. This playful aestheticization of the world is to be found both in architecture, which, in Jameson's view, is the cultural form closest to politics, and in film, in videos and MTV, in theory and in art. The tendency of resolutely postmodern art (which very few people, unfortunately, would admit to), is to be cheerfully agreeable. Jameson: 'In postmodern culture, "culture" has become a product in its own right; the market has become a substitute for itself and fully as much a commodity as any of its items it includes within itself: modernism was still minimally and tendentially the critique of the commodity and the effort to make it transcendent itself. Postmodernism is the consumption of sheer commodification as a process. The "lifestyle" of the superstate therefore stands in relationship to Marx's "fetishism" of commodities.'[117]

Escape into the playful, the cynical, the funny, into cheerful historicism and the motley affirmation of despair devalues postmodern culture and theory into an interesting but otherwise unimportant continuation of bourgeois neo-liberalism, advocating a vague pluralism and generally ending as pragmatism. One example of this might be the theory of Lyotard, who cannot define a minimum of cognitive and moral obligation 'that is necessary to establish the fronts between post-Marxist, radical democratic politics and postmodern neo-conservatism'.[118] In her critique of Lyotard Seyla Benhabib refers to the main problem of all forms of political liberalism as 'the neglect of the structural origins of inequality in terms of influence, available resources and power between competing groups'.[119]

On the level of cultural practice, postmodernism tends to neo-conservatism, because artists have lost the ethical definitions of modernism, and many are at a loss about their own aesthetic practice. The tendency towards pessimism and highly polished despair are also possibly due to the fact that artists observed the inadequacy of their own approaches, and saw no way out. After Godard, many critical film makers couldn't think of anything more to say. After punk and Cage the old form of composition was over. After conceptual art, painting struck many artists as a miserable retreat into history, and literature no longer knew how and what it should tell. This helplessness doubtless played a part in the rise of the old recipes rather than exciting experiments.

One further reason for the new praise of frivolity and cynicism doubtless lay in the origins of the theorists and artists, who were often not members of a minority but renegade representatives of the ruling bourgeoisie. The seriousness of the situation in the ghetto only permitted frivolity in the consciousness under certain conditions. The artists from the ghettos – whether the ghettos of poverty, of homosexuals, of the races or religions that suffered discrimination – were not desperate because they didn't know what to fight for; they fought out of despair. The history of DJ culture shows that this struggle was not fought stubbornly or hard-heartedly, but with a love of the artist's own production, which made the hardships of life in the ghetto liveable and to some extent even enjoyable, without losing sight of the political perspectives.

Maybe the ignorance of the approaches and aporias of modernism provide a great opportunity for artists who are working an unconsciously modernist way. Their freedom from manifestos and dogmas remains – it almost seems paradoxical – borne by their seriousness in attempting to keep alive the innovatory spirit of culture.

Jean-Paul Gaultier makes fashion and is quite sure: 'Everything is possible, you know? But everything possible doesn't mean that everything will be. It means that there is – *something to do*.'[120] If we understand postmodern openness as a mission to do not just *something* but *the right thing*, there is no time for pessimism or resignation. DJ culture, with its impetus of innovations and influence on art, fashion, literature and film/video makes it plain that the journey of reason through time and space is by no means over, and if it has come to an end it's only temporary. The sun will rise again. The Enlightenment has not yet done its work, and nowhere does the desire for more knowledge and more understanding of the world appear more urgent than in the ghettos of the marginalized, as a piece by Kool Moe Dee entitled 'Knowledge Is King' proves:

120. PANDISCIO, Richard: Jean-Paul Gaultier, in: INTERVIEW 1/1994, p. 73.

The wicked can rule ya but knowledge can stop it
Souls can't be controlled 'cause it's a spiritual thing
But ya got to have knowledge
Knowledge is king
Knowledge is king[121]

121. KOOL MOE DEE:
Knowledge is King, in: STANLEY,
Lawrence A., op. cit., p. 189.

122. HUYSSEN, Andreas/
SCHERPE, Klaus R.: Introduction, in:
idem, op. cit., p. 10.

Maybe the critique of reason and fear of knowledge are the privilege of those who already have the luxury of knowledge. Rappers and DJs from the ghetto think it a privilege to be able to read and write. And the members of the hip-hop nation who belong to the black middle class and attend university feel obliged to communicate knowledge and ideas to their black brothers and sisters in the ghetto. The euphoria with which rappers and DJs speak about books, ideas, ideologies and metaphysics reveals a massive thirst for ideas. After the civil rights, soul and Black Panther movements, hip-hop is the next great boost for the proud, intellectual self-determination of Afro-Americans in the USA. 'Knowledge Is King' also refers, of course, to aesthetic practice, whose self-reflexiveness and growing complexity requires knowledge as an underlying precondition.

The question of how necessary it is to locate DJ culture within the project of modernism must remain open, since the definition of modern/postmodern is a difficult enterprise which must remain vague because of the many different interpretations of the terms. It is just as senseless to condemn postmodern thinkers and artists as it would be wrong to ignore their approaches to problems. The vagueness of the term 'progress' corresponds to uncertainty about the form in which the project of modernism can be continued. Widespread helplessness and resignation about the question of the right way can also be seen as the chance for a new openness and tolerance, which reaches its limits where it relinquishes its fundamental grip on progressive practice.

'At the end of blind alleys, it isn't just regression when you shift into reverse,'[122] observe Huyssen and Scherpe in the introduction to their book about postmodernism. But how much better it is if parts of culture are spared the need to shift into reverse. Within the context of pop culture, DJ culture has made it clear that the possibilities of modernism are far from exhausted, but that there are new methods, means and ways, new strategies and goals that are worth fighting for, and which can without too much distortion be fitted into the development of a progressive course of history. The most interesting parts of a culture that seeks to be described as postmodernist should really be seen as 'high modernist'. The introduction of the term 'high modernist' only makes sense, however, if – in the strictly modernist sense – it is considered as an attitude of mind in which modernism becomes aware of itself. By virtue of this, pop culture would first of all escape the circle of high modernism, since this reflection does not consciously take place. But as exiles of (modern) high culture, as aliens and outsiders, the artists of DJ music find new solutions and approaches which had previously not been considered, or which had even been unthinkable. The contemporary nature of music, so relentless that it puts everything in the past in its shade, links up, through various contact points between modernism and pop culture, with an attitude of mind which, in its seriousness and ideological narrow-mindedness, is perceived by outsiders as something alien and even perhaps absurd. Nonetheless, these contact points – in the form of artists like Malcolm McLaren and Andy Warhol – always indicate that there are patterns, methods and affinities in the history of modernism that can easily be covered or sampled: consciously or unconsciously.

High modernism may be the bastard son of modernism or its abandoned child, which grew up without the help of its parents, rebelled against them and stood on its own feet relatively early. Hegel's cunning of reason makes the question of the affinity between modernism and high modernism a matter of secondary importance: what counts is their dialectical relationship in the progress of the world-spirit, which always knows where it is going. But sometimes high modernism, which – of course – exists only as a creation of the theorists, is one of the many helpful aberrations that gets the world-spirit out of time's blind alleys. The idea of a relief action carried out unconsciously by its actors fits into the proposed ideology of contingency. If modernism seeks to become aware of itself in high modernism, it perhaps does so most securely in the warm, friendly darkness of the unconscious. This is perhaps its greatest chance.

PROGRESS FOR MANKIND: LIFE IN THE SUBCULTURE

After the provisional failure of socialist and communist strategies to achieve power and set up a socialist society, many left-wing thinkers lost their faith and fell silent. Left-wing theorists and politicians, for whom being on the left was more than a faith, a way of life and a science, asked the question of how Marxist materialism and all forms of left-wing thought and politics could be kept alive into the 21st century.

The cultural battle for human rights and self-determination, for autonomies and minority rights, for enlightenment and co-determination reflects, in its disparity and frequent imprecision, the current state of confusion within left-wing theory. Orthodox Marxists like the theorists and philosophers of the Marxist Group refused all reflection on a cultural strategy of subversion, and restricted themselves to the political business of the days. Leftist thinkers in pop culture have few allies. Most politically left-wing groupings dress themselves up with 'agit-pop', which falls within the tradition of communist party propaganda of the early years of this century and practises the manipulation of consciousness in a practically anti-Enlightenment way. Today, the spectrum of this agit-pop in Germany extends from Konstantin Wecker (SPD) via BAP (The Greens) and Rio Reiser (PDS) to punk-rock bands like Slime, who play for the militant left. In this music, leftism is only apparent in the unambiguous writing of the lyrics. That cultural resistance could also be demonstrated and achieved by the aesthetic and the form of art production appears alien and extravagant.

The story of artists who were filled with (Leninist) partisanship and were nonetheless thrown out of the party extends from the Soviet Constructivists to Godard and Rainald Goetz, who was mocked by the Marxist Group. Despite this, these artists remained true to their ideas and went on working, free and unorganized, on their leftist art.

Apart from the black nationalism of hip-hop, DJ culture largely independent in party-political terms, and represents a new form of resistance. As the form of expression of minorities and ghettos, hip-hop originally had little to do with realism in the obvious sense. As everyone else in the audience was marginalized as well, a realism telling oppression on the semantic and narrative level would have been redundant. Hip-hop as a whole was the product of ghetto reality, and at first it wished not to reflect reality but to change it – the reality in which hip-hop came into being. It was a matter of conquering a space in which the members of minorities and the ghettos could dance and listen to music freely and undisturbed. The micropolitics of the subcultures was not interested in utopian promises or in changing the world, but wanted to create and structure the smallest niches of self-determination. The beginnings of disco lay in the clubs of the 'gay community'. They were part of the 'patchwork of minorities' (Lyotard) that replaced the united resistance of a class or a party and instead formed a resistance that was heterogeneous, the common denominator being the desire to be seen and acknowledged as minorities.[123] Sexuality and the body have only been political themes since 1968. When the dogma of identity was called into question by Marxism and the revolutionary process, 'the importance given to the body is one of the most important, if not essential elements'.[124] Foucault observed. The occupation and control of the body by power led to a rebellious rediscovery of the desires and yearnings of the body. The conquest of the body by power leads to 'responding claims and affirmations, those of one's own body against power, of health against the economic system, of pleasures against the moral norms of sexuality, marriage, decency. Suddenly, what had made power strong becomes used to attack it.'[125] The 'revolt of the sexual body'[126] fighting for a wide-ranging emancipation of the homosexual minority proved particularly violent.

The beginnings of disco were seen as political in exactly this sense, at the clubs and parties where pleasure could be experienced and celebrated against the repressions of the dominant morality. Disco was body music, and 'Move Your Body, Shake Your Body', the refrain of countless disco and, later, house tracks made the body

123. Cf. LYOTARD, Jean-François: Kleine Perspektivierung der Dekadenz und einiger minoritärer Gefechte, die hier zu führen sind, in: idem: Das Patchwork der Minderheiten, p. 38.

124. FOUCAULT, Michel: Body/Power, in: idem: Power/Knowledge, p. 57.

125. Ibid. p.56

126. Ibid. p.57

the subject of direct address, just as the music did when it compelled people to dance. For Foucault, addressing the body is 'more materialist' than constantly occupying the consciousness with ideologies. Analyses that prefer to examine ideologies are suspect because they still presuppose 'a human subject on the lines of the model provided by classical philosophy, endowed with a consciousness which power is then thought to seize on'.[127] DJ music is aimed directly at the dancing body, and thus tries to avoid being diverted via the consciousness, so it can pleasure the body directly.

The disco scene and the original house scene emerged from the gay community, and either partially broke down the ghettoization of homosexuals or else made the ghetto rather more agreeable and inhabitable. The first hip-hop DJs came from a real, identifiable ghetto in New York: the Bronx.

Until 1979 hip-hop was a local cultural form that barely attracted attention outside the Bronx. In the Bronx, however, it had undergone a fast and strong development, with deejaying, rapping, graffiti spraying and breakdancing all blossoming over the course of the previous four years. In a side-room off the general cultural history, an autarkic black culture was able to develop untroubled by the dominant white intellectual hegemonic power. It was far from the 'anonymous ideology' (Barthes) of a bourgeois society that forces all consumers to preserve and employ the traditional cultural forms of that society. Practically nothing in the everyday life of the Bronx was committed to the idea that the bourgeoisie had marshalled for itself and others 'of the relations between people and the world'.[128] And where Barthes reveals the traditional customs of every culture as something like a second, false nature in civilized societies, the ghetto, thanks to its socially marginalized status, becomes an experimental zone for new cultural forms. Only through life in the ghetto does the pseudo-nature of a bourgeois society appear as something strange, being perceived by the inhabitants as constructed and unnatural. The identification of ideological misuse and a reactionary, system-bolstering culture is, for the oppressed and the rejected of that culture, something quite natural, which white bourgeois intellectuals like

127. Ibid. p.58

128. BARTHES, Roland: Mythologies, p. 127.

Roland Barthes had to imagine their way into.

In the ghetto, bourgeois ideology appears only as a fragment. People who do not profit from the distribution of power within a society, but pay for it, are per se immune to the seductions of that ideology. In short: they cannot afford that ideology and its liberality of affluence. The movement 'by which the bourgeoisie transforms the reality of the world into an image of the world, history into nature',[129] stalls in the ghetto. Barthes defines the transition from reality to ideology in bourgeois society as 'the transition from anti-nature to pseudo-nature'.[130] And this transition does not occur in the ghetto.

Pop culture is a bastard. It can't decide whether it is a counterculture or the dominant culture. Generally, pop is both, and mostly it is the instrument with which counterculture is turned into the dominant culture. Nik Cohn has pop beginning with rock'n'roll, and in the first line of his history of pop he points out that rock'n'roll had its ancestors in black R&B, a minority culture. Until the late 60s, pop remained a rebellion against the establishment, but at the same time it prefigured the establishment. Under the tutelage of pop culture, many young pop rebels quickly found their way into bourgeois society after their 'wild years'. But the roots and, above all, the innovations and revolutions of pop music continued to emerge from the milieu of the minority cultures, principally that of ethnic, religious and sexual minorities.

The power and force of pop lives on the resistance of these subcultures. Paradoxically, these energies finally end up, via the mediation of pop culture, back in the hegemonic culture, which is almost always in a position to absorb all subcultures and use their strength for itself. Via pop, the (power) centre integrates the periphery, and 'uses it for its own purposes, for its internal dynamic'.[131] This function of relocation gives a special place to pop culture and everyone who works in it. They can create work of their own in relative independence of the hegemonic culture. But freedom (quickly) ends where the products of a subculture can no longer be incorporated within the dominant discourse. Then the police methods of the hegemonic

129. Ibid. p. 129.

130. Ibid. p. 130.

131. LYOTARD, Jean-François, op. cit., p. 7.

Alan Freed (centre) playing himself in Go, Johnny, Go! (1959)

power come into play, and begin to crusade against the menacing subculture. So pop culture should be enjoyed cautiously. Pop is always two things: promise and betrayal. The transition of hip-hop culture from a marginal culture to a form of pop culture tells the story of rebellion and conformity in a fascinating way. Black author Nelson George saw the marketing and industrialization of R&B as its falsification, decline and death. Now he observed the same thing in rap. 'At one point I thought rap was going to be a totally new thing both musically and businesswise, but it's been co-opted, just as R&B was, and in a more accelerated process.'[132] Despite the exploitation of hip-hop culture by the white-run entertainment companies – certainly correctly attested by George – hip-hop has made a contribution to consciousness-raising and politicization not only of young blacks. Many rap artists feel more powerful than the politicians. KRS One is disappointed by the more than 300 black mayors in America who have no 'juice', no power, to put across the concerns of the black minority: 'I got more juice as a rap artist than I would as a mayor.'[133] Ice Cube has something similar to say, and knows that all children and young people believe him because he has never lied to them on records or in interviews, or in his lectures at schools and universities. 'I think the rappers that are conscious are more qualified than these so-called leaders we have to bring about a sense of knowledge and wisdom in the community.'[134]

Many of the productions of 1994 are still directly connected, musically and philosophically, with the ghetto situation, and do not squint past the realities of society as pop likes to do. The link with the ghetto gives many of the musicians strength and confidence. A member of the Wu-Tang Clan, one of the most successful rap bands of 1994, declared at the New Music Seminar in New York that the most important thing is the family you surround yourself with. He didn't mean the family one is born into, and which is generally fragmented in the ghetto, but the 'family' which is constructed as a substitute authority of socialization. The posse or the clan surrounds rap music, creating a familiar atmosphere even when they cross over into white media to appear in the foreign

132. SPENCER, Neil: Full Nelson, in: STRAIGHT NO CHASER, Winter 1993, p. 33.

133. SMALL, Michael, op. cit., p. 81.

134. ESHUN, Ekow: Ice Cube, loc. cit., p. 90.

land of hegemonic culture outside of the ghetto. In these cases – and the Wu-Tang Clan is no exception – it isn't just a question of security and reticence, but also of not severing one's own roots and staying in close connection with the marginalized. The micropolitics of minorities is as strong and unbroken as it is because it has recognized that the greatest danger lurks in the alienation of the minority. 'Being black and proud' means not wanting to go into the centre's structures of order, morals and power, and insistence on autonomy and independence. While some minorities in the USA and Europe have tried to assimilate as generally as possible, the minorities in the field of DJ culture are strictly uncompromising in their reluctance to be subordinated. Because it pays off.

Non-members of minorities who feel linked to the culture of a minority dramatize themselves as a minority. The hipster as 'White Negro', as Mailer called him, puts himself at the margin of society because he finds that society morally and aesthetically unacceptable. The hipster as described by Mailer chooses a life of humiliation and danger that was exciting, violent and honest in comparison to that of the average American. In the 50s, the hipster was at once a masochistic psychopath and an artist, a philosopher and a narcissist who defined himself as part of an elite, who possessed not only his own values and norms but also a language of his own. The goal was to come as close as possible to the ideal of an absolute self-creation.
The hipster today is no longer an existentialist like the 'White Negro' of the 50s. The ghetto of the blacks has culturally conquered a wide territory in which members of non-minorities find space to live and work. DJ culture as a minority product freed 'white negroes' from the burden of paying for their connection to the marginalized by putting their lives at risk. Parallel to the 'white negro', the 'straight faggot' developed within disco and house culture, the heterosexual gay who not only felt solidarity with the life, romanticism and style of homosexuals, but also copied it and transferred it to a heterosexual existence. Other forms of hipsterdom were 'atheist Jews', 'Aryan mulattos', or the

'Communist Nazis' that the Slovenian band Laibach invented to reveal and circumvent repression through identity. Their appearance in Nazi uniforms with antlers while declaring their support for Yugoslavian Communism precisely embodies the semiotic campaign of the hipster, who subverts and destroys all forms of certainty.

DJ culture was able to do without the conceptual art of Laibach and the 'Neue Slovenische Kunst', because it grew almost organically out of social and political problem areas that required different forms of resistance from a totalitarian system in Eastern Europe. While the members of the minorities stressed their identity as minorities and manifested it in their culture, hipsters contributed to its erosion by means of their play with identities. As an elaborately elitist constructor of the 'self', the hipster negated every form of social seriousness and confused the fronts at which discrimination, oppression and hatred establish society's identity. The hipster, like the whole of DJ culture, has little interest in the old structure of the bourgeois subject, and sees the 'self' as a stylistic, aesthetic project, which demands serious work.

One of the chief concerns of the hipster is being totally up-to-date. The hipster knows what's going on in the world, and he's sure that his style, his behaviour and his view of the word are absolutely contemporary. The symbolic order of the centre of power is pleasurably confused. Paul Weller, singer with The Jam, declared in a hymn to the mods that one cover of a French Small Faces EP would make people forget every painting by Pablo Picasso.[135] His interest in the 'style years', the 'total look' from 1963 until 1967, is purely aesthetic and perhaps superficial, as he admits: '...very rarely does it extend past clothes, music, films and books.'[136] For Weller, the mods are the embodiment of a rebellion that made taste, dignity and strength available to the working-class teenager. 'The whole image is C-O-O-L: dancing into the small hours, blocked, finger clickin' to J.B. and the Famous Flames, even smokin' to Bluebeat!'[137]

Hipsterdom means rebelling about or for things that most people don't care about. Hipsterdom means

135. Weller even says he would piss on all of Picasso's paintings to prove it.

136. WELLER, Paul: The Total Look, in: STEWART, Tony: Cool Cats, p. 33.

137. Ibid.

resisting boredom and arguing for imagination, beauty and excitement. From that point of view the Situationist movement, as Greil Marcus describes it in *Lipstick Traces*, can also be read as the history of (artistic) hipsterdom. Indeed, all the semiotic rebellions from Dada to punk were pure hipsterdom.

The hipster is constantly on his way to new shores. Hipness is a seal of approval distributed within bohemia, Diederichsen wrote in 1985 in *Sexbeat*: 'What was hip was what went further. Parker improvised over more fixed structures than Miles Davis. Miles dropped the structures and improvised "modally". Plop, gone, off you go! Hip. Lennie Tristano was that bit freer as well. Hip. And then you get Coltrane. And so on.'[138] A further criterion for hipsterdom, in Diederichsen's view, is the question of authenticity or soul. 'The question of whether someone had really fought, worked, felt for something, or whether he was simply clever.'[139]

Now the dogma that the hipster mustn't be clever sounds touchingly old-fashioned. People laugh at authenticity and soul, if they look uncoded and crude. The delineation with the non-hip is also treated in a more cynical and distorted way. Cynicism is the reaction to a historical situation in which the straight options seem to have gone missing. But in the end cynicism can only have its beginning and its end in the morally rigid position that permits it.

Perhaps hipsterdom can be morally grounded, with the consequence that people no longer talk of the hip and the non-hip world, but of the good and the bad world. The hipsters as 'the first wind of a second revolution'[140] embodied a new form of resistance. After the disappointments of the last real rebellions against the abuses of capitalist society a new strategy comes into being in 1968. The dream of a universal coup is abandoned in favour of the modest creation of a small, good world, in which hipsters can keep themselves separate from the rest of society. Style becomes an external distinguishing feature of the moralists. Non-conformist and unalienated by earning money, the hipster, at least for himself and his comrades-in-arms, realizes the vision of a better world. He is a nightlife missionary, recruiting the next generation for the good

138. DIEDERICHSEN, Diedrich: Sexbeat, p. 24.

139. Ibid.

140. MAILER, Norman, op. cit., p. 232.

world via style and ease. His instinct makes greater reflection superfluous.[141]

Since the 80s, nightlife has been the hipster's ideal domain, and extends the ghetto of the marginalized strategically world-wide with sympathizers and the likeminded. Where DJ culture maintains its underground character – regardless of how far up the charts it gets – the battles of minorities and hipsters continue. The question of how effective the underground can be when it has become pop must remain unanswered. But perhaps the idea of the underground resistance is only a stale idea – a touching dream for the middle-class consumers of pop culture.

'We live in revolutionary times,' said George Lipsitz, commenting on the state of youth culture in the 90s. The last two decades in the US have made the situation of minorities worse rather than better. Between 1979 and 1989 the number of black children growing up in poverty rose from 41.2 to 43.7 per cent; over all, 2.2 million more children were living in poverty than in 1979. The mortality rate of black children is almost twice as high as the national average, and black men in the ghettos of Harlem, New York or South Central, Los Angeles have a lower life expectancy than men in the Third World country of Bangladesh.[142] In view of this, the word 'progress' rather sticks in the throat. And yet every form of micropolitics within DJ culture makes it plain that this progress is important, desirable and necessary. As we have said: any doubts about the notion of progress are at an end where they run into the political and cultural practice of those who are destroyed by prevailing conditions.

NEW DAWN

Strength and beauty provide confidence. The history of mankind advances. On MTV, Heavy D. presented a programme showing the best videos of hip-hop history, from the Sugar Hill Gang to Snoop Doggy Dogg. And by then it becomes clear how infinitely strong, powerful

141. Cf. POSCHARDT, Ulf: Die beste aller Welten, p. 125ff.

142. Cf. LIPSITZ, George: We Know What Time It Is, in: ROSS, Andrew/ ROSE, Tricia (Ed.), op. cit., p. 18.

and clever this DJ culture is, the magnificent and refined way in which it has developed, and how much respect and charm reigns in it. Female MCs mock the sexism of the men (Salt'n'Pepa: 'Shoop'), male MCs rescue the figures of black women from the diet-based terror of white women's magazines (Sir Mix-A-Lot: 'Baby Got Back'), and one of the first hip-hop bands makes a gripping pop video as a new version of socialist realism (Grandmaster Flash and The Furious Five: 'The Message'). In between one hears Heavy D. thanking Chuck D. for the educational work of Public Enemy. 'This was accordingly a glorious mental dawn.'[143] Without confidence there is no progress, no reforms, no revolutions, no dawn. Once enlightenment at the service of the present day had, for Horkheimer and Adorno, become the 'wholesale deception of the masses',[144] the enlightenment of enlightenment occurs as pop in the music of the ghettos. The horizon of freedom is infinite, and the small light of DJ culture gleams brighter and brighter, providing hope: a thrust to rebellion.

Let's talk to Hegel again. When the revolution began in France, Hegel was 19 years old, studying at Tübingen with Hölderlin and Schelling. Recalling the revolution, he writes: 'All thinking beings shared in the jubilation of this epoch. Emotions of a lofty character stirred men's minds at this time; a spiritual enthusiasm thrilled through the world…'[145] The whole Hegelian system is a machine of confidence and hope. Within it works the knowledge that a revolution is possible, that injustice doesn't necessarily remain injustice, and that 'liberty, equality, fraternity' are not merely empty formulae. Faith in the victory of reason is never unbroken. The spirit – and therefore culture as well – is the result of its activity. 'The life of a people ripens a certain fruit; its activity aims at the complete manifestation of the principle which it embodies. But this fruit does not fall back into the bosom of the people that produced and matured it; on the contrary, it becomes a poison-draught to it. That poison-draught it cannot let alone, for it has an insatiable thirst for it: the taste of the draught is its annihilation, though at the same time the rise of a new principle.'[146]

Dawn. The Beastie Boys order: 'Check Your Head.'

143. HEGEL, G.W.F., Philosophy of History, p. 447.

144. HORKHEIMER, Max/ ADORNO, Theodor W.: Dialectic of Enlightenment, p. 42.

145. HEGEL, loc. cit.

146. Ibid., p. 78.

Rainald Goetz, in his article 'Ästhetisches System': 'We can all explain to each other, through silence and through showing, or through speech, we were human children. And peacefully time drew us with affection onwards.'[147]

147. GOETZ, Rainald: Kronos, p. 401.

BONUSTRACK
('97) MOODY DUB)

REAWAKENING

Darkness has fallen upon the world. The machines are groaning, the bass is deeper than ever, and the loudspeaker systems no longer merely massage the diaphragm, they thump it. Your head beats against walls of sound that seem hard as concrete. From the walls, steel-grey computer graphics glare sternly down, showing the dancers the prison they are trapped in: Metalheadz – the DJs are called Grooverider, Fabio, Peshay, Kemistry & Storm and Goldie.

In the middle of the Leisure Lounge in London, a walkway has been erected, and gradually fills with dancers. The movements of their bodies obey two different options: some twitch at the frequency of beats per minute, others move to the lethargic off-beat of the vibrating bass. The faces of the dancers are blank, some expressions appear transfigured, transcendent. With closed eyes and a faint smile floating around their lips, they yield harmonically to the waves of sound. Many of them are sweating, they keep glancing at the DJ working in his gallery. His shouts of encouragement seem superfluous. The club breathes blissfully to the beat. A perfect night.

A day later, on Sunday, it is the Metalheadz night at the Blue Note, a famous old jazz club. The audience is blacker, not so stylish, and the mood more charged and heated than it was in the Leisure Lounge. The dancefloor is smaller, the soundwaves are even more relentless, and most of the dancers are grouped in a semi-circle around the DJ and the MC. Floorkillers are greeted with frenetic whistling and shrieking, loud howling interrupts the MC in his eulogy of the DJ, his music and club. If the audience is particularly into a particular track, the DJ presses the stop button and

Metalheadz flyer

coolly puts the needle back on the start. 'Rewind!' the homeboys in the audience shout: 'Rewind!' Goldie writhes around on the floor with enthusiasm, other homeboys pogo, girls jump on the spot like crazy gymnasts. It's a trip back to the future of DJ music and B-Boy culture.

Drum'n'bass, distilled out of jungle in the mid-90s, opened up new avenues for DJ music to lead out of its stagnation and into new kinds of adventures. The journey into the unheard-of is still going on, and it almost seems as though drum'n'bass, the most recent stage in the music's development, might promise a synthesis of all the DJ styles that have electrified the masses in the past: a hint of disco, a healthy portion of hip-hop, the digital aggressiveness of techno and plenty of darkness previously only heard in industrial and gothic. Particularly apparent is its similarity to hip-hop. Even more than this, anyone wishing to attest to such a thing will see drum'n'bass as the rebirth of hip-hop – this time in Europe, with a precise knowledge of the Bronx phenomenon that had a lasting effect on pop music in the mid-70s. At a time when the DJ was turning more and more into a filigree studio wizard in an ever more refined electronic dance music, whose products revealed only the barest rudiments of the old DJ structures, and who threatened to decline into a cliché as a cult figure and role model, in drum'n'bass the old concept of two turntables and a mixing desk came back into its own. As in the early days of hip-hop, the MC positioned himself at the DJ's desk to charge the intentional pauses and dramatic decrescendos with hysteria and power. The DJ is no longer just an entertainer producing a routinely good soundtrack for the night, but is now – and more visibly than before – the centre-piece of the club. Like the workers in the hive, the dancers in the Blue Note have grouped around the queen bee at the decks. The DJ scratches, mixes and cuts just like in the old days. Just as hip-hop was distinctly and autonomously created in the Bronx, now DJs, particularly from London and Bristol, can be seen as the ancestors of this new music.

Drum'n'bass is a kind of music which, as its name suggests, is defined primarily by its percussive structure. The rapid breakbeat lives on the disintegrating speeds of the dub-like bass sounds and the high-pitched drum elements like the hi-hat and the snare drum. Like the first breakbeat sounds, drum'n'bass is based around rhythmical bones that are not just a principle of construction but the music's actual unit of meaning. Two London DJs, Fabio and Grooverider, called their breakbeat sound – before it was given the name 'jungle' – 'strictly rhythm', because they maintained that concentration on the rhythm throughout their DJ careers from house via hip-hop to breakbeat techno. This meant that an unrestrained embellishment of the rhythmical structure was possible. In the process, two different schools have emerged: one delicately, almost esoterically intersperses the percussive hardbodies with jazzy and spherical sounds, while the other works with aggressive hip-hop samples, driving MC solos and raw techno sounds. Both kinds share a terrific level of abstraction and intellectual freedom.

The heart of darkness pumps sounds between the rhythmical pillars, whose terror lies primarily in their novelty. Impossible to locate, they seem to be derived from a secret mixture of moods, which otherwise exist as a soundtrack only in the unconscious, in sad dreams and despairing moments of loneliness. The sounds make fear audible, and thus offer a skewed kind of salvation. Records by Roni Size and Goldie play on a keyboard of the soul that seems never to have been touched before. Memory-banks pumped full of repressed threats and the scars they left are called up and voided. Good, dark drum'n'bass is the ultimate mind-fuck. Slip into this music and it swallows you whole. Only when the DJ brings the mind-fuck to an end do the listening dancers and dancing listeners recompose themselves as if they'd just been liberated. The journey through the interior of one's own psychical system is brought to an exhausted and happy conclusion.

Drum'n'bass is an open system. The 'drops' between the rhythmical skeletons leave room for the projections of the listeners. More than that: without the active participation that turns perception into co-authorship, the music falls apart. The dancers continue to move to the drops at the same speed of beats per minute; they go on tapping in rhythm. In this way what seem like breaks in the beat are drawn back, despite their floating character, into the rigid construction of the percussion. Just as abstract painting calls for a completely new form of visual perception, this abstract music attempts to open up the demand for co-authorship on the part of the recipient, so that that authorship is fertilized, in the act of dancing, by the intelligence of the body. In the rhythm-free sequences, the inaudible loops can be experienced in the movements of the body, and thus recorded into the psychical system of the dancer. At the same time, through the suggestive character of the dancefloors and their underhand emotional power, images and visions flow together from the memory of the psychical system and into the depths of the dancer. A kind of intoxicating ecstasy of perception is born.

Devotees of the music realize how calculated and open these attacks on current listening habits are when they are heard outside of the club, in a darkened room, on a damp country road or on a Walkman on the subway. Direct and demanding, the music drills into their headphones, without offering them a choice. Places of refuge are not presented, are not even on offer. To this extent drum'n'bass is a radical music, a radical aesthetic challenge.

The imagination of times, spaces and fictional realities, so important for the arts, is led by the nose in the psychic system of the clubbers. Because while journeys can float freely through the twists and sediments of past experiences and future desires, the DJs and MCs are constantly bringing these peregrinations back down to earth. The drops are linked by realistic samples of 'Inner City Life' (Goldie) to the features of late 20th century urban life. The dancefloor aura consists of the vibes of the age in which the music, its producers and consumers are located. The sounds of police sirens, the noises of space ships from science fiction movies or the sonic landscapes, familiar from twenty years of DJ music, of digital sound machines fuse into a sonic fingerprint of the age in which they came into being. More freely than in disco, hip-hop or house, drum'n'bass musicians avoid any conservative concept of realism. The sounds themselves are realistic. Consequently the desire to present sounds, signifiers of reality, as testimony to that reality, as the old concept of realism would have required, becomes superfluous. The sounds themselves bring forth the cities, clubs, living-rooms of loneliness, the fights in back courtyards, fast driving on the motorway, into the sonic network of the pieces. What is interesting is that the most contemporary forms of DJ music like electro, drum'n'bass or the Detroit techno sound appear to revolve only around their own constitution: speaking of their bass, of the blessings of modern technology and the pride of being ahead of all other arts in the use of this technology. And yet: where this music – British critic Kodwo Eshun calls it 'sonic fiction' – speaks by itself, it speaks of the state of the world, of its front-line positions, problems and its emotion. If we consider the history of DJ music as the proliferation of the melancholy state of being lost in the present, by '97 this sound has become a terribly sad and cheerful wailing wall, at once proud and vulnerable.

This music of darkness lives most powerfully in the gloom which, once daylight has vanished, fades out the world and retrieves its melancholy memories. Hope has quietly taken its leave; what remains is trust in the enjoyment that music can bring if it lets the audience stay alert and stay funky at the same time, that is, if it communicates directly with the body. Communication with the body is only possible if it sends stimulating signals that the body can transmit directly into motor movement. Abstract music works with brachial rhythmical patterns that activate the body and let its life and its experiences flow into the ecstasy of perception we described before. The body as a material satellite of the psychical system actually brings with it its own memories and stories. And if it is dark, it sees the apparatus of perception itself.

'Drops' are atmospheres and as such generally dangerous simulations of reality. 'As regards the individual things that occupy spaces,' Luhmann writes, 'atmosphere is always what they are not, which is to say: the other side of their form.'[1] Since in music form is only ever the immaterial projection of sound signals, the other side of that form can be taken as the

1. LUHMANN, Niklas: Die Kunst der Gesellschaft, p. 181.

emanation of the actual impulse that feeds into it. But this ad hoc definition is a difficult one to sustain, because in music form and atmosphere tend to merge. Hence atmosphere, Luhmann continues, is what would disappear if the individual objects that occupy spaces were to disappear: 'This explains the "unassailability" of the atmospheric along with its dependence on that which is given as the occupation of the space. To a certain extent, atmosphere is a surplus effect of difference of place.'[2] Drum'n'bass DJs let sound flourish: they set it free so that it uses its freedom, so that it does damage, it causes fear, it unsettles old listening habits, so that it prepares beauty and makes possible great art, which always means freedom. In his book *Silence*, John Cage described this freedom to think and compose as the result of a productive, wise uncertainty: 'This means for me knowing more and more not what I think a sound is, but what it actually is, in all of its acoustical details and then letting the sound exist, itself changing in a changing sonorous environment.'[3] And Schönberg, in his essay on twelve-tone music, pointed out that everything that happens at a particular point in a musical space has 'more than local meaning': 'It has not only one function on its own level, but in all other directions and levels, and is not without influence, even at remote points.'[4]

Cage calls the dialectic between form and the other side of form an 'intimacy of multiplicity and emptiness.'[5] Particularly given the otherwise strict mechanism of the rhythmical sequences, in drum'n'bass this relationship between multiplicity and void becomes a crucial element within a strict dramatic structure. Contrary to the old rules of dancefloor-oriented DJ music, clubgoers are left alone with their thoughts for long periods of up to two or three minutes without a groove. Londoner DJ Hype puts drops over each other to fill the grooveless time, so that the tension isn't lost but intensified. The pause as endless delay of the climax is employed as a dramatic effect in ever wilder ways – so wildly, in fact, that the craziness with which the drop begins reveals the DJ's technical perfection. As a sign of boundless ease, the record is repeatedly stopped just by using the stop button, and the void is allowed the opportunity to take

2. Ibid.

3. CAGE, John: Silence, p. 189f.

4. SCHÖNBERG, Arnold: Stil und Gedanke, p. 153.

5. CAGE, John, op. cit., p. 190.

over – but only because the non-void is such a powerful presence.

I ROCK THE PARTY THAT ROCKS THE BODY

6. For MC Lyte, the sample of Diana' Ross's 'Upside Down' for the remix of her song 'Cold Rock Party' was so valuable that she put a sticker on her LP, identifying the Motown disco sample as such: with full credit to the two song-writers Bernard Edwards and Nile Rodgers. Then Sean 'Puffy' Combs, a master of neo-funk remixed the whole thing and took it into the charts.

Disco was funk with an electronically twitchy charge. In the mid-90s, disco experienced a rebirth with the rediscovery of the legacy of funk in hip-hop and house tracks. Shortly after this came a reinterpretation of almost all the major disco numbers in every imaginable kind of DJ music. The gamut of enthusiastic reanimators runs from LL Cool J and MC Lyte[6] via Westbam and Armand van Hees to Jeff Mills and DJ Sneak. So from neo-soul via the endless series of funk bands to disco, all earlier forms of DJ music now live simultaneously in their contemporary form. Digital historicism means that the juxtaposition of all available family trees provides a panoramic view of the artist's own genesis. In ever more surprising nods and references, techno DJs and hip-hop MCs take parts of their history and make them not just audible but contemporary.

The recollection of disco and the recollection of hip-hop and reggae that happens in drum'n'bass reveals just how much DJ music identifies with its roots, despite its filigree ramifications. Progress occurs in step with history. From disco to disco.

The first bass guitar was built by the legendary Leo Fender in 1951, and rapidly became an indispensable element of the pop music that was just coming into being. The double bass that had been popular up until then, and which was used by both jazz combos and R&B bands, had found a less unwieldy successor. Available in various different lengths and with four or five strings, the bass has had an uneven history. It was important for the quality of group playing, it provided the rhythm, supplied a ground for the harmonies and established order in the band. But despite these merits and often virtuoso playing techniques, bassists remained marginal figures particularly in white pop bands – tolerated as a necessary evil rather than acknowledged as leaders.

While bands like Pink Floyd were sounding out the extremes of acoustic perception with the Azimuth generator, and thus giving the bass an experimental life of its own, it was black pop music above all that made the bass the protagonist of its arrangements with its stress on the rhythmical over the melodious. The development of reggae from the syncopated variety of R&B through ska and rock steady to reggae as we know it was essentially a fluid modulation of emphasis within the beat structure.

The transition from soul to funk also has a bass history. While in soul the melodies and sensitive vocals were a defining element within the music, in the variety of the music that goes by the name of funk, the arrangements slip towards the lower body. All instruments, including the singer's voice, become rhythm instruments. Everything puffed, groaned and sweated in time.

The origins of the words 'funk' and 'funky' in Afro-American slang date back to the Congo of the 17th century, where 'funk' was an expression for body odour. Up to our own times, the root 'funk' has been given various meanings, all of which have referred in one way or other to human physicality. Although these days the word 'funky' is generally positive in Afro-American slang, for a long time it had an ambivalent semantic which encompassed both the beautiful and the repellent. 'Funk is at the extremes of everything,' writes Rickey Vincent in his book *The Funk*.[7] Funk is earth, sex, rawness, nature, power, seduction. It has been used to refer to a style of music since the 50s. In Fab 5 Freddy's dictionary for homeboys, 'funky' is used for everything to do with music, fashion, culture or ideas that comes from a black background, and in a special sense for any cultural achievement inspired by the Godfather James Brown.

Parliament's P-funk in the mid-70s supplied even fatter bass-lines. P-funk was short for pure funk, also known as 'The Bomb' – the pure theory of something that was supposed to come over as dirty and sexy. The bass of Bootsy Collins, who had also played with James Brown, was plucked in such a dirty way that the whole

7. VINCENT, Rickey: Funk, p. 3.

music had a provocatively erotic and menacingly relaxed underlying mood. Afro-American musical theorist Greg Tate writes of the song 'P-Funk (Wants To Get Funked Up)' that the bass was 'another animal entirely', 'moving the groove along with fat gulps of syncopation that slithered and rumbled around your pelvis region until they punched erotic hotspots you never knew existed.'[8] In 'Flashlight', the 1978 hit, Collins' bass-playing was reinforced by the fat bass sounds that keyboard-player Bernie Worell drew from his Moog synthesizer.

Parliament's music was embedded in a mythology and metaphysics unparalleled in pop music. It became part of a fantasy of salvation that was both political and esoteric. Parliament mastermind George Clinton had discovered 'Funkentelechy'. A power that made funk stronger and more powerful, fired from the Bob Gun, the greatest invention of Dr Funkenstein, as Clinton liked to call himself. Funkentelechy as a force pulled people into the core of P-funk, propelled by their own powers as revitalized by the Bob Gun. The right dose of funk was enough to bring about a kind of personal self-renewal.

The term 'entelechy' comes from the Greek and means 'having a goal'. In Aristotle, entelechy is the form that is realized in matter, particularly the force within the organism that brings it to self-development and self-perfection. The entelechy of the organic, living body is the soul. In the vitalist philosophy of Driesch, entelechy becomes the 'whole-making' power of an organism. Funk as an address to the soul-filled body was to strengthen this holistic force among people who hadn't lost it, and restore it among people whose entelechy had suffered an injury. From this point of view, the deep, warm bass was at once balm, spiritual welfare and therapy. Salvation. In Clinton's metaphysical visions salvation through funk plays a central part. 'Splank' was the special term for the use of funk to protect both the consciousness and the rear end against constipation. In English the rather obscure word 'splanchnik' refers to the bowels and the kidneys. All kinds of constipation are to be dissolved, including, of course, that of the male genitalia. The music seeks total release. What is important is total 'selfsatis-function',

8 . TATE, Greg: Doin' it in your Earhole, in: Booklet for Parliament double CD 'Tear the Roof off', PolyGram 1993.

as Clinton calls it. Being one with the groove should shake people free.

Funk has – or so all the musicians who play it believe – always existed: as the rawest form of the primal groove. Clinton has the idea of the first beat as 'One' in which all other rhythms are already laid down. 'The One' is a 'meta-foolish perfection': 'Everything is on the One.'[9] In house music this primal groove is called 'Jack'. So funk has always existed, but only with James Brown and then Funkadelic was it able to appear in the raw, without a disguise. Of course it was a black thing, rooted in African rhythms, which allowed the Afro-Americans to go on living after their transportation, as a central legacy of their origins, and which thus became an important authority within their conception of identity. They had lost their own language and experienced alienation in the language of the masters, English, but in music they could cultivate the link with their lost homeland in Africa. The rhythm of the drums was the first immaterial medium of the transmission of messages, and in Africa it has a long tradition – not just as ritual music, but also as a direct form of communication.

The idea of liberation through funk is a memory of life before transportation. This motif also appears in a characteristic form in Clinton's work: in the form of the 'mother ship', the space ship that breaks into the world of the transported slaves to rescue them with funk. The scary idea, familiar from science fiction, of transporting human beings to an alien universe, was already part of the Afro-American past. Forced into big ships by white slave traders, another kind of evil extra-terrestrial, they were shipped to a completely alien world, and forced to live there. No wonder that rescue should be imagined in the form of a ship, albeit a space ship, by which space and time can be transcended. The funk of the mothership connection comes from the future, which only exists when the past and the roots of the Afro-Americans have been rediscovered. From this point of view funkentelechy acts as a high-tech connection to the lost homeland of Africa.

In Germany at the same time, Kraftwerk were experimenting, trying to fabricate danceable music

9. FUNKENSYCLO-P-DIA, in: Booklet for Parliament double CD 'Tear the Roof off', PolyGram 1993.

using the latest computer technology. While Clinton's funk seeks to have a holistic effect, curing constipated minds and genitalia, and funkentelechy wants to reconcile people with their own past, Kraftwerk's funk pretends to have been produced by androids. The colder the better, the more futuristic, the more beautiful.

But, as John Cage stresses, rhythm is not arithmetic,[10] and the resounding pocket calculators are just as alienated as the alienation of Kraftwerk itself. Kraftwerk played with alienation as the deliberate act of futurist fracture of something alienated already. The result was an orgy of alienation, which meant that with one of the supposed agents of this alienation, technology, something free could be produced, namely dance music. The correct use of the latest modern technology by the artist must, according to black techno musician Derrick May in the film *The Last Angel of History* (John Akomfrah, 1995), 'take it to the level of human instinct'. Kraftwerk succeeded in this via immense and, for them, necessary detours.

Kraftwerk were funky. A new kind of funk, industrial funk, as Rickey Vincent was to call it, white hardcore funk, as the black hip-hop DJs thought, when they made records by Kraftwerk the raw material of their first breakbeat mixes. Kraftwerk had not even tried to fake the sexiness of black music or find the primal funk within themselves. As white intellectuals, the direct path was blocked. In an interview, the musicians of A Tribe Called Quest once mentioned the possibility of reaching beyond the existing powers of life. For German intellectuals in the early 70s, that was difficult in every respect. Through the hundreds of kilometres of cables and spools in their cobbled-together Kling-Klang studio, the musicians of Kraftwerk took the detour they had to take to be funky. After the earthy, warm, smooth and 'pelvis-centred' erotic power of the primal bass, what Kraftwerk presented was the proud self-denunciation of merciless modernism and technology.

Hip-hop was above all the child of P-funk and James Brown, house was the child of disco, but without Kraftwerk both would have lost a crucial element: the calculated heartlessness of white musicians who love the black dance beat without wanting to emulate it.

10. Cf. CAGE, John: op. cit., p. 180.

Kraftwerk helped black musicians with structure and discipline, said black Detroit musician Carl Craig. Consequently the primal concept of funk and P-funk could be extended. What came out was what Kodwo Eshun has called 'Afrofuturism'. Black musicians could live without self-denunciation and the positivism of alienation. Maybe it's the privilege of the oppressed that they don't guiltily have to demonize themselves and their past, but can have confidence in themselves.

It is interesting that both Clinton and Kraftwerk refer to the vision of the future in Fritz Lang's *Metropolis* in one of their works. While in Clinton's latest video, Metropolis appears as the terrifying image of a de-functionalized world, in which people are robbed of pleasure and freedom, in which records are planed down and then destroyed and in which Clinton frees these same enslaved subjects as a terrorist using tapes and records, on Kraftwerk's 1977 LP *Man Machine*, Metropolis is presented as the perfect stage for the band's music. In Clinton's work, the (black) woman-machine Maria is rehumanized by having headphones playing loud funk put on her head, and there is a happy ending with dancing people. Kraftwerk gave up this confidence long ago. Dancing has become part of a meaningless world to which hopes of the past belong. Rhythm becomes a neurophysiological stimulus to which people react like androids equipped for the purpose.

The political struggle of the Afro-Americans is unfamiliar with this white intellectual cynicism – perhaps because the question of political emancipation presents itself with a quite different urgency for Afro-Americans. For Kraftwerk who, as veterans of '68, bore the stigma of a failed revolt, this confidence cannot exist, and must not exist. Afro-American musicians cannot allow themselves that luxury.

Pop music is funkier than ever. From Beck to Coolio, from George Michael to Carl Craig, from LFO to LTJ Bukem. Historical funk is fashionable again, it's sampled and copied, cloned and watered down, it's omnipresent. Clinton's musical conception has barely changed over the last 20 years. He still talks of the same funk and its consciousness-regenerating qualities. In a similar form, the new dancefloor music, post 1987, has returned to an archaic meaning of rhythm. But the medium of its presentation has become harder, more relentless and more materialistic. Since the introduction of digital methods of recording and reproduction, it has become possible to treat the sense of hearing in a quite different way. White DJs in particular have continued where Kraftwerk left off: to exploit technical innovations to the point where the increasing effect of the auratic and erotic vibrations of the bass can be replaced by the seductiveness of perfection, coldness, volume and, if necessary, by subsonic frequencies. When funk appears, it is only as a quotation or as a sampled temperature in sound.

LFO was an abbreviation, for Low Frequency Oscillator, and referred to a button used for frequency modulation on old synthesizers. This bass makes its presence felt, relentless, monstrous, in the aural channels. Where black musicians in particular seemed to like organically harnessing seductive bass sounds to the human sense of rhythm, the two white computer freaks operated in a more brachial way. They wanted to crush the people in the club, they rocked the computer and tortured the speaker systems: an acoustic violation which caused a strangely pleasant pain and which was infinitely sexy in its effect. The deeper the cooler. The 'deeper' which, in garage house, meant both the sound and the penetration of sexual intercourse, had assumed a new quality. But while eroticism and melancholy found particular expression in garage house or 'deep house', LFO picked up on the approach of Kraftwerk, creating rhythms with a technoid, cool elegance close to the state of the western white nations and their young avant-garde. As breakdancers and techno fans from the earliest days, they had seen it as part of their mission to reinterpret the black Detroit sound of Juan Atkins and Derrick May, and, bringing to it a sensitivity of their own, achieve their own sound. Detroit techno, which had come into being in the mid-80s, also saw itself as underground resistance music: black music that was completely incompatible with mainstream music and bore within it a typically Afro-American hope of a technological future; techno as the opportunity to use computers, samplers and a futuristic sound to flee the here and now.

In situations in which built-up aggressions cannot react outwardly and thus subside, they turn inwards, against oneself. The more 'fragmented' white dancefloor music was not the only threat to the physical wellbeing of the audience. The growing heaviness, not only of the bass-lines, has had other consequences. For years, doctors had been warning about growing levels of damage to the ears, particularly among young people between the ages of eighteen and twenty-five. If it was up to the medics, young people should only put on their Walkmans for an average of 4.8 minutes per day. And many clubs and raves had to put up signs saying the sound systems were 'severely damaging to the health'. Ninety decibels – according to the noise abatement society in Berlin – is the maximum level if serious aural damage is to be avoided. In decent clubs the volume is turned up beyond a hundred and ten decibels, and the same is true of well-made Walkmans with mega-bass amplification.

The call for a ninety-five-decibel volume limit for clubs and Walkmans is currently under debate – because noise can lead to death, and the life expectancy of people in cities varies from district to district. Where things are particularly loud, people die younger, especially of heart attacks, which are now – doctors say – one of the commonest causes of death. The trend is growing. Almost one in every three young people in Germany has had their hearing damaged between the frequencies of two and six kiloherz – the predominant range of both speech and music. But it is not only DJs and clubbers who yearn for the ultimate noise: heavy-metal devotees, car stereo fanatics and even the average Phil Collins fan yield to the rule of noise.

Perhaps the rebellious character of DJ music could be defined as a violaton of the noise level. Perhaps the new, heavy club music is a good inoculation against this vulnerability to noise. But perhaps the music is only a first dose of noise that will at some point lead to deafness or death.

In Los Angeles, the bass has become a religion. Gene Hester, a 19-year-old from LA, owns the most powerful subwoofer system that has ever been fitted in a car. He has twenty-four loudspeakers, three amplifiers of eight hundred watts each, powered by four car batteries. Because of people like Gene Hester, there's a new crime in LA called 'noise pollution' – the cops are now empowered to go after decibel violations as well as traffic violations. In the spring of 1996 Hester was arrested when he'd turned subwoofer speakers up full on Ventura Boulevard, shattering his windshield in the process. When Hester drives down the street with his system turned up, the alarms of the parked cars are set off, one after another, by the soundwaves. And the same soundwaves disturb the television reception of the local inhabitants, whose pictures flicker when Hester cruises past.

Gene Hester calls himself a bass-head. He describes his pleasure as follows: 'I can hear everything. I immerse myself in the sound, I listen to the small details, I feel unknown vibrations, I let it take hold of me, my whole body vibrates, I feel the friction on my skin, under my ass, and I can distinguish rhythmic patterns. And I can even feel my nerve-endings... I experience more than other people. It's like an adventure in perception.'[11]

Hester's car is a Chevy Suburban, a minivan with an enormous interior space that acts as an echo-chamber and thus guarantees more bass. He blow-dries his girlfriends' hair with the soundwaves, and chases other guys in the hood with his sound attacks if they've strayed into the wrong patch. The bass and his technical command of it at its loudest have become a status symbol and a kind of symbol of authority in the hood. Hester (and other followers of the 'bass movement') see their resolute journey into deafness as a real alternative to gang rivalry with guns and the acute risk of death.

If we define the occupation of spaces, districts and streets as one of the fundamental motifs of the gang, the use of sound waves makes twice as much sense. If, in the animal world, boundaries are drawn with scent, among human beings – apart from colours and the uniforms of gang members, which present a visual definition of one's own territory – the possibility of sonic annexation becomes increasingly important. The idea of the ghetto blaster was that of a mobile battle station, with which the owners could sonically occupy streets, courtyards and sports grounds. In Spike Lee's

11. KUMMER, Tom: Bässe machen Mädchen wild, in: SZ-Magazin 37/1996, p. 45.

film *Do the Right Thing* a race riot breaks out at the moment when the Italian pizza-baker smashes a proud homeboy's ghetto-blaster, the homeboy's weapon against the Italian culture of pop, baseball and food. With this act of destruction of the sound machine, the peaceful if tense co-existence of two cultures, the Italian and the Afro-American, comes to an end. From this point of view the ghetto blaster has emerged triumphant as a weapon of attack.

The battle with decibels and bass sound waves runs through the whole history of DJ music. The Jamaican sound systems, as a kind of larger-than-life mobile disco, were the medium of a generally peaceful argument between various gangs in the slums and ghettos of Jamaica. And in the 50s, the bass-line of a sound system was the deciding criterion for its quality. There was a similar principle at the beginning of hip-hop culture, when the first DJs engaged in DJ battles against one another. Kool DJ Herc, who may be seen as the first breakbeat DJ, defended his cultural primacy chiefly via the power of his speakers. For a long time, DJ and MC battles, breakdance competitions and graffiti wars were a cultural means of bringing peace to the particularly brutal gang wars of the 70s, or at least of keeping them within limits.

For Andrea Parker, one of the currently most innovative figures in DJ music, the bass-line is the most important element of a track. To build up bass-lines, she uses various techniques. If she is using the sound of a bass guitar, she adds the bass of an analogue synthesizer to make the bass-line denser, more voluminous and more multi-layered. As a musician and DJ, constantly on the lookout for new sounds, her research is always taking her out on expeditions with her DAT recorder. She records the deep bass noises of an aeroplane or a passing car, both miles away. And even in the silence of the forest, where there is no bass to be heard, the DAT recorder picks up sounds that can be used later. 'There is no such thing as silence,' John Cage says in his book *Silence*. 'Something is always happening to make a sound.'[12] The fact that powerful bass-lines can be built from this – from apparently nothing – might have surprised even Cage. Digital

12. CAGE, John: op. cit., p. 191.

recorders have assumed the role of presentation. But silence is only one idea for a fat bass-line. For one of her most recent tracks, Andrea Parker drove her car through a car wash, filtered the deepest sounds out of the recordings of the rattling and roaring and constructed a bass-line out of it.

A fat bass – to define it for a moment – is a bass fed with as many sounds as possible. It needs as many ideas and technical treatments as possible to be more defined, designed and complex. Following the same logic, we might answer the question that frequently pops up in hip-hop, 'Bass how long can you go?' by saying that it goes further the better fed the bass is, the better the attached amplifiers and speakers can keep the fat basses marching. But the basic equipment (and nourishment) has to come from the artist.

On his track 'Kenuri' (on Mo'Wax), the Japanese musician DJ Krush, who produces a form of hip-hop essentialism that is at once ascetic and modernist, used a surprising trick. He sampled the sound of a steel drum being struck with drumsticks under water. He got exactly the sound he wanted: the illusion, now a sonic truth, of a gigantic bass drum, that sounded not only deep and fat but also cold and technological.

At the beginning of all his tracks is the production of a drum loop and then the construction of a bass-line. If these two elements – Krush calls them the 'basement' of his tracks – are not stable and convincing, the track sinks. His models for this kind of song production are EPMD, who created all their pieces around the bass-line. Unlike most hip-hop musicians, DJ Krush is bored by the unchanging bass-line based on James Brown's funk. When he uses these classics, he slows them down dramatically and then takes only fragments out of the sound spectrum until everything sounds as dark and ghostly as he wants. His bass experiments mean that he has to buy a new loudspeaker almost every week, because they regularly explode. Krush's neighbours regularly complain because the bass-lines make their furniture slide through their apartments. In Japan he is rarely able to complete the final mix of his tracks because the bass is so misunderstood there. Most engineers and studio technicians come from jazz or rock music, and want a clear, tame bass, while hip-hop – according to Krush – needs a dirty and menacing bass. For that reason he primarily produces in the USA and sometimes in England.

Never have so many different varieties of DJ music been defined by the use of the bass or defined themselves as bass terrorism. Apart from the drum'n'bass examined above, there is the Detroit bass sound, a gloomy, melancholy variation of the breakbeats that underlay the first hip-hop, and the bastard child of Detroit techno – a new variety of industrial funk with shatteringly depressing lyrics and an incredibly dirty-mixed bass backdrop that sounds decidedly cheap.

The only conciliatory variant is Miami bass rap, a sub-species of rap built for big auto-subwoofers, and the neo funky bass sound of the West Coast rappers. What all these variations share is the manipulative force that this sound exerts on people. They are all powerful sounds, some of them overwhelming, some of them frightening the first time you hear them, but they tend to be addictive for people who have got used to this manipulation. Bass-heads want to be immersed in the heaviness of it all without losing their sensitivity to the gentle, quiet notes. To this extent, drum'n'bass above all, but also the Detroit bass sound with its hyper-sensitive high-pitch landscapes, satisfy these desires.

Andrea Parker has said in an interview that she was inspired by a documentary film showing babies responding happily to deep frequencies in the womb, while higher frequencies disturbed them. Similar effects of deep frequencies are used in music therapy and by tribes in Africa and Asia. Interestingly, children and young people who were born deaf or with severe hearing damage often have a passion for techno clubs, because they are places where you can not only hear the bass but feel it as well. So music can be perceived with senses other than that of hearing. Because the fat bass sound creates a leap in musical perception that would have fascinated Hegel. If hearing is considered as theoretically a perceiving sense, and touch as a practical sense, the bass can be said to have achieved a direct and dialectical connection between the two. This might be a reason for the pleasure that we all take in the new basses.

Andrea Parker says women react more strongly to the bass than men do. Or more precisely: more women than men react to the bass at all. Apart from her personal research, Parker adduces the evidence of the Renegade Soundwave track entitled 'Women respond to Bass'. For Fetish, one of the three musicians in Turntable Terranova, the bass is 'the mother and the abyss of my soul'. No wonder the bass has become so important: it may be the final passion of a generation driven less by ideals than by radical perceptions and the promises of happiness that go with them.

In London drum'n'bass clubs like Metalheadz, people are said to have developed nosebleeds as a result of the heavy bass sound. Ecstasy demands its blood sacrifices.

HOMEWORK

French duo Daft Punk put the possibility of a reconciliation between funk, disco, house, techno and industrial to a new test. Like Detroit veterans Jeff Mills and Carl Craig, they combined the rawness and heaviness of the sounds with the warmth and seductiveness of the old disco and funk grooves. What was new was the experimental, multi-layered way in which Daft Punk take their songs so close to the edge of collapse that rescue looks impossible. A danger apparent in 'Pump Up the Volume' by M/A/R/R/S – and now it's back again, ten years later and more relaxed and freestyle than ever. Daft Punk aren't afraid of quotation, and with their desire for wild collage they are constantly challenging their own musicality, turning many individual fragments into a track. Like many other musicians in DJ culture, Daft Punk have published their musical ancestral line, which in this case extends from Sun Ra and Red Crayola via Roxy Music and Television to Grandmaster Flash and Carl Craig. These are their teachers, whom they don't hate but love, as the song 'Teachers' makes apparent. These, then, are the teachers who have set their 'homework'.

In the list of songs, next to the title there is an exercise book with the title of the album where you would expect the name of the school subject. This idea of an innovative record as homework, conveyed through the band's own models and ancestors, is another flirtatious and confident game on the part of Thomas Bangalter and Guy-Manuel de Homem-Christo: respect means obligation, and it finds fulfilment. The statements of gratitude and respect are rounded off with a quotation from Beach Boys mastermind Brian Wilson, which, in its passion, openness and freedom from ideology, sums up the Daft Punk sound: 'I wanted to write joyful music that made other people feel good. Music that helps and heals, because I believe that music is God's voice.'

Homework: a suggestion of DIY, of work done in the home, of imperfection. The record almost lives up to the idea of presenting the incomplete and sketchy as such – if one didn't, in the end, have the feeling that the two French musicians had lured us into a trap with the idyllic notion that we are looking over their shoulders while they produce their tracks. The incomplete sounds complete, the sketchy sounds perfect, and all the snapshots on the cover and the inner sleeve are merely further proof that the gesture of 'homework' is thoroughly thought out and cleverly glued together. From the live party intro 'Daftendirect' to the final track 'Funk Ad', a backwards-dubbed jingle from 'Da Funk': here, as in many works this century, the fragmentary is not one of 'some contingent particular', rather the fragment is 'that portion of the totality of the art work that resists being integrated'.[13] Art can never be perfect, but while it knows that and accepts it affirmatively, fragmentation and 'disjointedness' (Adorno) can innocently try for perfection. 'Art of the highest calibre pushes beyond totality towards a state of fragmentation.'[14] Adorno recognized the fragmentary nature of all the modern art that he valued and considered important: from Kafka to Schönberg. The problem of closure in an art work must be seen against the background of a traditional understanding of art. Daft Punk insists on the idea of 'homework' (or DIY) in order to close the art work, ostentatiously retracting claims to completeness. The closure of the work grants it the possibility of becoming pop. For Adorno, this

13. ADORNO, Theodor W.: Aesthetic Theory, p. 67.

14. Ibid. p. 212.

Inner sleeve of Daft Punk double album Homework

stabilization of the fragmentary would be unacceptable, for pop music it isn't.

Daft Punk's biggest hit is called 'Da Funk', and it made the charts across Europe. Once again the state of the perceptual arts allowed the wider public to do something that is hard for cultural critics to understand: the avant-garde as such was ignored, and simply swallowed and honoured as an entertaining, fun, funky new thing – and more importantly, it sold. 'Da Funk' has a romantic guitar loop, a murderous bass-line and a number of fades that are mixed as crudely as if the two musicians had produced the track on a simple DJ mixing desk. It crashes and hammers, hisses and whirrs, and all the notes and sounds seem to be driven apart by a powerful centrifugal force. Once again it is the bass, Da Bomb in physical form, that keeps together something that strives for freedom and independence. Nothing seems to fit together, and at the end of the song everything has meshed: crude, riven, yet addictive to listen to.

The crowning glory is the video for the track, which has been shown on MTV since February 1997, and whose stylistic peculiarity corresponds to the music at the highest level. Disguised as a clip from a film, we see a well-built man with scruffy clothes, his leg in plaster and a ghetto blaster in his hand walking through downtown New York. Only for the very first moment, the first nanosecond, do you see the protagonist as a man. After that he has a dog's head and dog's paws. He's walking through the streets and no one turns to look at him. Two street-boys laugh at the way he limps, and tell him at the traffic light, when the hefty bass-line begins on the off-beat, that they like the music coming out of his ghetto blaster. He thanks them politely, and the next moment someone jostles him in passing. Someone asks directions of him, but won't accept the answer because he's only been there for a month. When buying a book at a street stall he is badly treated because his music is too loud. In this scene he is seen rummaging in his wallet before buying a book entitled *Big City Nights*, and briefly losing himself in an old family photograph. The photograph shows a typical American in a typical driveway, washing his late 70s BMW, and at the edge a child helping him wash it, with the arms and head of a young dog. Finally he ends up at the window of a deli, through which he sees a pert and pretty girl doing her shopping. He runs his paw over his long ears and goes into the deli to greet the woman. She's surprised, and reacts in a shyly friendly way. After a brief pause he reveals himself as her former neighbour Charles, who grew up with her. Only at that moment does she recognize him, and throws herself around his neck. She invites him to her place, and they wait at a bus stop. When the bus comes, the woman gets in straight away, and polite Charles waits until everyone has got off. But then he spots a notice saying 'No Radios. No Smoking. No Spitting.' He is frightened, and the bus drives off without him. Surprised and disappointed we see the young woman looking out. With his shoulders hunched, Charles lifts up his ghetto blaster. 'No Radios' – he can't get on. He trots alone and lonely to the next crossing. The video is over.

The dialogue in the video is mixed as if in a film, the music is jerkily faded out. The aesthetic of the clip is that of an American mainstream movie with a hint of independent authenticity. There's nothing to suggest that it's a fairy tale or a fantasy film. The dissonance between the appearance of the dog-man and the reactions of the people around him make the video an indigestible masterpiece.

Charles is excluded because he has his leg in plaster, because he listens to loud music on his ghetto blaster and because he's new to the city; the fact that he is a dog seems to be a problem only for the audience. Charles' kind and friendly demeanour, his mixture of shyness and openness, his sad expression and his melancholy way of dressing are upsetting – much more upsetting than characters in video clips ever normally are. The banality of the scenes and the relaxed way in which they are incorporated in the film force us repeatedly to abandon our own stereotypical perception. The puzzle of the video can't be cracked: the absurdity is never broken down into a form of comprehensibility or something that can be controlled. Unlike Kafka's *Metamorphosis*, there is no breakdown or analysis of the whole. Absurdity in normality is normality.

With this video, Daft Punk present their work just as smartly as their music: skilfully disguised as mainstream and constantly referring beyond it. The VJs stand there helplessly, like little children, when they have to go on presenting after the clip. The actual trick of the video is a constant contradiction between what the viewer sees and expects and the reality of the video in which the most significant motif, man as dog, is not commented upon by the story on display. The reactions of the characters in the video give us an image of Charles which – ignoring his canine physiognomy – refers to a sad life in normality: with his leg in plaster, a tattered book and the look of an Everyman. Behind Charles' external appearance, which one would expect to define him entirely, the video forces the viewer to imagine the person that sees and deals with his surroundings in the video. An awkward task that makes it clear with what semantic fine-tuning Daft Punk, after a hundred years of modern art, try to tear apart reality and the reproduction of reality in art and leave it disturbing and unresolved for the recipient.

THE NEW NORMALITY

DJs now enjoy the respect they deserve. On Germany's Viva music tv channel, there's a programme in which disc jockey's like Carl Craig, Carl Cox and Westbam present their work at the record decks. By dividing the screen into three, the skilful process can be seen very precisely. The interviews with DJ Disko and Sabine Christ – both of them working as DJs – prepare the ground for these sets and explain the musical background and artistic strategies of the DJs. After an initial blind sympathy for the techno sound of rave, this programme has now opened up to almost all kinds of DJ sound, and clearly freed itself from the potentially clichéd stereotypes of a rave programme.

Berlin record label K7 began, with its series *DJ-Kicks*, to release on vinyl and CD DJ sets that had previously existed only as either authorized or bootleg tapes. The sets, limited to 80 minutes each, were originally recorded in the studio and then released, but now more

#1 PUNKS
Means Being sullen, liking reggae and looking dead cool (The Clash axis). Swearing and self-destructing (Sex Pistols axis). Together they promised Sten guns in Knightsbridge and were nasty about the Queen
Cause of failure Taking money and scarpering to Malibu. Or accepting a post on *The Guardian*
Legacy Jon Savage's books. Tony Parsons on TV. Green Day
Influence on mainstream politics Jeremy Paxman's interview technique

They Tried To Change The World...

#2 CRUSTIES
Means Scupper the wicked capitalist machine by dodging the DSS and refusing to buy evil consumer items like soap and combs
Cause of failure The Levellers. Members deserting to join hedonistic "Goa Trance" faction
Legacy Buskers. Leeds students. Megadog
Influence on mainstream politics Ongoing chain-yourself-to-JCBs road protest mayhem

#3 MODS
Means Keep Britain tidy looking
Cause of failure Socio-political leanings of early Weller ("That's Entertainment", "Eton Rifles") soon forgotten in favour of songs about "wood", "sun" and "trees". New clobber over new world order
Legacy Ocean Colour Scene. That month when Blur decided they were "mod". Return of *Quadrophenia*
Influence on mainstream politics Undetectable. Not Major's suits

#4 GOTHS
Means Pretending to be a vampire
Cause of failure Obsession with necrophilia, Bela Lugosi and The Mission unable to gain stranglehold on Middle England's village greens
Legacy A generation of males able to apply lipstick without smudging
Influence on mainstream politics John Redwood

#5 HIPPIES
Means We shall overcome by dropping acid, being scruffy and liking the Grateful Dead
Cause of failure Apathetic sit-down manifesto at odds with forwarding the revolution. Marketing jobs accepted immediately on leaving university
Legacy Glastonbury Festival. The inexplicable phenomenon that is the continued career of Hawkwind. And The Orb. And Kula Shaker
Influence on mainstream politics Bill Clinton

#6 ACID HOUSE
Means Drug and hug your way to a better future
Cause of failure Unifying aspect of large-scale communal gatherings hampered by having to spend the next three days in bed. As a design for life, kissing your mates and dancing badly not exactly *Das Kapital*
Legacy Advertisers inheriting the phrase "sorted"
Influence on mainstream politics Strangely, politicians remain largely unenamoured of the hedonistic joys of repetitive beats. They've even passed a law against them

#7 INDIE KIDS
Means Being sensitive, misunderstood and unable to pull at parties. More recently, indie's pulled its socks up, losing its cardigan-and-glasses stigma. Or at least it's pretending it's being "ironic"
Cause of failure Spinelessness of Eighties faction means they never had the balls to put Margaret On The Guillotine. Jarvis' recent Michael Jackson hijack promises a zanier rebirth
Legacy The Fall still releasing albums
Influence on mainstream politics Oasis' place on the Blair household stereo already confirmed

#8 HIP HOP
Means Marxist-style power to the people through a mic, turntables and a sampler
Cause of failure Insurrectionary approach (Public Enemy) binned in favour of waving guns about. Tendency to shoot own party members a problem
Legacy Adidas shoes. Booming small-arms industry
Influence on mainstream politics To be fair, quite considerable in US. "Cop Killer" furore results in man called Tracey (Ice-T) being accepted as socio-political icon

#9 JUNGLE
Means Parent-baffling souvenir of hardcore days. Difficult to dance to
Cause of failure Trotsky-like failure to compromise militant underground manifesto. Aural terrorism hard to take seriously after "Touch 'n' Fresh" ad. Plus failure, post-Baby D, to set the charts alight
Legacy Really noisy traffic lights in south London
Influence on mainstream politics Swinging New Labour almost certain to reflect "the kids'" love of drum and bass. Jack Straw to promise he'll be "ruff" on crime

They were great at changing their hairstyles, but less successful at altering history. GARETH GRUNDY on 30 years of subcultural under-achievement

The end of utopias: 30 years of resistance rituals (page from The Face 1/1997)

Carl Craig

Stacey Pullen's DJ Kicks album: Detroit genius for the museum

and more DJs tend to prepare their mix digitally with additional technology, incorporating loops and samples, and mixing in individual channels. The conception of the series, designed to bring the DJ's mixing arts to as large a section of the buying public as possible, as authentically as possible and with good sound quality, was extended, and a hybrid form between remix, DJ set and track production emerged. Artists were granted maximum freedom, within the framework of the concept, to produce their idea of a master mix. The selection of pieces, most of which feature recent tracks, not only permits a glance into the record box, but at the same time presents a compressed form of the DJ's style and its component parts. Affinities, passions and historical roots are understood in discographic terms, and rendered listenable. Munich's DJ Hell used his X-mix record to make a 'pure version' of his history of electronic music accessible. Carl Craig sampled a little of all his pieces and at the end of his mix he presented a piece of his own made up almost entirely from the previous tracks – as if to prove that DJ music lives on the internalization and honouring of the DJ's personal preferences, and that something new and original can or – perhaps – must emerge out of it.

Everything has become quite natural. DJ sets as an art form have become as normal as the productions of many DJs, in which the record deck has vanished from the production process. Works with orchestras, rock bands or jazz musicians testify to the choice that artists from DJ backgrounds allow themselves. At the same time there are always practices, concerts or club evenings in which this work finds its way back to the basic unit of turntable plus mixing desk. DJ music has entered a stage of relaxed ease, in which its rootedness in its origins is so conscious, so informing, that those roots no longer need to be presented ostentatiously. The replacement of one stage of development by the next has become a simultaneity of the means and methods with which DJ music can be produced. Just as drum'n'bass re-established the roots element within DJ music a few years ago, countless freestyle experiments, from electronic music via jazz to world music are including every imaginable mixing opportunity in terms

DJ BOOTH ETIQUETTE

1. Say *"HI"* -- then *"BYE"*!! (Better yet, wave from the dance floor).

2. If DJ is in this position 🎧 he obviously cannot speak to you.

3. No person in this booth is employed by a record store.

4. The dance floor is where all the people are dancing -- **NOT HERE!**

5. Since the DJ doesn't dj in the lounge, then loungers shouldn't lounge in the DJ booth.

6. When in the DJ booth, if you find yourself saying *"Excuse me"* more than once, then you should excuse yourself from the booth.

(These DJ booth rules and regulations were created by RBM, XTCee, and Sasha. They shall be enforced by club management, security and DJ's around the world). We thank you for your full cooperation, support, and most of all, your sense of humor!

T-shirt with advice on behaving at the DJ desk

of arrangement and composition. Electronic music's modern dream of using all sources of notes and sounds side by side is realized without unnecessary drama. The success of DJ music depends not least on freedom in the choice of media, and the ease and curiosity with which these complex possibilities are used. While current pop music and rock music – which always sounds stuck in the past – are trapped within an old structure, the system of DJ culture is revealed as an open one.

The confidence of belonging to a kind of music that has a future only strengthens the artists' determination to strike out in new directions and conquer unknown territories. The concept of the avant-garde, on the other hand, has lost its validity because none of its drama and pathos is apparent in this kind of music. For DJ musicians, the new is normal, the old has become meaningful tradition. Drum'n'bass DJs like Fabio, Grooverider, Peshay and Goldie have stated this time and again in interviews. Nomadic wandering between different kinds of style, instrumentation and production structure casually produces sounds that have never been heard before. With each new step, countless new options are uncovered, ready to be used. While the old conception of DJ music, whose document and manifesto forms the heart of this book, was still greatly influenced by the historical dialectic of dissolution and new beginning, the present nature of the music proves to be seductively multi-layered and significantly indefinable. The common denominator, however, remains the aesthetic centre of the music, which can still be found in the turntables plus mixing desk.

The development goes on, and engineers are constantly inventing new instruments and computers with which the audible universe can be captured and manipulated. The confidence with which this music allows us to look into the future seems boundless. This confidence lives in the sense – despite twenty years of history – of belonging to a pioneer unit for whose discoveries no horizon has yet been found. The fate of classical Modernism has shown us how quickly pioneers can become conservatives. But Modernism made a quite different claim: it wanted to created new things for dogmatic reasons as well as passionate ones. The dogmatic respectability of DJ culture will at least spare it the great disappointment at the end of its explorations. But who knows, perhaps the disillusion will be just as great.

Although cultural history, like all forms of historiography, should avoid making predictions, there are good reasons for this confidence. The proliferation of computer technology appears above all to promise a great deal to an art form which, from the start, when computers were still unwieldy monsters, believed in and profited from that technology. For staking everything on what we now know to have been the future, electronic artists have been richly rewarded. The struggle against aporias and paradoxes that was fought so desperately by classical artists is something that DJ culture has been spared. 'Thus technical appliances,' says Hegel, 'make their appearance when a need for them is experienced.'[15]

15. HEGEL, G.W.F., The Philosophy of History, p. 410.

BIBLIOGRAPHY

ADORNO, Theodor W.: Musikalische Schriften VI, Gesammelte Werke Vol. 19, Frankfurt/Main 1984
– Aesthetic Theory, Trans. C. Lenhardt, London 1984

AITKEN, Hugh G.J.: The Continuous Wave: Technology and American Radio, 1900–1932, Princeton (New Jersey), 1985

BALDWIN, James: The Fire Next Time, New York 1993

BANNERMAN, R. LeRoy: Norman Corwin and Radio – The Golden Years, Alabama 1986

BARCK, Karlheinz et al: Aisthesis. Wahrnehmung heute oder Perspektiven einer anderen Ästhetik, Leipzig 1990

BARNARD, Stephen: On The Radio – Music Radio in Britain, Milton Keynes 1989

BARTHES, Roland: Mythologies, Trans. Annette Lavers, London 1972
– The Rustle of Language, Berkeley – Los Angeles 1989

BAUSCH, Hans: Rundfunk in Deutschland, Vol. 1, Munich 1980

BEADLE, Jeremy J.; Will Pop Eat Itself? Pop Music in the Soundbite Era, London 1993

BECKMAN, Janette/ ADLER, B.: Rap, New York 1991

BEERMANN, Wilhelm, et al:
– Fünf Interviews zur Veränderung des Socialen, Stuttgart 1992

BELZ, Carl: The Story of Rock, New York 1973 (2nd edition)

BERGMAN, Billy/ HORN, Richard: Recombinant Do-Re-Mi, New York 1985

BENJAMIN, Walter: Illuminations, Trans. Harry Zohn, London 1970
– One-Way Street and

Other Writings, Trans. Edward Jephcott and Kingsley Shorter, London 1979

BENNETT, Tony et al (Ed.): Rock and popular music – politics, policies, institutions, London – New York 1993

BLOCH, Ernst: Tübinger Einleitung in die Philosophie, Frankfurt/Main 1985

BLOCK, Ursula/ GLASMEIER, Michael (Ed.): Broken Music. Artist's Recordworks, Berlin – The Hague – Grenoble 1988

BODY, Veruschka/ WEIBEL, Peter (Ed.): Clip, Klapp, Bum. Von der visuellen Musik zum Musikvideo, Cologne 1987

BOLZ, Norbert: Die Welt als Chaos und als Simulation, Munich 1992

BONSON, Manfred et al: Lexikon Pop. Ein Sachwort ABC der Unterhaltungsmusik von Operette und Schlager bis Folk, Jazz und Rock, Wiesbaden 1977

BOSSE, Heinrich: Autorschaft ist Werkherrschaft, Munich – Vienna – Zürich 1981

BOULEZ, Pierre: Orientations. Collected Writings, London 1990

BRADLEY, Dick: Understanding Rock'n'Roll. Popular Music in Britain 1955–1964, Buckingham – Philadelphia 1992

BRADLEY, Lloyd: The Rock Yearbook 1989, New York 1988

BROMBERT, Craig: The Wicked Ways of Malcolm McLaren, New York 1989

BROWN, James (with TUCKER, Bruce): The Godfather of Soul, New York – London 1986

BUSBY, Linda/ PARKER, Donald: The Art and Science of Radio, Boston et al 1984

CAGE, John: Silence, London 1968

CANTOR, Louis: Wheelin' On Beale. How WDIA-Memphis Became the Nation's First All-Black Radio-Station and Created the Sound that Changed America, New York 1992

CARR, Roy, et al: The Hip. Hipsters, Jazz and the Beat Generation, London – Boston 1986

CHAMBERS, Ian: Urban Rhythms. Pop Music and Popular Culture, New York 1985

CHAPPLE, Steven/

GAROFALO, Reebee: Rock'n'roll is here to pay: the history and politics of the music industry, Chicago 1977

CHIPP, Herschel B. (Ed.): Theories of Modern Art. A Source Book by Artists and Critics, Berkeley – Los Angeles – London 1968

COHN, Nik: AwopBopaLooBop AlopBamBoom. Pop from the Beginning, London 1969

COSTELLO, Mark/ WALLACE, David Foster: Signifying Rappers. Rap and Race in the Urban Present, New York 1990

CROSS, Brian: It's Not About a Salary… Rap, Race and Resistance in Los Angeles, London – New York 1993

CURTIS, Jim: Rock Eras. Interpretations of Music and Society, 1954–1984, Bowling Green (Ohio) 1987

DeCURTIS, Anthony: Present Tense. Rock'n'Roll and Culture, Durham – London 1992

DELEUZE, Gilles: Kleine Schriften, Berlin 1980
– Idem/ GUATTARI, Félix: The Anti-Oedipus. Capitalism and Schizophrenia, Trans. R. Hurley, M. Sear and H.R. Lane, London 1977
– Idem/ GUATTARI, Félix: Rhizome, Paris 1976

DeLONG, Thomas A.: The Mighty Music Box. The Golden Age of Musical Radio, Los Angeles 1980

DESCARTES, René: A Discourse on Method, Meditations and Principles, Trans. John Veitch, London 1992

DIEDERICHSEN, Diedrich: Sexbeat, Cologne 1985
– Freiheit macht arm, Cologne 1993
– Schocker, Stile und Moden der Subkultur, Reinbek bei Hamburg 1983
– DJ Yearbook 1994, London 1993

DUFRESNE, David: Yo! Révolution Rap: l'histoire, les groupes, le mouvement, Paris 1991

EBERLY, Philip K.: Music in the Air. America's Changing Tastes in Popular Music, 1920–1980, New York 1982

EHRENSTEIN, David/ REED, Bill: Rock on Film, New York 1982

EISEN, Jonathan (Ed.): The Age of Rock. Sounds of the American Cultural

Revolution, New York 1969

ERB, Ernst: Radios von gestern, Lucerne 1991

EWALD, François: Pariser Gespräche, Berlin 1989

EWING, Sam: You're on the Air, Blue Ridge Summit (Pennsylvania) 1972

FAB 5 FREDDY: Fresh Fly Flavor: words and phrases of the hip-hop generation, Stamford 1992

FERNANDO, S.H.: The New Beats. Exploring the Music, Culture and Attitudes of Hip-Hop, New York 1994

FEYERABEND, Paul: Wissenschaft als Kunst, Frankfurt 1984

FOUCAULT, Michel: Language, Counter-Memory, Practice, Trans. Donald F. Bouchard and Sherry Simon, Cornell 1977
L'Ordre du Discours, Paris 1971
The Order of Things, London 1970

FREDERKING, Klaus (Ed.): Rock Session 8, Sound and Vision, Reinbek bei Hamburg 1985

FRITH, Simon (Ed.): Facing the Music, New York 1989
– Sound Effects. Youth, Leisure and the Politics of Rock'n'Roll
– Idem/ GOODWIN, Andrew: On Record – Rock, Pop and the Written Word, London 1990
– Idem/ HORNE, Howard: Art into Pop, London – New York 1987

GATES, Henry Louis Jr.: The Signifying Monkey. A Theory of African-American Literary Criticism, Oxford (et al) 1988

GEORGE, Nelson: The Death of Rhythm & Blues, Harmondsworth 1988
– Buppies, B-Boys, Baps & Bohos. Notes on Post-Soul Black Culture, New York 1992

GILLESPIE, Dizzy/ FRASER, Al: Dizzy – To Be or Not to Bop. The autobiography of Dizzy Gillespie, London – Melbourne – New York 1982

GILLETT, Charlie: The Sound of the City. The Rise of Rock and Roll, London 1984 (2nd edition)

GLASER, Peter (Ed.): Rawums. Texte zum Thema, Cologne 1984

GODARD, Jean-Luc: Godard on Godard; Critical Writings. Edited by Jean Narboni and Tom Milne, New York, 1972

– Nouvelle Vague – Presseheft, Munich 1990

GODFREY, John (Ed.): a decade of i-Deas – the encyclopaedia of the '80s, London 1990

GOETZ, Rainald: Irre, Frankfurt am Main 1983

– Hirn, Frankfurt am Main 1986

– Kontrolliert, Frankfurt am Main 1988

– Kronos. Berichte, Frankfurt am Main 1993

GOLDMAN, Albert: Disco, New York 1978

– Sound Bites, New York 1992

GÖÖCK, Roland: Erfindungen – Radio Fernsehen Computer, Künzelsau 1989

GOODWIN, Andrew: Dancing in the Distraction Factory – Music, Television and Popular Culture, Minneapolis 1992

GORDY, Berry: To Be Loved. The Music, the Magic, the Memories of Motown: an Autobiography, New York 1994

GRAVES, Barry/ SCHMIDT-JOOS, Siegfried: Das neue Rock-Lexikon, 2 vols., Reinbek bei Hamburg 1990

GREENBERG, Clement: The Collected Essays and Criticism, 2 vols

GÜLDEN, Jörg/ HUMANN, Klaus (Ed.): Rocksession 2, Reinbek bei Hamburg 1981 (2nd edition)

GUNDEN, Keneth von: Postmodern Auteurs – Coppola, Lucas, De Palma, Spielberg and Scorsese, Jefferson (North Carolina) – London 1991

HAGER, Steven: Hip Hop. The Illustrated History of Break Dancing, Rap Music, and Graffiti, New York 1984

HALBSCHEFFEL, Bernward/ KNEIF, Tibor: Sachlexikon Rockmusik, Instrumente, Stile, Techniken, Industrie und Geschichte, Reinbek bei Hamburg 1982

HALPER, Donna L.: Radio Music Directing, Boston – London 1991

HANSON, Kitty: Disco Fever. The Beat, People, Places, Styles, Deejays, Groups & the Latest Disco Steps, New York 1978

HARTMANN, Walter/ POTT, Gregor (Ed.): Rock Session 6, Reinbek bei Hamburg

1982
HAUSER, Arnold: Kunst und Gesellschaft, Munich 1988
HEATLEY, Michael: The Ultimate Encyclopedia of Rock, New York 1993
HEBDIGE, Dick: Subculture, London – New York 1979
– Cut'n'Mix. Culture, Identity and Caribbean Music, London 1987
HEGEL, G.W.F.:
– Aesthetics, Trans. T.M. Knox, Oxford 1975
– Elements of the Philosophy of Right, Trans. H.B. Nisbet, Cambridge 1991
Lectures on the History of Philosophy. Trans. E.S. Haldane, 3 Vols, London 1892–96
– Phenomenology of Spirit, Trans. J.N. Findlay, Oxford 1977
– Philosophy of History, Trans. J. Sibree, New York 1991
HEIDEGGER, Martin: Being and Time, Trans. John Macquarrie & Edward Robinson, London 1962
– Basic Writings, Trans. D.F. Krell, London 1978
– Die Technik und die Kehre, Pfullingen 1988 (7th edition)
HELMS, S. (Ed.); Schlager in Deutschland, Wiesbaden 1972
HERMAN, Gary: Rock'n'Roll Babylon, New York 1982
HOLMAN, Michael: Breaking and the New York City Breakers, New York 1984
HORKHEIMER, Max: Zur Kritik der instrumentellen Vernunft, Frankfurt am Main 1991
– Idem/ ADORNO, Theodor W.: Dialectic of Enlightenment, Trans. John Cumming, London 1997
HUBER, Jörg (Ed.): Wahrnehmung von Gegenwart, Basel – Frankfurt am Main 1992
HÜNDGEN, Gerald (Ed.): Chasin' a Dream. Die Musik des schwarzen Amerika von Soul bis Hip Hop, Cologne 1989
HUYSSEN, Andreas/ SCHERPE, Klaus R.: Postmoderne – Zeichen eines kulturellen Wandels, Reinbek bei Hamburg 1986
– Ice T: The Ice Opinion. Ice T as told to Heidi Siegmund, New York 1994
– Jackson, John A.: Big Beat Heat. Alan Freed and the Early Years of Rock'n'Roll, New York

1991
JAKOB, Günther: Agit-Pop. Schwarze Musik und weisse Hörer, Berlin 1993

JAMESON, Frederic: Postmodernism, or the Cultural Logic of Late Capitalism, Durham (North Carolina) 1991

JOE, Radcliffe A.: This Business of Disco, New York 1980

JONES, K. Maurice: Say it Loud! The Story of Rap Music, Brookfield (Connecticut) 1994

JONES, LeRoi: Blues People, Edinburgh 1993

KAFKA, Franz: Tagebücher 1910–1923, Frankfurt am Main 1986

KAMPER, Dietmar/REIJEN, Willem van (Ed.): Die unvollendete Vernunft. Moderne versus Postmoderne, Frankfurt am Main 1987

KITTLER, Friedrich A.: Grammophon Film Typewriter, Berlin 1985
– Aufschreibesysteme 1800/1900, Munich 1985
– Draculas Vermächtnis. Technische Schriften, Leipzig 1993

KOCHMANN, Thomas: Rappin' and Stylin' Out. Communication in Urban Black America, Urbana – Chicago – London 1972

KOSSELECK, Reinhart/MEIER, Christian: Fortschritt, in: BRUNNER, Otto et al (Ed.): Geschichtliche Grundbegriffe, Vol. 2, Stuttgart 1975

KOSUTH, Joseph: Interviews 1969–1989, Stuttgart 1989

KREYE, Andrian: Aufstand der Gettos. Die Eskalation der Rassenkonflikte in Amerika, Cologne 1993

KÜHN, Helmut/WIEDMANN, Franz (Ed.): Die Philosophie und die Frage nach dem Fortschritt, Munich 1964

LAZARSFELD, Paul F./STANTON, Frank N. (Ed.): Radio Research 1941, New York 1979
– Radio Research 1942–1943, New York 1979

LICHTY, Lawrence W./TOPPING, Malachi C. (Ed.): American Broadcasting. A Source Book on the History of Radio and Television, New York 1986

LUHMANN, Niklas: Soziale Systeme. Grundriss einer allgemeinen Theorie, Frankfurt am Main 1987

– Die Kunst der Gesellschaft, Frankfurt am Main 1995

LYOTARD, Jean-François: Das Patchwork der Minderheiten, Berlin 1977

MacDONALD, J. Fred: Don't Touch That Dial! Radio Programming in American Life, 1920–1960, Chicago 1979

MacFARLAND, David T.: The Development of the Top 40 Radio Format, New York 1979

MAILER, Norman: The Long Patrol, New York 1971

MAJOR, Clarence: Juba to Jive. A Dictionary of African-American Slang, New York 1994

MARCUS, Greil: In the Fascist Bathroom, London 1993

– Lipstick Traces. A Secret History of the Twentieth Century, London 1997

– Mystery Train, London 1975

MARLOW, Curtis: Breakdancing, Cresskill (New Jersey) 1984

MARX, Karl: Capital, Chicago – London 1990

– Critique of Hegel's 'Philosophy of Right', Trans. Annette Jolin and Joseph O'Malley, Cambridge 1967

– A Contribution to the Critique of Political Economy, London – Moscow, 1970

– Idem/ ENGELS, Friedrich: The German Ideology, Moscow 1976

– Idem: The Holy Family, Moscow 1956

Idem: Über Kunst und Literatur, Vol. 1, Frankfurt am Main 1968

McLUHAN, Marshall: Understanding Media, London 1964

McQUISTON, Liz: Graphic Agitation. Social and Political Graphics since the Sixties, London 1993

MELLY, George: Revolt into Style. The Pop Arts in the 50s and 60s, Oxford 1989

MELTZER, R.: The Aesthetics of Rock, New York 1970

MEYER, Hazel: The Gold in Tin Pan Alley, Philadelphia – New York 1958

MIDDLETON, Richard: Studying Popular Music, Milton Keynes – Philadelphia 1990

MIEZITIS, Vita/ BERNSTEIN, Bill: Night-Dancin', New York 1980

MILLER, Jim: The Rolling Stone

Illustrated History of Rock & Roll, New York 1980

NELSON, Havelock/ GONZALES, Michael A.: Bring the Noise. A Guide to Rap-Music and HipHop Culture, New York 1991

NEWMAN, Mark: Entrepreneurs of Profit and Pride. From Black-Appeal to Radio Soul, New York 1988

NEWQUIST, H.P.: Music and Technology, New York 1991

NIETZSCHE, Friedrich: On the Genealogy of Morals, Trans. Walter Kaufmann and R.J. Hollingdale, New York 1967

NOBLE, Peter L.: Future Pop. Music for the Eighties, New York 1983

NOELLE-NEUMANN, Elisabeth et al (Ed.): Fischer Lexikon Publizistik Massenkommunikation, Frankfurt am Main 1991

OAKLEY, Nik/ GOTZ, Dave: The Music Spinners. Britain's Radio DJs, London 1976

OLIVER, Paul: Black Music in Britain. Essays on the Afro-Asian Contribution to Popular Music,
Milton Keynes – Philadelphia 1990

OSSI, Rapneck/ MOONDUST, Ziggie: Hiphop. Rap, graffiti, scratching, break-dance, Bergisch-Gladbach 1984

PASSMAN, Arnold: The Deejays, New York 1971

PECK, Abe (Ed.): Dancing Madness, New York 1976

PECK, Ira: The New Sound/ Yes!, New York 1966

PEELLAERT, Guy/ COHN, Nik: Rock Dreams, New York 1982

PIELKE, Robert G.: You Say You Want a Revolution. Rock Music in American Culture, Chicago 1986

POLLOCK, Bruce: When Rock was Young. A Nostalgic Review of the Top 40 era, New York 1981

PYNCHON, Thomas: The Crying of Lot 49, London 1967

– Gravity's Rainbow, London 1973

RAMSEY, Dan: How to be a Disc Jockey, Blue Ridge Summit (Pennsylvania) 1981

REDHEAD, Steve: The End-of-the-century Party. Youth and Pop Towards 2000,

Manchester – New York 1990

REDON, Odilon: A Soi-même, Paris 1961

REINHARDT, Ad: Art as Art: the Selected Writings of Ad Reinhardt, ed. B. Rose, New York 1975

REYNOLDS, Simon: Blissed Out. The Raptures of Rock, London 1990

RIEDEL, Heide: 60 Jahre Radio, Berlin 1987

RIESE, Utz: Falsche Dokumente, Postmoderne Texte aus den USA, Leipzig 1993

RIHA, Karl (Ed.): Dada Berlin. Texte, Manifeste, Aktionen, Stuttgart 1982

RITTER, Joachim: Fortschritt, in: idem (Ed.): Historisches Wörterbuch der Philosophie, Vol. 2, Basel – Stuttgart 1972, pp. 1032–1059

ROSE, Cynthia: Design after Dark. The Story of Dancefloor Style, London 1991

ROSE, Tricia: Black Noise. Rap Music and Black Culture in Contemporary America, Hanover (New England) – London 1994

ROSS, Andrew/ ROSE, Tricia (Ed.): Microphone Fiends.

Youth Music & Youth Culture, New York – London 1994

RUCKER, Rudy et al: Mondo 2000 – A User's Guide to the New Edge, New York 1992

RUSHKOFF, Douglas (Ed.): The GenX Reader, New York 1994

RYZIN, Lani van: Disco, New York – London 1979

SALZINGER, Helmut: Rock Power. Oder wie musikalisch ist die Revolution, Frankfurt am Main 1975

SAVAGE, Jon: England's Dreaming. Sex Pistols and Punk Rock, London 1992

SCHEURER, Timothy E. (Ed.): American Popular Music, Volume II: The Age of Rock, Bowling Green (Ohio) 1989

SCHÖNBERG, Arnold: Stil und Gedanke, Leipzig 1989

SEDLMAYR, Hans: Die Revolution der modernen Kunst, Hamburg 1955

SEEGER, Charles: Studies in Musicology 1935–1975, Berkeley – London – Los Angeles 1977

SERRES, Michel: Esthétiques sur

Carpaccio, Paris 1980
- Le Parasite, Paris 1975
- L'Hermaphrodite. Sarrasine sculpteur, Paris 1987
SHANNON, Doug: Off the Record, Cleveland 1982
SHAW, Arnold: Dictionary of American Pop/Rock, New York – London 1982
- Rock'n'Roll. Die Stars, die Musik und die Mythen der 50er Jahre, Reinbek bei Hamburg 1978
- Black Popular Music in America. From the Spirituals, Minstrels and Ragtime to Soul, Disco and Hip-Hop, New York – London 1985
- Soul. Von den Anfängen im Blues zu den Hits aus Memphis und Philadelphia, Reinbek bei Hamburg 1980
- The Rock Revolution, New York – London 1969
- Honkers and Shouters. The Golden Years of Rhythm & Blues, New York 1978
SILBERMANN, Alphons; Musik als Phänomen sozialer Gruppen- prozesse, in: HOFFMANN-RIEM, Wolfgang/ TEICHERT, Will (Ed.): Musik in den Medien: Programmgestaltung im Spannungsfeld von Dramaturgie, Industrie und Publikum, Baden-Baden 1986, pp. 113–125
SKLAR, Rick: Rocking America. How the All-Hit Radio Stations Took Over, New York 1984
SMALL, Michael: Break it Down. The Inside Story from the New Leaders of Rap, New York 1982
SONTAG, Susan: A Susan Sontag Reader, New York 1982
SPENCER, Jon Michael: Protest & Praise. Sacred Music of Black Religion, Minneapolis 1990
STANLEY, Lawrence A. (Ed.): Rap: the Lyrics. With an introduction by Jefferson Morley, New York 1992
STEWART, Tony: Cool Cats. 25 years of Rock'n'Roll style, New York 1982
STOCKHAUSEN, Karlheinz: Texte zur Musik 1963–1970, Vol. 3, Cologne 1971
STONE, Terri: Music Producers. Conversations with Today's Top Record Makers, Emeryville (California) 1992

STRAUSS, Neil (Ed.): Radiotext(e), New York 1993

TATE, Greg: Flyboy in the Buttermilk, New York 1992

TAYLOE, Paul: Impresario. Malcolm McLaren and the British New Wave, New York 1988

THEWELEIT, Klaus: Buch der Könige (Vol. 1). Orpheus (und) Eurydike, Frankfurt am Main 1988

TOBLER, John: This Day in Rock: Day by Day Record of Rock's Biggest News Stories, New York 1993

TOOP, David: Rap Attack. African Rap to Global Hip Hop, London – New York 1991 (revised and expanded edition)
– Ocean of Sound. Aether talk, ambient sound, and imaginary worlds, London – New York 1995

TOSCHES, Nick: Unsung Heroes of Rock'n'Roll. The Birth of Rock in the Wild Years before Elvis, New York 1991

TZARA, Tristan, Sept manifestes Dada, Paris 1921

USLAN, Michael/ SOLOMON, Bruce: Dick Clark's the First 25 Years of Rock & Roll, New York 1981

VASARI, Giorgio: The Lives of the Painters, Sculptors and Architects, Trans. A.B. Hinds, London 1927

VILARI, Jack/ VILARI, Kathleen Sims: (The Official Guide to) Disco Dance Steps, Northbrook (Illinois) 1978

VINCENT, Rickey: Funk. The Music, the People, and the Rhythm of the One, New York 1995

VOLOSINOV, Valentin N.: Marxism and the Philosophy of Language, Trans. Ladislav Matejka and I.R. Titunik, New York – London 1973

WALLIS, Brian (Ed.): Art after Modernism. Rethinking Representation, New York 1989

WARHOL, Andy: From A to B and Back Again. The Philosophy of Andy Warhol, New York – London 1975

WHITCOMB, Ian: After the Ball. Pop Music from Rag to Rock, New York 1972

WICKE, Peter: Bigger than Life. Rock & Pop in den USA, Leipzig 1991

WOODMANSEE, Martha/ JASZI, Peter: The Construction of

Authorship. Textual
Appropriation in Law
and Literature,
Durham – London
1994
WOLFE, Tom: The
Kandy-Kolored
Tangerine-Flake
Streamline Baby,
London 1966
– The Pump-House
Gang, New York 1993
WOLFF, Janet: The
Social Production of
Art, New York 1993

MAGAZINE ARTICLES

ALETTI, Vince: Lost in Music. The Dancing Machinery: An Oral History, in: Village Voice – Rock'n'Roll Quarterly, Summer 1993, pp. 15ff. + 23

AMARETTO, Joel: Neue Europäische Elektroschule, in: Frontpage 2/1995, p. 42f.

BAKER, Lindsay: Funki Like a Dred, in: The Face 4/1989, pp. 60–64

BÖHM, Thomas: Was ist House Music, in: Musik Express 5/1988

BORROMINI, Franco: Bye, Bye, Phil! in: FAZ, 23.3.1982

BÜCKERT, Heike: Bam! Bam! Bam!, in: Frontpage 10/1991, p. 6f.

BUG, Christian: Tanz den Hitler!, in: Tip, 18.8.1988

CHUCK D.: Arbeiten wie James Bond, in: Spiegel Spezial 'Pop und Politik' 2/1994, pp. 55–59

COSGROVE, Stuart: The DJs They Couldn't Hang, in: NME, 6.8.1986

—Pump it Up, Homeboy, in: NME, 12.9.1987

CRYSELL, Andy: Mo Wax Than Most, in: Dazed & Confused 9/1994, p. 53

DALTON, Steve: Herb Crawlers, in: NME, 15.2.1992

DENIS, Reginald C.: 25 Old School Turning Points, in: The Source 11/1993, p. 54f.

DENSELOW, Robin: Here Comes the Wolfman, in: The Guardian, 27.10.1981

DIEDERICHSEN, Diedrich: Wer fürchtet sich vor dem Cop Killer? Zehn Thesen, in: Spiegel Spezial 'Pop und Politik' 2/1994, pp. 23–27

– Copy Right, in: Konkret 12/1987

– Vom Ende der Wahrheit, in: Konkret 5/1990

ENGELHARDT, Ingo: Herr der Rille, in: Tip, 2.8.1990

ESHUN, Kodwo: Ice Cube, in: The Face 2/1994, pp. 86–91

FREEDBERG, Michael: You Can Dance to It, But is It Worth a Listen?, in: New York Times, 29.4.1990

FUCHS-GAMBÖCK, Michael: Kraftwerk, in: Wiener 7/1991, pp. 107–113

GEORGE, Nelson: Hip-Hop's Founding Fathers Speak the Truth, in: The Source 11/1993, pp. 44–50

GOETZ, Rainald/KERN, Michi: Sven Väth – Maniac Love. The Tokio Tapes, in: Tempo 9/1994, pp. 70–80

GORRIS, Lothar: Der Acid-Bluff, in: Tempo 5/1989

– Kraftwerk, in: Zeit Magazin, 11.10.1991, pp. 113–118

GRAF, Andreas: Chipsy Kings, in: Musik Express 7/1991, p. 44ff.

GROTELÜSCHEN, Frank: Kartoffeln-Sound, in: Spex 11/1988, pp. 42–45

HARVEY, Steven/BATES, Patricia: Behind Groove, in: DJ 3/1993, pp. 4–10

HÜETLIN, Thomas: Der Gott aus der Maschine, in: Der Spiegel, 8.11.1993, p. 212ff.

—Drei Jungs im Mull, in: Der Spiegel, 1.8.1994, p. 140ff.

HUGHES, Walter: Feeling Mighty Real. Disco as Discourse and Discipline, in: Village Voice – Rock'n'Roll Quarterly, Summer 1993, pp. 7–11 + 21

JACOBSON, Harlan: Wild Style, in: Film Comment 6/1983, pp. 64–66

JARRETT, Michael: Beastie Boys, in: Pulse 7/1994, pp. 48–52 + 104f.

JONES, Allen: Howl of the Wolfman, in: Melody Maker, 6.9.1975

KELLER, Hans: Rap, in: Sounds 11/1981, pp. 44–48

KLINKMANN, Uwe/SCHNEIDER, Markus: Peace, Love, so was in der Art, in: Spex 10/1990, p. 11

KUMMER, Tom: Bässe machen Mädchen wild, in: SZ-Magazin

37/1996, p. 45

KÜNZLER, Hans-Peter: Acid Jazz, in: Wiener 5/1989

LAARMANN, Jürgen: Words Don't Come Easy, in: Frontpage 2/1995, p. 58ff.

LÜCKNER, Michael: Tenorsaxophon Lysergsäure Bleep, in: Spex 12/1991, pp. 78–81

MANSCH, Jenny: Bomb the Bass. Leader of the Pack, in: Zitty, 19.5.1988

MARCUS, Tony: Acid's Back, in: i-D 7/1992

McCANN, Ian: Nothing Compare to Huge, in: NME, 2.3.1991, p. 17

McCREADY, John: A–Z of Techno, in: The Face 12/1991, p. 56ff.

MI.: Beutezug der Klang–Klauer, in: Musik Express 7/1989

MIKE D.: Yo, Wuss Thu? – An Impromptu Car Phone Conversation with Russell Simmons, in: Grand Royal Autumn/Winter 1993, p. 4f.

MIXMAG 3/1993, Definitive A–Z of Dance Music and Clubbing

MYERS, Caren: Dead Ringer, in: Details 5/1994, p. 154f.

NEGATIVLAND: (Copyright) Fair Use & the Law, in: Keyboards 6/1994, pp. 88–94 + 134–140

NIEMCZYK, Ralf: Coldcut/ Justified Ancients of Mumu und die anderen, in: Spex 5/1988, p. 36ff.

Age of the DJ (Part: Early Rococo), in: Spex 11/1988, p. 8f.

NIESWANDT, Hans: Vive la résistance, in: Spex 12/ 1991, p. 26f.

O'HAGAN, Sean: Life on M/A/R/R/S, in: NME, 14.11.1987

– The Wild Bunch, in: The Face 2/1995, pp. 42–46

OWEN, Frank: Hip-Hop's Original DJ is Back at the Turntables, in: New York Newsday, 11.10.1993

PANDISCIO, Richard: Jean-Paul Gaultier, in: Interview 1/1994, pp. 70–75 + 109

PHILLIPS, Dom: The World's Biggest Remixer, in: Mixmag 7/1993, p. 46f.

POSCHARDT, Ulf: Die beste aller Welten, in: Spiegel Spezial 'Pop und Politik' 2/1994, pp. 117–120

– 1968er Aufstand, Popkultur und Technik. Eine fast vergessene Geschichte, in: Eichholzbrief – Zeitschrift für politische Bildung 3/1994, pp. 81–88

– Klang eines Schatten, in: Vogue 1/1995, p. 84

REINBOTH, Michael: It's All In The Mix, in: Musik Express 1/1994, p. 30f.

ROBERTS, Todd C.: Don't Sweat the Technics, in: Urb August 1992, p. 48

RULE, Greg: The Good, the Bad and the Noisy, in: Keyboards 5/1994, pp. 31–40

– 'They're Making Samplers Wrong', in: Keyboards 5/1994, pp. 45–53

SANDALL, Robert: Soul II Soul, in: Rolling Stone, 12.7.1990, p. 105ff.

SAVAGE, Jon: Machine Soul. A History of Techno, in: Village Voice – Rock'n'Roll Quarterly, Summer 1993, pp. 18–21

SCHEURING, Dirk: Die LP des Jahres, in: Vogue 5/1991, p. 112

SHARP, Elsa: Disco Dave, in: DJ 3/1993, p. 12

SINKER, Mark: Bytes and Pieces, in; NME, 14.11.1987

SNOW, Mat: Sampling Secrets of Sound Scientists, in: The Guardian, 8.7.1988

SPENCER, Jon Michael (Ed.): The Emergence of Black and the Emergence of Rap. A Special Issue of Black Sacred American Music: a Journal of Theomusicology, 1/1991

SPENCER, Neil: Full Nelson, in: Straight No Chaser, Winter 1993, pp. 30–33

STERNE, Adam Keane: Quest for Fire, in: Seconds 27, 7/1994

THE BELIEFS OF UNIVERSAL ZULU NATION, in: The Source 11/1993, p. 49

THOMAS, Anthony: The House the Kids Built, in: Outlook 5, Summer 1989, pp. 24–35

THOMPSON, Ben: All Shipshape and Bristol Fashion, in: Independent Review, 26.5.1991, p. 18

TOOP, David: Disco, in: The Face 9/1992, pp. 49–56

TOPE, Frank: Holding On, in: DJ 2/1994, p. 26f.

TORELLA, Chris et al: Explorer's Guide to House, 2nd edition, in: Streetsound 8/1993, pp. 20–25

– Exlorer's Guide to House, 3rd edition, in: Streetsound 8/94, pp. 22–29

USLAR, Moritz von: Ha! Ha! Superdoof?, in: Tempo 11/1993, pp. 98–102

– 'Wir haben prima Laune. Aber wir sind nicht geisteskrank.' In: SZ. Magazin, 21.1.1994, pp. 18–22

– 'Ich bin nur zufällig hier. Meine Kleidung ist mitgekommen, ohne mich zu fragen.' In: SZ-Magazin, 3.3.1995, pp. 32–39

VAIL, Mark: Roland CR-78, Tr-808 & TR-909, in: Keyboards 5/1994, pp. 82–86

VERRICO, Lisa: Welcome to Portishead. Please Read Carefully, in: Dazed & Confused 9/1994, p. 94f.

WALTERS, Barry: Last Night a DJ Saved my Life, in: Village Voice, 7.7.1988

WILSON, Tony: Juan Atkins, in: i-D 8/1993, p. 51

WITTER, Simon: Moving House, in: NME, 20.6.1987

– Back to Jack, in: NME, 15.8.1987

ZABEL, Sebastian: Warp – Subsonic Business, in: Spex 6/1991, pp. 29–31

– Children of the Rave-O-lution, in: Spex 10/1990, pp. 6–12

INDEX

A

ABC 27, 284
Above the Law 150
AC/DC 269
Ace, Johnny 85
Acid 315
Adorno, Theodor 33, 47,
    52f., 54, 228f., 249f.,
    259f., 280, 338f., 357,
    371, 407
Aerosmith 279
Africa Islam 146
Afrika Bambaattaa (& The
    Soul Sonic Force) 151,
    159, 160ff., 166, 175–81,
    191, 194, 196f., 201, 204,
    209, 217f., 223f., 227.,
    229ff., 273, 326, 361f.,
    178
à;Grumh 319, 321
Ahearn, Charlie 144, 201,
    213ff.
Alcapone, Dennis 158
Aletti, Vince 111, 137, 140
Allam, Paul 144
Allman, Duane 353
Amazing Birth 160
Anderson, Laurie 170, 216,
    171
Andy, Bob 158
Angus, Colin 291
Animals 279
Aphex Twin(*see also* James,
    Richard) 315, 325,
Aristotle 418
A.R. Kane 262

Armstrong, Louis 153
Astor, Patti 213
Atkins, Juan 317f., 422, *317*
A Tribe Called Quest 298,
    389
Aurra 273

B

B-52s 200
Baby Ford 318
Bacall, Lauren 105
Bach, Johann Sebastian 370,
    372
Badlam, John 140
Baez, Joan 79
Baker, Arthur 217, 223, 280
Bakhtin 377
Baldwin, James 153f.
Bananarama 284
Bangalter, Thomas 429
Banks, Mike 286
BAP 398
Barrett, Syd 364f.
Barrows, Geoff 298
Barthes, Roland 37, 40, 72,
    188, 376–80, 381, 400f.
Baryshnikov, Mikhail 136
Basquiat, Jean-Michel 200
Bataille, Georges 316
Baxter, Blake 318
Beach Boys 278
Beadle, Jeremy J. 179, 182,
    194, 207, 266f., 271f.,
    274, 277f.
Beastie Boys 199, 268–71,

276, 279, 300, 304, 369, 407, *268, 270*
Beatles 68, 76ff., 82, 95, 105, 180, 278, 328
Beatmasters & Cookie Crew 274
Beck 421
Beckett, Samuel 320
Bee Gees 112, 140f.
Beethoven, Ludwig van 33, 249, 370, 372
Bell, Al 92
Bell, Mark 323
Bell, Thom 118
Bellote, Pete 121
Benhabib, Seyla 394
Benjamin, Walter 33, 220f., 228, 280, 370
Bennett, Tony 49, 203
Benson, Al 87
Berliner, Emil 15, 41
Bernstein, Bill 146
Berry, Chuck 54, 61, 90, 282
Big Audio Dynamite 280
Big Black 223
Big Bopper (*see also* Richardson) 67
Big Daddy Kane 150, 231, 292
Billboard 55
Bisset, Jacqueline 136
Biz Markie 34, 232
Black, Matt 275f.
Black Box 115
Black Sheep 298
Blackmore, Richie 245
Bloch, Ernst 338
Block, Martin 45–9, 55, 74, 87, 350f., *46*
Blondie (Deborah Harry, *see also* Harry, Debbie) 200, 204f., 209, 270
Blow, Kurtis (Kool DJ Kurt, *see also* Walker, Curtis) 172, 174, 181, 197f., 204, 216, 268
Blue Notes 117
Bobby O. 241
Bogart, Neil 121
Bomb The Bass 272–5, 280,

284, 290, 300, 364
BoogieDown Productions 191
Booker T and the MGs 107
Botticelli, Sandro 370f.
Boulez, Pierre 354
Bow Wow Wow 205f., 208
Boy George 294
Bracken, James 67
Brahms, Johannes 372
Brathwaite, Fred 199
Brecht, Bertold 350f.
Bredow, Hans 43, 44
Brice, Will 61
Brown, Dennis 158
Brown, H. Rap 188
Brown, James 91ff., 105, 110, 116f., 121, 124f., 138, 160, 177, 180, 201, 264, 270, 327, 387
Brown, John 160
Browne, Tom 264
Brunner, Reinhold 320f.
Burning Spear 158
Burroughs, William 191, 297, 313f., 319, 377f., 393, 377
Busy Bee 214
Butler, Jerry 68
Byrd, Gary 88, 94

C

Caberet Voltaire 280
Cage, John 108, 415, 420, 425
Caine, Michael 177
Cale, J.J. 222
Calloway, Cab 153
Campbell, Jo-Ann 64
Campbell, Clive 160
Can 95, 225
Cantor, Louis 85
Capote, Truman 73, 106, 136
Cappello, Michael 110
Carr, Roy 130
Carter, Betty 153
Carter, Vivian 67
Castor, Jimmy 105, 118, 264
Cat Mother 107
Cauty, Jimmy 275
Caz 194

Cerrone 147, 241
Cervantes 370
Change 115
Chapple, Steven 45, 47f., 50, 61
Charles Ray 90f.
Checker, Chubby 103f.
Cherry, Neneh 294, 298
Chicago 107
Chip E 286
Christ, Sabine 434
Chuck D. (*see also* Public Enemy) 152, 187, 346, 407
Cimabue 370
Circus, Martin 243
Clapton, Eric 353
Clark, Dave 90
Clark, Dick 63–66, 103, 128, 64
Clark, Thomas 42
Clash 239
Clay, Cassius (Muhammad Ali) 153, 178,
Clinton, George 88, 143, 418ff., 421
Cocteau, Jean 104
Cohn, Nik 21, 35f., 53, 59f., 63, 66ff., 75ff., 91, 92, 95ff., 104, 119, 126ff., 132ff., 140f., 277ff., 318, 391f., 401
Coke la Rock 183
Cold Crush Brothers 194, 214
Coldcut 271–5, 280, 284, 322, 364
Cole, Nat 'King' 50
Collin, Matthew 270, 287, 289, 292
Collins, Albert (Jazzbo) 49
Collins, Bootsy 417f.
Coltrane, John 292, 314, 387, 405
Como, Perry 50, 60
Conrad, Frank 42
Contours 92
Coolio 421
Coquelin, Oliver 102
Cosgrove, Stuart 243ff., 247,

255, 263f.
Cowboy (*see also* Wiggins, Keith) 183f.
Cowley, Patrick 241
Cox, Carl 434
Craig, Carl 421, 428, 434, 436
Criminal Element Orchestra 264
Crocker, Frankie 94, 125
Crystals 277
Culshaw, John 277
Curtis, Bill 88
Curtis, Jim 112
Cybotron 317

D

Daddy-O (Vernon Winslow) 86
Daddy-O-Daylie 86
DAF (Deutsch-Amerikanische Freundschaft) 305
Daft Punk 428f., 432ff.
Dalí, Salvador 373
Danny & the Juniors 103
D'Aquisito, Steven 110
Darnell, August 137
Darwin, Charles Robert 337
Davis, Miles 218, 405
Davis, Richard 317
Day, Doris 54, 60
Dean, James 73, 351
Debord, Guy 206, 265
Deee-Lite 147
Def Jam 269
DeForest, Lee 40f.
Deleuze, Gilles 38, 190, 283, 381f., 388
Del Tha Funky Homosapien 234
Der Plan 305
Descartes, René 383
Diaz, Maria 'Smokin'' 243
Dibango, Manu 119
Diederichsen, Diedrich 27f., 35ff., 86, 146, 163, 178f., 188, 251, 269, 282, 286, 307, 315, 342f., 405
Digital Underground 364
Dillinger 158

Disco King Mario 180
Disposable Heroes of
    Hiphoprisy 150, 378, *377*
Distl, Gottfried 306
Divine 241
DJ Adamski 291, 318
DJ Adonis 286
DJ Bam Bam 286
DJ Electrifying Mojo 317
DJ Fabio 410, 438
DJ Goldie 410–13, 438
DJ Grooverider 410, 412,
    438
DJ Hell 309ff., 436
DJ Hollywood 151, 181f.,
    192, 194
DJ Hype 415
DJ Kemistry & Storm 410
DJ Krush 257, 274, 301f.,
    426f., *302*
DJ Norman Jay 292
DJ Olaf 311
DJ Peshey 410, 438
DJ Pierre 33, 286, *285*
DJ Shadow 301
DJ Sleazy D 286
DJ Sneak 416
DJ Takemura 301
DJ Theodore (Grand Wizard
    Theodore) 168ff., 172,
    214
DJ Woody 311f.
Dodd, Clement 158
Dokoupil, Georg 306
Donahue, Tom 81ff., 352f.
Donovan 279
Donovan, Jason 284
Dorell, Dave (*see also*
    M/A/R/R/S) 262f., 266
Dostovesky, Fyodor
    Mikhailovitch 377
Double Exposure 124
Double Trouble 193, 214
Dr Hep Cat (Lavanda Durst)
    86
Driesch, Hans 418
Dr. Jeckyl & Mr. Hyde 198
Drummond, Bill 275
Drummond, Don 158
Duchamp, Marcel 16, 207,

211, 363, 367, 372, 380,
    383
Duchin, Peter 102
Duck Rock 209ff.
Duke of Bedford 102
Duke of Windsor 102
Dune 318
Duran Duran 284
Dyer, Richard 112
Dylan, Bob 79, 82

E

Edison, Thomas Alva 15,
    219f.,
808 State 223, 287, 364
Eisenstein 370
El Dorado 54
Electric Force Dancers 214f.
Ellington, Duke 259
Engels, Friedrich 21, 336f.,
    340ff., 374
Eno, Brian 325
EPMD (*see also* Sermon, Eric)
    202, 233, 364, 426,
Eric B & Rakim 235, 262,
    264, 271f.
Eshun, Kodwo 414, 421
Extrabreit 305

F

Fab 5 Freddy (Fred
    Brathwaite) 150ff., 159,
    172, 181, 199–203, 204,
    213, 231, 235, 417, *201*,
    202
Fantastic Freaks 214
Farley, Terry 291
Fatback Band 193
Fats Domino 54
Fehlfarben 305
Fender, Leo 416
Fessenden, Reginald A. 15,
    40, 349
Fetisch 428
Feyerabend, Paul 348, 371
Fitzgerald, Ella 153
Flash 163
Flaubert, Gustave 375
Fleetwood Mac 280
Flowers, Pete (Grandmaster

Flower) 160, 176, 199
Fonda, Jane 106
Fonteyn, Margot 104
Ford, Henry 102
Foucault, Michel 17, 38,
    113f., 150, 166, 283, 316,
    339f., 348, 375f., 379,
    381f., 399f.
Four Seasons 67
Fowlkes, Eddie Flashin 318
Fox, Samantha 284
Frankie D. 199
Franklin, Aretha 107, 120,
Freed, Alan 48, 57–65, 74f.,
    78, 82, 84, 90, 120, 242f.,
    351f., *58, 59, 60, 401*
Freeman, Bobby 81
Frith, Simon 25, 81, 113,
    145, 207f., 222, 276
Front 319, 321
Fugs 79
Funkadelic 419
Funky Four Plus One 273
Futura 2000 200

G

Gaillard, Slim 129
Gamble, Kenny 117f.
Gang Starr 202, 302, 388
Garbo, Greta 104
Gardner, Ava 102
Garland, Judy 104
Garofalo, Reebee 45, 47f.,
    50, 61, 203
Gaultier, Jean-Paul 395
Gaynor, Gloria 112, 124, 241
George, Nelson 19, 65, 68,
    84, 87ff., 92ff., 125, 159,
    161f., 166, 170, 173, 177,
    180–84, 192, 194–9,
    202f., 215, 235, 269, 343,
    402
Gibbons, Beth 298
Gibbons, Walter 123f.
Gibson, Jack 89
Gillespie, Dizzy 89, 129, 301
Gillet, Charlie 54, 58, 67, 82,
    104
Giotto, G. di Bondone 370
Glaser, Peter 27, 305f.

Godard, Jean-Luc 16, 22,
    163, 263, 284, 370, 394,
    398
Goetz, Rainald 27, 305–13,
    325, 378, 398, 408, *311*
Goldman, Albert 102, 106,
    109f., 136
Gonzales, Kenny 124
Gonzales, Michael A. 174,
    200, 269
Goodman, Benny *46*
Goodwin, Andrew 113, 222,
    276, 280ff.
Gordon, Roscoe 85
Gordy, Berry 86, 92
Gorris, Lothar 292, 309
Graham, Billy 65
Grand Funk Railroad 180
Grandmaster Caz 194
Grandmaster Flash (& The
    Furious Five) 18, 156,
    159ff., 161, 166, 167–75,
    180f., 183ff., 194, 196,
    198, 204f., 209, 214–17,
    222, 227, 234f., 268, 302,
    355f., 359–61, 391, 407,
    428, *167, 168, 169*
Grandmixer D.ST 214, 218
Grateful Dead 79, 82
Greenberg, Clement 387
Griffiths, Marcia 158
Grosso, Francis 107–12, 118,
    124
Guattari, Félix 38, 283,
    381f., 388

H

Hager, Steven 160ff., 166,
    169, 180, 185, 194, 196
Haley, Bill 53f., 59, 61, 282,
    351
Halper, Donna 46
Hamilton, Richard 73
Hancock, Herbie 218, 223
Handel, George Frideric 15,
    41, 349
Hank Ballard & the
    Midnighters 103
Hanson, Kitty 120f., 136,
    139

Happy Mondays 289
Hardy, Ron 257, 286
Haring, Keith 18, 200, 201f.
Harrison, George 77
Harry, Debbie 205
Hauser, Arnold 371–4
Hausmann, Raoul 163
Hayes, Isaac 105, 118, 155, 180, 282, 287
Haza, Ofra 271
Healey, Jeff 276
Heard, Larry (Mr Fingers, Fingers Inc.) 245, 257
Heaven 17 27, 284
Heavy D 233
Hebdige, Dick 129, 138, 156, 158, 351
Hees, Armand van 416
Hegel, G.W.F. 16f., 37, 249, 336ff., 370f., 393, 407, 427, 439
Heidegger, Martin 30, 250, 356f.
Henderson, Douglas 'Jocko' 88, 105
Hendrix, Jimi 80, 216, 353
Hernandez, Patrick 135
Herold, Charles D. 42
Hertz, Heinrich 40
Hester, Gene 423f.
Hölderlin, Friedrich 356, 407
Hollaway, Loletta 243
Holly, Buddy 67
Homen-Christo, Guy-Manuel de 429
Hooker, John Lee 68
Hooper, Nellee (see also Soul II Soul) 293f.
Horkheimer, Max 47, 52f., 250, 357, 407
Horn, Trevor 209
Horne, Howard 207
Hot Mix 5 257
Huelsenbeck 265
Hues Corporation 115
Huff, Leon 117f.
Hughes, Walter 113–16, 246
Human Resource 322
Humphries, Tony 124, 240, 244, 257, 245

Hunter, Ivory Joe 58
Hurley, Steve 124, 259
Hütter, Ralf (see also Kraftwerk) 31, 225, 354, 365, 369
Hyatt, Slim 102

I

Ice Cube 231, 402
Ice T 146, 188f., 199, 269, 190
Incredible Bongo Band 161
INXS 381

J

Jack'n'Chill 274
Jackson, Michael 232
Jackson, Millie 155
Jagger, Bianca 136
James, Richard (see also Aphex Twin) 315, 324f., 355f., 381, 325
James, Rick 172
Jameson, Frederic 393
Jarman, Derek 28
Jarvis, Al 45f., 55
Jazzie B (see also Soul II Soul) 293, 293
Jazzy Fives 264
Jazzy Jay 209
Jefferson Airplane 82
Jefferson, Marshall 244, 257
JM (Jackmaster) Silk 246, 259
Joey Dee and the Starliters 104
Johns, Jasper 72
Johnson, Linton Kwesi 157
Jones, Grace 115, 136
Jones, Pete 160, 168, 176, 199
Jones, Rocky 257
Jones, Tom 299
Jordan, Louis 49
Joyce, James 370
Julien, Isaac 142–6

K

Kafka, Franz 299, 375, 429
Karnik, Olaf 93, 124

Keith, Farley (Farley Jackmaster Funk) 243, 247
Keller, Hans 170, 172
Kennedy, Jackie 104
Kerouac, Jack 129
Kern, Michi 312, 316, 325
Key, Scott 243
Khlebnikov, Welimir 350
Kid Creole 137, 184
Kid Frost 149
Kid Paul 381
King, B.B. (Riley B. King) 85, 89
King, Evelyn 243
King, Martin Luther 93, 179, 345
King, Rodney 345, *345*
King Tim III 195
Kippenberger, Martin 306
Kipps, Charlie 120
Kittler, Friedrich A. 30f., 41, 43, 70, 73, 170, 216, 219, 278, 309, 316, 348f., 355f., 365
KLF (The Timelords) 275, 280, 322
Kneif, Tibor 59f., 83, 126, 157, 222, 236
Knight, Gladys and the Pips 68, 107
Knuckles, Frankie 244f., 257, *244*
Kool DJ Herc 107, 159–63, 166, 173–6, 181ff., 194, 196f., 360, 425
Kool Moe Dee 196, 395f.
Kosuth, Joseph 387
Kraftwerk (*see also* Hütter, Ralf; Schneider, Florian) 31, 96, 138, 172, 204, 217, 219, 222, 224–7, 243f., 316ff., 348, 352–4, 364ff., 369, 381, 419–22, 422, *369*
Kreye, Andrian 36
Kröher, Michael O.R. 307
KRS One 202, 402

L

Lacan 186

Laibach 404
Laine, Frankie 60
L.A. Mix 275
Lang, Fritz 421
Lang, Helmut 231, 340f.
L.A. Sunshine 196
Lavelle, James 300f., *300*
Lazarsfeld, Paul F. 50ff.
Leaders of the New School 298
Led Zeppelin 108, 180, 269
Lee, Spike 424f.
Lenz, Fabian 326
Leonardo da Vinci 374
Levan, Larry 146, 239f., 243
Lewis, Jerry Lee 62, 65
LFO 323f., 422f., *324*
Lichtenstein, Roy 72
Lipsitz, George 406
Little Richard 68
Livingston, Gene 170
Livingston, Jennie 256
LL Cool J 199, 282, 416
Lord, Arnie 106
Lorraine 273
Lottmann, Joachim 27, 306
Lovin' Spoonful 82
Lowe, Chris 241
LTJ Bukem 421
Lucas, George 57, 62
Lydon, John 210
Lyotard, Jean-François 112, 394, 399–401

M

MacDougald, Duncan Jr. 51
MacFarland, David T. 52–6
Machine 115
Mackintosh C.J. 262f.
Madonna 27, 147, *28*
Mad Professor 297
Magritte, René 359
Mailer, Norman 59, 73, 129ff., 403
Major Force 301f.
Makeba, Miriam 180
Malcolm X 151, 179, 345
Malevich, Casimir 138, 226, 363, 371f.
Mancuso, David 111
Marconi, Guglielmo 40

Marcus, Greil 21f., 24, 35, 62, 79, 82, 188, 207, 392, 405
Marcuse 357
Markus 305
Marley, Bob 158
M/A/R/R/S (see also Dorell, Dave; Young, Martin) 261–6, 268, 270–5, 280, 284, 290, 300, 316, 322, 364, 383, 428, 263
Martha and the Vandellas 92
Martin, George 278f., 352, 364
Martina (Singer) 299
Marvellettes 93
Marx, Karl 21, 33f., 336ff., 341f., 374, 398f.
Marx, Olaf Dante 307
Massive Attack 294–300, 363, 380, 391, 295
Master Ace 202
Master, D. 199
Mathew, Brian 96
Maureen 273
May, Derrick 318, 420, 422
Mayfield, Curtis 118
McCarthy, Joseph Raymond 59, 65
McCoy, Clyde 45
McCoy, Van 109, 120f.
McCrae, George 222
McCready, John 314
McFive 79
McLaren, Malcolm 25, 205–13, 265, 268, 270, 389, 392f., 397, 206
McLuhan, Marshall 41, 47, 351
MCA 276
MC Lyte 416
MD 11 286
Mean Machine 216
Mel& Kim 284
Melle MeL (Grandmaster Melle MeL) 184, 217
Melvin, Harold 117, 244
Merlin 273
MFSB Orchestar 117f.
Michelango 370, 374

Michael, George 421
Michigan And Smiley 158
Mike D 270, 276, 369
Miller, Larry 81
Mills, Jeff 317, 416, 428
Minnelli, Liza 138
Minogue, Kylie 284
Mintz, Leo 58f.
Miracles 92
Mitchell, Rob 323
MK (Mark Kinchen) 381
Modell 500 286
Moholoy-Nagy, Laszlo 228f., 349f., 355
Monday Michíru 300
Monkees 180
Monroe, Marilyn 73
Montana Sextet 264
Moog, Robert A. 71
Mooney, Art 49f.
Morales, David 17, 248
Morley, Jefferson 149, 173
Moroder, Giorgio 109, 121, 223, 241, 300
Morris, David Burton 80
Most, Mickie 279
Moulton, Tom 123f.
Mountain 279
Murcia, Bill 206
Murray K. (Murray Kaufman) 74–8, 82, 75
Musto, Tommy 124
Myers, Elman 42

N

Negro, Joey 109, 122
Nelson, Havelock 175, 193, 200, 213, 269,
Nelson, Shara 294
Nena 305
Newman, Mark 84, 87, 92
New Order 27, 147, 284
New York Dolls 206
Nicolette 297
Nietzsche, Friedrich 19f., 37, 154
Nightmares on Wax 323, 323
Nixon, Richard 78, 112
Noel, Terry 107
Nunnally, Keith 259

O

Oakenfold, Paul 285, 290, 291
O'Brien 201
Ochs, Phil 79
Ohio Players 118
O'Jays 117, 244
Oliver, Mickey 243
Orridge, Genesis P. 319
Osbourne, Johnny 158
O'Sullivan, Gilbert 232
Overdose 286
Owen, Frank 160, 166, 197

P

Pakula, Alan J. 106
Palmer, Robert 353
Pappalardi, Félix 279
Parker, Andrea 425–8
Parker, Charlie 314
Passman, Arnold 41f., 44ff., 48, 59–62, 74, 87f.
Peel, John 97
Perkins, Carl 66
Perry, Lee Scratch 158f.
Persuaders 118
Pet Shop Boys (see also Tennant, Neil) 15, 27, 147, 241, 284
Peterson, Gilles 292
Petrillo, James Caesar 44
Philipps, Peter 73
Phuture 286
Piaf, Edith 180
Picabia, Francis 16
Picasso, Pablo 320, 404, 416
Pink Floyd 248, 279, 297, 301, 302, 316, 325, 352f., 364ff., 381, 417
Plant, Robert 108
Portishead 298–300, 389
Pressure Drop 264
Presley, Elvis 54, 66, 73, 85, 182, 328
Primal Scream 289
Prince Buster 156
Prince Paul 232
Proust, Marcel 375
Pryor, Richard 172
Prysock, Red 58

Public Enemy (see also Chuck D.) 152, 190f., 199, 299, 301, 345f., 407
Pynchon, Thomas 19, 36, 68–72, 73f., 95

Q

Queen Latifah 202

R

Rachmaninov 301
Rampling, Danny 285
Randle, Bill 49, 55, 62, 343
Rapper 3 D 297
Rare Earth 160
Ray, Johnnie 49, 343
Ray, Nicholas 73
Rebel MC 150
Red Crayola 428
Redon, Odilon 373
Reed, Jimmy 68
Reid, Duke 156f.
Reid, Jamie 206, 208
Reinhardt, Ad 384f., 391
Reiser, Rio 398
Reynolds, Simon 247–51, 280–2
Richards, Keith 353
Richardson, Jape 67
Rivette 163
Roberts, Todd C. 235f.
Robinson, Bobby 195f., 199
Robinson, Sylvia 193, 194f., 199
Rock Steady Crew 209, 211, 214
Rohe, Mies van der 363
Rolling Stones 67, 82, 95, 105, 180, 216
Rolling Stone 301
Ronettes 277, 279
Roni Size 412
Rosario, Ralphie 243
Rose, Cynthia 303
Roosevelt, Franklin Delano 51
Rose, Filipe 140
Rose, Tricia 36, 256, 258, 355, 406
Rosenquist, James 73

Rosko, Emperor 97
Rossini, Gioacchino 41
Roxy Music 27, 428
Rubin, Rick 199, 269, 279f.,
  327
Rule, Greg 233
Run DMC 198, 233, 268,
  279
Russell, Leon 222

S

Salinger, Jerome D. 95
Salt 'n' Pepa 407
Salzinger, Helmut 80
Saunders, Jesse 244
Saunderson, Kevin 318
Savage, Jon 207, 317
Saville, Jimmy 96f.
Schäffer, Pierre 353
Scharf, Kenny 200
Schelling, Friedrich Wilhelm
  Joseph von 407
Scheuring, Dirk 296
Schneider, Florian (see also
  Kraftwerk) 225, 365
Schoenfeld, Herm 55
Schönberg, Arnold 258, 372,
  386, 429
Schopp, Markus 316
Scott-Heron, Gil 178
Sears, Al 58
Seeger, Pete 79
Sequence 216
Sermon, Eric (see also EPMD)
  233
Serres, Michel 17, 20, 37, 38,
  203
Sex Pistols 24, 145f., 200,
  206ff., 210
Shaheed 386, 389, 399
Shanon, de 230
Shannon 115
Shapiro, Brad 125
Shaw, Arnold 19, 35, 48f.,
  51, 54, 59, 61f., 65f., 68,
  82ff., 86, 91ff., 104, 121,
  135, 153, 157, 287
Sherman, Cindy 320
Shields, Del 93f.
Silver Convention 135

Simenon, Tim (see also Bomb
  The Bass) 272ff.
Simmons, Russell 194f.,
  197ff., 202, 269, 199
Sinatra, Frank 50f.
Sir Coxsone 156, 158f.
Sir Mix-A-Lot 407
Sister Sledge 135
Sklar, Rick 60, 74f.
Slayer 279
Slick Rick 199, 231
Slime 398
Sly and the Family Stone 105,
  177, 232
Smooth, Joe 257
Snoop Doggy Dogg 406
Soul Patrol 143f.
Soul Sonic Force 217, 227
Soul II Soul 293–6, 298, 363
Sound Factory 250
Sovine, Red 182
Spandau Ballet 27
Spanky 285
Spector, Phil 277ff., 352, 364
Spinners 118
SPK 319
Spoonie Gee 175, 195f., 204
Stansfield, Lisa 294
Steppenwolf 80
Stewart, Sylvester 81
Stirling, James 363
Stock, Aiken & Waterman
  241, 284
Stockhausen, Karlheinz 175,
  300f., 324, 353
Stone, Christopher Reynolds
  96
Stone Roses 289
Stone, Sly 81, 90
Stooges 79
Storz, Todd 53
Strayhorn, Billy 259
Streisand, Barbra 180
Stylistic 118
Sugar Hill Gang 193–6, 216,
  361, 406
Summer, Donna 108, 110,
  121
Sun Ra 428
Sutherland, Donald 107

Sylvester 135, 137ff.

T

Talking Heads 200, 239
Tambala, Rudi 262
Tangerine Dream 96, 225
Tate, Greg 33, 188, 418
Taylor, Liz 253
Taylor, Paul 206, 208, 210f.
Technotronic 318
Teddy Bears 277
Television 428
Tennant, Neil (*see also* Pet
    Shop Boys) 15, 241
Terry, Todd 124
Thatcher, Maggie 296
The Band 62
The Byrds 79, 82
The Cream 83, 279
The Heptones 158
The Jam 404
The Shamen 290, 291
The Skatalites 158
The Source 159
The Wailing Souls 158
Theweleit, Klaus 30
The Who 95, 180
The World's Famous Supreme
    Team 210
13th Floor Elevators 79
Thomas, Carla 85, 92
Thomas, Rufus 85, 90, 92
Throbbing Gristle 291, 319ff.
Thunderbirds 273
Thunders, Johnny 206
Thurn und Taxis, Princess
    Gloria 25
Timelords 275
Todd, David 119
Toffler, Alvin 366f.
Toop, David 35, 86ff., 105,
    107, 116, 123f., 148, 152,
    162, 168, 180, 182, 183,
    188, 192f., 196, 217, 227
Toots And The Maytals 158
Tope, Frank 254
Travolta, John 140f., 141
Treacherous Three 196
Tricky 298–300, 389, *299*
Tricky Disco 324

Tristano, Lennie 405
Trouble Funk 218, 264
Trudeau, Pierre Elliot 136
True, Sybil M. 42
Truffaut, François 263
Turing, Alan Mathison 31
Turner, Ike 279
Turner, Tina 279
Turntable Terranova 428

V

Vail, Mark 223, 224
Valens, Richie 67
Varley, Jez 323
Vasari, Giorgio 370f.
Vasquez, Junior 124
Väth, Sven 311f., 316, 327f.,
    311, 328
Vega, Little 'Louie' 124, 240
Velvet Underground 79
Vicious, Sid 207, *23*
Vilari, Jack 136
Vilari, Kathleen 136
Village People 115, 137,
    138ff., 147, *137*
Vincent, Gene 54
Vincent, Rickey 417, 420
Volosinov, Valentin N. 187,
    189f.

W

Wagner, Richard 277
Walker, Curtis 197
Warhol, Andy 16, 72, 204,
    206f., 226, 250, 253, 283,
    367, 373, 383, 397
Waters, John 241
Watford, Michael 254, 255
Wayne, John 105
Weatherall, Andrew 'Andy'
    290f., *291*
Wecker, Konstantin 398
Weller, Paul 404
Wells, Mary 92
Welsch, Wolfgang 26
Westbam (Maximilian Lenz)
    256, 310f., 315, 325ff.,
    416, 434, *326*
Westwood, Vivienne 206, 208
White, Barry 155, 243

Whodini 198
Wiggins, Keith 183f.
Wild Bunch 294
Williams, Dyanna 94
Williams, Tennessee 104
Wilson, Brian 278, 429
Wilson, Delroy 158
Winter, Johnny 276
Wolfe, Tom 19f., 36, 73–8,
  126f., 129, 133f.,
Wolff, Janet 16, 374, 377,
  380
Wolfman Jack 57, 263, *57*
Wolman 264
Wonder Mike 195
Wonder, Stevie 92

Wu-Tang-Clan 402f.

X
X-Ray Spex 143

Y
Yello 291
Young, Martin (*see also*
  M/A/R/R/S) 232, 263, 266
Youngbloods 279
Young Soul Rebels 284, *143*

Z
Zabel, Sebastian 290
Zephyr 200

PICTURES:

Cover photograph: Simon, back cover: Joachim Gern, p. **18**: Arne Bockelmann, p. **28**; Arsenal Filmverleih, p. **46**: Frank Driggs Collection, p. **58**: Bildarchiv Engelmeier, pp. **59, 60**: Steve Petruszyn, p. **64**: Edgar S. Brinker. p, **75**: Frank Driggs Collection, p. **85**: WDIA advertisement 1949, p. **137**: TCI, p. **141**: Bildarchiv Engelmeier, p. **143**: Kinowelt, pp. **164, 165**; Arsenal Filmverleih, pp. **167–169**: Pat Bates, p. **171**: Archiv Block, p. **178**: Bob Gruen/Starfile, p. **190**: Ryme Syndicate Records/Jesse Frohman, p. **199**: Def Jam, p. **201**: Arsenal Filmverleih, p. **221**: Archiv Paul Metall, p. **234**: VG Bild/Kunst, p. **237**: Akai Professional, p. **240**: Panasonic Deutschland GmbH, p. **244**: Norma Caloca/Virgin, p. **245**: Ulf Poschardt, p. **263**: Tom Sheehan/Photoselection, p. **268**: Arne Bockelmann, p. **270**: Ari Marcopoulos/ Capitol Records, p. **285**: Wolfgang Tillmans, p. **291**: Grant Peden/Rough Trade, p. **293**: Virgin, p. **295**: Mondino/Virgin, p. **299**: Mercury, p. **300**: Marlboro Music – Mo'Wax, p. **302**: Marlboro Music – Mo'Wax, p. **311**: Rainald Goetz, p. **317**: Wolfgang Tillmans, p. **323**: Vanya Balogh/Rough Trade, p. **324**: Paul Evans/Rough Trade, **325**: Rough Trade, p. **326**: Michael Reinboth archive, p. **328**: Rainald Goetz, pp. **329–31**: Ulf Poschardt, p. **345**: George Holliday, p. **360**: Arne Bockelmann, p. **369**: EMI, p. **377**: BMG Ariola/Island, p. **385**: Verlag Silke Schreiber, p. **410**: Paul Metall archive, p. **436**: Studio K71 Ali Kepenek, p. **437**: Paul Metall.

RESPECT TO:

Torsten and Granddad, Thomas and Lullamy, Denis 'Kaos' Kaun.

THANKS TO:

Claudius Seidl, John Warwicker + Tomato, Eberhard Delius, Birgit Politicky, Kodwo Eshun, Klaas Jarchow, Louis 'Onkel' von der Borch, Dr. Dr. Rainald Goetz, Arsenal Filmverleih, Kinowelt Filmverleih, Sophie Raml/ BMG Ariola, Marlboro Music – Mo' Wax, Prof. Friedrich A. Kittler, Diedrich Diederichsen, Niko Hansen, Thomas Baecker, Bernd Kühn, Rafael 'Rafi' Honigstein, Susanne Knecht, Mattias Reihs, Andreas Reim, Johanna Adorjan, Arne Bockelmann, Markus Kiersztan, Thomas Hintermaier (The Master Cutter).